Aerial view of a breathtaking
mountain landscape in Gates
of the Arctic National Park.
SCOTT DICKERSON

HIKING ALASKA

A GUIDE TO ALASKA'S GREATEST HIKING ADVENTURES

Third Edition

Mollie Foster

GUILFORD, CONNECTICUT

A person on foot, on horseback or on a bicycle will see more, feel more, enjoy more in one mile than the motorized tourists can in a hundred miles.

Edward Abbey (1927–1989)

Dedicated to those everywhere who have worked to keep Alaska wild.

FALCONGUIDES®

An imprint of Globe Pequot
Falcon and FalconGuides are registered trademarks and Make Adventure Your Story is a trademark of Rowman & Littlefield.

Distributed by NATIONAL BOOK NETWORK

British Library Cataloguing-in-Publication Information available

ISSN 1558-6316
ISBN 978-1-4930-2559-6 (paperback)
ISBN 978-1-4930-2560-2 (e-book)

Printed in the United States of America

∞™ The paper used in this publication meets the minimum requirements of American National Standard for Information Sciences—Permanence of Paper for Printed Library Materials, ANSI / NISO Z39.48–1992.

The author and Rowman & Littlefield assume no liability for accidents happening to, or injuries sustained by, readers who engage in the activities described in this book.

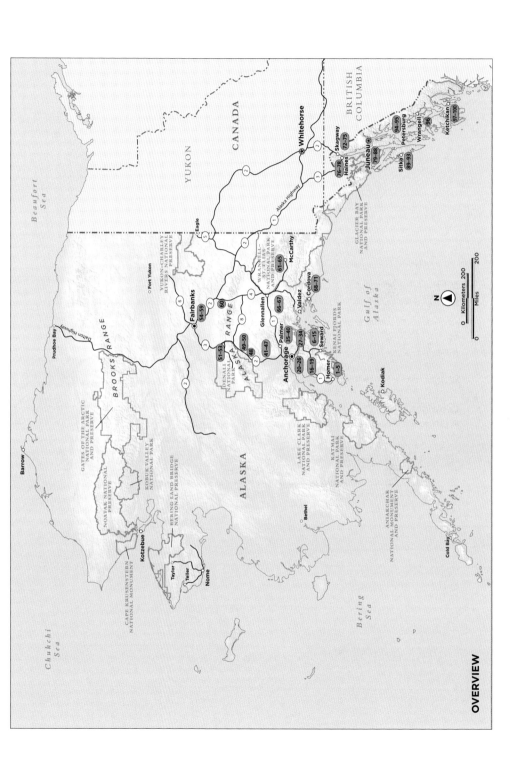

OVERVIEW

The 4-mile Harding Icefield Trail winds through forest and meadows and climbs well above tree line with breathtaking views in every direction. HAGEPHOTO

THE HIKES

MEET YOUR GUIDE   x

MAP AND ICON LEGENDS   xii

TRAIL FINDER   xiv

BEFORE YOU HIT THE TRAIL   xxi

Southcentral Alaska

Homer   2

1. Kachemak Bay Beach   3
2. Wynn Nature Center   8
3. Grace Ridge Trail   11
4. Grewingk Valley   15
5. China Poot Lake   21

Seward/Eastern Kenai   27

6. Caines Head   28
7. Exit Glacier   34
8. Harding Icefield   38
9. Lost Lake   42
10. Ptarmigan Lake   47
11. Johnson Pass   50
12. Crescent and Carter Lakes   54
13. Russian Lakes   58
14. Resurrection Pass   63
15. Devil's Creek   68

Kenai National Wildlife Refuge   72

16. Fuller Lakes and Skyline Ridge   73
17. Kenai River   77
18. Skilak Lookout, Bear Mountain, and Vista Trails   80
19. Seven Lakes   84

Hope to Girdwood   88

20. Gull Rock   89
21. Hope Point   93
22. Trail of Blue Ice   95
23. Byron Glacier   99
24. Portage Pass   102
25. Winner Creek   106
26. Crow Pass   111

Chugach State Park South   116

27. Bird Ridge   117
28. Falls Creek   121
29. McHugh and Rabbit Lakes   124
30. Turnagain Arm Trail   129
31. Flattop Mountain   134
32. Ship Lake Pass   138
33. Williwaw Lakes   142
34. Wolverine Peak   147

Chugach State Park North   150

35. South Fork Eagle River   151
36. Eagle River Valley   156
37. Mount Baldy and Blacktail Rocks   163
38. Ptarmigan Valley and Roundtop   167
39. Twin Peaks Trail   169
40. Bold Ridge Trail   174

Matanuska and Susitna Valleys   178

41. Pioneer Ridge   179
42. Lazy Mountain and Matanuska Peak   184
43. West Butte   189
44. Mint Glacier Valley   192
45. Reed Lakes   197
46. Snowbird Mine and Glacier Pass   201
47. Independence Mine   204

Talkeetna   207

48. Talkeetna Lakes Park   208

Denali State Park   211
  49. Byers Lake   212
  50. Kesugi Ridge   215

Interior Alaska

Denali National Park and Preserve   221
  51. Triple Lakes Trail   224
  52. Mount Healy Trail   229
  53. Savage River Valley   233

Fairbanks   237
  54. Creamer's Field   238
  55. Granite Tors   242
  56. Angel Rocks   246
  57. Chena Dome   250
  58. Pinnell Mountain   255
  59. Summit Trail   260

Delta Junction   265
  60. Quartz Lake State Recreation Trails   266

Wrangell–St. Elias National Park and Preserve   269
  61. Root Glacier and Stairway Icefall   271
  62. Bonanza Ridge   275
  63. Caribou Creek   278
  64. Trail and Lost Creeks   281
  65. Skookum Volcano   285

Glennallen to Valdez   288
  66. Tonsina River   289
  67. Worthington Glacier   291

Cordova   295
  68. Power Creek and Crater Lake   296
  69. Sheridan Mountain Trail   301
  70. McKinley Lake   304
  71. Saddlebag Glacier   307

Southeast Alaska

Skagway 310
72. Laughton Glacier 311
73. Chilkoot Pass 313
74. Dewey Lakes 320
75. Sturgill's Landing 324

Haines 326
76. Mount Ripinsky and 7 Mile Saddle 327
77. Mount Riley 332
78. Seduction Point 337

Juneau 340
79. Perseverance Trail 341
80. Mount Juneau and Granite Creek 345
81. Dan Moller Trail 350
82. East Glacier and Nugget Creek 354
83. West Glacier 359
84. Montana Creek and Windfall Lake 363
85. Auke Nu Trail 367
86. Herbert Glacier 371
87. Amalga Trail 374
88. Point Bridget 378

Sitka 382
89. Indian River 383
90. Sitka National Historical Park 387
91. Harbor Mountain and Gavan Hill 390
92. Starrigavan Bay 394
93. Beaver Lake and Herring Cove Trail 397

Petersburg 400
94. Three Lakes and Ideal Cove 401
95. Petersburg Lake 404

Wrangell 408
96. Rainbow Falls and Institute Creek 409

Ketchikan   414

  97. Deer Mountain   415
  98. Ward Lake and Ward Creek   420
  99. Perseverance Lake   423
  100. Naha River   426

Off the Beaten Path: Discovering
Wilderness Alaska   431

  Gates of the Arctic   433
  Arctic National Wildlife Refuge   435
  Wrangell–St. Elias   437
  Katmai   439
  Lake Clark   441
  Northwest Alaska   443

  Appendixes
  1. Information Sources   445
  2. Cabin Reservations   446
  3. Further Reading   447
  4. Sample Backpacking Checklist   448
  Hike Index   449

Alaska-based editor, photographer, and writer **Mollie Foster** is passionate about storytelling, specializing in outdoor lifestyle and adventure. She loves to spend her time exploring by human power—hiking, biking, skiing, and packrafting. Mollie has been a contributing editor to *Alaska Magazine*, has directed and guided week-long educational programs, and teaches field-based photography courses in Denali. She moved to Alaska, fell in love with the Alaskan lifestyle, and now can't imagine living anywhere else. She splits her time between Anchorage and Denali.

ACKNOWLEDGMENTS

The foundation for this guidebook is the work of Dean Littlepage, the author of the first and second editions of the book. Dean hiked, researched, and wrote about literally every detail covering the one hundred hiking trails around the state, in both editions. He is the reason this guidebook exists, for this and future editions. This is simply a revision of his groundwork.

In addition to Dean, I'd like to send a big thank you to the following people, agencies, and organizations.

Justin Wholey for his dedicated attention to detail with the trails in Alaska State Parks; Beth Trowbridge with the Alaska Center for Coastal Studies; Seth Spencer of Wynn Nature Center; Jacob Marshall of Kenai Fjords National Park; Irene Lindquist and Carolyn Seramur of Chugach National Forest; Darcy Harris of Alaska State Parks; Eric Haggstrom and Mark Goetsch of Matanuska-Susitna Borough; Molly McKinley and Jared Zimmerman of Denali National Park; Lynne Brandon with Sitka Trail Works; Mark Ross with Department of Fish and Game; Tim DuPont and

Eric Yeager with Bureau of Land Management; Lee Hart with Levitation 49; and Dave Zastrow (Cordova), Gina Meucci (Petersburg), Corree Delabrue (Wrangell), and Jon Regetz (Ketchikan) with the USDA Forest Service.

A special thanks to all the contributing photographers in this edition: Willie Dalton, Justin Wholey, Will Koeppen, Matt and Agnes Hage, Scott Dickerson, Nathaniel Wilder, Haley Johnston, Sarah Stehn, Mike Ausman, Ynez Slaymaker, Andy Hedden, Craig Brandt, Erica Watson, Mike Records, Carl Battreall, Harrison Scheib, Jason Reppert, Alexander Lee, Chelsea Haisman, Beezer Muth, Lee Kuepper, Ryan Delaney, Charity Hommel, Rachel Deehan, and Ilona Singh.

Thanks to Kirsten Anderson with Ramble Out Yonder Design, for the illustrations.

Thanks to all my friends and family for their support. A special thanks to Joe Meyer for his continued encouragement and expertise throughout a big project.

Thanks to friends and family for wonderful company on the trail: Joe Meyer, Willie Dalton, Sarra Khlifi, Sam Longacre, the Shea Family, Sharon Howrey, Bruce Bland, Sean Sweeney and Gena Layman, Nathaniel Wilder, Michael Howard, Emily Myhre, and off the trail to Kent Foster, Nick and Niki Goddard, and Terry Boyd. For the generous hospitality of Chuck Klemer and Dulce Havill, for sharing their home with the best view in Denali, while I edited this book. Not to forget our four-legged hiking buddies: Spur, Reese, Stewart, and Scout.

Finally, thanks to this edition's editors: Dave Costello, David Legere, and Julie Marsh. A special thanks to Dave Costello for his attention to detail and considerate approach to creating this edition of the guidebook.

Map and Icon Legends

ICON LEGEND

 BEST
FOR PHOTOS

 HIKES FOR
FAMILIES

 HIKES FOR
WATERFALLS

 DOG-FRIENDLY
TRAILS

 FINDING
SOLITUDE

Each hike begins with **The Rundown**, a summary that describes the length of the trip and the basic geography. For day hikes, most entries indicate the approximate time required for the hike, using these three categories as general rules of thumb, based on an average adult hiking pace and decent trail conditions: "Short day hikes" are, generally, hikes of 3 hours or less; "half-day hikes" take roughly 3 to 5 hours; and "long hikes" will keep you outdoors more than 5 hours and up to an entire sunset-free day in midsummer. There are options for shorter hikes on most of the longer trips covered; options are listed in "Shorter hikes" at the end of the narrative.

Distances shown are the actual distance of the trail or route. For traverses or loops, this is the entire distance of the trip. Distances shown as "one way" indicate out-and-back hikes; if you do the entire round-trip, you'll cover double the listed trail mileage.

Difficulty ratings give a general sense of how strenuous a hike is. The ratings correspond to elevation gain, tempered by the grade, length, and hiking surface.

Easy: can be completed without difficulty by hikers of all abilities
Moderate: is challenging for novices
Strenuous: may tax even experienced hikers
Very strenuous: difficult even for experienced hikers

Trail type refers to the degree of development of the trail. Accessible trails are packed and graded and suitable for mobility-impaired people, including those who use wheelchairs. "More-developed" trails are planned and constructed trails with some combination of trail structures like bridges or foot logs over streams, switchbacks, steps, bench-cut tread on side slopes, boardwalk in wet areas, signs, and for the most part, a clear path and relatively even tread.

"Less-developed" trails may in places have structures like more-developed trails, but they are generally rougher and will take longer to hike. While there is a tread to follow in most places, it may be only the tread other hikers have made with their boot soles. Less-developed trails are usually maintained less frequently. They are common in Alaska's state parks.

A "route" may be marked with rock cairns, wooden posts, or fiberglass stakes and follow intermittent sections of tread laid down by hikers' feet, but is rough and may be difficult to follow in places. "Cross-country" refers to travel following a line of geography like a stream or ridgeline without any marking or tread to follow. "Path" as used here refers to any tread hikers can follow on the ground.

Total elevation gain is a figure in vertical feet that reflects all the uphill grade on the hike; if there are significant ups and downs, the figure includes a rough total of all the "ups," so in many cases it's more than the elevation of the destination minus the elevation of the trailhead.

Note that some of the geographic features in the text and on the maps make use of an Alaska convention for referring to important features that do not have official names, as is the case with much of Alaska's geography. The convention is to combine the generic name of the type of feature with its elevation in feet, for example, Peak 6,430 and Knob 2,211.

HOW TO USE THE PROFILES AND MAPS

This book uses elevation profiles to provide an idea of the elevation changes you will encounter along each route. This, in turn, will help you understand the difficulty of the hike. In the profiles, the vertical axes of the graphs show the total distance climbed in feet. In contrast, the horizontal axes show the distance traveled one way in miles. It is important to understand that the vertical (feet) and horizontal (miles) scales can differ between hikes. Read each profile carefully, making sure you read both the height and distance shown. This will help you interpret what you see in each profile. Some elevation profiles may show gradual ascents and descents to be steep and steep ones to be gradual. Elevation profiles are not provided for hikes with little or no elevation gain.

The maps in this book that depict a detailed close-up of an area use color to portray relief. These maps will give you a good idea of elevation gain and loss. They are a good reference, but should not replace USGS Topographic Maps that should be used as the navigational tool.

ABOUT THE MAPS

Topographic maps are an essential companion to the activities in this guide. Falcon has partnered with National Geographic to provide the best mapping resources. Each activity is accompanied by a detailed map and the name of the National Geographic TOPO! map (USGS).

If the activity takes place on a National Geographic Trails Illustrated map, it will be noted. Continually setting the standard for accuracy, each Trails Illustrated topographic map is crafted in conjunction with local land managers and undergoes rigorous review and enhancement before being printed on waterproof, tear-resistant material. Trails Illustrated maps and information about their digital versions, that can be used on mobile GPS applications, can be found at natgeomaps.com.

MAP LEGEND

—②—	State Highway
—9578—	County/Forest/Local Road
------	Featured Route on Trail
▬▬▬▬	Featured Route on Road
▬▬▬▬	Featured Route on Unpaved Road
•••••••••	Featured Off-Trail Route
- - - - -	Trail
•••••••••	Off-Trail Route
🪑	Bench
‿	Bridge
🛥	Boat Ramp
🏠	Cabin
△	Campground
•—•	Gate
▢	Glacier
🛏	Inn/Lodging
⛏	Mine
▣	National Park
P	Parking
‿	Pass/Gap
🌲	Park
▲	Peak
🎋	Picnic Area
□	Point of Interest
👫	Ranger Station/Park Office
📷	Scenic View
⊏	Shelter
🎿	Ski Area
🔍	Spring
①	Trailhead
?	Visitor/Information Center
〰	Waterfall

	BEST PHOTOS	FAMILY FRIENDLY	WATER FEATURES	DOG FRIENDLY	FINDING SOLITUDE
HOMER					
1. Kachemak Bay Beach	●	●	●	●	●
2. Wynn Nature Center		●			●
3. Grace Ridge Trail	●		●		●
4. Grewingk Valley	●		●		●
5. China Poot Lake		●	●		●
SEWARD/EASTERN KENAI					
6. Caines Head	●		●		●
7. Exit Glacier	●	●	●		
8. Harding Icefield	●				
9. Lost Lake	●		●	●	●
10. Ptarmigan Lake		●	●	●	
11. Johnson Pass	●	●	●	●	●
12. Crescent and Carter Lakes			●		●
13. Russian Lakes	●	●	●		
14. Resurrection Pass	●		●	●	●
15. Devil's Creek	●		●	●	●
KENAI NATIONAL WILDLIFE REFUGE					
16. Fuller Lakes and Skline Ridge			●	●	●
17. Kenai River	●	●	●	●	
18. Skilak Lookout, Bear Mountain, and Vista Trails	●	●	●		
19. Seven Lakes	●	●	●	●	●

	BEST PHOTOS	FAMILY FRIENDLY	WATER FEATURES	DOG FRIENDLY	FINDING SOLITUDE
HOPE TO GIRDWOOD					
20. Gull Rock	•		•	•	•
21. Hope Point	•		•	•	•
22. Trail of Blue Ice		•	•	•	
23. Byron Glacier	•	•	•	•	
24. Portage Pass	•	•	•	•	•
25. Winner Creek		•	•		•
26. Crow Pass	•		•		•
CHUGACH STATE PARK SOUTH					
27. Bird Ridge	•			•	•
28. Falls Creek			•	•	•
29. McHugh and Rabbit Lakes	•		•	•	•
30. Turnagain Arm Trail	•	•	•	•	
31. Flattop Mountain		•			
32. Ship Lake Pass	•	•	•	•	•
33. Williwaw Lakes	•		•	•	•
34. Wolverine Peak	•		•	•	•
CHUGACH STATE PARK NORTH					
35. South Fork Eagle River	•	•	•	•	•
36. Eagle River Valley		•	•	•	
37. Mount Baldy	•	•		•	
38. Ptarmigan Valley and Roundtop			•	•	
39. Twin Peaks Trail	•		•	•	•
40. Bold Ridge Trail	•		•	•	•

	BEST PHOTOS	FAMILY FRIENDLY	WATER FEATURES	DOG FRIENDLY	FINDING SOLITUDE
MATANUSKA AND SUSITNA VALLEYS					
41. Pioneer Ridge	•				•
42. Lazy Mountain and Matanuska Peak	•				•
43. West Butte	•	•		•	
44. Mint Glacier Valley	•		•	•	•
45. Reed Lakes	•		•		•
46. Snowbird Mine and Glacier Pass	•		•	•	•
47. Independence Mine		•	•		
TALKEETNA					
48. Talkeetna Lakes Park		•	•	•	•
DENALI STATE PARK					
49. Byers Lake	•	•	•	•	
50. Kesugi Ridge	•		•	•	•
DENALI NATIONAL PARK AND PRESERVE					
51. Triple Lakes Trail		•	•		•
52. Mount Healy Trail	•				
53. Savage River Valley	•	•	•		
FAIRBANKS					
54. Creamer's Field		•	•	•	•
55. Granite Tors	•			•	•
56. Angel Rocks	•		•		•
57. Chena Dome					
58. Pinnell Mountain				•	•
59. Summit Trail				•	•

	BEST PHOTOS	FAMILY FRIENDLY	WATER FEATURES	DOG FRIENDLY	FINDING SOLITUDE
DELTA JUNCTION					
60. Quartz Lake State Recreation Trails		•	•	•	
WRANGELL–ST. ELIAS NATIONAL PARK AND PRESERVE					
61. Root Glacier and Stairway Icefall	•	•	•		
62. Bonanza Ridge	•		•		•
63. Caribou Creek			•	•	•
64. Trail and Lost Creeks			•	•	•
65. Skookum Volcano	•		•		•
GLENNALLEN TO VALDEZ					
66. Tonsina River		•	•	•	
67. Worthington Glacier	•	•			
CORDOVA					
68. Power Creek and Crater Lake	•	•	•	•	•
69. Sheridan Mountain Trail	•		•	•	•
70. McKinley Lake	•	•	•	•	•
71. Saddlebag Glacier	•	•	•	•	
SKAGWAY					
72. Laughton Glacier	•	•	•		•
73. Chilkoot Pass	•		•		•
74. Dewey Lakes		•	•		•
75. Sturgill's Landing	•		•		•

	BEST PHOTOS	FAMILY FRIENDLY	WATER FEATURES	DOG FRIENDLY	FINDING SOLITUDE
HAINES					
76. Mount Ripinsky and 7 Mile Saddle	•		•	•	•
77. Mount Riley	•		•	•	•
78. Seduction Point	•	•	•		•
JUNEAU					
79. Perseverance Trail		•	•	•	
80. Mount Juneau and Granite Creek	•		•	•	•
81. Dan Moller Trail	•		•	•	•
82. East Glacier and Nugget Creek		•	•		
83. West Glacier	•		•		
84. Montana Creek and Windfall Lake		•	•	•	•
85. Auke Nu Trail	•		•	•	•
86. Herbert Glacier		•	•	•	•
87. Amalga Trail	•		•	•	•
88. Point Bridget	•	•	•	•	•
SITKA					
89. Indian River	•	•	•	•	•
90. Sitka National Historical Park		•	•		
91. Harbor Mountain and Gavan Hill	•			•	•
92. Starrigavan Bay		•	•	•	
93. Beaver Lake and Herring Cove Trail	•	•	•	•	

	BEST PHOTOS	FAMILY FRIENDLY	WATER FEATURES	DOG FRIENDLY	FINDING SOLITUDE
PETERSBURG					
94. Three Lakes and Ideal Cove		•	•		
95. Petersburg Lake	•		•		•
WRANGELL					
96. Rainbow Falls and Institute Creek	•	•	•		•
KETCHIKAN					
97. Deer Mountain	•		•	•	•
98. Ward Lake and Ward Creek		•	•	•	
99. Perseverance Lake		•	•	•	
100. Naha River		•	•		•

Brown bear feeding on salmon at the
confluence of Funnel and Moraine Creeks
in Katmai National Park and Preserve.
HALEY JOHNSTON

BEFORE YOU HIT THE TRAIL

Alaska! the midnight sun in the Arctic, the rain forest along the twisting coastline of the Southeast, the towering peaks and glaciers along the Gulf of Alaska, alpine ridges rolling like ocean waves across the Interior—it's all waiting for hikers to explore.

The state is enormous, and the name fits: "Alaska" is a corruption of an Aleut word that translates to "great land." From the heavily forested Southeast to the expansive Arctic plain, the Great Land is a mosaic of forests, glaciers, fjords, islands, mountains, rivers, muskeg, and tundra, stretching 1,400 miles north to south and 2,300 miles east to west. Alaska is about a fourth the size of the entire Lower 48 states.

It's also the wildest state, by far, in the United States; Alaska contains fifteen national parks, preserves, monuments, and national historical parks, including Wrangell-St. Elias National Park and Preserve, the largest national park in the country, as well as the Tongass and Chugach National Forests, the two largest national forests in the country.

REGIONS AND CLIMATES

Southeast Alaska, a land of islands, ocean, mountains, and forest, is the southernmost region of the state. Except for Haines and Skagway, the Southeast is accessible from outside only by air or state ferry. The largest areas of uncut temperate rain forests in the world are here; this is Alaska's mildest and rainiest region.

May and June are the driest months, but some of the high country, especially in the northern Southeast, is not snow-free until late June or early July. Hot summer days may top 80 degrees Fahrenheit, but a cloudy day with a high in the 60s is more typical. The low-elevation hiking season is a long one, even year-round in the south if you don't mind hiking in the winter rain. Winter is wet; October usually brings the first major winter storms.

Southcentral Alaska lies north of the Gulf of Alaska and south of the arc of the Alaska and Aleutian ranges. Southcentral is the home of 70 percent of the state's residents, the most extensive road system, and the most developed hiking trails. Chugach National Forest on the Kenai Peninsula and Chugach State Park outside Anchorage are the most developed hiking areas.

Southcentral is also the region with the most natural diversity, with coastal, interior, and transitional forests, fjords and tidewater glaciers, great rivers, and major mountain ranges. The climate is transitional too, from the wetter, milder climate of the southern coast to the drier, colder climate of the interior.

During the snow-free season, average rainfall increases gradually from May to September. On average, August and September are the peak precipitation months of the year. In Southcentral's mountains, June is typically "posthole" month, when hikers punch through the snow that lingers at higher elevations. A hot summer day can take temperatures into the 80s. Autumn in the high country can begin as early as late August.

Interior Alaska, the largest of Alaska's regions, is the part of the state between the Alaska and Brooks Ranges. The Interior holds many of Alaska's longest rivers, including the Yukon River. The Interior is connected by highway to Southcentral, and there is a system of gravel roads to the more remote country north of Fairbanks.

Snow melts more quickly in spring in the Interior than in Southcentral, and there is a thunderstorm season with frequent forest fires early in summer. Midsummer can bring temperatures in the 90s, but the weather cools significantly by September.

Southwest Alaska, accessible mainly by air, runs 1,400 miles down the Alaska Peninsula and the Aleutian Island chain. It's a wet, windblown land of sea and volcano, the home of Katmai National Park and several other conservation areas.

Western Alaska is mainly a tundra zone, stretching north along the Bering Sea from Bristol Bay to Kotzebue Sound. There are millions of acres of seldom-visited preserves and refuges here.

Arctic Alaska, another remote region, lies north of the Arctic Circle, mostly beyond North America's northern tree line, and includes the Brooks Range. There are several large national preserves in the Arctic: the Arctic National Wildlife Refuge and four National Park Service areas—Gates of the Arctic, Noatak, Kobuk Valley, and Cape Krusenstern.

The Arctic has 24 hours of daylight a day in midsummer, but the warm-weather season is short; only from June through September are average daily temperatures above freezing. In the Interior, the light snow cover melts relatively early, but arctic fronts can blow in from the north with fresh snow anytime in the summer.

THE NATURE OF ALASKA

Wildlife. Alaska has the full, natural range of northern wildlife. In the charismatic megafauna department, there are bears and wolves, mountain (Dall) sheep and goats, moose, black-tailed deer, and caribou. Smaller but no-less-important mammals like lynx, coyote, fox, river otter, mink, marten, wolverine, marmot, pika, ground squirrel, beaver, lemming, and vole all inhabit the state as well. Elk and bison are not native, but have been introduced to a few areas. Sport and subsistence hunting of moose, deer, and Dall sheep is popular; hunting season generally begins in mid-August.

Humpback and gray whales, orcas, dolphins, porpoises, sea otters, sea lions, harbor seals, and twenty other varieties of marine mammals spend at least part of the year in Alaska's coastal waters. About 300 species of birds visit or live permanently in Alaska.

Fish. Alaska's pristine waters support five species of salmon, rainbow trout, steelhead, char, grayling, Dolly Varden, lake trout, pike, sheefish, and other fish; Alaska's salmon runs are world famous. If you plan to fish, be sure to buy a license and read up on the regulations before you wet a line. Even if you don't fish, seeing a run of salmon in a small stream is an unforgettable sight. For detailed information, check out Alaska Department of Fish and Game online: www.adfg.state.ak.us.

Plants. Seeing three dozen species of Alaska wildflowers in a day of June or July hiking is not all that unusual; there are 1,500 species of flowering plants in Alaska. Tundra, the low-growing mix of mosses, lichens, sedges, grasses, herbs, and shrubs, is widespread in the mountains (alpine tundra) and beyond the northern tree line (arctic tundra).

Only fifteen Alaska tree species commonly grow taller than 30 feet. The two main types of forest are boreal, or northern, forest, the forest of white and black spruce in the Interior, and coastal forests, mainly Sitka spruce and western hemlock, found in Southeast Alaska and the coastal parts of Southcentral.

Berries and mushrooms are abundant in Alaska's wilds. Blueberries, salmonberries, huckleberries, and raspberries are favorites among the berries, as are shaggy manes, hedgehogs, and king boletes among the mushrooms. The first rule of berry and mushroom hunting, however, is to know positively what you're looking at before you munch; there are several poisonous berries and mushrooms in the state.

TRAILS AND THE HIKING LANDSCAPE

Almost all of the state's developed hiking trails are in Southcentral, Interior, and Southeast regions of the state. Many of the state's national parks have few or no established trails; they're largely remote wilderness parks with rugged hiking conditions.

The condition of Alaska's hiking trails and routes varies greatly. There are graded and graveled nature trails, easy front-country trails, well-developed backcountry trails, trails on miles of boardwalk, routes that are barely scratched out on the ground or that are marked only with rock cairns, and routes with no trails at all—where orienteering skills are needed.

Glaciers are the high point of some of Alaska's hikes; in general, hikers without training and glacier-travel equipment should not venture onto glacial ice, which can hide dangerous crevasses and holes.

Some hikes will travel through the ever-present "brush zone" between forest and alpine country in Southeast and Southcentral. This band of tall grasses, perennials, and intertwined shrubs, especially alders, can make hiking off-trail quite difficult.

Many of Southeast's trails are highly developed, including miles of boardwalk. Long boardwalk hikes can be tough on knees and hips, and boardwalks can be slick when wet.

THE HIKER'S ESSENTIALS

Preparation is the key to a good hike. Pick a hike within the abilities of all members of your party. Pack gear and supplies based on the trip you're planning. Leave word of your plans with someone who will be responsible for calling for help in the event you are overdue on your return and check the weather forecast before you leave.

When you're out in the backcountry, adopt wilderness time, paying close attention to what the land, the water, and the weather are telling you. If you have a plane to catch or a job to get back to, and it's on the other side of an unbridged, raging river, or getting there involves venturing out of a dry tent into a howling storm, you're probably better off letting nature dictate your schedule.

The Ten Essentials for day trips, as usually quoted, include food and water, extra clothing, rain gear, map, compass, matches and fire starter, knife, first-aid kit, flashlight, and sunglasses.
KIRSTEN ANDERSON/RAMBLE OUT YONDER DESIGN

The idea of the "Ten Essentials" is widespread and a good general concept, but remember that each trip carries its own requirements. The Ten Essentials for day trips include: food and water, extra clothing, rain gear, map, compass, matches and fire starter, knife, first-aid kit, flashlight, and sunglasses.

See the sample backpacking checklist in appendix 4.

STREAM CROSSINGS

There are bridges on many of Alaska's trails, but there are many others where wading is the only way to cross streams. Stream crossings can be very dangerous without knowledge and preparation; many experienced wilderness wanderers consider stream crossings the riskiest aspect of backcountry travel. With planning and patience, however, hikers can expand their hiking universes to include the wider wilderness without bridges. A few tips:

- Pick the safest route (see below). Consider depth and width of the stream, the strength of the current, and water clarity.
- Alaska water is cold, and cold water can quickly rob you of heat and energy and the feeling in your feet, making any crossing risky. Wear your boots; they offer

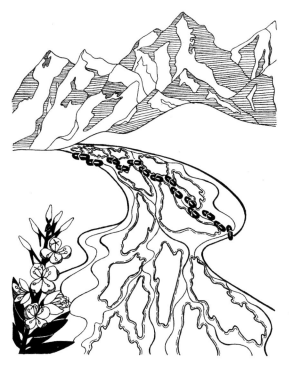

A braided stream, with footprints showing what is usually the safest route among the braids, gravel bars, and islands.
KIRSTEN ANDERSON/
RAMBLE OUT YONDER
DESIGN

more foot protection. One good strategy for dry feet after a crossing is to put on dry socks and add a waterproof layer between your fresh socks and wet boots. For dry-foot comfort later on, bring light camp shoes.

- Cross carefully, one step at a time, testing your footing with each step. Angle downstream along a riffle or a submerged sand/gravel bar if possible. The current is usually strongest in the middle of the stream, so if the current feels strong to you, soon after stepping into the water, it's probably best to retreat and find a different crossing.

IT'S A PUZZLE: PICKING A ROUTE ACROSS A STREAM

Safely crossing a stream means taking the time to scout the best route.

- Pick a wide or braided section of the stream ("braided" refers to sections where the stream widens and splits into several channels, a common feature of streams fed by glaciers). The water is likely to be slower and shallower here. Look for small, closely spaced riffles, which indicate shallow water running over a relatively smooth bottom.
- Walk upstream and downstream to find the best crossing for all the members of your party. In some cases there may not be a safe crossing, and you may have to hike back the way you came.

The best method for river crossing is to go in a group, with the strongest person in the front with a trekking pole, and the smallest member of the group in between larger people. Face upstream and cross slowly, allowing your feet to feel for placement, before shuffling your other foot.
KIRSTEN ANDERSON/RAMBLE OUT YONDER DESIGN

- Check depth by tossing in large rocks. If the rock makes a ka-thump sound when it hits the water, the stream is deep. If you can hear rocks bouncing downstream in the current, the water is too swift.

AVOIDING AN ENCOUNTER WITH BEARS

Bears generally will avoid humans if we don't surprise them. When hiking in bear country, let them know you're there by making plenty of noise. Sing, talk loudly, or clap your hands, and turn up the volume if you're approaching an area where the lay of the land or the vegetation limits your vision. Bear bells may not be effective; they're generally not loud enough for a bear to hear over the sounds of wind or water rushing along a stream. Here are a few other tips for traveling in bear country:

- If you see a cub, retreat immediately. Its mother is probably not far away, and she may attack in defense of her cub.
- Be especially cautious early in the summer when the higher country is still under snow; both humans and bears are confined to lower elevations during this time of year.
- Don't intrude on a bear's personal space; if you do, they may respond aggressively. There is no safe distance for approaching a bear; some may feel comfortable at 50 yards, but others have charged people from more than a quarter mile away. Give bears lots of room, especially mothers with young.

FOOD AND OTHER BEAR ATTRACTIONS

Bears are curious and always on the lookout for a meal, and they have a highly developed sense of smell. If you attract a bear to your food, you may be in danger, and afterward the bear may associate humans with food, creating a dangerous situation for all the hikers who come after you. The first order of business is to keep strong smells, of food and anything else, under control.

- In camp, set up separate cooking and sleeping areas 100 yards apart. Cook downwind of your sleeping area and change clothes if you spill food on them.
- Put your food and other smelly items in bear-safe canisters at night or anytime you're not in the immediate vicinity of your pack and its contents. Store the bear-safe canister of food at least 100 yards from your tent.

CLOSE ENCOUNTERS OF THE BRUIN KIND

The most common situation is a surprise encounter that may bring on a defensive reaction from the bear. A few guidelines apply here:

1. Let the bear know you're not a threat by speaking to it in a normal voice, as you would to an agitated dog. Face the bear, and don't run; no one can outrun a bear, and running might excite a predatory response.

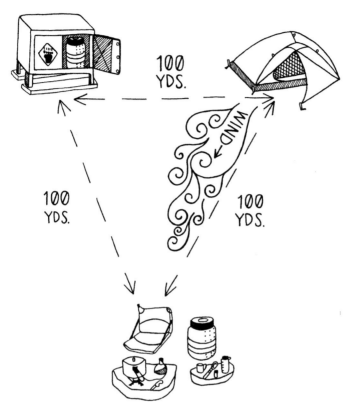

Set up your camp in a triangle, with your cooking area downwind, and your tent and bear-resistant canister with scented items all at least 100 yards away from each other.
KIRSTEN ANDERSON/RAMBLE OUT YONDER DESIGN

2. If a bear charges defensively and gets so close that contact is imminent, at the last second, drop to the ground and play dead. Keep your pack on your back for protection, and lie flat on your stomach or roll up in the fetal position with arms over your head. If the bear appears to leave, don't get up immediately; it may be only a short distance away and could renew the attack if it senses your movement.

For more information, refer to *Bear Attacks: Their Causes and Avoidance* (Stephen Herrero, Lyons Press, 2002), the most extensive and authoritative treatment of the subject in print. Also, at this writing, the Bureau of Land Management has bear information on their website: https://www.blm.gov/ak/st/en/prog/recreation/rec_info/bearsafety.html.

BEAR SPRAY AND OTHER ALTERNATIVES

Most experts recommend carrying pepper spray ("bear spray") in bear country. It's a defensive spray, made of cayenne pepper and packaged in a small aerosol can, that is designed to burn the mucous membranes of a bear's eyes, nose, and lungs. As such, the spray is intended to be shot into a bear's face, not used as a repellent; don't spray yourself or your gear with it!

Bear spray is effective only at close range, no more than 25 feet, and is ineffective when used in the wind.

Pepper spray must be carefully packed and carried; puncturing a can is an unmitigated disaster. If you're taking a flight to a remote area, tell your pilot if you have bear spray along; it has to be packed away for safety.

Some veteran outdoor users carry portable air horns or flare guns as bear deterrents.

Carrying firearms for protection should never be used as a substitute for good bear-country behavior. On trails near cities and towns, where hiker traffic is relatively heavy, firearms pose a significant danger to people.

While hiking be cautious, but enjoy yourself. Given the numbers of people who use the outdoors and the infrequency of bear encounters, the risk of injury from a bear attack is extremely low; it's statistically more dangerous to drive to a trailhead than to hike a trail in bear country.

OTHER HAZARDS

Moose. Moose are plentiful in Southcentral and the Interior, and present but less abundant in other parts of the state. Give any moose a wide berth, and keep dogs under control. If a moose responds aggressively, keep a tree between you and the animal until you are able to move away.

Foxes. Foxes in the Arctic occasionally contract rabies. Keep your distance if you suspect from its erratic behavior that a fox may be sick.

Insects. There are twenty-eight species, and they all bite. They can be thick and voracious, especially in the Interior, the Arctic, and in wetlands, lowlands, and forests anywhere. The latter half of June is usually the height of mosquito season, but in some places they can be annoying until the first frosts.

Some hikers consider a head net or a bug jacket necessary gear during peak mosquito season. Traveling and camping in open country where there is a breeze, for example, along river bars and open ridges, helps keep them away.

In some years, wasps and hornets are fairly abundant; they typically nest in brush or downed, decaying logs. There are also several types of tiny gnats, or "no-see-ums," some of which bite. One type, with a touch of white on its feet and therefore known as a "white sock," can cause significant swelling with its bite.

Plants. There are several poisonous or irritating plants to avoid. Baneberry is a common and poisonous Southcentral berry, and poisonous water hemlock and death camas may be confused with other, edible plants. There are several other poisonous flowering plants and fungi, so know what you're eating before you put any part of any plant in your mouth.

Cow parsnip, a tall, widespread meadow plant, can cause severe blistering and skin irritation in the presence of sunlight. Stinging nettle, which causes relatively minor skin irritation in its Alaskan incarnations, is found in Southeast and near-coastal Southcentral.

Near the Southeast and Southcentral coasts, keep an eye out for devil's club, a well-armed shrub with big, palmate leaves. If you get any of the spines stuck in your skin, they may become sore and possibly fester.

OUTDOOR ETHICS
Plan your trip to minimize its impact
1. Limiting group size to no more than six people is best for the land.
2. Know the regulations and special concerns for the area you're about to visit.
3. If it's wet, consider waiting for drier conditions to start your hike.
4. Pack items that will help reduce your impact. Taking a water bag along will help you minimize trips and trampling on the route between your camp and water source, saving stream banks and fish habitat in the process. Bring along a trowel for digging holes for human waste.
5. Stay on the trail. Use switchbacks, and hike on the established tread even if it is a bit wet.

If you packed it in, pack it out
1. Bring along several airtight plastic bags for garbage.
2. Before your trip, remove excess packaging from food and other items you carry to minimize your garbage and lessen the chance you will accidentally leave garbage behind.
3. Plan meals so you won't have leftovers. If you do, carry them out as you would garbage; don't try burning or burying them.
4. Look around thoroughly before leaving a trail rest stop or campsite to be sure you have everything you brought in.

Leave it the way you found it
1. Replace rocks and logs you move from your campsite, and don't tear out clumps of vegetation for your camp.
2. Take care not to burn any tundra with your camp stove.
3. Enjoy the occasional wild edible plant, but don't deplete the population.
4. Leave all cultural artifacts in place. Taking artifacts from public lands is illegal.
5. Respect private property; there are many private cabins and landholdings in the Alaska backcountry.

iking up Pepper Peak
5,450 feet, opens to a
unning panoramic view of
mile-long Eklutna Lake.
e Twin Peaks Trail hike.
OLLIE FOSTER

HOMER

HOMER, THE TOWN AT the end of the road on the southwestern Kenai Peninsula, has no national parks, forests, or refuges, but Alaska State Parks and two private, nonprofit groups manage trails near town and across Kachemak Bay from the city.

Across the bay is huge, wild Kachemak Bay State Park (KBSP), Alaska's first state park, 400,000 acres big, with more than 80 miles of trails, good backcountry camping, and several fee cabins for overnighters. See the Grewingk Valley and China Poot Lake hikes for samples of what you can do in KBSP.

In addition to the Carl Wynn Nature Center, the Center for Alaskan Coastal Studies operates the Peterson Bay Field Station across Kachemak Bay from Homer. The center (907-235-6667; www.akcoastalstudies.org) runs day tours that include hiking the field-station trails and learning about the bay's forest and marine ecology, and also offers overnight tours by special arrangement for school or private groups of ten or more.

The Kachemak Heritage Land Trust (907-235-5263; www.kachemaklandtrust .org) maintains several miles of trails in the Homer "metro" area. One of the most popular and scenic is the Homestead Trail; one end of the trail is on Diamond Ridge Road about 2 miles west of West Hill Road. The other end of the trail is on Rogers Loop, 3 miles north on the Sterling Highway from downtown Homer.

1. KACHEMAK BAY BEACH

WHY GO?

Walking on a coastal beach with chances to view sea life, shorebirds, tide pools, and breathtaking views of mountain peaks and Kachemak Bay.

THE RUNDOWN

Distances: A 7-mile traverse or out-and-back hikes of 3 to 7 miles round-trip

Special features: Beach walking, mountain views, tide pools, birds, and marine mammals. Impassable at extreme high tides; best walked at low to mid-tide levels. Rubber boots recommended

Location: Two trailheads about 1 and 6 miles from downtown Homer

Difficulty: Easy to moderate

Trail type: A beach route; the Diamond Gulch access is a more-developed trail

Total elevation gain: About 500 feet if you hike out via Diamond Gulch; otherwise, none

Best season: May–Oct, although you can hike from Bishop's Beach essentially anytime with favorable tides

Fees/permits: None

Maps: National Geographic *Kachemak Bay State Park*

Contact: Homer Chamber of Commerce Visitor Information Center, PO Box 541, 201 Sterling Hwy., Homer, AK 99603; (907) 235-7740; www.homeralaska.org

FINDING THE TRAILHEAD

For the trailhead at Bishop's Beach, turn south off the Sterling Highway at the intersection with Homer's Main Street, about a mile from downtown Homer. (If you're driving into town, the turnoff is about 0.3 mile beyond the signed left turn to downtown on Pioneer Avenue.) Once on Main Street, travel 1 block and turn left (east) onto East Bunnell Avenue, and then turn right (south) in 1 block, onto Beluga Avenue, which leads into the Bishop's Beach parking area.

For Diamond Gulch, drive to Sterling Highway Milepost 167, about 6 miles from downtown Homer, at the intersection with Diamond Ridge Road to the north. On the south side of the highway, a few feet west of Diamond Ridge Road, a side road leads south toward the coast. Turn here and follow the gravel access road for about a mile, which leads to a dead end at the trailhead.

WHAT TO SEE

Just outside Homer, the beach hike between Bishop's Beach and Diamond Gulch is a wonderful sample of what makes Kachemak Bay special. The bay is a National Estuarine Research Reserve, a designation that recognizes the bay's importance as an intact, very productive northern ecosystem. (An estuary is a body of water where saltwater and freshwater meet and mingle.)

Recommendation number one for this trip is to leave plenty of time for glassing the water for sea otters, seals, and seabirds, watching eagles and shorebirds, exploring the tide pools at Overlook Point and Bluff Point, and just generally enjoying yourself and the views along the beach. Rubber boots are the best footwear choice; examining tide pools, strolling on soft, wet sand, and crossing tidal rivulets and streams are part of the package on this hike. Pick a minus-tide day for the best in tide pooling, and don't forget the binoculars.

The beach is impassable at extreme high tides and is at its best at low to mid-tide levels, so plan to start out 2 to 3 hours before low tide if you're doing the traverse or a longer out-and-back trip. The Homer Visitor Information Center carries printed tide tables, and the center's website lists tide predictions; see "Contact" above. At lower water levels, the pools left behind by the receding tide are easy and fun to explore. Also, if the tide is out, you can hike the sand and gravel of the lower beach, which is much easier walking than the shifting cobbles of the upper beach.

This is about a 6.5-mile stretch of beach, accessed by a road at the end nearest Homer (Bishop's Beach) and a 1.5-mile hike from the Sterling Highway at the trailhead farther from town (Diamond Gulch). At Bishop's Beach, the beach walking begins right out your car door. The catch is that it's busier than Diamond Gulch, with a greater chance of encountering four-wheel-drive or all-terrain vehicles on the beach. For a short beach walk, or early in spring when the Diamond Gulch Trail may still be snowed in, Bishop's Beach is a good choice.

Diamond Gulch Trail is the longer but less-traveled way to the beach, although from either end, once you're a couple of miles from the trailhead, you'll likely find decent solitude. If you're doing the traverse, start at Diamond Gulch to save yourself 500 feet of climbing at the end. If you want to do a more energetic, secluded hike but don't want to shuttle a car, try an out-and-back trip from Diamond Gulch.

Bishop's Beach. At this end there is a small park with picnic tables and restrooms, but no camping or overnight parking. To the left, as you enter the parking area, is the Beluga Slough Trail, a short walk on a decked trail along the edge of the slough, with good birding for shorebirds in spring. (Wait until there is some water in the slough to take this walk; the water level rises and falls with the tides.)

Diamond Gulch. Start hiking the well-beaten footpath (very slick when wet) along the edge of the gulch, reaching the beach at the mouth of the gulch about half a mile from the trailhead.

Overlook Park: This small, isolated state park parcel is about the same distance, roughly 4 miles, from either trailhead. A local nonprofit, the Kachemak Bay Conservation Society, is in charge of the park.

If you do this hike in high summer, the park will be mainly a landform curiosity you examine from the beach, a spot where the usual tall vertical bluffs along Homer's coastline fall away in favor of a flat shelf a short climb above the beach. The nearly flat shelf is dotted with wetlands and ponds, making it a great bird habitat. There are no established trails in the park, and by midsummer tall grasses and shrubs are reaching to the sky, making hiking very difficult. The best time to explore here is early in spring, just after the snow is gone and before the vegetation has grown up. A good plan is to go on a naturalist-guided hike here during the Kachemak Bay Shorebird Festival in early May.

Be aware that there is unmarked private land in the vicinity of Overlook Park, and please don't disturb the private cabin at Bluff Point. If this hike piques your interest about the ocean, pay a visit to the Alaska Ocean and Islands Visitor Center, 0.1 mile east of Main Street on the Sterling Highway.

Aerial view of 7-mile-long Kachemak Bay Beach Trail, between Bishop's Beach and Diamond Gulch in Homer. Kachemak Bay is a geographically protected bay where freshwater streams, glacial meltwater, and tidally driven ocean waters merge.
SCOTT DICKERSON

A woman walks
on the Kachemak
Bay Beach Trail
during sunset.
SCOTT DICKERSON

Exploring the Kachemak
Bay Beach Trail on
sunny, spring evening
MOLLIE FOSTER

MILES AND DIRECTIONS

From Diamond Gulch		From Bishop's Beach
0.0	Begin/end at Diamond Gulch Trailhead.	7.0
0.5	Arrive at Diamond Gulch Beach.	6.5
1.5	Explore the tide pools at Bluff Point.	5.5
3.0	Reach Overlook Park/Point.	4.0
5.0	Cross Bidarki Creek.	2.0
7.0	End/begin at Bishop's Beach Trailhead.	0.0

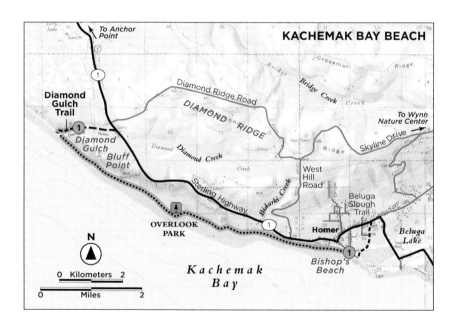

2. WYNN NATURE CENTER

WHY GO?

Walking trails for all activity levels with interpretive loops, overlook platforms, and information at a private, nonprofit nature center on the bluff above Homer.

THE RUNDOWN

Distances: From about 0.2 mile to 2 miles

Special features: Wildflower meadows, interpretive trails, birding, guided hikes, spectacular views

Location: On East Skyline Drive, 5 miles from downtown Homer

Difficulty: Easy

Trail type: Accessible to more developed

Total elevation gain: Essentially none

Best season: Open mid-June to Labor Day, 10 a.m. to 6 p.m. daily

Fees/permits: Trail-use fee

Maps: Wynn Center trail map and nature trail booklet, available at the center

Contact: Center for Alaskan Coastal Studies, PO Box 2225, Homer, AK 99603; (907) 235-6667; www.akcoastalstudies.org

FINDING THE TRAILHEAD

 From the corner of Lake Street and Pioneer Avenue in downtown Homer, drive 0.8 mile east on East End Road, the eastern extension of Pioneer Avenue. Turn left onto East Hill Road and climb 2.5 miles, merging onto East Skyline Drive near the top of the bluff behind Homer. Continue about 1.5 miles east to the entrance to the Wynn Center on the left.

WHAT TO SEE

There's a lot to recommend about the Carl E. Wynn Nature Center. First, there's an accessible, 0.2-mile boardwalk leading to a viewing platform overlooking a pretty wildflower meadow that comes alive in June. Then there's the Dogwood Loop, a 0.4-mile self-guided interpretive loop trail; the landscape along the trail is laid out in a well-written booklet that's keyed to numbered, miniature metal moose spiked into the ground at appropriate spots.

Meadows full of wildflowers finger into forest all over the property, and if you want to add a few to your life list, wooden signs near the entrance identify many of the more common flowers. You can also hike to a raised viewing deck on the Lutz-Fireweed Loop, a platform that overlooks the natural elements that

Walk through dense boreal forest on the Lynx Link Trail at the Wynn Nature Center. WYNN NATURE CENTER

The boardwalk trail leading to a Chocolate Lily meadow at the Wynn Nature Center. WYNN NATURE CENTER

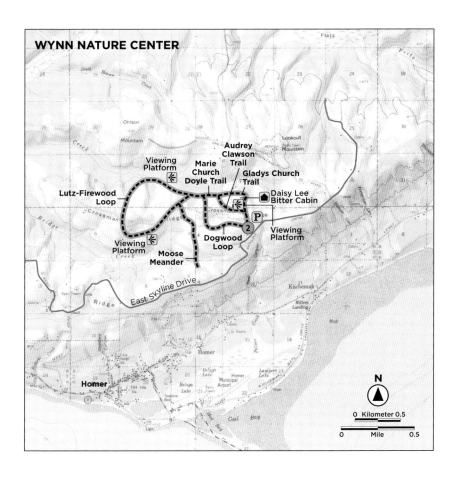

WYNN NATURE CENTER

make Homer special: meadows, tall groves of Lutz spruce, Kachemak Bay, and the glacier-gouged Kenai Mountains across the bay.

Lutz spruce, in case you're curious, is a natural hybrid of Sitka spruce, the common coastal spruce as far south as Oregon, and white spruce, one of the dominant trees of Alaska's interior, "boreal" forest to the north. Lutz thrives in the transition zone between the temperate coast and the subarctic, which is the setting of the Wynn Center and Homer.

From the trailhead, follow the boardwalk onto the center grounds and take the right fork to the Wynn Center headquarters, otherwise known as the Daisy Lee Bitter cabin (the name honors a longtime Homer resident, homesteader, and conservation leader). Drop your trail fee in the box, check out the posted list of plants in bloom and recently sighted animals, and pick up copies of the trail map, the Dogwood Loop interpretive booklet, and plant and bird checklists. You can also join a guided walk, which center staff offer daily; call ahead or check the website for times.

3. GRACE RIDGE TRAIL

WHY GO?

Grace Ridge Trail provides alpine ridge hiking with stunning views of Kachemak Bay State Park, with Kachemak Bay, Eldred Passage, and Cook Inlet volcanoes among the highlights.

THE RUNDOWN

Distances: 8.9 miles one way

Special features: Spectacular hike on an alpine ridge with views of Sadie Cove, Tutka Bay, and the Homer Spit

Location: 10–16 miles from the Homer Spit via water taxi

Difficulty: Strenuous

Trail type: From Kayak Beach: More developed to alpine. Cairns mark much of the route to the summit. Less developed trail at alpine. The trail leading south from the summit (toward South Grace Ridge Trailhead) is an alpine route with intermittent tread

More developed route in the last mile before reaching South Grace Ridge Trailhead

Total elevation gain: 3,100 feet

Best season: Mid-June through Sept

Fees/permits: None

Maps: National Geographic *Kachemak Bay State Park*; Alaska State Parks brochure Kachemak Bay State Park Hiking Trails

Contact: Alaska State Parks, Kenai Area Office, PO Box 1247, Soldotna, AK 99669; (907) 262-5581; http://dnr.alaska.gov/parks/

FINDING THE TRAILHEAD

To get to Grace Ridge Trail, take a water taxi from the boat harbor on the Homer Spit. The spit is at the end of the Sterling Highway, about 4 miles south of downtown Homer.

At this writing, there are two conveniently located water taxis serving the trails: Mako's (907-235-9055; mako@xyz.net) and Smoke Wagon (907-399-2340; 907-235-2341; smokewagon@homerwatertaxi.com), both located on the east side of Homer Spit Road, just north of the harbormaster's office. For a complete, current list of operators, check the Alaska State Parks website (see "Contact" above) or contact the Homer Chamber of Commerce Visitor Information Center (201 Sterling Hwy.; 907-235-7740; info@homeralaska.org).

Kayak Beach is 10 miles by water taxi, South Grace Ridge is 16 miles by water taxi. The landing is wide open to Kachemak Bay and the weather from the west, so during storms or in the afternoon after the wind has come up, landing a boat on the beach can be a problem. There are markers visible from the water at each trailhead.

WHAT TO SEE

The most popular route is to make this an out-and-back day hike from the Kayak Beach Trailhead, however, the best vistas are along the ridge, southeast of the summit.

The trail is more developed from north to south, so it's easier to travel in this direction and traverse from Kayak Beach to South Grace Ridge.

KAYAK BEACH TRAILHEAD

Begin by hiking an old road lined with overgrown alders, then continue climbing through an old growth Sitka Spruce forest. At Mile 1.4, look for views of Sadie Knob. The route crosses a small creek at Mile 1.6, which provides as an excellent water source. It's a good idea to fill up water here, before climbing into alpine. At Mile 2.9, an alpine knob (1,745 feet) provides an excellent destination for a shorter day hike. The trail follows rolling terrain, then begins to follow large rock cairns to the summit. To continue, follow the marked route through the alders to the southeast, cross a saddle, and climb the alpine ridgelines to the peak. The alpine portion of the trail is unmarked, but it is easy to follow the narrow ridges. Keep in mind, it is easy to get lost when the ridge is obscured by clouds (even with the cairns), so it is best to proceed only when there is good visibility. If the weather is clear, the alpine views are incredible with Eldred Passage, Sadie Peak, Cook Inlet volcanoes in sight. Keep an eye out for mountain goats, golden and bald eagles, and black bears (bears are known to frequent this trail). As the route enters into the brush, hikers need to be alert to route finding, as it can be easy to miss the trail, especially in late-summer when vegetation is overgrown. Descending into the alders again, the trail switchbacks into the spruce forest, ending at Tutka Bay.

Kayak Beach is the more popular campsite. South Grace Ridge is less popular for camping, but has a few spots with limited space. Yurts are available to reserve in advance from www.alaskayurtrentals.com, at both Grace Ridge trailheads.

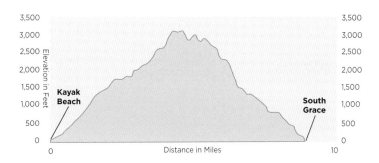

MILES AND DIRECTIONS

From Kayak Beach		From South Grace Ridge
0.0	Begin/end at the Kayak Beach Trailhead.	8.9
1.4	Views of Sadie Knob.	7.5
1.6	Stream to fill up water.	7.3
2.9	Arrive at Alpine Knob.	6.0
4.5	Highest point in trail (3,100 feet).	4.4
8.9	Begin/end at South Grace Ridge Trailhead	0.0

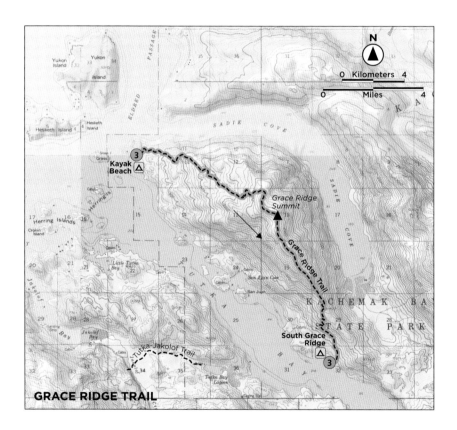

GRACE RIDGE TRAIL

A hiker traverses the summit along the southeast side of the Grace Ridge Trail. Tutka Bay is visible on the right, Sadie Cove is on the left.
JUSTIN WHOLEY

Sunset at the South Grace Ridge Trailhead on Tutka Bay.
JUSTIN WHOLEY

TIDBIT

Before heading into the park, take the time to check on the weather, the progress of snowmelt in early summer, and trail conditions (deadfall from beetle-killed spruce can block the trails). The best local information sources are water-taxi operators and the chamber's visitor center (contact information above).

4. GREWINGK VALLEY

WHY GO?

A variety of hikes, from an easy half-day to a rugged 2-to-3-day backpack, to Grewingk Lake, Grewingk Glacier, and alpine ridges overlooking the valley.

THE RUNDOWN

Special features: A glacial lake, views of Grewingk Glacier, alpine ridge rambling. Access is by water taxi from Homer

Location: In the Halibut Cove area of Kachemak Bay State Park, 8–10 miles across the bay from Homer

Trail type: Less-developed trails to routes

Best season: Grewingk Lake: Mid-May to mid-Oct. Grewingk Glacier: June through Sept. Alpine Ridge: July through Sept

Fees/permits: None

Maps: National Geographic *Kachemak Bay State Park*; Alaska State Parks brochure *Kachemak Bay State Park Hiking Trails*

Contact: Alaska State Parks, Kenai Area Office, PO Box 1247, Soldotna, AK 99669; (907) 262-5581; http://dnr.alaska.gov/parks/

KEY DISTANCES, DIFFICULTIES, AND TOTAL ELEVATION GAINS:

Grewingk Lake from Glacier Spit: 3.2 miles one way, easy, 200 feet

Glacier Spit to Saddle Trailhead via Grewingk Lake: 4.2-mile traverse, moderate, 500 feet

Grewingk Glacier from Glacier Spit: 6.5 miles one way, strenuous, 1,000 feet

Alpine Ridge from Saddle Trailhead: 3.0 miles one way, strenuous, 2,200 feet

Alpine Ridge from Grewingk Lake: 3.8 miles one way, strenuous, 2,000 feet

Alpine Ridge from Glacier Spit: 5.0 miles one way (6 miles if you visit the lake), strenuous, 2,200 feet

FINDING THE TRAILHEAD

 To get to the Grewingk Valley trails, take a water taxi from the boat harbor on the Homer Spit. The spit is at the end of the Sterling Highway, about 4 miles south of downtown Homer.

At this writing, there are two conveniently located water taxis serving the trails: Mako's (907-235-9055; mako@xyz.net) and Smoke Wagon (907-399-2340; 907-235-2341; smokewagon@homerwatertaxi.com), both located on the east side of Homer Spit Road just north of the harbormaster's office. For a complete, current list of operators, check the Alaska State Parks website (see "Contact" above) or contact the Homer Chamber of Commerce Visitor Information Center (201 Sterling Hwy.; 907-235-7740; info@homeralaska.org).

The Glacier Spit Trailhead is a boat landing on a gravel beach 8 miles east of Homer. The landing is wide open to Kachemak Bay and the weather from the west, so during storms or in the afternoon after the wind has come up, landing a boat on the beach can be a problem.

The Saddle Trailhead, 10 miles from Homer, is in a small rocky bay inside Halibut Cove. The landing is rocky but more protected than the Glacier Spit landing, so water-taxi operators typically prefer to do drop-offs and pickups there on windy summer afternoons.

There are markers visible from the water at each trailhead.

Before heading into the park, take the time to check on the weather, the progress of snowmelt in early summer, and trail conditions (deadfall from beetle-killed spruce can block the trails). The best local information sources are water-taxi operators and the chamber's visitor center (contact information above); Alaska State Parks no longer has a fully staffed office in Homer.

WHAT TO SEE

Choosing your destination(s) and water-taxi drop-off and pickup points are the most complicated logistics about this trip. Probably the easiest way to see the whole area is to start at Glacier Spit, hike to Grewingk Lake and Glacier, and then hike out via the Saddle Trail, with a side trip to the Alpine Ridge. For a day trip on the Alpine Ridge, the Saddle Trail is definitely the better choice; starting at Glacier Spit is better for day trips and backpacks in and north of the Grewingk Valley. A popular day trip is a drop-off at Glacier Spit, a hike to the lake and then south over the Saddle Trail, ending with an afternoon pick up at the Saddle Trailhead.

If you want to camp near Glacier Spit and day-hike from there, the spit is a fine beach-camping area (bring water).

Grewingk Lake (via Glacier Lake Trail). The trail from Glacier Spit begins in coastal forest and hugs the south side of the glacier's rocky outwash, passing progressively younger stands of cottonwood and alder. At an intersection a bit over a mile from the trailhead, a trail leads north toward the face of Grewingk Glacier. At about 2.7 miles the Saddle Trail splits off to the south, and the lakeshore is another 0.5 mile beyond.

If the sun's out when you reach trail's end at Grewingk Lake, the blue ice of Grewingk Glacier will be sparkling in the distance at the head of the lake. Gaggles of gulls, shorebirds, and glacier icebergs and bergy bits will likely greet you on the gravel shoreline, as well as wildflowers like dwarf fireweed, yellow oxytrope, and yellow dryas. The retreating glacier has exposed the lakeshore only in recent times, so alders and wildflowers are the only colonizers so far.

If you plan to camp near the lake, look for sheltered tent sites back in the alders, away from the lake and higher up on the lake flats; the park makes a point of warning campers that landslides from the higher country around the lake can kick up large waves that may engulf the shoreline. Please practice low-impact camping and human-waste disposal here; use has increased in recent years, and the lakeshore could suffer if hikers and campers aren't mindful of their impact. In good weather this is a popular area.

The lake's water is glacial and silty—let it settle before treating it, or melt a piece of the glacial ice near shore for fresh water. (There are lots of birds along the shallow edge of the lake, so give your water a good boil.) Better yet, hike back to the Saddle Trail and follow it about 0.1 mile to water in the small draw to the right of the trail.

Grewingk Glacier. From the intersection of the Glacier Lake Trail and Grewingk Tram Spur Trail, a bit over a mile from Glacier Spit, bear left, or north, to head to the glacier. The Grewingk Tram Spur Trail cuts across the glacier's outwash plain another mile to Grewingk Creek; a hand tram—a car on cables with pulleys—is the means to get across the foaming creek. The tram is best with a team of at least two; one hiker pulling in the car and one pulling from shore. Wearing gloves helps.

North of Grewingk Creek one section of the Emerald Lake Loop Trail splits off to the left, leading 2.2 miles to a boat landing, campsite, and trailhead at Humpy Creek. (The pink-salmon runs in both Grewingk and Humpy Creeks attract black bears in midsummer.) Heading east from the tram the Emerald Lake Loop Trail climbs to a high point with a view from Foehn Ridge (a foehn, pronounced fayn, is a strong wind down a lee slope of a mountain). The ridge is a good destination in itself, about 3 miles from Glacier Spit. The Emerald Lake Loop Trail then descends to the glacial plain again. To visit the glacier, stay right at the Emerald Lake Loop Trail/Blue Ice Trail Junction. Follow the less developed trail to a rocky overlook close to the glacier. Watch for rock cairns marking the trail.

Camping options off the glacier trail include the flats near Grewingk Creek north of the tram, with water from small ponds a short way out the Humpy Creek Trail, and sites near a small stream in the glacial flats, east of Foehn Ridge. Another camping option is Emerald Lake, about 800 feet of climbing and 2.3 miles away, high above the Grewingk Valley at the edge of alpine country. There are a few campsites, including two tent platforms, and one bear resistant container for campers to store food in. To reach Emerald Lake from the glacier, take the right fork uphill at the Emerald Lake Loop Trail/Blue Ice Trail junction. This part of the park is at its best later in the summer; snow can linger around Emerald Lake and on the Portlock Plateau

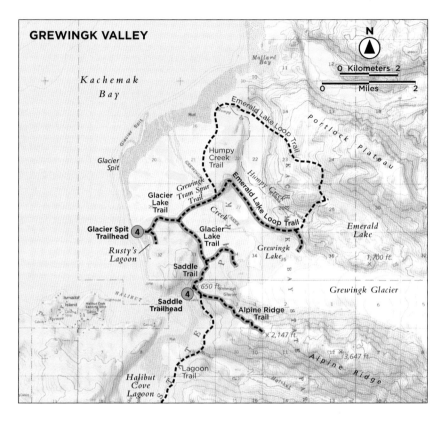

GREWINGK VALLEY

to the north well into July. The Emerald Lake and Humpy Creek Trails connect to form a difficult 13-mile loop from Grewingk Creek; check on current conditions before trying it.

Alpine Ridge. The climb to the Alpine Ridge overlook is a bit stiff, but the view on a good day is fantastic, and wandering out on the ridge from the overlook could keep you entertained for an entire midsummer day. The trail begins in a deep, quiet spruce forest in the saddle between Grewingk Lake and the Saddle Trailhead, with the distant sound of the ocean in the background. Turn east, or uphill, at the junction, and in about 0.2 mile, bear left at the intersection with the Lagoon Trail.

Hiking on the Alpine Ridge Trail, accessible from the Saddle Trail in the Grewingk Valley. The Grewingk River drains the Grewingk Glacier lake into Kachemak Bay in the valley below.
SCOTT DICKERSON

A hand tram—a car on cables with pulleys—is the means to get across Grewingk Creek. The tram is best with a team of at least two; one hiker pulling in the car and one pulling from shore (wearing gloves helps).
BEEZER MUTH

The climb begins to level out at about 1,400 feet elevation, where the forest opens to the first distant views of the village of Halibut Cove, more of the park's ice-blanketed mountains to the south, the Homer Spit across the bay, and the Grewingk Creek valley to the north. Above the brush the trail is marked with a few cairns, but the hiker's path is well worn and easy to follow if the trail is snow-free. The first good overlook of the Grewingk Glacier is on an alpine knob at 2,100-foot elevation. The knob is the end of the Alpine Ridge Trail, but it could be just the beginning of an alpine adventure. The basin below the knob has some fine meltwater ponds, wildflowers, and blueberries, and the ridge stays broad and fairly gently sloped for almost 4 more miles, with fine views of the intricately crevassed glacier below.

Aerial view of the lake and glacier visible along the Glacier Lake Trail, in Grewingk Valley. SCOTT DICKERSON

5. CHINA POOT LAKE

WHY GO?

The trail passes through forest, two small lakes with gorgeous views of Poot Peak and China Poot Lake.

THE RUNDOWN

Distances: China Poot Lake: 2.5 miles one way. Poot Peak's southeast shoulder: 6 miles one way. Moose Valley Loop: a 10-mile loop

Special features: A lake, alpine scenery, fishing, fee cabins, good camping. Access is by water taxi from Homer

Location: In the Halibut Cove Lagoon area of Kachemak Bay State Park, 13 miles across the bay from Homer

Difficulty: China Poot Lake: moderate. Poot Peak's southeast shoulder: strenuous. Moose Valley Loop: strenuous

Trail type: More developed but steep in places

Total elevation gain: China Poot Lake: 600 feet in, 450 feet out. Poot Peak's southeast shoulder: 2,100 feet in, 500 feet out. Moose Valley Loop: 1,500 feet

Best season: June through mid-Oct; July through Sept for the higher elevations around Poot Peak

Fees/permits: Fee for cabin use

Maps: National Geographic *Kachemak Bay State Park*; Alaska State Parks brochure Kachemak Bay State Park Hiking Trails

Contact: Alaska State Parks, Kenai Area Office, PO Box 1247, Soldotna, AK 99669; (907) 262-5581; http://dnr.alaska.gov/parks/

FINDING THE TRAILHEAD

The trailhead is at the floating dock at the head of Halibut Cove Lagoon, about 13 miles by water from Homer, accessible by water taxi from the boat harbor on the Homer Spit. The spit is at the end of the Sterling Highway, about 4 miles south of downtown Homer.

At this writing, there are two conveniently located water taxis serving the trails: Mako's (907-235-9055; mako@xyz.net) and Smoke Wagon (907-399-2340; 907-235-2341; smokewagon@homerwatertaxi.com), both located on the east side of Homer Spit Road just north of the harbormaster's office. Another possibility is to charter a floatplane in Homer and fly to China Poot Lake. For a current list of water- and air-taxi operators, check the Alaska State Parks website (see "Contact" above) or contact the Homer Chamber of Commerce Visitor Information Center (201 Sterling Hwy.; 907-235-7740; info@homeralaska.org).

The narrow, shallow channel into Halibut Cove Lagoon from Halibut Cove is navigable only at or near high tide; check the tides at www.homeralaska.org/tidetabl.htm while you're planning your trip.

Before heading into the park, take the time to check on the weather, the progress of snowmelt in early summer, and trail conditions (deadfall from beetle-killed spruce can block the trails). The best local information sources are water-taxi operators and the chamber's visitor center (contact information above); Alaska State Parks no longer has a fully staffed office in Homer.

WHAT TO SEE

The dock at the head of Halibut Cove Lagoon may be busy with boaters and salmon anglers in midsummer, but decent solitude is just up the trail. Since the tides control when you can get in and out, you might as well relax and stay awhile, at least overnight—and two or three nights is even better. There's a fee cabin at China Poot Lake and two campsites near Moose Valley Creek, and in the subalpine country of Garden Lakes south of Poot Peak. You could also opt to day-hike the trails, overnighting in one of the three fee cabins at the head of the lagoon, or camping in the camping area near the West Cabin. (To reserve a cabin, use the state parks website [see "Contact" above], or contact the Alaska Department of Natural Resources [DNR] Public Information Center at 550 West 7th Ave., Suite 1260, Anchorage, AK 99501-3557; 907-269-8400.)

To get started on your hike, follow the boardwalk above the dock to the ranger station, go down the steps past the station into a clearing, and look for the path on the right side of the clearing that crosses a footbridge; this is the start of the short Estuary Trail.

The trail does plenty of climbing and dipping on its way to China Poot Lake. In 0.4 mile the Estuary Trail meets the China Poot Lake Trail at a junction (The China Poot Lake Trail officially starts on a beach to the west of the dock and cabins), stay left for the lake. The right fork leads about 0.5 mile back to the lagoon (China Poot Lake Trail), the West Cabin, and the lagoon camping area. About halfway to the lagoon, a left fork heads about 1.5 miles to China Poot Bay along the Coalition Trail, a good day-hike option if you're overnighting at one of the cabins or in the camp area along the lagoon.

The "coalition" in the name of this side trail is the coalition of local groups that banded together to save this part of the park from logging and other threats. Where the Coalition Trail reaches China Poot Bay, there is a tent platform with a seasonal stream for water. There is also a yurt available (alaskanyurtrentals.com). Alaska State Parks has also built a section of trail that loops back from the bay to China Poot Lake, but the loop section has been infrequently maintained in recent years, so check on conditions before committing yourself to hiking it.

Back on the China Poot Lake Trail, you'll pass two smaller lakes, and at the second, Two Loon Lake, 1.2 miles into the hike, the Moose Valley Trail leads off to the left, or east. Taking the trail up Moose Valley, over the saddle south of Poot Peak, and back to this point via China Poot Lake adds up to a 10-mile loop. The best camping along the way is near the creek crossings about 2.5 and 3 miles from Two Loon Lake, and in the Garden Lakes area in the subalpine country on the south side of Poot Peak. In midsummer, cow parsnip is tall and healthy in Moose Valley, so wear long sleeves and pants if you're sensitive, and stay alert if you want to keep to the trail in the tall grasses and shrubs.

Beyond Two Loon Lake the China Poot Lake Trail crosses a grassy cottonwood flat before reaching the pretty, forested lake and the fee cabin. Poot Peak hangs above the east side of the lake like a big chocolate drop, and Cronin Island, a piece of private land, rises out of the lake toward the south end. There are a few campsites near the lake on Moose Valley Creek, which enters the lake along the trail south of the cabin. Beyond the creek, the trail twists along the hilly shorelines of the lake and Fourth Lake to the south.

Just beyond the Moose Valley Creek campsites, a very rough, eroded gully of a route leads up from the trail toward the north side of Poot Peak. This route used to be the main access to Poot Peak, but now it is officially unmaintained. Do yourself and the land a favor and skip it; the next trail junction, another mile ahead, is the better trail to the alpine country around the peak. Called the Poot Peak Trail, South Route, it climbs steeply through a gap south of the peak and emerges onto the peak's incredible southeast shoulder at about 1,700 feet in elevation.

The country here is a mountain wonderland, with acres of chocolate lilies, forget-me-nots, lupine, and columbine and views of glaciers, mountains, and alpine meadows. The Garden Lakes country stretches out ahead, and the trail drops into Moose Valley as the Moose Valley Trail. To the left, the Poot Peak Trail, South Route, leads around the peak, tying into a very rough, backcountry route to the Poot Peak summit, elevation 2,600 feet, in less than a mile. Loose scree, rotten rock, and, earlier in the summer, steep snowfields make this a climb suitable for seasoned scramblers only. If hiking in a large group, be sure to avoid hiking lower on the slope from other hikers, as the loose scree can be very dangerous. If you try the peak route, the mountain's north shoulder, well below the summit at 2,100-feet in elevation, is a good stopping point for most, with an amazing view of the peaks and glaciers all around.

The main north-south trail, south of the South Route junction, climbs a low hill and then drops into the wide, braided valley of the Wosnesenski River, about 5 miles from the Halibut Cove Lagoon Trailhead. The open gravel flats offer good campsites and a decent likelihood of a breeze to keep the bugs at bay. A trail leads about 10 miles down "The Woz" (often overgrown, rugged trail) to a landing at Haystack Rock, another possible pickup point if the trail down the river has been cleared recently.

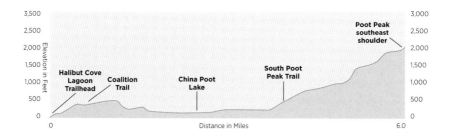

MILES AND DIRECTIONS

0.0   Begin at the Halibut Cove Lagoon Ranger Station.

0.4   Pass the junction with the Coalition Loop Trail.

1.2   Arrive at the Moose Valley Trail junction.

2.5   Reach China Poot Lake.

3.8   Join the Poot Peak Trail, South Route.

6.0   Top out on the southeast shoulder of Poot Peak.

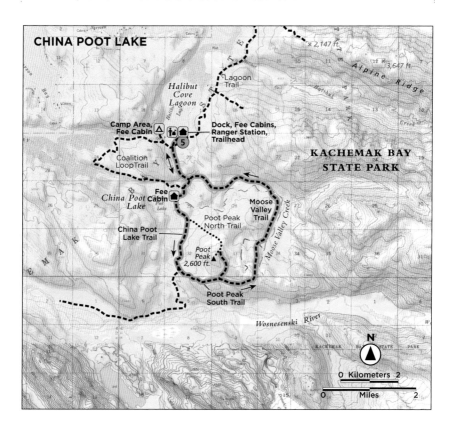

Aerial view of China Poot Lake and Poot Peak accessible from China Poot Lake Trail.
SCOTT DICKERSON

Sunset at Poot Peak and China Poot Lake.
JUSTIN WHOLEY

Shorter hikes: Staying in one of the fee cabins at the lagoon and day hiking the China Poot Lake or Coalition Trail is a good family trip and can be combined with salmon fishing in the lagoon in mid- to late summer.

Fishing: There are rainbow trout in China Poot Lake in addition to salmon in the lagoon.

SKELETON TREES, BARK BEETLES, AND A WARMING CLIMATE

Kachemak Bay State Park's fine coastal spruce forests are history, as you'll quickly notice on the Halibut Cove trails. The trees that once shaded a lush, open understory now stand as gray skeletons over tall grasses and brushy stands of alder. The immediate cause of the die-off is the spruce bark beetle, a tiny insect that lays its eggs in "galleries" it bores into the phloem layer under the bark of a tree. The phloem layer is the tree's veins and arteries, and if enough beetles bore into it, they can block the flow of nutrients and starve the tree to death. The Kenai beetle epidemic, which extends over most of the peninsula, is the largest single insect-kill of forest in North America in at least the last 250 years.

Bark beetles are a natural part of the cycle of change in forests where they live, but the Kenai plague of the 1990s was beyond anything foresters had ever seen. The pattern of mild winters and hot, dry summers that began its steamroller run through Alaska in the early 1990s is the real culprit. The summers stressed the trees, making them unable to ward off the beetles, and the mild winters boosted beetle survival. Normally spruce bark beetles have a two-year life cycle, but apparently the long, warm summers of recent years have enabled them to compress their life cycle into one year, effectively doubling their population.

The Kenai isn't the only place in the North where forests are in danger. The white spruce forests of Interior Alaska and western Canada are also being attacked, in their case by spruce budworm infestations, also thought to be as severe as they are because of the warming climate. Eventually, veteran foresters think, as climate change advances, the conifer forests of the northern interior country will die off completely, and grassy, aspen parklands will replace them.

SEWARD/EASTERN KENAI

THE MOUNTAINS OF THE eastern Kenai have the most extensive system of developed, longer hiking trails in the state, thanks to the Chugach National Forest's Seward Ranger District. The Seward District's trail and campground scene, while similar to many national forests in the Lower 48, is unique in Alaska. Besides the trails described here, try the short trails to Golden Fin Lake (Seward Highway Mile 12), Grayling and Meridian Lakes (Seward Highway Mile 13), Rainbow Lake (Cooper Lake Road), and Victor Creek (Seward Highway Mile 20).

The Kenai Mountains offer experienced cross-country hikers some fine high-ridge trekking. Try heading up onto alpine ridges at Summit Lake (Seward Highway Mile 48), Turnagain Pass (Seward Highway Mile 68.5), and near the headwaters of Palmer Creek outside Hope (up Resurrection Creek Road and Palmer Creek Road).

6. CAINES HEAD

WHY GO?

Along the coastline of Resurrection Bay, this trail offers ocean wildlife, coastal scenery, fishing, history, cabins, and camping.

THE RUNDOWN

Distance: North Beach: 4.5 miles one way. Fort McGilvray: 7.4 miles one way

Special features: Coastal scenery and wildlife, World War II–era Fort McGilvray, two fee cabins, beach walking, and surf fishing. The beach section of the hike, 2.5 miles long, is passable only at a tide of 3 feet or lower

Location: 2.5 miles south of Seward

Difficulty: Moderate

Trail type: More developed trail; beach section is an easy route

Total elevation gain: About 400 feet to North Beach; another 650 feet to Fort McGilvray

Best season: May to mid-Oct, but be especially prepared for stormy weather early and late in the season

Fees/permits: Parking fee or state parks pass; fee for cabin use

Maps: USGS Seward A-7 (SW, SE) and Blying Sound D-7; Alaska State Parks brochure Caines Head State Recreation Area; National Geographic *Kenai Fjords National Park*

Contact: Alaska State Parks, Kenai Area Office, PO Box 1247, Soldotna, AK 99669; (907) 262-5581; http://dnr.alaska.gov/parks/

FINDING THE TRAILHEAD

 Drive into Seward on the Seward Highway, which becomes 3rd Ave. as it enters town. Continue south to the end of 3rd Ave. and take a right (west) onto Railway Avenue, which becomes Lowell Point Road as it curves south and skirts the west edge of Resurrection Bay. Follow this gravel road just over 2 miles to Martins Road, about 0.1 mile south of a sharp left curve in the road. Turn right and then take an immediate right at the sign for the Lowell Point State Recreation Site. The trailhead is at the far end of the parking area.

WHAT TO SEE

Caines Head is the site of Fort McGilvray, a military garrison built to protect Seward's harbor during World War II, and the state recreation area it anchors also features fee cabins at Callisto Canyon and Derby Cove, backcountry camping areas at Tonsina Creek, South Beach, and North Beach, a side trail into alpine country below Callisto Peak, and a trail to the more remote South Beach.

Harbor seals, Steller sea lions, sea otters, porpoises, and humpback whales cruise the coast, and the seabird population includes pigeon guillemots, cormorants, murrelets, scoters, oystercatchers, and harlequin ducks. Don't forget the rain gear; the Gulf of Alaska coast is notoriously wet.

The main logistics of the hike revolve around the 2.5 miles of beach between Tonsina Point and Derby Cove, which is passable only at a tide of 3 feet or lower. (Check tide predictions prior to hiking, see "Contact" above.) The danger here is steep, extremely slick rock outcrops that jut out across the beach into the water; they're too dangerous to climb over (one hiker died in the attempt), so you have to hike it at lower tide levels. The best plan is to leave the trailhead about 2 hours before low tide, allowing plenty of time to cover the 1.5 miles to Tonsina Point and still do the beach section before the tide creeps up to the edge of the outcrops again. Day-hiking Caines Head is possible during the long days of midsummer, but it would be a very long day; once you made it to Caines Head, you would have to wait nearly 12 hours for the next low tide to hike back to the trailhead.

From the trailhead, the hike climbs and then drops fairly steeply to Tonsina Point and Tonsina Creek. The point is an alluvial fan laid down by the two forks of the creek, one north and one south of the point.

Cross the bridge and just before the trail hits the beach, the Tonsina camping area offers tables and an open-sided shelter. If you don't make the low tide, this is a good place to camp, and it's an ideal destination for a kid's first backpack (short hike, plenty to see and do, a shelter if the weather turns ugly). Don't forget the rain gear; the Gulf of Alaska coast is notoriously wet. The Tonsina camp area is also a good place to fish off the beach for Dolly Varden all summer and for silver salmon in late summer and fall. Salmon run up Tonsina Creek, and there may be a black bear or two in the neighborhood when the fish are in.

The Callisto Canyon fee cabin is in the upland forest near the end of the beach section of the hike. The Derby Cove fee cabin is well back in the trees at the end of a short trail from the northwest end of Derby Cove, the cove at the south end of the beach hike and just north of Caines Head. (To reserve one of the cabins, use the state parks website listed above, or contact the Alaska DNR Public Information Center at 550 West 7th Ave., Suite 1260, Anchorage, AK 99501-3557; 907-269-8400.)

The trail from Derby Cove to North Beach begins at the far, southeast end of the Derby beach. It climbs over the north point of Caines Head, connecting with the

Alpine Trail, a 3-mile hike that climbs to rolling alpine tundra at about 1,500 feet in elevation. The Loop Trail connects the Alpine Trail to the South Beach Trail, making a scenic loop passing waterfalls of more than 50 feet in the 5.5-mile route. North Beach is a good base camp for exploring the rest of Caines Head; besides a few good campsites (with bear lockers), there is a ranger station and two open-sided shelters (not for camping) in the trees behind the beach. The trail, actually an old army road, leads south to Fort McGilvray and South Beach. At the Y intersection a mile down the trail, take a left and continue another mile to the fort or bear right another 1.5 miles to South Beach.

The U.S. Army built Fort McGilvray to protect Seward, the main supply port for the military in Alaska, after the Japanese attack on the Aleutians in 1943. You can explore the innards of the old fort, but take a flashlight or headlamp to find your way through the dark, dripping passageways. A short hike up to the grassy summit south of the entrance to the fort leads to the fort's gun platforms and a fine view of Resurrection Bay and the wide-open waters of the Gulf of Alaska.

South Beach is a stony, exposed beach that faces the wind and weather of the outside of Resurrection Bay. It's much more isolated than North Beach. Remains of the army ghost town, the fort's living quarters, lie back in the woods.

Boating to Derby Cove or North Beach is another option for seeing Caines Head. (Avoid South Beach unless it's completely calm; the beach is exposed and often a very rough place to land a boat.) If you boat in, you'll still have plenty of energy for exploring Caines Head once you arrive, and you also won't be tied to the schedule of the tides. Miller's Landing, Mile 3 Lowell Point Road (0.3 mile beyond the trail-head), (907) 224-5739, (866) 541-5739, offers a charter-boat drop off and pick up service, rents kayaks and gives lessons if you want to paddle to Caines Head on your own, and runs a campground where late-arriving hikers can camp before starting the hike the next day.

Campfires are allowed only on the beaches. Please leave all artifacts in place so everyone can enjoy them.

MILES AND DIRECTIONS

- 0.0   Begin the hike at Lowell Point.
- 1.5   The trail drops steeply to Tonsina Creek, where camping is available.
- 3.5   The Callisto Canyon fee cabin is in the upland forest.
- 4.0   The Derby Cove fee cabin is set well back in the trees.
- 4.3   The trail connects with the Alpine Trail.
- 4.5   North Beach (camping, ranger station) is a good base camp for exploring the rest of Caines Head.
- 5.5   The trail forks to South Beach (1.5 miles).
- 7.4   The trail ends at Fort McGilvray.

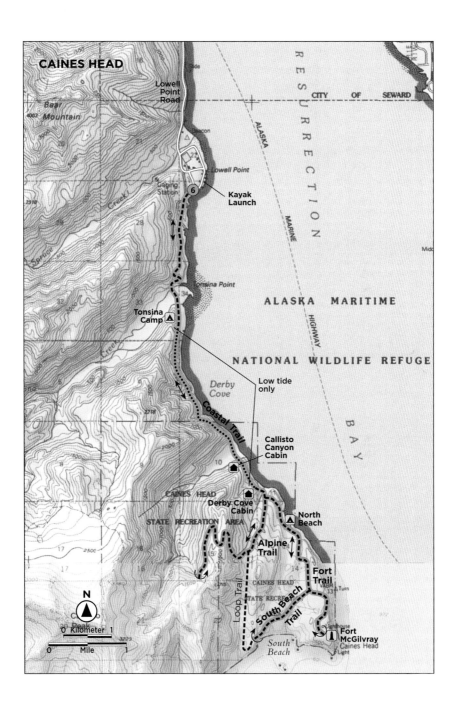

A WWII-era pier at Nort
Beach on the 6.5-mil
Caines Head Tra
ALASKA STATE PARK

A view from the Alpine
Trail, about 4 miles from
the Caines Head Trailhead.
ALASKA STATE PARKS

...kers walk the beach near ...nsina Point on a clear ...mmer afternoon. ...ARRISON SCHEIB

Shorter hikes: Tonsina Creek, 1.5 miles from the trailhead, makes a good day hike or family camping trip.

Fishing: You can surf-fish for Dolly Varden and, starting in late July, for silver salmon, although the best silver fishing is later, in August and September. If you can see silvers jumping, you might have a chance to land one here.

> **TIDBIT**
>
> Read tide tables before hiking this trail. The 2.5-mile section from Tonsina Point to Derby Cove follows an intertidal zone, and can only be hiked during low tide of 3 feet or lower. Also, remember your rain gear.

7. EXIT GLACIER

WHY GO?

Two short day-hiking trails, within view of a glacier, and the only road access within Kenai Fjords National Park.

THE RUNDOWN

Distances: Glacier View: 1-mile loop. Edge of the Glacier 1.5-miles one way

Special features: Exit Glacier, interpretive displays, guided hikes and programs, and a small nature center/bookstore. No pets

Location: 12 miles northwest of Seward

Difficulty: Easy

Trail type: Accessible to more developed

Total elevation gain: Up to 100 feet

Best season: May through Sept

Fees/permits: Entry fee or national parks pass

Maps: USGS Seward A-7 (NW) (trails not shown); *Kenai Fjords National Park* brochure

Contact: Kenai Fjords National Park, PO Box 1727, 1212 4th Ave., Seward, AK 99664; (907) 422-0500; www.nps.gov/kefj

FINDING THE TRAILHEAD

 Three miles north of downtown Seward, turn west off the Seward Highway onto Herman Leier Road, drive about 8.6 miles to the Exit Glacier area of Kenai Fjords National Park and park in the parking area at the end of the road. Follow the paved trail that leads out of the parking area to begin your hike.

The Forest Service's Resurrection River Trailhead (see the Russian Lakes hike) is on the right (north) side of the road to Exit Glacier, about 7 miles from the Seward Highway.

WHAT TO SEE

Exit Glacier is one of the thirty-five glaciers that flow off the 500-square-mile Harding Icefield, the central feature of Kenai Fjords National Park, and the Exit Glacier area is the only road-accessible section of the park. The glacier is now approximately 2.5 miles long, but it has retreated rapidly in the last couple of hundred years; in earlier days the terminus was 8 miles down the Resurrection River valley, roughly where the valley meets the Seward Highway today.

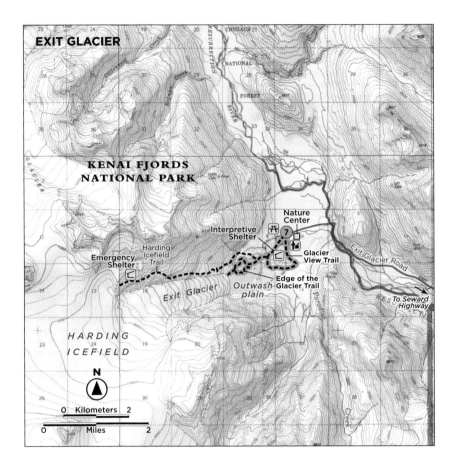

These two designated short trails are a good introduction to glaciers and the landscape they leave behind as they retreat—an especially hot topic these days as so many Alaska glaciers are shrinking in the warming climate. There is a seasonal ranger station and nature center near the trailhead and a small, tent-only, walk-in campground nearby. In summer park staff usually lead hikes to the glacier and give talks and children's programs at the nature center; see the website or contact the park for details.

The first 0.2 mile of the trail system is paved and accessible, leading to an interpretive shelter that houses displays about the glacier and the animals that live in the glacier's neighborhood. Beyond the shelter, the two forks of the trail system divide. Walking all the trails adds up to a stroll of roughly 4 miles.

Exit Glacier Trail ends with intimate views of the 2.5-mile-long glacier, in the only road-accessible section of the Kenai Fjords National Park.
YNEZ SLAYMAKER

The Resurrection River Valley collects water melting out of Exit Glacier and flows southeast into Resurrection Bay (This view is visible above the Exit Glacier entrance area trails.)
WILL KOEPPEN

Glacier View Trail. The Glacier View Trail is an accessible loop winding through the forest to a sweeping view of the Exit Glacier valley. The overlook provides a panoramic view of Exit Glacier flowing from the Harding Icefield, to the toe at the outwash plain.

Edge of the Glacier. The more moderate Edge of the Glacier Trail leads over deglaciated bedrock to the edge of the glacier. A wall of blue ice looms ahead as you stroll to a close up view point: For safety's sake, keep your distance: A number of years ago falling ice killed a visitor posing for a photo next to the face of the glacier.

While exploring the Exit Glacier area, look to the north of the glacier for black bears and mountain goats feeding on the brushy slope. You're more likely to spot animals here early in the summer; they follow the retreating snow line up, feeding on new green growth as it emerges. Also look and listen for warblers, magpies, swallows, and golden-crowned sparrows near the trails.

The trail to the Harding Icefield overlook branches off the Exit Glacier trails. The Exit Glacier trails are open only to foot and wheelchair traffic, and no pets are allowed. There are several shuttle-service options from Seward to Exit Glacier for travelers without vehicles; check the park website or contact the park for details.

TIDBIT

It is not recommended that visitors go to the terminus of the glacier because the creek is deep, fast moving, and constantly changing.

8. HARDING ICEFIELD

WHY GO?

This long day hike in the Exit Glacier area of Kenai Fjords National Park winds through the forest and climbs above tree line to an ice age experience with stunning panoramic views of the icefield.

THE RUNDOWN

Distance: About 4 miles one way

Special features: Exit Glacier and the Harding Icefield, great views and wildlife, especially mountain goats. No pets allowed

Location: 12 miles northwest of Seward

Difficulty: Strenuous

Trail type: Generally more developed; the last 0.8 mile is less developed

Total elevation gain: 3,000 feet

Best season: Late June to mid-Sept

Fees/permits: Entry fee or national parks pass

Maps: USGS Seward A-8 (trail not shown); Kenai Fjords National Park brochure; National Geographic *Kenai Fjords National Park*

Contact: Kenai Fjords National Park, PO Box 1727, 1212 4th Ave., Seward, AK 99664, (907) 422-0500; www.nps.gov/kefj

FINDING THE TRAILHEAD

Three miles north of downtown Seward, turn west off the Seward Highway onto Herman Leier Road, drive about 8.6 miles to the Exit Glacier area of Kenai Fjords National Park, and park in the parking area at the end of the road. Follow the paved trail that leads out of the parking area for about 0.2 mile to an interpretive shelter. Just beyond the shelter, turn right onto the Harding Icefield Trail.

WHAT TO SEE

Start early and bring a camera for this hike to the edge of the Harding Icefield, where dark peaks poke out of a sea of ice. The trail climbs gradually through forest and brush, alpine wildflower meadows, and finally rock and snow to an overlook of the icefield. The moderate, switch backing grade is courtesy of Student Conservation

Association trail workers—high school students hailing from all over the United States—who worked for several years building this spectacular trail.

Fog, rain, and poor visibility are common, and weather can change quickly, so carry warm, waterproof clothes, even on sunny days. Be prepared to retreat if bad weather moves in; you probably couldn't see anything anyway. If the weather is decent, it is well worth the trek.

From the Exit Glacier parking area, pick out the route on the sloping ridge between Exit Glacier and the rocky peaks to the north. A steady climb leads to a viewpoint at 1.5 miles on a brushy knob above tree line; at 2.5 miles, in a rocky alpine area, the view is even better. The last 0.8 mile is a route beaten by many feet over snow and loose rock, following a lateral moraine and exposed bedrock above Exit Glacier. The destination is a wild scene of ice and dark rock, a definite payoff for the climb. Remember that travel on the glacier below the overlook is potentially dangerous and only for people trained and equipped for it.

There is a shelter below the overlook for emergency use only. Camping near the icefield is possible but limited; if you do camp here, please camp on gravel, bare rock,

Aerial view of Harding Icefield, covering 700 square miles and a central feature in Kenai Fjords National Park.
SCOTT DICKERSON

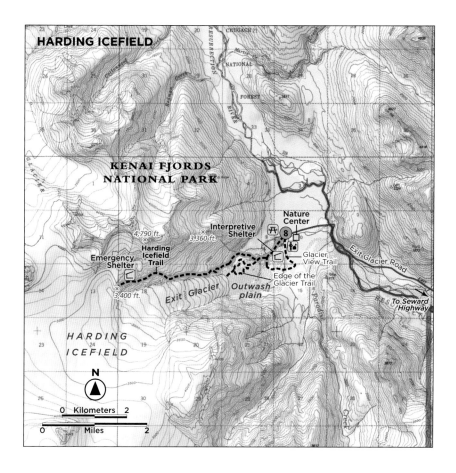

or snow and not on the sparse, easily damaged vegetation. However, if you want to spend the night in the park, you can also tent at the small campground on the park road, leaving you free to carry a daypack up the climb to the icefield.

Mountain goats are fairly common in the high country. Look for black bears, especially earlier in the summer, when they munch on new green plant growth. The trail is for foot traffic only, and no pets are allowed.

Most years, Kenai Fjords rangers lead occasional hikes to the icefield. Check the website, ask at the visitor center in Seward, or corral a ranger at the Exit Glacier ranger station for more information. Also plan to take in the Exit Glacier trails while you're here.

view along the 4-mile hike of
e expansive Harding Icefield,
hich begins on the valley floor.
ARRISON SCHEIB

Shorter hikes: The viewpoints at 1.5 and 2.5 miles make good turnaround points for shorter day hikes.

MILES AND DIRECTIONS

0.0   Begin at the interpretive shelter.

1.5   A steady climb leads to a viewpoint at about 1,600-foot elevation.

2.5   An even better viewpoint is reached at about 2,600-foot elevation.

3.2   The constructed/maintained trail ends.

4.0   Climb to the Harding Icefield overlook.

TIDBIT

Check on trail conditions prior to heading out, the upper section of the trail is typically covered with snow through early July, and there may be avalanche danger. Be prepared for storms, high winds, intense sunlight, and sudden temperature changes.

9. LOST LAKE

WHY GO?
Camping, fishing, long day or backpack trip options, and miles of alpine access are the big draws to Lost Lake.

THE RUNDOWN

Distance: 7 miles one way to the closest edge of the lake, via either the Primrose or Lost Lake Trails, or a traverse of 15 miles from one trailhead to the other

Special features: Alpine meadows, tundra rambling, fishing, and one fee cabin near the trail

Location: 12 miles north of Seward

Difficulty: Moderate

Trail type: More developed

Total elevation gain: 2,300 feet northbound, 2,000 feet southbound

Best season: July through Sept

Fees/permits: Fee for cabin use

Maps: USGS Seward A-7 (NE) and B-7, National Geographic *Kenai Fjords National Park*

Contact: Chugach National Forest, Seward Ranger District, PO Box 390, Seward, AK 99664; (907) 288-3178; www.fs.usda.gov/chugach/

FINDING THE TRAILHEAD

Lost Lake Trailhead. Five miles north of downtown Seward, turn west off the Seward Highway onto Scott Way. The intersection is 0.3 mile south of the Mormon church and 0.1 mile north of the Bear Creek fire station. As signs indicate, follow subdivision roads through several name changes to the trailhead. At 0.2 mile turn left, and after another 0.2 mile, turn right. Follow this road 0.4 mile to its end at the trailhead.

Primrose Trailhead. Seventeen miles north of Seward, and just south of the Snow River Bridge at Kenai Lake, turn northwest off the Seward Highway onto the road to the Primrose Landing Campground. Drive about a mile to the campground entrance; if you aren't camping in the campground, park in the entrance area near the boat launch, as there is no parking at the trailhead. The trailhead is about 0.2 mile from the car park, at the back of the campground.

WHAT TO SEE

Lost Lake is an alpine lake 2 miles long, set at the edge of a huge expanse of alpine country. Long, low tundra ridges finger into the lake at several points, and many smaller lakes and ponds dot the low hills to the east of the lake. To the west, Mount Ascension looms more than 3,000 feet above.

Good camping, fishing, and miles of alpine rambling are the big draws to Lost Lake. An alpine cross-country route to the west leads across miles of tundra, and Mount Ascension attracts mountaineers.

The two trails to the lake, the Primrose Trail from the north from Kenai Lake and the Lost Lake Trail from the south from Seward, offer either an out-and-back trip from one of the two trailheads or a traverse from one trailhead to the other. The Lost Lake Trail is more of a subalpine and alpine hike; the Primrose Trail is more of a forest trail at lower elevations, but from the Primrose end, you can camp in the roadside campground on Kenai Lake and do day hikes without driving. Hiking the 15-mile traverse beginning on the Primrose side saves a bit of climbing and offers slightly better views of Resurrection Bay once you're south of Lost Lake. For shuttle purposes, the road distance between the trailheads is also about 15 miles.

The Lost Lake Trail is a beauty, with great views of the Kenai Mountains and Resurrection Bay, wildflower meadows, subalpine groves of mountain hemlock, and salmonberries and blueberries for the picking. A side trail at Mile 4 leads 1.5 miles to the Clemens Cabin, a Forest Service fee cabin available for reservation at www. reserveusa.com or (877) 444-6777.

There are some possibly confusing forks on the Lost Lake Trail in the first mile. Initially, the hiking trail bears right to avoid a steep, eroded section of trail; the two sections rejoin above. Above, the winter trail to Clemens Cabin (steep, wet, eroded, and not recommended for summer travel) forks off to the right; stay left on the hiking trail.

After 2 miles in the forest, you emerge from the trees on the edge of the V-shaped gorge of Box Canyon Creek, and the glaciated Resurrection Peaks come into view. The brush yields to subalpine meadows by Mile 4, and alpine tundra begins about Mile 5. The first view of Lost Lake is from the 2,200-foot trail summit about Mile 6. It's a well-beaten path that crosses the lake's outlet creek, joins the Primrose Trail (just a matter of trail semantics; it's a continuous trail), and skirts the east side of the lake.

From the north end of the lake, you can wander to the west on easy tundra through a low pass between glaciated peaks into the Martin Creek drainage. This alpine jaunt makes a good day trip while you're camped at Lost Lake, and also is the first whiff of a more challenging backpack; you can keep going through a series of low passes into the upper valleys of Ship and Boulder Creeks, eventually tying in with the Rainbow Lake or Russian Lakes Trails and Snug Harbor Road (see the Russian Lakes hike). If you try this high-country route, take the relevant topo maps with you.

From the north trailhead, the Primrose Trail leads through forest for 4.5 miles, passing a winter trail on the left at about 0.8 mile, a rough side path to Primrose Falls at about Mile 2, and a cabin from the historic Primrose Mine at about Mile 3.5. The actual mine was below the trail, along the stream. There is a current claim, and the claimant has a permit to work the mine and to use an all-terrain vehicle on the trail.

Above the forest the trail follows a 2,100-foot subalpine ridge to Lost Lake. On either side of the ridge, wedged into nooks and crannies, are several small lakes and ponds, some with good campsites. This part of the trail can be really wet and slick in rainy weather.

The south end of Lost Lake is a popular camping and lunch spot. Ice often remains on the lake until July.
WILL KOEPPEN

The alpine section of the Lost Lake Trail makes for spectacular hiking, running, and biking with a well-defined track through rolling hills.
WILL KOEPPEN

Shorter hikes: On the Primrose Trail, hike 2 miles one way to Primrose Falls or 3.5 miles to the Primrose Mine site. The side trail to Primrose Falls is rough; be especially careful along the edge of the canyon at the end of the path. On the Lost Lake Trail, hiking 2 miles one way leads to views above Box Canyon Creek, and a 4-mile one-way jaunt leads to the subalpine meadows near the Clemens Cabin Trail junction. Take a shorter forest hike from either trailhead for berry picking later in the summer.

Fishing: Lost Lake has fair fishing for rainbow trout. Like most rainbows on the Kenai, these are a hatchery strain raised locally from Pacific Northwest stock.

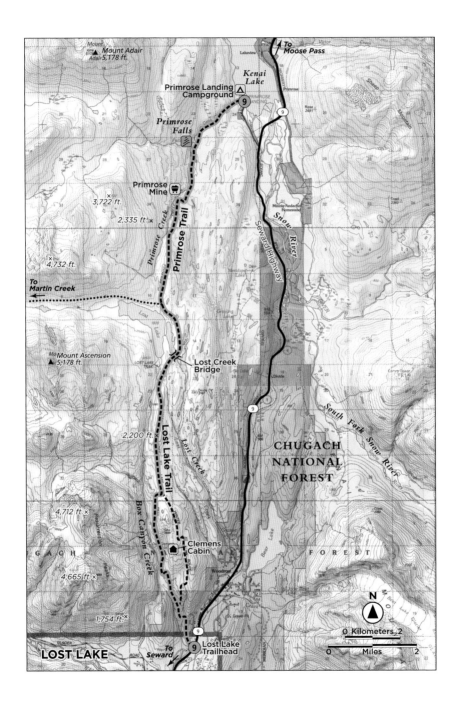

Mount Adair
Mount Adair 5,178 ft.

Kenai Lake

Lakeview

To Moose Pass

Primrose Landing Campground

9

9

Primrose Falls

Primrose Mine

3,722 ft.

2,335 ft.

4,732 ft.

Primrose Creek

Primrose Trail

Seward Highway

Snow River

Minnow Aviation Homestead

To Martin Creek

Mount Ascension 5,178 ft.

Lost Creek Bridge

LOST LAKE TRAIL

L. Divide

9

Lost Lake Trail

Lost Creek

South Fork Snow River

2,200 ft.

CHUGACH NATIONAL FOREST

4,712 ft.

Box Canyon Creek

Resurrection

Clemens Cabin

Boy Lake

FOREST

4,665 ft.

1,754 ft.

N

0 Kilometers 2

9

9

Lost Lake Trailhead

0 Miles 2

LOST LAKE

To Seward

Bearberry covers the alpine tundra among the carpet of autumn foliage on the west side of Lost Lake.
MOLLIE FOSTER

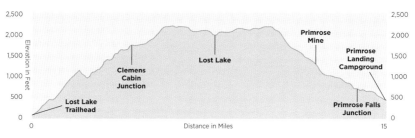

MILES AND DIRECTIONS

From Seward–Lost Lake Trailhead		From Kenai Lake–Primrose Trailhead
0.0	Begin/end at the Lost Lake Trailhead.	15.0
4.0	Intersect the trail to the Clemens Cabin.	11.0
6.0	Pass the trail's high point at 2,200 feet.	9.0
7.0	Arrive at the south end of Lost Lake.	8.0
7.5	Cross the Lost Creek Bridge.	7.5
8.0	Arrive at the north end of Lost Lake.	7.0
11.5	Pass the Primrose Mine.	3.5
13.0	Meet the side path to Primrose Falls.	2.0
15.0	End/begin at the Primrose Trailhead.	0.0

10. PTARMIGAN LAKE

WHY GO?

Camping, fishing, berries, and a beautiful glacially-fed lake are top reasons for hiking the Ptarmigan Lake Trail.

THE RUNDOWN

Distance: 3.5 miles one way to the west end of Ptarmigan Lake; 7.5 miles to the east end

Special features: Camping, wildlife, berries, fishing in the lake and in Ptarmigan Creek

Location: 23 miles north of Seward

Difficulty: Easy to the west (near) end of the lake; moderate to the east (far) end

Trail type: More developed

Total elevation gain: About 500 feet in and 200 feet out

Best season: June through early Oct

Fees/permits: None

Maps: USGS Seward B-7 and B-6; National Geographic *Kenai National Wildlife Refuge*

Contact: Chugach National Forest, Seward Ranger District, PO Box 390, Seward, AK 99664; (907) 288-3178; www.fs.usda.gov/chugach/

FINDING THE TRAILHEAD

Turn east off the Seward Highway into the Ptarmigan Creek Campground, 23 miles north of Seward and 6 miles south of Moose Pass. There's an immediate fork; go right into the day-use area and drive to the end of the road to the trailhead parking area, a total of about 0.2 mile from the highway.

WHAT TO SEE

A long, blue-green glacial lake set below the icy summit of Andy Simons Mountain, Ptarmigan Lake makes a fine family backpack trip, a fairly easy hike of 3.5 miles from the trailhead to the west shore of the lake. The trail continues another 4 miles to the east end of the lake. If you aren't up for a backpack trip, consider camping at the Ptarmigan Creek Campground and day hiking to the west end of the lake. Though the trail is popular, the lake still offers decent solitude. Watch and listen for moose, bears, and coyotes in the neighborhood.

The trail follows the Ptarmigan Creek valley to the lake, staying close by the stream for a bit over a mile from the trailhead. It then veers away from the creek, but determined anglers can continue cross-country upstream to more fishing holes. Climbing higher on the north side of the valley, the trail reaches a viewpoint on a brushy open slope at about 2.3 miles, with a fine vista of the Ptarmigan valley, deep-green forests, and snowy peaks. In another mile the trail drops to the lake, at 750 feet in elevation. A side path to the right

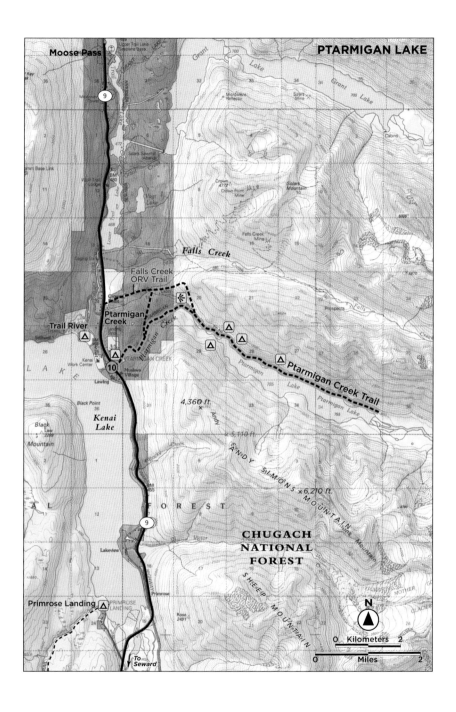

PTARMIGAN LAKE

Moose Pass

Falls Creek

Falls Creek
ORV Trail

Ptarmigan
Creek

Trail River

Ptarmigan Creek Trail

4,360 ft.

5,110 ft.

Kenai
Lake

Black Point

Black

Mountain

CHUGACH
NATIONAL
FOREST

FOREST

ANDY SIMONS MOUNTAINS ×6,210 ft.

SHEEP MOUNTAIN

Primrose Landing

To
Seward

N

0   Kilometers   2

0   Miles   2

(south) leads to the most popular day-use and camping spots, but there are several better spots off the main trail as it works its way east along the lakeshore.

The lower end of the lake is thickly forested. At the upper end, things open up a bit, with a view up the valley along the route of the abandoned trail that once crossed Snow River Pass into Paradise Valley. (It's a horrific bushwhack now, so although it's still possible to make your way there on foot, taking a floatplane to Lower Paradise Lake is a better idea these days.) To the south of Ptarmigan Lake is Andy Simons Mountain, a good mountaineering peak that's usually approached from the Victor Creek Trail, which runs up the next valley to the south.

MILES AND DIRECTIONS

0.0   Begin at the trailhead.

2.3   Reach a viewpoint on a brushy slope.

3.5   Arrive at the west end of Ptarmigan Lake.

7.5   Reach the east end of Ptarmigan Lake.

Shorter hikes: Take the Ptarmigan Creek Trail about 2.3 miles one way to the valley viewpoint, or hike and fish along the creek for 1 to 2 miles.

Fishing: The lake has a small population of Dolly Varden, and Ptarmigan Creek has Dolly Varden and rainbow trout. There are red salmon in the creek beginning in late July, but all salmon fishing is prohibited.

FISHING THE KENAI BACKCOUNTRY LAKES

While the fishing isn't as spectacular, the eastern Kenai Peninsula's backcountry mountain lakes are a lot quieter than the road-accessible streams of the western Kenai, where anglers often stand shoulder to shoulder, flailing away for salmon. The trout and grayling in the high lakes aren't as big or as famous as the salmon of the lower elevations, but they do make for decent fishing in a fine mountain setting.

For the best fishing, try the lakes soon after the ice goes out in late spring and early summer and in late summer and fall when temperatures drop again.

11. JOHNSON PASS

WHY GO?

A popular overnight hike in the Kenai Mountains through alpine with two backcountry lakes and options for out-and-back or thru-hikes from north or south trailheads.

THE RUNDOWN

Distance: About 10 miles to the pass or a 23-mile traverse

Special features: Alpine country, lake fishing, varied scenery

Location: The two trailheads are 32 and 64 miles north of Seward

Difficulty: Moderate

Trail type: More developed

Total elevation gain: About 900 feet southbound, 1,100 feet northbound

Best season: Mid-June through Sept

Fees/permits: None

Maps: USGS Seward C-6 and C-7; National Geographic *Kenai National Wildlife Refuge*

Contact: Chugach National Forest, Seward Ranger District, PO Box 390, Seward, AK 99664; (907) 288-3178; www.fs.usda.gov/chugach/

FINDING THE TRAILHEAD

Both trailheads are located off the Seward Highway between Turnagain Pass and Seward. For the north trailhead, turn south onto the signed access road 5 miles south of Turnagain Pass; the trailhead is at the end of the road, about 0.5 mile from the highway. The south trailhead is 32 miles north of Seward and 0.2 mile west of the Trail Lake Fish Hatchery, on the north side of the highway.

WHAT TO SEE

One of the easier overnight hikes on the Kenai, Johnson Pass makes a good, longer family backpack with kids who can carry their own gear. Think of it as a shorter Resurrection Pass hike without the cabins.

There is good camping and decent fishing at both Bench and Johnson Lakes, which are less than a mile apart on opposite sides of gentle, alpine Johnson Pass. Steeper, cross-country hiking into the higher country from Bench Lake is excellent, though best in the first half of the summer before the brushy vegetation has grown up.

The trail over Johnson Pass, first known to Europeans as the Sunrise Trail, was one of the Kenai's earliest "highways." The trail is one of the segments of the historic Iditarod Trail from Alaska's Gold-Rush era, and the hike today still follows some of the original sections of the trail. Groundhog Creek, about 5 miles from the north trailhead, was the site of an early mining operation; the original, bench-cut wagon road is still visible there.

The north trailhead is the more popular, as it's closer to Anchorage and closer by trail to the pass and lakes. From the north, the trail crosses bridges over Center Creek (just over 2 miles) and its tributary Bench Creek (just under 4 miles). Beyond the Bench Creek crossing, the hike cuts through subalpine meadows that can be brushy and overgrown if unmaintained—watch for cow parsnip and stinging nettle.

The two lakes are practically at the same elevation, but Bench Lake is alpine and Johnson Lake is partly subalpine and partly forested. The trail south of the lakes is uniformly forested and rolling; the southern 3.5 miles more or less parallel the shoreline of Upper Trail Lake.

There is good camping all along the trail as well as at the lakes, including seven signed sites, several of them provided with bear-proof food-storage boxes. Bear and moose are fairly common, so exercise reasonable caution. Dall sheep and mountain goats inhabit the high country. Johnson Pass is one of the more popular mountain-biking trails on the Kenai.

One of the many well-maintained bridges to cross a waterway. WILL KOEPPEN

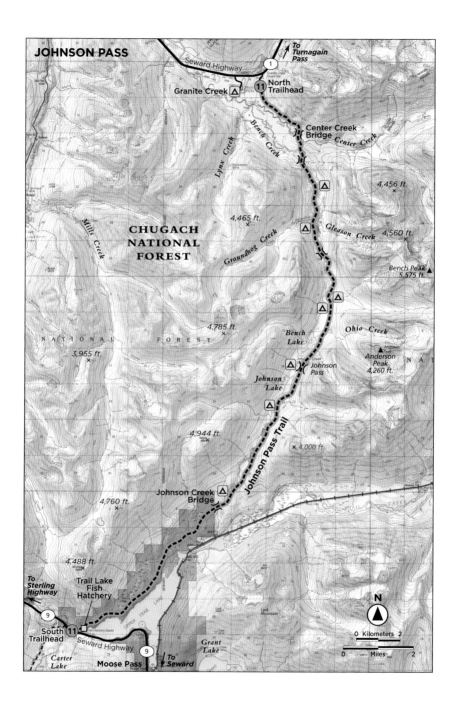

Looking south along the Johnson Pass Trail. The trail is very popular with mountain bikers in the spring and fall.
WILL KOEPPEN

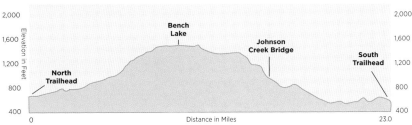

MILES AND DIRECTIONS

North trailhead		South trailhead
0.0	Begin/end at the north trailhead.	23.0
2.0	Cross the Center Creek Bridge.	21.0
5.0	Arrive at Groundhog Creek.	18.0
9.5	Arrive at alpine Bench Lake.	13.5
10.0	Hike over Johnson Pass.	13.0
10.5	Reach Johnson Lake.	12.5
16.0	Cross the Johnson Creek Bridge.	7.0
23.0	End/begin at the south trailhead.	0.0

Shorter hikes: From the north trailhead, hike just over 2 miles one way to the Center Creek Bridge or just under 4 miles to the lower Bench Creek Bridge. From the south trailhead, a short walk on the trail through the forest by Upper Trail Lake rates as pleasant, but with no single outstanding destination.

Fishing: Fish for rainbow trout in Johnson Lake and for grayling in Bench Lake.

12. CRESCENT AND CARTER LAKES

WHY GO?

A trail traveling by subalpine lakes, with options for day trips or longer overnight treks in the Kenai Mountains.

THE RUNDOWN

Distances: Crescent Creek Trail: 6.5 miles one way to the west end of Crescent Lake

Carter Lake Trail: 2 miles one way to Carter Lake and an additional 1.5 miles one way to the east end of Crescent Lake

Crescent Lake Primitive Trail: unmaintained 8 miles one way, linking the two trailheads for an 18-mile thru-hike

Special features: Subalpine lake and mountain scenery, fishing, 2 fee cabins

Location: 34 miles north of Seward

Difficulty: Moderate

Trail type: Crescent Creek and Carter Lake Trails: more developed. Crescent Lake Trail: less developed

Total elevation gain: Crescent Lake via Crescent Creek Trail: 1,000 feet in, 100 feet out. Carter Lake via Carter Lake Trail: 1,000 feet. Traverse: 1,500 feet from Carter Lake, 1,400 feet from Crescent Creek

Best season: Mid-June through early Oct

Fees/permits: Fee for cabin use

Maps: USGS Seward C-7, B-7, and C-8; National Geographic *Kenai National Wildlife Refuge*

Contact: Chugach National Forest, Seward Ranger District, PO Box 390, Seward, AK 99664; (907) 288-3178; www.fs.usda.gov/chugach/

FINDING THE TRAILHEAD

Crescent Creek Trail. Drive 7 miles west of the Seward/Sterling Highway Y junction and turn south onto Quartz Creek Road. Drive about 3.5 miles, past the Crescent Creek Campground, to the parking area on the left (north) side of the road. The trail begins on the south side of the road.

Carter Lake Trail. The trailhead is 34 miles north of Seward on the Seward Highway, on the south side of the road, about 0.7 mile west of the Trail Lake Fish Hatchery.

WHAT TO SEE

Crescent Lake, 6 miles long and 0.5 mile wide, wraps around the rocky alpine peaks of Wrong Mountain, in the shape of a narrow (you guessed it) crescent. It's brushy and subalpine at the east end, and partially forested with spruce and cottonwood on the south and west sides. Carter Lake is a smaller subalpine lake set in meadows, brush, and scatterings of weather-beaten mountain hemlocks.

There are good campsites on Carter Lake and the east and west ends of Crescent Lake, with fewer sites on the less-developed trail around Crescent Lake. The Crescent Lake fee cabin is on the west end of the lake, and the Crescent Saddle Cabin is on the south side of the lake about midway on the trail between the lakes. Each cabin has a rowboat for cabin occupants. Make a cabin reservation at www.reserveusa.com or (877) 444-6777.

Carter Lake Trail. The trail begins as a switchbacking, abandoned roadbed and climbs 1,000 feet, most of it in the first mile, to Carter Lake. The trail skirts the west edge of the lake, with good camping and fishing spots just off the path. The pass between the two lakes is essentially flat. Near the end of the maintained trail at Crescent Lake, the signed Crescent Lake Trail splits off to the left, at the top of an open hill before the lake is completely in view.

Crescent Creek Trail. The path up Crescent Creek cuts over a low divide to join the creek, and then follows it to Crescent Lake. The first bridge, at about 3.5 miles, is just beyond a major avalanche chute, where hardened slabs of snow may linger into early summer.

A second bridge crosses the creek at the mouth of the lake. For the Crescent Lake Cabin, cross the bridge and walk another 0.1 mile. To continue around the lake on the Crescent Lake Trail, stay on the south side of the creek and don't cross the bridge. There are popular campsites near the cabin.

View from the west end of the Crescent Lake, 6.5 miles from the trailhead, it's an additional 0.1 mile to Crescent Lake Cabin. YNEZ SLAYMAKER

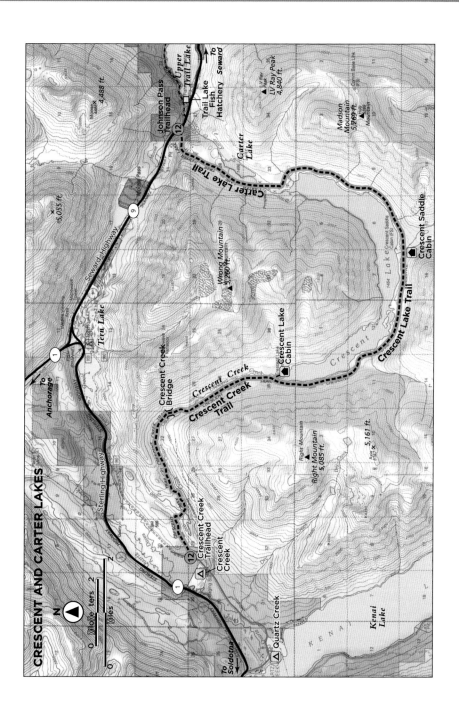

CRESCENT AND CARTER LAKES

N

Kilometers
Miles

Crescent Lake Primitive Trail. The less-developed 8-mile trail along the south shore of Crescent Lake is best hiked in early summer and fall. By midsummer the narrow trail is passable but thickly overgrown in grasses and shrubs, much of it cow parsnip, so if you're sensitive, wear long sleeves and pants. Expect head-high vegetation in places, and if there has been rain or dew, expect to get soaked. There are a few unbridged stream crossings; one that could be difficult at high water is a steep, fast-flowing stream about two trail miles south of the northeast end of Crescent Lake. Crossing the Carter Lake inlet stream also requires a ford, but it isn't usually difficult.

Campsites are limited around the lake, as the shoreline is mostly sloping and brushy; there is one signed site about 2 miles up the lake from the lower (Crescent Creek) end. The Crescent Saddle Cabin sits on a partially forested knob above the lake. A historic trail once ran through the saddle behind the cabin to Kenai Lake.

The three trails are open to hiking and mountain biking, and after June 30 to pack and saddle stock. The Crescent Lake Trail is suitable only for hiking.

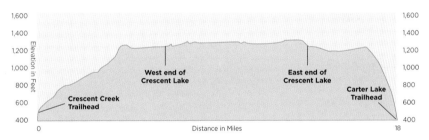

MILES AND DIRECTIONS

From Crescent Creek		From Carter Lake
0.0	Begin/end at the Crescent Creek Trailhead.	18.0
3.5	Cross the Crescent Creek Bridge.	14.5
6.5	Reach the west end of Crescent Lake	11.5 (0.1 mile to Crescent Lake Cabin)
11.0	Arrive at Crescent Saddle Cabin.	7.0
14.5	Reach the east end of Crescent Lake.	3.5
16.0	Skirt the shoreline of Carter Lake.	2.0
18.0	End/begin at the Carter Lake Trailhead.	0.0

Shorter hikes: Two good destinations are Carter Lake, 2 miles one way on the Carter Lake Trail, and the Crescent Creek Bridge, 3.5 miles one way on the Crescent Creek Trail.

Fishing: Crescent Lake supports grayling; the west end of the lake offers good fishing for large grayling. Carter Lake is stocked with rainbow trout.

13. **RUSSIAN LAKES**

WHY GO?

This trail has two large mountain lakes, boating, camping, and fishing, as the sockeye salmon runs attract all types of wildlife, including humans.

THE RUNDOWN

Distances: Russian River Falls: 2.4 miles one way. Lower Russian Lake/Barber Cabin: 3.3 miles one way. Upper Russian Lake/Cabin: 9.5 miles one way. Russian Lakes traverse: 21.5 miles

Special features: Large mountain lakes, fishing, boating, fee cabins; the falls and the lower lake are a fine family hike

Location: 100 miles south of Anchorage in the Cooper Landing area

Difficulty: Russian River Falls and Lower Russian Lake: easy. Upper Russian Lake and Russian Lakes traverse: moderate

Trail type: Mostly more developed; the trails to the falls and lower lake

are rated at a "difficult" accessible level

Total elevation gain: Lower Russian Lake: about 300 feet in and 200 feet out. Upper Russian Lake from Cooper Lake: about 400 feet. Russian Lakes traverse: about 1,000 feet

Best season: June–Sept

Fees/permits: Fee for cabin use

Maps: USGS Seward B-8; National Geographic *Kenai Fjords National Park*

Contact: Chugach National Forest, Seward Ranger District, PO Box 390, Seward, AK 99664; (907) 288-3178; www.fs.usda.gov/chugach/

FINDING THE TRAILHEAD

Russian River Trailhead: At Sterling Highway Mile 52.5 (about 5 miles west of the bridge over the mouth of Kenai Lake), turn south onto the signed road to the Russian River Campground. Continue straight ahead 1 mile to the trailhead on the left. If the station is open, stop at the campground entrance station for a free trailhead parking permit.

Cooper Lake Trailhead: Turn onto Snug Harbor Road at Mile 48 of the Sterling Highway, 0.1 mile southwest of the bridge over the mouth of Kenai Lake. Drive 11 miles on the gravel Snug Harbor/Cooper Lake Road to the signed trailhead on the left.

WHAT TO SEE

The Russian Lakes, two large lakes in the Russian River drainage, offer good camp-sites, trout fishing, and great scenery. Each lake has a fee cabin with a rowboat for cabin occupants, and there is a third cabin between the lakes at Aspen Flat (make reservations at www.reserveusa.com or 877-444-6777). A 21.5-mile trail runs along the Russian River valley, connecting the lakes and the river with trailheads on the lower Russian River (elevation 500 feet) and the Cooper Lake Trailhead (elevation 1,300 feet).

The Russian River's two sockeye-salmon runs attract gulls, eagles, and yes, bears, for the feast, so practice good bear-country behavior on the trail when the salmon are in, from midsummer on.

You have several options for sampling the Russian Lakes backcountry:

Russian River Falls and Lower Russian Lake. From the Russian River Trail-head, it's a popular and easy trip to Russian River Falls and Lower Russian Lake. The trails are maintained to a "difficult" level of wheelchair accessibility, and the Barber Cabin on Lower Russian Lake is equipped with a ramp and an accessible floatplane dock.

A spur trail leads 0.7 mile from the Lower Russian Trail down Rendezvous Creek to the falls, ending at two viewing decks, one barrier-free, overlooking the rocky cascades and falls. From midsummer on, you can usually see scores of bright red sockeye salmon milling around in the pools below the falls and making great leaps to try to get above them; brown bears sometimes hang around the falls, gorging

A mountain biker rides along the Lower Russian Lake, on a 21.5-mile traverse of the complete trail connecting Russian River Trailhead with Cooper Lake Trailhead. MOLLIE FOSTER

themselves on salmon. The tunnel on the opposite side of the river is a fish pass that the Department of Fish and Game opens only at high water to allow salmon to bypass the falls; under normal conditions they have to do the work themselves.

At a fork about 2.5 miles up the Lower Russian Trail, take the wide, gravel trail angling down to the right about 0.8 mile to the lake, the Barber Cabin, and lakeshore campsites. The narrower trail to the left at the fork is the main trail up the valley; it crosses an open slope above the lake and continues up the Russian River to Upper Russian Lake and the Cooper Lake Trailhead.

MILES AND DIRECTIONS

Lower Russian Lake (Russian River Trailhead)

0.0   Begin at the Russian River Trailhead.

1.7   Reach the Russian River Falls Trail (0.7 mile to falls).

2.5   Bear right on the Barber Cabin Trail.

3.3   Arrive at Barber Cabin.

Upper Russian Lake. Upper Russian Lake is a giant body of water, 3 miles long and up to a mile wide. It's a 9.5-mile hike from the Cooper Lake Trailhead and a 12-miler from the Russian River Trailhead, so starting from Cooper is easier if Upper Russian is your main destination. Between Cooper and Upper Russian, the trail runs through a wide, forested gap in the Kenai Mountains, crosses an almost imperceptible divide, and then descends to Upper Russian. Between the trailhead and the lake, there are two signed campsites, at about 2.5 and 4.5 miles, and not many other possible tent sites. The Resurrection River Trail, 5.5 miles from the Cooper trailhead, leads south toward Exit Glacier and Seward.

The trail follows the Upper Russian shoreline for only a short distance near the cabin at the northwest end of the lake. If you rent the cabin and take the cabin rowboat out, you can explore the trail-less, seldom-visited shoreline of the rest of the lake. Just north of (below) Upper Russian are a series of beautiful cottonwood groves along the river flats, with several nice campsites. The lake's outlet stream, the famous Russian River, is near the cabin and the cottonwood campsites, and for several miles below the lake, the river is a popular rainbow-trout fishery. Much of the backcountry use of the Russian Lakes area is concentrated along this stretch of the trail.

Russian Lakes Traverse. The 21.5-mile, 2-to-4-day traverse can be done in either direction, but if you start at Cooper Lake, the hike is downhill overall with a few moderate ups and downs along the way.

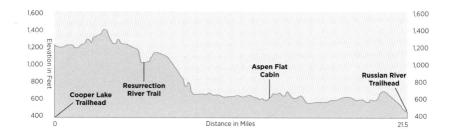

Except for the open slopes above Lower Russian Lake (an avalanche zone in winter and spring), the entire hike is in the forest, making it a good stormy-weather choice over higher-elevation hikes like Resurrection Pass. The forest canopy is open, so tall grasses and brush, including cow parsnip and stinging nettle, grow in profusion. If the trail hasn't been cleared recently, it can be nearly overgrown in places.

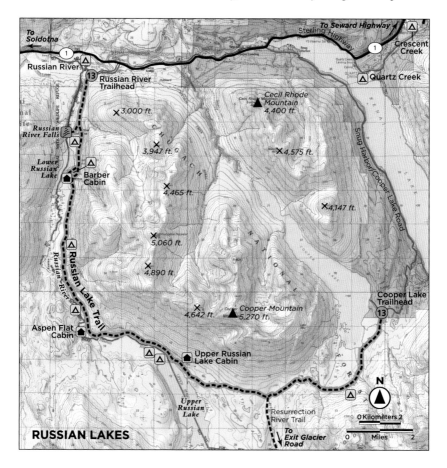

Renting the cabin or camping at Upper Russian is a highlight of the traverse. There's another cabin—the Aspen Flat Cabin—in the forest by the river 3 miles below (north of) Upper Russian, at the end of a 0.3-mile spur trail.

MILES AND DIRECTIONS

Upper Russian Lake and Thru-hike (Cooper Lake Trailhead)

0.0   Begin at the Cooper Lake Trailhead.

5.5   Continue west at the junction with the Resurrection River Trail.

9.5   Arrive at the Upper Russian Lake Cabin.

12.5   Intersect with the spur trail to the Aspen Flat Cabin (0.3 mile to cabin).

17.0   Reach the upper end of Lower Russian Lake.

19.0   Meet the junction with the Barber Cabin Trail (0.8 mile to cabin).

21.5   End the thru-hike at the Russian River Trailhead.

Resurrection River Trail. The trail into the Resurrection River valley intersects the Russian Lakes Trail about 4 miles east of the Upper Russian cabin, leading 16 miles south to the trailhead on the Exit Glacier Road out of Seward. The trail more or less follows the river, which is thick with bears and salmon in late summer and fall.

From the Exit Glacier Road Trailhead (see the Exit Glacier Hike), the lower section of the trail is in good shape and a relatively easy hike for the first 4.5 miles. After that point, expect slow going, unbridged stream crossings, many fallen logs, and more than the usual trail adventure if you try it. When melting snow raises stream levels in early summer and the usual late-summer rains swell them again, the stream crossings may be dangerous or impossible. Be sure to check on trail conditions before setting out on this one (see "Contact" above).

Fishing: The Russian River below the falls is the original home of combat fishing, drawing elbow-to-elbow crowds, but the upper river is much quieter. Fish the upper river and the two lakes for rainbow trout and Dolly Varden, but check the regulations before you fish.

TIDBIT

Hikers looking for more of an adventure can link the Russian Lakes Trail with the Resurrection Trail for a 60-mile traverse. The Resurrection Trailhead is 0.5 mile west on the Sterling Highway from the Russian River Campground/Trailhead Road.

14. RESURRECTION PASS

WHY GO?

Resurrection Pass is one of the most popular longer hikes on the Kenai. The trail covers stunning scenery climbing from forest floor into alpine tundra, with numerous alpine creeks, cabins, and backcountry lakes along the route.

THE RUNDOWN

Distance: 39 miles one way

Special features: Alpine scenery, large lakes, fishing, and a series of fee cabins

Location: Between Hope and Cooper Landing, about 100 miles south of Anchorage

Difficulty: Moderate

Trail type: More developed

Total elevation gain: About 2,200 feet in either direction

Best season: Mid-June through Sept

Fees/permits: Fee for cabin use

Maps: USGS Seward B-8, C-8, and D-8; National Geographic *Kenai National Wildlife Refuge*

Contact: Chugach National Forest, Seward Ranger District, PO Box 390, Seward, AK 99664; (907) 288-3178; www.fs.usda.gov/chugach/

FINDING THE TRAILHEAD

Hope. About 70 miles south of Anchorage, turn northwest off the Seward Highway onto the Hope Highway. Drive 16 miles to the outskirts of Hope and turn left (south) onto Palmer Creek Road. In about 0.6 mile, bear right at a road fork onto Resurrection Creek Road; continue to the signed trailhead, a total of 4 miles from the Hope Highway.

Cooper Landing. The marked trailhead is on the north side of the Sterling Highway at Mile 53, about 15.5 miles west of the junction of the Seward and Sterling Highways and 0.2 mile west of the second Kenai River Bridge.

WHAT TO SEE

The most popular longer hike on the Kenai, the Resurrection Pass Trail features a string of eight fee cabins that make the trip a great 3-to-6-day cabin-to-cabin hike—if you can reserve the right cabins in advance. Make reservations early, at www.reserveusa.com or (877) 444-6777, if you want to do the hike without pitching a tent. There are plenty of good campsites along the trail, many of them cleared and marked by the Forest Service, and some are provided with bear-proof food-storage boxes. Signed campsites are spaced no more than a mile or two apart the entire length of the trail, except for about a 5-mile stretch roughly centered on Resurrection Pass.

The southern part of the trail wanders through the lake basin of Juneau Creek. The basin's three large, forested lakes, all with fair fishing, are Trout Lake (7.5 miles from the south trailhead), Juneau Lake (9.5 miles), and Swan Lake (13 miles). Beyond Swan Lake, the trail climbs in switchbacks into Juneau Creek's alpine upper valley.

Devil's Pass Cabin is in a treeless zone and is equipped with a fuel-oil stove; cabin occupants are responsible for bringing their own fuel. The Devil's Creek Trail intersects the Resurrection Pass Trail at the cabin, leading 10 miles east to the Seward Highway and connecting with the Resurrection to create two other trail options: either a 27-mile hike between the Devil's Creek and Cooper Landing trails, or a 31-miler between Devil's Creek and Hope.

The Resurrection is an alpine hike for about 7 miles, between the top of the Swan Lake grade and a point a short distance above American Creek. The trail crosses Resurrection Pass at 2,600 feet in elevation. Just south of where the trail enters the trees, roughly 2 miles north of the pass, experienced cross-country ramblers can head west off the trail into the alpine watersheds of Afanasa, Abernathy, and American Creeks.

The north end of the trail is rolling and forested, with some scenic bluffs above Resurrection Creek between Fox Creek and tree line. The lower end of the north

Although not all of the trail is above tree line, grassy meadows filled with fireweed are a common sight.
WILLIE DALTON

The bridge over Fox Creek is one of six that signal the presence of a public use cabin. Keep an eye out for bears at these junctions.
ILLIE DALTON

trail threads through a mixed conifer forest of Sitka and white spruce and its natural hybrid, Lutz spruce. Caribou Creek, Fox Creek, and East Creek cabins and nearby campsites are good destinations from the Hope Trailhead.

The Hope end of the trail passes gold-dredge tailings and an overgrown mine site, each a good reminder of the area's past. The lower part of the trail is on an old mining road, following an easement across mining claims.

Some backpackers tie this trail together with the Russian Lakes Trail for a 60-mile trip between Hope and Cooper Lake.

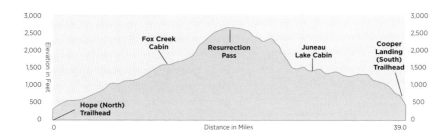

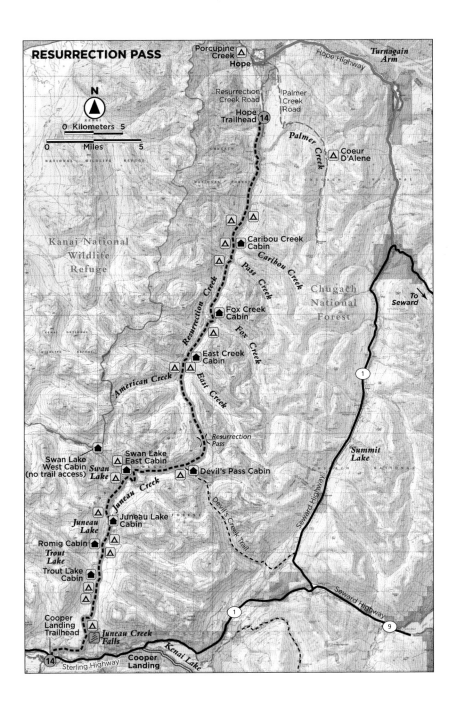

RESURRECTION PASS

N

0 Kilometers 5

0 Miles 5

Porcupine Creek
Hope
Hope Highway
Turnagain Arm

Resurrection Creek Road

Palmer Creek Road

Hope Trailhead 14

Palmer Creek

Coeur D'Alene

Kenai National Wildlife Refuge

Caribou Creek Cabin

Caribou Creek

Pass Creek

Chugach National Forest

Resurrection Creek

To Seward

Fox Creek Cabin

Fox Creek

American Creek

East Creek Cabin

East Creek

1

Resurrection Pass

Summit Lake

Swan Lake West Cabin (no trail access)

Swan Lake East Cabin

Devil's Pass Cabin

Swan Lake

Juneau Creek

Devil's Creek Trail

Juneau Lake Cabin

Seward Highway

Juneau Lake

Romig Cabin

Trout Lake

Trout Lake Cabin

1

Cooper Landing Trailhead

Seward Highway

Juneau Creek Falls

9

14 Sterling Highway

Cooper Landing

Kenai Lake

MILES AND DIRECTIONS

From Hope		From Cooper Landing
0.0	Begin/end at the Hope (north) Trailhead.	39.0
7.0	Arrive at Caribou Creek Cabin.	32.0
11.5	Pass by the Fox Creek Cabin.	27.5
14.5	Arrive at East Creek Cabin.	24.5
19.5	Cross Resurrection Pass.	19.5
21.5	Arrive at Devil's Pass Cabin/Trail.	17.5
26.0	Arrive at Swan Lake Cabin.	13.0
29.5	Reach Juneau Lake Cabin.	9.5
30.0	Arrive at Romig Cabin.	9.0
32.0	Meet the Trout Lake Cabin/Trail (0.5 mile to cabin)	7.0
35.0	Arrive at Juneau Creek Falls.	4.0
39.0	End/begin the hike at Cooper Landing (south) Trailhead.	0.0

Fishing: There are rainbow and lake trout, burbot, and whitefish in Trout Lake; the same species plus grayling in Juneau Lake; and lake trout, rainbow trout, and Dolly Varden in Swan Lake. Fish Resurrection Creek for pink salmon and Dolly Varden, and Juneau Creek for Dollies. Check current fishing regulations before wetting a line.

TIDBIT

Resurrection Pass is popular for both hiking and mountain biking; be prepared for bike encounters. Hunters use the trail, especially from the north, for moose and caribou hunting in the fall.

---

15. DEVIL'S CREEK

WHY GO?

Devil's Creek Trail crosses a variety of terrain: through forest, streams, lakes, and into the alpine. The route includes access to Resurrection Pass Trail for a longer traverse.

THE RUNDOWN

Distance: 10 miles to the pass or thru-hikes of 27 to 31 miles connecting with the Resurrection Pass Trail

Special features: Alpine terrain, a fee cabin, and options of longer backpacking trips

Location: 85 miles south of Anchorage

Difficulty: Moderate

Trail type: More developed

Total elevation gain: About 1,500 feet in and 100 feet out to Devil's Pass Cabin

Best season: Mid-June through Sept

Fees/permits: Fee for cabin use

Maps: USGS Seward C-7 and C-8; National Geographic *Kenai National Wildlife Refuge*

Contact: Chugach National Forest, Seward Ranger District, PO Box 390, Seward, AK 99664; (907) 288-3178; www.fs.usda.gov/chugach/

FINDING THE TRAILHEAD

The trailhead is on the west side of the Seward Highway at Mile 39.5, about 2 miles north of the Seward/Sterling Highway junction and 6 miles south of Summit Lake Lodge.

WHAT TO SEE

A gradual climb into high alpine country, the Devil's Creek Trail follows its namesake valley into the high country near the Resurrection Pass Trail. The 10-mile trail ends at the Devil's Pass Cabin on the Resurrection, 2 miles south of Resurrection Pass. Connecting with the Resurrection, you can keep going to the Cooper Landing trailhead (about 27 miles total distance) or to the trailhead outside Hope (about 31 miles).

At 2 miles a marked side trail leads a short distance to a backcountry campsite the Forest Service calls the Beaver Pond site; with a name like that, be sure to boil or filter the water. Camping is limited between here and the upper valley, at about Mile 8; there is one site at the unnamed creek at about 5.5 miles.

Past tree line at 3 miles, the view of Devil's Creek's deep, V-shaped valley and several Kenai Mountain peaks gets progressively better. Once into the high country, there is good off-trail hiking to seldom-walked ridges and valleys like Gilpatrick's Mountain and the headwaters of Devil's Creek. The pass (8.5 miles) and Devil's Pass Lake (9 miles) lie in heavenly high alpine country. The Devil's Pass Cabin (Mile 10) is an A-frame with a large sleeping loft; make reservations at www.reserveusa.com or (877) 444-6777. If you want to camp in the area, please respect the privacy of people staying in the cabin and camp well out of sight.

The 10-mile Devil's Creek Trail is a gradual climb into high alpine country, ending at the Devil's Pass Cabin on the Resurrection, 2 miles south of Resurrection Pass.
MIKE RECORDS

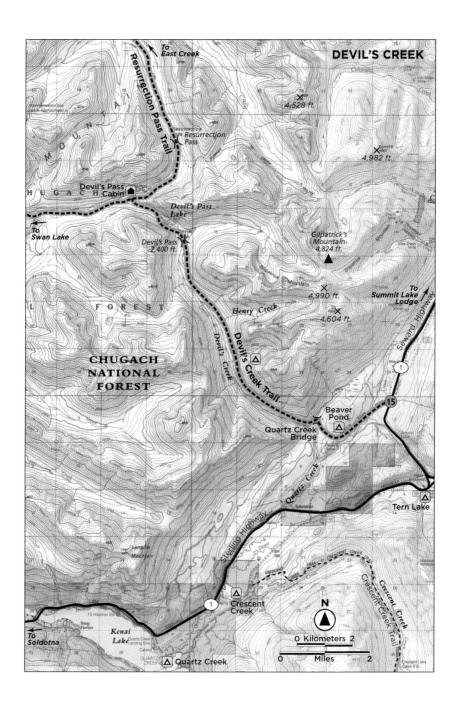

DEVIL'S CREEK

To East Creek

Resurrection Pass Trail

Resurrection Pass

M O U N T A I N

Devil's Pass Cabin

C H U G A C H

Devil's Pass Lake

To Swan Lake

Devil's Pass 2,400 ft.

4,528 ft.

4,982 ft.

Gilpatrick's Mountain 4,824 ft.

4,990 ft.

4,604 ft.

To Summit Lake Lodge

Henry Creek

F O R E S T

CHUGACH NATIONAL FOREST

Devil's Creek

Devil's Creek Trail

Beaver Pond

Quartz Creek Bridge

Seward Highway

1

15

Tern Lake

Quartz Creek

Sterling Highway

Crescent Creek

Crescent Creek Trail

Langille Mountain

1

Crescent Creek

N

To Soldotna

Kenai Lake

Quartz Creek

0 Kilometers 2

0 Miles 2

A mountain biker rides along the 10-mile Devil's Creek Trail on a September afternoon. MIKE RECORDS

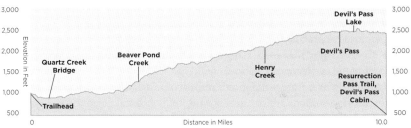

MILES AND DIRECTIONS

0.0   Begin at the trailhead.

0.5   Arrive at the Quartz Creek Bridge, an option for a shorter hike.

2.0   A marked side trail leads to the Beaver Pond campsite.

3.0   Arrive at tree line.

5.5   Arrive at an unnamed creek and campsite.

6.0   Cross Henry Creek.

8.5   Cross Devil's Pass.

9.0   Reach Devil's Pass Lake.

10.0   The trail ends at Devil's Pass Cabin/Resurrection Pass Trail.

Shorter hikes: The 0.5-mile (one way) walk to the Quartz Creek Bridge is a short stroll through forest and berry bushes, and hiking three or more miles up the trail leads into open country with good views.

KENAI NATIONAL WILDLIFE REFUGE

THE 1.9-MILLION-ACRE KENAI NATIONAL Wildlife Refuge started out in 1941 as a refuge for the unique Kenai moose, but the 1980 Alaska Lands Act made it much more than a moose range. Bears, wolves, caribou, Dall sheep, mountain goats, salmon, and trout are all part of the refuge's mission these days.

Most of the refuge's hiking trails are in the section of the refuge off the Skilak Lake Loop Road. The Skilak area, where the Kenai River emerges from the Kenai Mountains, offers good hiking as well as good fishing. With trails, campgrounds, and lake and stream fishing, it's a great outdoor and family vacation spot. The Skilak area also provides a welcome respite from the hordes of anglers on the lower river near the towns of Kenai and Soldotna.

The refuge also has a few remote trails. The Surprise and Cottonwood Creek Trails, accessible only by boat across the Kenai River and Skilak Lake, lead to high country in the Kenai Mountains. The Emma Lake Trail, accessible by boat or float-plane at the road less end of Tustumena Lake, leads to a trail shelter at the lake and an alpine area beyond.

16. FULLER LAKES AND SKYLINE RIDGE

WHY GO?

Fuller Lakes Trail has fishing, camping, and off-trail access to the high country in the Mystery Creek section of the Kenai Wilderness.

THE RUNDOWN

Distances: Lower Fuller Lake: 2 miles one way. Upper Fuller Lake: 3 miles one way. North end of Upper Fuller Lake: 3.5 miles

Special features: Lakes, fishing, access to alpine ridge hiking

Location: 37 miles east of Soldotna

Difficulty: Moderate

Trail type: More developed to the south end of Upper Fuller Lake; less developed beyond

Total elevation gain: About 1,400 feet

Best season: June through Sept

Fees/permits: None

Maps: USGS Kenai B-1 (NE) and C-1 (SE); National Geographic *Kenai National Wildlife Refuge*

Contact: Kenai National Wildlife Refuge, Ski Hill Rd., PO Box 2139, Soldotna, AK 99669; (907) 262-7021; www.fws.gov/refuge/kenai/

FINDING THE TRAILHEAD

 The trailhead is at Mile 57.2 of the Sterling Highway, 37 miles east of Soldotna, about 0.6 mile east of the Kenai Refuge visitor contact station, and about 2 miles west of the signed eastern boundary of the Kenai Refuge. The trail begins on the north side of the highway.

WHAT TO SEE

Nestled into subalpine bowls between the alpine summits of Round Mountain and the Mystery Hills, the Fuller Lakes are relatively easy to reach on foot. The trail offers good camping, fishing, and off-trail access to the high country. The entire hike is in the Mystery Creek portion of the Kenai Wilderness.

The hike gains most of its elevation from the trailhead to the lower lake, and then gains only another 100 feet to the upper lake. The lower trail passes through spruce and birch forest with a few beautiful groves of aspen. Toward the top there is a fine view back toward Skilak Lake.

Lower Fuller Lake, at about 1,600 feet in elevation, is in the last large pocket of timber below tree line. The trail crosses the outlet stream and continues along the west side of the lake toward Upper Fuller, passing two smaller ponds on the way. This section of the trail may be wet or flooded early in summer.

The upper lake, just across a barely discernible divide from the lower lake at 1,690 feet in elevation, is set among scattered, small white spruce just below tree line. The lower lake drains directly to the Kenai, while the upper lake is part of the Mystery Creek watershed. A less-developed trail leads along the east shore to the far end of the lake.

There are good campsites at both lakes. Please use a camp stove and avoid building campfires, and filter or boil the water.

A backpacker hiking along Upper Fuller Lake in the Kenai National Wildlife Refuge on the Kenai Peninsula.
HAGEPHOTO

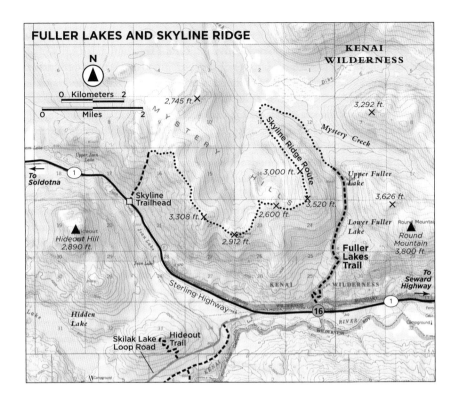

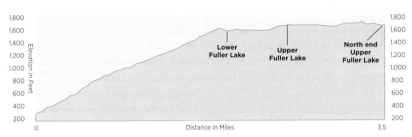

MILES AND DIRECTIONS

0.0   Begin at the trailhead.

2.0   Arrive at Lower Fuller Lake.

3.0   Reach Upper Fuller Lake.

3.5   Arrive at Upper Fuller Lake's north end; continue beyond for Skyline Ridge.

Beyond Upper Fuller Lake. The Mystery Hills are tantalizingly close to Upper Fuller, separated from the lake by a thin strip of brushy mountain hemlock, willow, and dwarf birch. To get to the Mystery Hills ridgeline, there is a well-beaten route to follow that avoids major bushwhacking. At the north end of the lake, continue beyond the maintained trail, crossing the lake's tiny outlet creek and following the route that side-slopes up to the northwest. It's roughly 1.5 miles to the lower ridgeline at about 2,300 feet in elevation, and then about the same distance again to the first peak, Peak 3,520 to the south. Even if you go only part of the way, the route has a good view into the Mystery Creek valley.

Once you're on the ridgeline, you're just at the beginning of the Mystery Hills traverse, an outstanding but tough 11-mile, up-and-down hike following the ridge's peaks and saddles, gaining more than 3,000 feet in elevation, finally descending steeply to the Skyline Trailhead at Sterling Highway Mile 61. The trailheads are close enough for an easy shuttle by bicycle. A topographic map, compass, and decent weather are requirements for this very long, hard hike. Carrying an overnight pack would be limited fun on this up-and-down route, so for most hikers, it's best done as a very long day trip. Plan on doing it during the longest days of midsummer to allow plenty of time, as it will take longer than the distance would lead you to believe, as much as 12 hours even for hikers in decent shape.

Fishing: There are a few grayling in Lower Fuller and possibly still a few Dolly Varden in Upper Fuller.

TIDBIT

Along the trail to the lower lake, there are wonderful views of the Kenai Range. Near the upper lake, climb the surrounding peaks for incredible birds-eye views of the area.

---

17. KENAI RIVER

WHY GO?

Kenai River trails offer a range of hikes for all activity levels winding through forest, with a beautiful turquoise river in view.

THE RUNDOWN

Distances: Upper Kenai River: 2.8 miles one way. Lower Kenai River: 2.3 miles one way

River Loop: a 2.5-mile loop. The Kenai River Grand Tour: about 6.5 miles round-trip

Special features: A forest and river hike, fishing

Location: In the Skilak Lake area, east of Soldotna

Difficulty: Easy/moderate

Trail type: Less developed

Total elevation gain: 250 to 500 feet, depending on the route chosen

Best season: May through mid-Oct

Fees/permits: None

Maps: USGS Kenai B-1 (NE); National Geographic *Kenai National Wildlife Refuge*

Contact: Kenai National Wildlife Refuge, Ski Hill Rd., PO Box 2139, Soldotna, AK 99669; (907) 262-7021; www.fws.gov/refuge/kenai/

FINDING THE TRAILHEAD

 Drive to the east junction of the Skilak Lake Loop Road with the Sterling Highway at Mile 58, 36 miles east of Soldotna, 3 miles west of the signed eastern boundary of the Kenai Refuge, and 0.1 mile west of the refuge visitor contact station. Turn south onto the Skilak Road; drive 0.7 mile to the Upper Kenai River Trailhead or 2.4 miles to the Lower Kenai River Trailhead. The trailheads are on the south side of the road.

WHAT TO SEE

The Kenai River Trail meanders along two sections of the river through forests of spruce, aspen, cottonwood, and birch. This trail is the only place to hike anywhere along the Kenai River, a world-class trout and salmon stream. Scenery, fishing, and late-summer berries are all in good supply. Eagles, waterfowl, terns, and gulls hang out along the river, and bears are fairly common here during the big sockeye-salmon runs in June and July.

An old fire burned years ago, and now is a mix of boreal forest and shrubs; look for fireweed, wild rose, and raspberries. Check out the interpretive panels on the south side of the Skilak Road at Mile 2.5, 0.1 mile west of the Lower Kenai River Trailhead.

The two trailheads offer a variety of hikes.

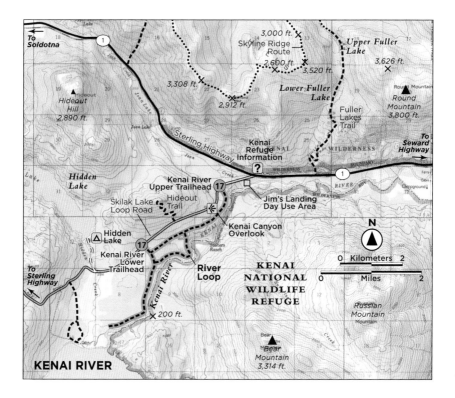

Upper Kenai River. The upper (eastern) trail traverses low hills, follows the river briefly, and crosses a section of the 1991 burn before reaching the lower (western) trailhead in about 2.8 miles. There is an overlook of the Kenai River Canyon at 0.4 mile. If you plan to hike this section of the trail as a one-way hike with a car or bicycle shuttle, it saves some elevation gain to start the trip from the west trailhead. (No bikes are allowed on any of the refuge trails.)

From the Upper Kenai Trailhead, elevation about 350 feet, follow the trail out of the parking area about 0.2 mile and turn right at the signed intersection. (The trail leading straight ahead continues another 0.1 mile to a fishing hole on the river.) Follow the path up onto the bluff above the river, reaching the canyon overlook in another 0.2 mile. The trail then drops down to the river, which here is a beautiful green stream flowing smoothly over a cobbled bed.

The trail then climbs away from the river and crosses the burn. At a junction about 2 miles from the east trailhead, take the right fork for the shortest path to the west trailhead, at about 550 feet in elevation. Getting back to the east trailhead involves a return trip or a 1.8-mile road walk.

Lower Kenai River. The Lower Kenai Trail leads down to the river and follows it to a beautiful cottonwood flat, a good spot for camping and fishing. Beyond the flat, a fishing route continues downriver.

The Kenai River Trail winds along two sections of the river through forests of spruce, aspen, cottonwood, and birch. This trail is the only place to hike anywhere along the Kenai River, a world-class trout and salmon stream.
LEE KUEPPER

The River Loop. From the west trailhead, hikers can also take the River Loop, a 2.5-mile loop that follows the river a short distance, passing a set of foaming rapids, before returning to the west trailhead.

The Kenai River Grand Tour. To have it all, do the grand tour, about 6.5 miles plus the 1.8-mile road walk if you haven't shuttled a vehicle. Hike out to the river on the Lower Kenai Trail, cut back to the Upper Kenai Trail via the lower, southern section of the River Loop, and hike out to the east trailhead.

Hideout Trail. For a bird's-eye view of this section of the Kenai River as it emerges from the Kenai Mountains, hike to the lookout point 1.5 miles and 850 feet of elevation up the Hideout Trail, which runs north from the Skilak Lake Loop Road at Mile 2, between the Upper Kenai and Lower Kenai trailheads.

Shorter hikes: Hike about 0.4 mile one way to the Kenai Canyon overlook from the east trailhead. Take care with kids along the edge of the canyon.

Fishing: Most anglers on this section of the Kenai River are after rainbow trout (catch and release only) and sockeye salmon, but there are also Dolly Varden and runs of silver salmon in the river. The sockeye runs are in June and July, the silver run is in late summer and fall, and rainbow and Dolly Varden fishing is good throughout the summer and fall. Check the Alaska Department of Fish and Game regulations; the river is usually closed to all fishing until mid-June to protect spawning fish, and special regulations are in effect at other times.

18. SKILAK LOOKOUT, BEAR MOUNTAIN, AND VISTA TRAILS

WHY GO?

A variety of hikes and terrain, with stunning views of the 15-mile-long Skilak Lake in the valley below.

THE RUNDOWN

Distance: Skilak Lookout: 2 miles one way. Bear Mountain: 0.8 mile one way. Vista: 1.5 miles one way

Special features: Great views, good hikes for hearty families

Location: In the Skilak Lake area, east of Soldotna

Difficulty: Moderate

Trail type: More to less developed

Total elevation gain: Skilak Lookout: 700 feet. Bear Mountain: 500 feet; Vista: 800 feet

Best season: Mid-May through early Oct

Fees/permits: None

Maps: USGS Kenai B-1 (NW); National Geographic *Kenai National Wildlife Refuge*

Contact: Kenai National Wildlife Refuge, Ski Hill Rd., PO Box 2139, Soldotna, AK 99669; (907) 262-7021; www.fws.gov/refuge/kenai/

FINDING THE TRAILHEAD

Drive to the east junction of the Skilak Lake Loop Road with the Sterling Highway at Mile 58, 36 miles east of Soldotna, 3 miles west of the signed eastern boundary of the Kenai Refuge, and 0.1 mile west of the refuge visitor contact station. Turn south onto the Skilak Road. The Skilak Lookout Trailhead is at Mile 5.3; park on the right (north) side of the road and begin the hike from the trailhead on the south side. The Bear Mountain Trailhead is at Mile 6; the trailhead and parking area are on the north side of the road.

The Vista Trail begins in the Upper Skilak Lake Campground. Drive to Mile 8.5 of the Skilak Lake Loop Road, turn south onto the signed campground access road, and drive about 2 miles to the entrance. About 200 feet beyond the information kiosk and fee station, at a fork in the road, curve left into the day-use area; park here. Walk down the road to the boat launch, and in about 200 feet, cross a pedestrian bridge to the left and join the campground road. Walk about 50 feet to the right on the road, where you'll find the trailhead on the left, across from the "A" Loop pit toilets.

WHAT TO SEE

These three short trails climb to fine views of the Skilak Lake country and the Kenai Mountains. Skilak Lookout, directly above the lake, is a longer hike; Bear Mountain is a shorter hike with a good view, but it's farther from the lake. Vista, farther west, looks out on the lake and the distant, wetland-dotted lowlands of the Kenai Peninsula. Don't forget the binoculars for these hikes.

Skilak Lookout. The Skilak Lookout Trail is a bit steep, wet, with roots in a few places, but it still makes a decent longer family hike.

The trail climbs gradually through an open-canopied spruce forest and across open slopes that were scorched by the 1996 Hidden Creek Fire. As the trail nears the rocky peak, it climbs steeply. The view first unfolds to the east and southeast, where the Kenai River and the glacial Skilak River, with its huge delta, enter the lake.

At the top, where the wind will likely be blowing from the southeast (check out the growth of the limbs on the trees at the summit), there is a 180-degree view of the lake, and you can see how big this 15-mile-long lake really is. The alpine ridges of the Kenai Mountains stretch into the distance to the south of the lake.

Be on bear alert late in the summer when raspberries and mountain ash berries are ripe. Look for moose feeding in the openings, gray jays in the trees at the summit, and a riot of wildflowers in June.

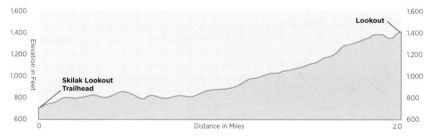

Bear Mountain. The trail skirts the east flank of a bald ridge, climbing steeply with occasional level stretches as it threads through open forests and patches of brush, passing several rocky ledges and outcrops along the way. Just below the summit, the first views of Skilak Lake and the Skilak River open to the southeast. The trail's summit adds much more to the view: the Kenai River, the Skilak Lake Lookout peak, and the western end of the Kenai Mountains.

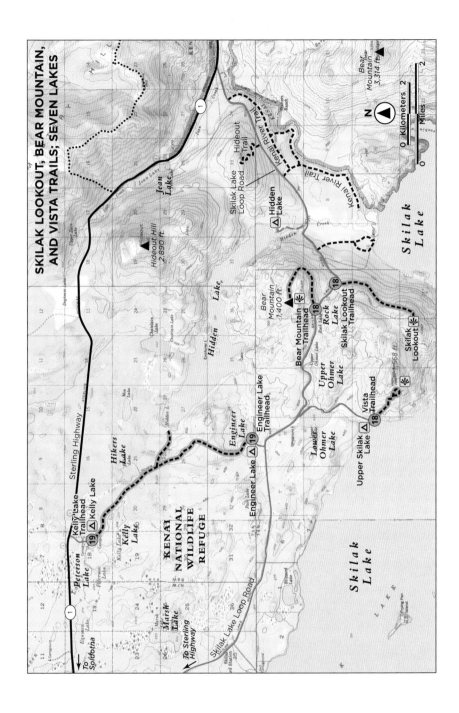

SKILAK LOOKOUT, BEAR MOUNTAIN, AND VISTA TRAILS; SEVEN LAKES

Vista. The Vista Trail, built over the summers of 2000 to 2004 by Student Conservation Association high school work crews, winds and climbs through a portion of the 1996 Hidden Creek Fire and a smaller 2002 burn. The burns grow luxuriant in tall grasses and shrubs by midsummer, and the open slopes yield great views on the way up. Near its high point at 1,100 feet foot in elevation, the trail makes a short loop, or you can continue blazing your own trail in the alpine. Unless it's windy or rainy, you'll want to linger a bit and take in the sights from the top.

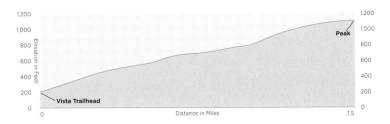

Two hikers admire the 15-mile-long Skilak Lake from a panoramic view at the summit of Skilak Lookout trail. To the south, the alpine ridges of the Kenai Mountains stretch into the distance; to the east, the Kenai River and the glacial Skilak River, enter the lake.
MOLLIE FOSTER

19. SEVEN LAKES

WHY GO?

Seven Lakes Trail is an adventure suitable for the whole family, with low elevation gain, traveling by multiple lakes, and plenty of fishing opportunities.

THE RUNDOWN See map on page 82.

Distance: 4.4 miles one way

Special features: Lakes, fishing, wildlife

Location: In the Skilak Lake area, east of Soldotna

Difficulty: Easy

Trail type: Less developed

Total elevation gain: About 150 feet

Best season: May through mid-Oct

Fees/permits: None

Maps: USGS Kenai B-1 (NW), C-1 (SW), and C-2 (SE); National Geographic *Kenai National Wildlife Refuge*

Contact: Kenai National Wildlife Refuge, Ski Hill Rd., PO Box 2139, Soldotna, AK 99669; (907) 262-7021; www.fws.gov/refuge/kenai/

FINDING THE TRAILHEAD

Kelly Lake. The Kelly Lake turnoff is at Sterling Highway Mile 68.5, 26 miles east of the Kenai Spur Road junction in Soldotna. It's between the two junctions of the Skilak Lake Loop Road: 7 miles east of the west junction and 10 miles west of the east junction. Turn south off the highway here and continue about 0.7 mile to Kelly Lake, taking the left (east) fork of the road at about the halfway point. The trail leaves the parking area at the far end on the left, by the boat launch.

Engineer Lake. If you're coming from the west, turn right (south) onto the Skilak Lake Loop Road at Sterling Highway Mile 75 (19 miles east of the Kenai Spur Road junction in Soldotna) and drive about 9.5 miles east on the loop road. If you're coming from the east, turn left (south) onto the Skilak road at Sterling Highway Mile 58 (3 miles west of the signed eastern boundary of the Kenai Refuge and 0.1 mile west of the refuge visitor contact station) and drive about 9.5 miles west on the loop road. Either way, turn north at the signed Engineer Lake turnoff and continue 0.3 mile to the lake; the trailhead is next to the boat launch.

WHAT TO SEE

Seven Lakes is a lake and lowland trail that reaches the shorelines of four lakes: Engineer, Hidden, Hikers, and Kelly Lakes. Shuttling a car between the trailheads is an easy way to hike this trail if you have two vehicles with your party.

If you're counting, the fifth, sixth, and seventh lakes lie north of the Sterling Highway. Before the Sterling was built, the Skilak road was the highway, and the trail extended down a chain of seven lakes to the East Fork of the Moose River. Now it's no longer maintained north of Kelly Lake and the Sterling Highway, and four lakes are all you get.

It's a flat to rolling walk with wildlife all around—look for moose and beaver and their sign, and sign of bear, wolf, and lynx. Use your binoculars at the lakes to pick out loons, scoters, mergansers, terns, cranes, and other waterfowl and shorebirds. Sit quietly by the lakes in early morning or evening and listen for the calls of loons and cranes. There are campsites on Kelly, Hidden, and Engineer Lakes, but Hikers Lake pretty much belongs to the moose. About a third of a mile from the Kelly Lake trailhead is a rustic log cabin available by reservation.

The country along the lakes is flat with low-growing spruce forest, and the rolling hills between the lakes are covered with stands of bright-green aspens that turn their trademark gold in autumn. Near a meadow north of Engineer Lake, some of the aspens are as much as 2 feet in diameter. From the low ridge between Hidden and Hikers Lakes, the trail overlooks acres of aspens.

The lightly used, 0.5-mile side trail to the roadless end of Hidden Lake forks off the main trail on a small ridge between Engineer Lake and Hikers Lake. The trail fades as it approaches the lake, but leads across a small stream to a good campsite, which is also accessible by boat from the Hidden Lake Campground at the other end of the lake.

If you're visiting in midsummer, don't forget the bug spray, and anytime you go, take along binoculars for wildlife viewing.

Two hikers walk along the shore of Kelly Lake. From the north trailhead the first mile of the route sticks to the edge of the lake. MOLLIE FOSTER

About a third of a mile from the north trailhead is a public use cabin, and a rowboat available by reservation, with easy access to the lake.
MOLLIE FOSTER

A small group of swans swim across Kelly Lake, as visible from the lakeside trail, on a sunny autumn evening.
MOLLIE FOSTER

MILES AND DIRECTIONS

From Engineer Lake		From Kelly Lake
0.0	Begin/end at Engineer Lake Trailhead.	4.4
1.0	Reach the north end of Engineer Lake.	3.4
2.5	The Hidden Lake spur trail forks off the main trail.	1.9
3.0	Pass Hikers Lake.	1.4
3.5	Arrive at the east end of Kelly Lake.	0.9
4.1	Pass a public use cabin	0.3
4.4	Arrive at/start from the Kelly Lake Trailhead.	0.0

Shorter hikes: From the south trailhead, hike along Engineer Lake as far as you like, or from the north trailhead, try a short hike on the shoreline of Kelly Lake.

Fishing: Shore fishing is fair in the lakes along the trail. Engineer Lake may still have some hatchery silver salmon from previous stockings, but it is no longer stocked because of the fear that hatchery fish might mix with wild Kenai silvers lower in the watershed. The most plentiful fish in Hidden Lake are lake trout and kokanee (landlocked salmon), and there are also rainbows and Dolly Varden; most anglers use boats. Kelly Lake has rainbows. Northern pike, a predatory game fish not native to this part of the state, may now inhabit Hidden Lake. If you catch one, don't return it to the lake; pike can wreak havoc on the area's native fish.

HOPE TO GIRDWOOD

THE HOPE-TO-GIRDWOOD SECTION OF the Chugach National Forest curls around Turnagain Arm, a fjord that lies in the basin between the Chugach and Kenai Mountains.

The mountains along Turnagain Arm were the toughest country on the historic Iditarod Trail, back when dog teams and prospectors braved deep snow and avalanches on the winter trail in the early 1900s. Now Southcentral Alaskans are building a commemorative Iditarod Trail north from Seward, the ice-free port that was the gateway to the trail; see "Reviving a Forgotten Trail" in the Winner Creek hike.

20. **GULL ROCK**

WHY GO?

A trail with loads of diversity: birch woods, overlooks with mountain and ocean views, tundra slopes, an avalanche gully (that can hold snow into June), and mossy forests of hemlock and Sitka spruce.

THE RUNDOWN

Distance: 5.1 miles one way from campground

Special features: Coast and forest scenery, historic interest

Location: At the end of the Hope Highway, outside Hope

Difficulty: Moderate

Trail type: More developed

Total elevation gain: About 600 feet in each direction

Best season: May to mid-Oct

Fees/permits: None

Maps: USGS Seward D-8; National Geographic *Kenai National Wildlife Refuge*

Contact: Chugach National Forest, Seward Ranger District, PO Box 390, Seward, AK 99664; (907) 288-3178; www.fs.usda.gov/chugach/

FINDING THE TRAILHEAD

Drive 70 miles south of Anchorage and turn northwest onto the Hope Highway. Drive about 18 miles through the outskirts of the town of Hope, and take a left 500 ft. before Porcupine Campground, drive 0.25 mile to Gull Rock/Hope Point Trailhead.

WHAT TO SEE

The trail crosses the forested slope above Turnagain Arm to Gull Rock, a prominent headland that projects well out into the arm. This is one of the earliest hikes to open on the Kenai Peninsula in the spring. Watch for mountain bikes; the trail is popular with bikers, and the narrow trail dips and twists enough that visibility is limited. The trail is a popular hike or ride for campers at the Porcupine Creek Campground.

The Gull Rock hike is loaded with variety: leaf-carpeted birch woods, bluffs with mountain and ocean views, small streams gushing through quiet forest, a pretty talus and tundra slope, an avalanche gully that can hold snow into June (take care crossing it), and dark, mossy forests of hemlock and Sitka spruce. The trail crosses several small creeks, but the only large stream is Johnson Creek, about 0.3 mile from the end of the trail.

The hike leaves the national forest and enters the Kenai National Wildlife Refuge a few minutes before reaching Johnson Creek. Not far beyond the boundary, look for stumps from the timber cutting of a century ago; the trail follows the route of a wagon road that once led to a sawmill at Johnson Creek, where workers cut ties for the Alaska Railroad in the early 1900s.

The sound of wind in the trees will probably be your first clue that you're nearing Gull Rock. The wind is Gull Rock's nearly constant companion, and it usually blows from the east, as you'll see from the spreading, low-growing spruce trees on the headland.

The maintained trail peters out as it reaches Gull Rock, forking into several fainter trails. Follow the side trails to explore the headland. Rocky outcrops provide great views over the coast; watch for gulls wheeling in the breeze, listen for surf crashing on the rocks, and if the tide has retreated, look for wild ripple patterns in the mudflats below. Keep your distance, though: The mudflats are like quicksand.

There are a few decent campsites in sheltered spots under the trees; the nearest fresh water is back at Johnson Creek. Please use your camp stove and don't build a fire here. The Kenai bark-beetle epidemic has taken many of Gull Rock's spruces, and the combination of dead trees and high winds may be a significant windthrow hazard, so be cautious where you camp or hang out.

Before hiking out, enjoy a moment of peace listening to the birds, the surf, and the wind.

A rainbow appears along the Gull Rock Trail, overlooking the Turnagain Arm
JUSTIN WHOLEY

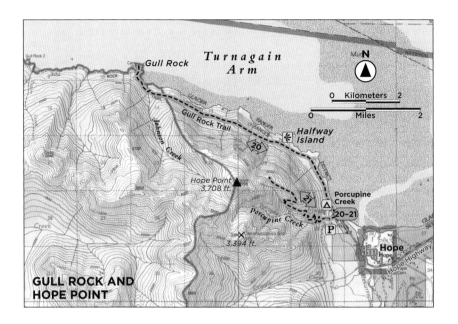

GULL ROCK AND
HOPE POINT

MILES AND DIRECTIONS

0.0   Begin at the Porcupine Creek Campground.

2.0   A short side path leads to a lookout point above Halfway Island.

4.8   Cross Johnson Creek.

5.1   Reach Gull Rock.

One of the many beautiful contouring sections of the Gull Rock Trail. This is one of the earliest hikes to open on the Kenai Peninsula in the spring. JUSTIN WHOLEY

Shorter hikes: Near Halfway Island, a bit less than 2 miles from the trailhead, a short side path leads to a nice lookout point.

21. HOPE POINT

WHY GO?

Hope Point Trail is a great day hike, with the first stretch of trail suitable for families, while the route beyond is for more adventurous hikers, with opportunities to connect to other peaks in the Kenai Mountains.

THE RUNDOWN See map on page 91.

Distance: 3.5 miles one way

Special features: Starts in the forest and climbs to gorgeous views of the Resurrection Creek Valley, Turnagain Arm, and Chugach Mountains

Location: At the end of the Hope Highway, outside Hope

Difficulty: Strenuous

Trail type: More developed

Total elevation gain: About 2,300 feet

Best season: May to mid-Oct

Fees/permits: None

Maps: USGS Seward D-8; National Geographic *Kenai National Wildlife Refuge*

Contact: Chugach National Forest, Seward Ranger District, PO Box 390, Seward, AK 99664; (907) 288-3178; www.fs.usda.gov/chugach/

FINDING THE TRAILHEAD

 Drive 70 miles south of Anchorage and turn northwest onto the Hope Highway. Drive about 18 miles through the outskirts of the town of Hope, and take a left 500 ft. before Porcupine Campground, drive 0.25 mile to Gull Rock/Hope Point Trailhead.

WHAT TO SEE

Hope Point Trail begins with a gradual grade for the first mile with switchbacks, through a forest of cottonwood, spruce, and alder. The start of the route briefly runs parallel to Porcupine Creek. The trail continues and transitions to more moderate to strenuous, climbing from the creek to the alpine meadows covered with wildflowers in early summer. The switchback route continues above tree line to a mix of grassy mountainsides and rocky knolls with views of Resurrection Creek Valley below. Look for edible berries as you climb on the trail, especially in late summer/early fall. It is an easy route to follow, on what used to be used as a trail to a microwave tower site. From the tower site to the Hope Point summit, the

On the 3.5-mile Hope Point trail, hikers are rewarded with breathtaking views of the Resurrection Creek Valley, Turnagain Arm, and Chugach Mountains.
ILONA SINGH

route is not marked, but is obvious. Be ready to do a bit of scrambling if you're going to the summit.

Keep an eye out for wildlife, as its bear and moose country, and scan the water in Turnagain Arm for beluga whales.

MILES AND DIRECTIONS

0.0   Begin at Gull Rock Trailhead.

0.3   Hope Point Trail splits off from Gull Rock Trail.

1.0   Trail changes from gradual to moderate grade.

3.5   Maintained trail ends, path to Hope Point.

TIDBIT
Bring plenty of water, layers, and a windbreaker if you plan on hiking to the ridgeline.

22. TRAIL OF BLUE ICE

WHY GO?

A fully-accessible trail for all hiking abilities, winding through forests, streams, and lakes with vistas of the surrounding mountains and glaciers.

THE RUNDOWN

Distances: 5 miles one way

Special features: Spruce and cottonwood forests, streams and lakes

Location: In the Portage Creek valley, off Portage Glacier Road

Difficulty: Easy

Trail type: Developed

Total elevation gain: 30 feet

Best season: All year

Fees/permits: None

Maps: USGS Seward D-5 and D-6; National Geographic *Kenai National Wildlife Refuge*

Contact: Chugach National Forest, Glacier Ranger District, PO Box 129, 145 Forest Station Rd., Girdwood, AK 99587; (907) 783-3242; www.fs.usda.gov/chugach/

FINDING THE TRAILHEAD

At Mile 78.9 of the Seward Highway, 11 miles south of Girdwood, turn east onto Portage Glacier Road. The trail is accessible from two main trailheads: at Moose Flats Day Use Area, 1.5 miles from the highway turnoff on north side of the road. The other end of the trail begins at the Begich, Boggs Visitor Center, just over 5 miles on the Portage Glacier Road.

WHAT TO SEE

Portage Valley is one of the most popular visitor destinations, and for good reasons, with easy access to mountains, glaciers, and the Prince William Sound. The valley's blue ice and glacial scenery is spectacular, and many visitors only stop at the Begich, Boggs Visitor Center, stay for a brief visit, and leave for another adventure. If you want to explore more, the Trail of Blue Ice is one the whole family can enjoy.

The Trail of Blue Ice is a fully-accessible trail for all hiking abilities, running the length of the Portage Valley, paralleling the Portage Glacier Road, and connecting the valley's many points of interest. The route travels through spruce forests, cottonwoods, alder, and willow, the 5-mile gravel path is wide and open, leaving plenty of opportunities to take in the views of the mountains and glaciers of the Portage Creek Valley.

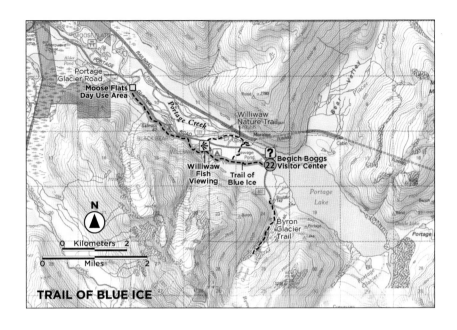

TRAIL OF BLUE ICE

A fully accessible picnic table at the Moose Flats Day Use Area along the Trail of Blue Ice. The trail covers the length of the Portage Valley, paralleling the Portage Glacier Road, and connecting the valley's many points of interest.
MOLLIE FOSTER

A hiker strolls through the forest of spruce, cottonwoods, alder and willow, along the 5-mile-long Trail of Blue Ice.
MOLLIE FOSTER

A glassy pond creates a reflection of the Kenai Mountains on a calm spring evening.
MOLLIE FOSTER

At the trailhead by the visitors center and lake, the trail climbs 30 feet, and slightly higher than accessibility guidelines allow. There's another route option to avoid the grade: travel along the shoulder of the road, and it will meet where the route crosses the intersection of Portage Lake Loop Road and Byron Glacier Road. From this point, the trail has a well maintained paved surface to Williwaw Campground.

Other trails: The Williwaw Nature Trail, which runs from the Williwaw Fish Viewing Area (Mile 4.1 of Portage Glacier Road), follows Williwaw Creek, and look for spawning salmon in late July and August. At the Moose Flats Day Use Area (Mile 1.5 of Portage Glacier Road), try the 0.3-mile wetland interpretive trail, built by the Forest Service in cooperation with Ducks Unlimited.

TIDBIT

Bring rain gear, in case the valley's frequent, pelting rains strike while you're on the trail. Also, be on the lookout for avalanche run out areas where the trail is close to the mountain slopes (between Williwaw Campground and Five Fingers).

23. BYRON GLACIER

WHY GO?

This trail is an easy, fully-accessible trail traveling along a glacial creek, through lush forest and ending with a stunning view of the Byron Glacier.

THE RUNDOWN

Distance: 1.4 mile one way

Special features: A mountain glacier and a permanent snowfield

Location: 17 miles south of Girdwood

Difficulty: Easy

Trail type: More developed

Total elevation gain: 100 feet

Fees/permits: None

Best season: June through early Oct

Maps: USGS Seward D-5 (SW); National Geographic *Kenai National Wildlife Refuge*

Contact: Chugach National Forest, Glacier Ranger District, PO Box 129, 145 Forest Station Rd., Girdwood, AK 99587; (907) 783-3242; www.fs.usda.gov/chugach/

FINDING THE TRAILHEAD

Turn east off the Seward Highway onto the Portage Highway, 11 miles south of Girdwood and 10 miles north of Turnagain Pass. Drive about 5.4 miles, turn on Portage Lake Loop Road and follow the signs to the trailhead parking lot, located approximately one mile from the Begich, Boggs Visitor Center via the Byron Glacier Road. Take the path out of the far (south) end of the parking lot, next to the trailhead sign and bulletin board.

WHAT TO SEE

Portage Valley is one of the most popular visitor destinations in Alaska, but don't let that scare you away. The valley's blue ice and glacial scenery is outstanding, and many visitors simply stop at the Begich, Boggs Visitor Center, enjoy the surroundings a bit, and leave for the next attraction. If you stick around for a short hike to Byron Glacier, you'll be glad you did. Bring rain gear along, however, in case the valley's frequent, pelting rains strike while you're on the trail.

The hike parallels the road a short distance and then turns to follow Byron Creek upstream along its alder-and-cottonwood-covered bank. As you approach the glacier, the cottonwoods disappear, the alders grow shorter, and the air grows cooler. Leaving the brush behind, the trail emerges near the bank of foaming Byron Creek as it rushes through the rocky valley below Byron Glacier and frosty Byron Peak.

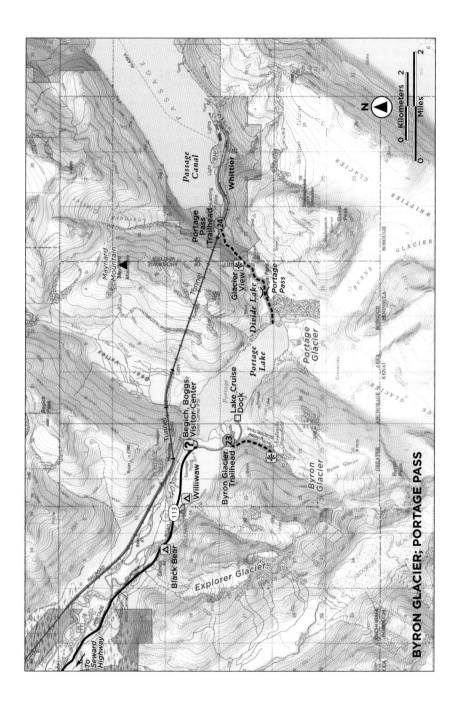

BYRON GLACIER; PORTAGE PASS

Byron Creek as it flows through the rocky valley below Byron Glacier, along the 1.4-mile one-way trail. YNEZ SLAYMAKER

Byron Glacier, visible in the twisting canyon upstream, is a hanging glacier; it isn't retreating as fast as Portage Glacier (see "Disappearing Portage Glacier," in the Portage Pass hike). Ahead, the creek pours out of a massive snowfield, a permanent feature built up of the hardened avalanche snow of many previous winters. If you want to wander out onto the snowfield, do so with caution, staying well clear of fissures and the ceiling of the stream-cut cavern; they're potentially very dangerous, as are occasional avalanches into the Byron valley as late as early June.

Forest Service naturalists lead "ice-worm safari" hikes on the Byron Glacier Trail during the summer; check at the Begich, Boggs Visitor Center (907-783-2326) for the schedule. Yes, ice worms are for real; they're tiny, black, threadlike worms that munch on pollen and algae near the surface of snow or ice. They're best found at twilight or on overcast days.

To learn more about Portage Valley, glaciers, and glacial geology, pay a visit to the Begich, Boggs Visitor Center.

Other trails: The Gary Williams Nature Trail, adjacent to the visitor center, is a 0.25-mile loop which is mostly wheelchair accessible.

24. PORTAGE PASS

WHY GO?

Portage Pass Trail is a great family outing, with stunning views of subalpine terrain, Passage Canal, Portage Lake, and the Glacier.

THE RUNDOWN See map on page 100.

Distances: Portage Glacier viewpoint: 1 mile one way. Portage Lake: 2 miles one way

Special features: A glacial landscape, alpine scenery, and historic interest

Location: Just outside Whittier, 50 miles southeast of Anchorage

Difficulty: Moderate

Trail type: More developed trail to route

Total elevation gain: 700 feet to the glacier viewpoint; 700 feet in and 600 feet out to Portage Lake

Best season: July through Sept

Fees/permits: None for the hike, but the road from Portage to Whittier is a toll road

Maps: USGS Seward D-5 (SW)

Contact: Chugach National Forest, Glacier Ranger District, PO Box 129, 145 Forest Station Rd., Girdwood, AK 99587; (907) 783-3242; www.fs.usda.gov/chugach/

FINDING THE TRAILHEAD

Getting to the start of this hike in Whittier, involves driving the Portage-Whittier toll road south of Girdwood, which passes through a one-lane, shared auto/train tunnel with specific periods during the day when it is open to automobile traffic in each direction. (At this writing, the typical pattern from May 1 to September 30 is a short opening in each direction approximately hourly from about 5:30 a.m. to 11:00 p.m.) For current information on the toll and schedule, see www.dot.state.ak.us/creg/whittiertunnel. The toll is not inexpensive; plan to stay awhile for the hike and maybe take a walk around Whittier while you're there—the town is a world of its own, to put it mildly.

The details: At Mile 78.9 of the Seward Highway, 11 miles south of Girdwood, turn east onto Portage Glacier Road. Drive about 5 miles to a fork and bear left toward Whittier (the right fork leads to Portage Lake, the Forest Service's Begich, Boggs Visitor Center, and the Byron Glacier Trailhead). Drive through the short, first, auto-only tunnel, pay your toll, and proceed 2.5 miles through the second, longer, shared auto/train tunnel.

As you exit the tunnel, look to the right to see the trail climbing toward an obvious pass (you guessed it: Portage Pass). Drive almost 0.2 mile, turn at the first right, cross the railroad tracks, take a right at the "Y." The trail begins roughly 200 feet ahead, near the end of this road, as a closed and abandoned roadbed heading south through a green tunnel of alder and salmonberry. Look for a sign at the trailhead.

WHAT TO SEE

Portage Pass is a beautiful spot in its own right, and this hike is also the easiest way to get a good view of the face of Portage Glacier since it melted back out of sight of the Begich, Boggs Visitor Center, in 1993. A moderate hike to an outstanding destination, this trip offers a reward-to-effort ratio that's right up there with the best Southcentral Alaska has to offer.

Portage Pass is a gap gouged out of the earth long ago by a lobe of Portage Glacier and opened up for hikers by the glacier's retreat of the last century. The trail has history too; in the 1890s, when the Alaska gold rush brought in the first big influx of non-natives, steamships docked at the foot of Portage Pass, where Whittier is now, and dropped off prospectors headed for gold strikes near Hope and Sunrise on Turnagain Arm.

The trail initially follows an old roadbed on a wide, easy course to the glacier viewpoint (1 mile one way, at 750 feet in elevation), where the crevassed, jumbled face of Portage Glacier stands out in the distance. Bear right on a branching path to a knob with an even better view. The knob is a good destination for a shorter hike, but if you've got the time and energy to continue down to Portage Lake, you'll remember the lake and its amazing glacial landscape as the highlight of the trip.

The abandoned roadbed disappears for a moment at the viewpoint; follow a narrower trail down and left to pick it up again. The wide path drops down to Divide Lake and Portage Pass, at about 550 feet in elevation, about 1.5 miles into the hike. The trail continues down to the stony beach at Portage Lake, a wonderful lunch or resting stop.

The view from the lakeshore is fantastic on a clear day, and there are plenty of good campsites and routes for rambling through the newly exposed landscape. Walking to the Burns Glacier outlet stream through the jumble of glacial rocks and boulders is a great side hike.

The wide and rocky trail at the top of Portage Pass, the high point of the trail, with Portage Glacier visible in the background.
WILLIE DALTON

A hiker explores the tundra covered rocky landscape of Portage Pass during sunset, Portage Glacier in the background.
WILLIE DALTON

At 700 feet of elevation, Prince William Sound and the road to the Whittier tunnel are visible from the summit of Portage Pass.
WILLIE DALTON

Wildlife highlights here are resident mountain goats and, in season, migrating birds. If you do the hike in September, you might be lucky enough to spot a flock of swans flying through the pass on their southerly migration.

Forest Service naturalists stationed at the Begich, Boggs Visitor Center occasionally lead hikes to Portage Pass. Check at the center (907-783-2326) for the schedule.

No connecting trail exists between the trail and Begich, Boggs Visitor Center, but paddlers can access it via a water route on the northeast shore of Portage Lake, beginning at the Bear Valley pullout.

MILES AND DIRECTIONS

0.0   Begin at the trailhead.

1.0   Stop at the Portage Glacier viewpoint.

1.5   The path drops down to Divide Lake and Portage Pass.

2.0   Arrive at Portage Lake.

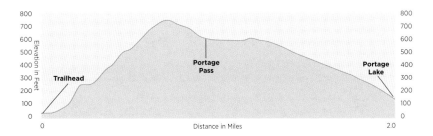

DISAPPEARING PORTAGE GLACIER

A century ago the blue ice of Portage Glacier nearly filled Portage Valley. The glacier began to retreat about 1914, exposing Portage Lake, and the retreat turned into a sprint a few decades ago. Visitors to the Forest Service's Begich, Boggs Visitor Center, built in 1986 to showcase the glacier, lost sight of the galloping glacier in 1993, when the face of the ice inconveniently disappeared around a bend in the lake. So, if you want to see the face of the glacier now, your choices are to take a lake cruise on a tour boat, hike the Portage Pass Trail from Whittier, or paddle to the end of the trail along the lakeshore from Bear Valley. As late as the early 1970s, you could drop down about 300 feet in elevation from the high point on the trail and touch the glacier; now you have to get to 700 feet in elevation for a distant view of the glacier's face across the upper end of Portage Lake. Translation: A lot of ice has melted since the 1970s.

Portage Glacier is in good company with glaciers and other kinds of ice all over Alaska. Glaciers are shriveling, permafrost is thawing, sea ice is retreating, and the Arctic ice pack is shrinking, all at barely believable rates, and all in synch with rising temperatures in the North. Since about 1970, the average year-round temperature in the state has jumped five degrees, and winter temperatures have risen by eight degrees in parts of the state. The leap in warming is already well within the range of climate scientists' predictions of how much the entire earth will warm by the end of the century.

The Portage Glacier is a good illustration of what's going on with climate change in Alaska.

25. WINNER CREEK

WHY GO?

A trail for all abilities, with a variety of options: a short or longer day hike option, or a longer overnight traverse climbing into the alpine country.

THE RUNDOWN

Distances: Winner Creek Gorge and Glacier Creek Tram: 2.5 miles one way. Hike/bike loop: About 8 miles

Special features: Lush forest, a gorge on lower Winner Creek, and a hand-tram crossing of the Glacier Creek canyon

Location: In the Girdwood valley, near Alyeska Ski Resort

Difficulty: Easy to moderate

Trail type: More developed

Total elevation gain: About 300 feet in and 200 feet out

Best season: June through early Oct

Fees/permits: None

Maps: USGS Seward D-6 (NW); National Geographic *Kenai National Wildlife Refuge*

Contact: Chugach National Forest, Glacier Ranger District, PO Box 129, 145 Forest Station Rd., Girdwood, AK 99587; (907) 783-3242; www.fs.usda.gov/chugach/

FINDING THE TRAILHEAD

Drive 35 miles south of Anchorage on the Seward Highway to the Alyeska Highway junction. Turn east toward Girdwood and Alyeska Ski Resort, and drive 3 miles, past the Girdwood town site, to a T intersection in front of the resort. Turn left here, onto Arlberg Avenue, following signs to the Alyeska Hotel. In a mile, pass the hotel entrance, follow the road as it loops back to the left, and park in the visitor area by the shuttle-bus stop.

From there, signs to the Winner Creek Hiking Trail lead you on a roundabout, unnecessary loop on bike trails and gravel paths around the south end of the hotel, a total of about half a mile, to the trailhead.

For a far easier and shorter walk from the parking area to the beginning of the hike, take the pedestrian path to the left as you face in the direction of the hotel from the parking area, back the way you drove in. Curl around the north end of the hotel, reaching the tram terminal in about 0.2 mile. Cut through the walkway between the terminal and the hotel, and turn immediately left onto a signed gravel path; the path leads under the tram line to the signed trailhead.

WHAT TO SEE

The Winner Creek Trail is a bit of a suburban wildland hike, but there are plenty of rewards: a beautiful trail, temperate rain forest, and the narrow gorges of Winner and Glacier Creeks. Across Glacier Creek, 2.5 miles into the hike, the trail connects with the Girdwood Iditarod Trail, a "natural tread" trail that parallels Crow Creek Road and leads about 3 miles to the Girdwood School. From the school, you can walk or bike 2.5 miles of paved bike path back to the trailhead at the Alyeska Hotel. This entire 8-mile loop, both forest trail and paved path, is open to bicycles.

Leaving the bustling extravagance of the hotel at the trailhead, you'll make a quick transition to the muffled sounds of the old-growth forest along the trail. Sitka spruce, western hemlock, feathery ferns, prickly devil's club, lush blueberry bushes, and equisetum, the fernlike horsetail, are abundant along the trail. This is the same coastal spruce-hemlock forest type that extends all the way south to Oregon, but these stands are the last you'll see if you're making your way north.

Bridges and boardwalk cross the many small creeks, seeps, and bogs in the first section of the trail. At about 1.5 miles, just after the trail passes a pretty meadow and climbs a low rise, it descends to the bluff above Winner Creek and meets a trail that runs up and down the creek. Turn left at this T intersection, heading downstream (west) toward the gorges. The east fork, to the right, is the upper Winner Creek Trail, described briefly under "Other trails" below.

About 0.6 mile toward the gorges from the T junction, ignore the snowcat trail and bridge to the right, except maybe to go sit on the bridge and watch the creek rush under you. Continue straight ahead, and in another 0.2 mile the trail crosses a narrow bridge over Winner Creek Gorge, where the foaming creek crashes through a narrow bedrock slot.

The trail continues on the far side of the bridge, climbing a steep but short hill, reaching the hand-operated tram over Glacier Creek in another 0.2 mile. This is the heart of the Girdwood valley, the confluence of three of the major streams here: Glacier, Winner, and Crow Creeks. Crow joins Glacier just upstream of the tram, and Winner Creek enters just downstream.

The tram is a car hung on a cable over the gorge, with a thick cable rope you pull to propel the car across. Even if you're turning back at Glacier Creek, be sure to take the tram to the other side; there's a fine view once you're out over the canyon, and propelling a tram is fun, especially if it's a new experience. It's hard work for a lone hiker, but a good upper-body workout if you've got some strength in that part of the anatomy. However, it's best to have two people pulling, someone on one of the platforms as well as someone in the car. Gloves also help.

The Iditarod Loop. On the west side of Glacier Creek, look for the Girdwood Iditarod Trail bearing upstream from the tram. It leads 0.8 mile to Crow Creek Road, at a point 2.9 miles from the Alyeska Highway. (The Alyeska Highway–Crow Creek Road intersection is 1.9 miles from the Seward Highway.) At Crow Creek Road the trail crosses the road and continues a bit more than 2 additional miles to the Girdwood School, crossing the road again at 1.6 miles from the Alyeska Highway.

To add your bicycle into the mix, spot it at either of the Crow Creek Road trail-heads or, for a longer distance on foot, leave it at the school, which is located in the Girdwood townsite at the north end of Hightower Drive. (Hightower intersects the Alyeska Highway 2.1 miles from the Seward Highway.) The 5.5 miles of the loop from the hotel to the gorges to the school is soft, "natural tread" trail that is the most suitable and scenic for hiking, and the 2.5 miles via the shortest route from the school to the hotel is paved bike path. No matter where you leave your bike, lock it securely to something solid.

The hand-operated tram over Glacier Creek, is the only way to cross the fast moving water. This is the heart of the Girdwood valley, the confluence of three major streams: Glacier, Winner, and Crow Creeks.
WILLIE DALTON

MILES AND DIRECTIONS

0.0 Begin at the trailhead.

1.5 Turn left at the Winner Creek T intersection.

2.3 Arrive at the Winner Creek Gorge.

2.5 Take the Glacier Creek Tram to the west side of the creek.

Other trails: The upper Winner Creek Trail is being rebuilt as part of a major new trail project. The new trail alignment will lead up Winner Creek, over alpine Berry Pass, and down the Twentymile River valley to the south and will be suitable for a 2-to-4-day traverse.

Shorter hikes: A short out-and-back walk from the hotel, about half a mile to a mile one way, is a good option for sampling Alaska's northernmost rain forest and picking a few blueberries in season; the forest is a kids' paradise. Another option is to park at Mile 2.9 of Crow Creek Road and walk the 0.8-mile section of the Girdwood Iditarod Trail to the Glacier Creek Tram.

> **TIDBIT**
>
> This trail includes a creek crossing by a modern hand-operated tram, a car on a cable with a with a thick manila rope to propel the car across. The crossing is easiest with a two-person team, and gloves help too.

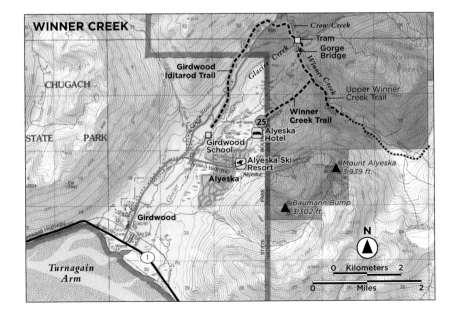

REVIVING A FORGOTTEN TRAIL

Most people who follow Alaska outdoor sports know that the Iditarod Trail Sled Dog Race runs from Anchorage to Nome, but few know that Seward was the southern gateway to the historic Iditarod Trail. Seward was the nearest year-round ice-free port and served as the jumping-off point for the winter trail to Iditarod and the other goldfields of western Interior Alaska.

Over the years since the early 1900s heyday of the trail, roads and railroads have taken over most of the historic route between Seward and Anchorage, but the Iditarod in this part of the state is making a comeback. Building on the previous work of trail lovers in Seward and Girdwood, the Chugach National Forest has put together a large-scale plan to revive the trail south of Anchorage. It's one of the most ambitious trail projects in Alaska in many years.

Several new trail segments will parallel roads and highways, connecting lakes, trails, and other points of interest, as the terrain of the Kenai and Chugach Mountains dictates. The new Trail of Blue Ice in the Portage Valley and an improved Portage Pass Trail are part of the recent progress. Also, in the future a new trail, connecting the Twentymile River, north of Portage, and Girdwood's Winner Creek, over Berry Pass. There's going to be some big backcountry fun on the twenty-first-century version of the Iditarod Trail.

26. **CROW PASS**

WHY GO?

Crow Pass Trail travels through a variety of terrain: glaciers, waterfalls, wildflowers, and mining ruins, plus the pass is the highest point on the historic Iditarod Trail and one of the top day hikes in Southcentral Alaska.

THE RUNDOWN

Distances: Crow Pass: 3.5 miles one way; Traverse of Crow Pass: 24 miles

Special features: An alpine pass, mountain glaciers, mining and Iditarod Trail history, wildlife, and access to off-trail wilderness rambles; one of Southcentral Alaska's classic alpine traverses

Location: 7 miles north of Girdwood

Difficulty: Strenuous

Trail type: More developed to Crow Pass; less developed north of the pass

Total elevation gain: Crow Pass: about 2,000 feet. Traverse: from Crow Pass, 2,000 feet; from Eagle River, 3,100 feet

Best season: Late June through Sept

Fees/permits: Fee for cabin use; parking fee at Eagle River trailhead

Maps: USGS Anchorage A-6 and A-7 (NE); Imus Geographics *Chugach State Park*

Contact: Chugach State Park, 18620 Seward Hwy., Anchorage, Alaska 99516; 907-345-5014; http://dnr.alaska.gov/parks/. (17 miles of the trail) Chugach National Forest, Glacier Ranger District, PO Box 129, 145 Forest Station Rd., Girdwood, AK 99587; (907) 783-3242; www.fs.usda.gov/chugach/ (4 miles of the trail)

FINDING THE TRAILHEAD

The trail begins at the end of the Crow Creek Road outside Girdwood. To get there, drive 35 miles south of Anchorage and turn northeast onto the Alyeska Highway. Drive 1.9 miles, turn left (north) onto Crow Creek Road, and follow it 6 miles to the trailhead. The road is often rough but is passable during the snow-free season.

If you're doing the traverse to or from the Eagle River Trailhead, get there by taking the Eagle River exit off the Glenn Highway, 13 miles north of Anchorage. Turn east, take a right turn onto Eagle River Road, and drive 12 miles to the end of the road at the Eagle River Nature Center. The trail begins behind the center.

WHAT TO SEE

Glaciers, waterfalls, wildflowers, and mining ruins add some spice to the hike to Crow Pass, as if it needed any. The pass is the highest point on the historic Iditarod Trail and one of the top day hikes in Southcentral Alaska. If you're backpacking, you can continue over the pass to the Eagle River Nature Center on a grand, 24-mile traverse through the Chugach Mountains.

Arctic ground squirrels, marmots, and mountain goats inhabit the high country near Crow Pass, and bears, moose, and Dall sheep are frequently spotted too, especially on the Eagle River side of the pass. The Eagle River valley has a significant bear population. Salmonberries and blueberries can be a trail prize for hikers later in summer.

The trail is relatively snow-free by late June, though the Crystal Lake basin south of the pass and some of the gullies north of the pass may hold snow well into the summer.

The mining history starts even before you reach the trailhead: The Crow Creek and Girdwood Mines, both just off Crow Creek Road, were two of the earliest mining claims in this part of the state.

Crow Pass Trail. The trail starts in the brush zone above tree line and climbs steadily up the old Monarch Mine Road. Tram cable, a boiler, and the remains of an ore-crushing mill and a compressor mark the site of the mine. The miners had their "base camp" (a bunkhouse, cookhouse, and blacksmith shop) there, and they hacked the ore out of the mountains above the trail.

Beyond the mine the trail starts a series of switchbacks, and a short, rough side trail leads to Crow Creek's cascades. A second trail, steeper than the main trail, cuts away from the switchbacks not far above the creek's lower cascades. This is an alternate trail toward the pass that avoids some early-season, snow-covered sidehilling on the main trail.

At 3 miles and 3,500 feet in elevation is the Crystal Lake basin and the Forest Service's Crow Pass fee cabin (reservation required: www.reserveusa.com or 877-444-6777). At Crow Pass, 0.5 mile farther and only about 100 feet higher, the main event is a view of Raven Glacier. The crevassed glacier can be dangerous; don't travel on the ice unless properly trained and equipped. There are plenty of peaks and ridges nearby for ice-free side trips.

Some hikers, apparently lulled by how short a hike this is, do the trip in shorts, T-shirts, and running shoes with no backup clothing; this is not a good plan. No matter how good the weather looks at the trailhead, don't leave the warm layers and rain gear behind.

The Crow Pass–Eagle River Traverse. The trail continues from Crow Pass down Raven Creek and the Eagle River about 20.5 more miles to the Eagle River Nature Center; about 10 miles of the 24-mile traverse are above tree line. Campsites for larger parties are fairly limited in the Raven Creek valley between Crow Pass and the Eagle River. There are sites at Clear Creek and Raven Gorge, and it's also possible to sleuth out a place or two at Turbid Creek and in the forest before the final descent into Eagle River Valley. The valley has loads of campsites of all sizes; see the Eagle River Valley hike.

Rock cairns mark the way through the glacial rubble (on a lateral moraine) just north of the pass. Take care while crossing steep snow slopes here (bringing an ice axe or similar gear is helpful if traversing early in the season); if they're hard packed, you may need to climb or descend to get around them. The trip involves two stream fords, one at Clear Creek, at Mile 5.5, and one at a marked ford across Eagle River, at Mile 12. Carrying extra foot gear is worth the weight.

Some of the highlights of the traverse are Raven Glacier and the glacially sculpted terrain below it; Raven Gorge, where water blasts through a rock arch in a tight bedrock canyon; Eagle River's upper valley and Glacier Lake; and the many side canyons, waterfalls, mountain walls, and glaciers of Eagle River. Several strenuous cross-country hikes are possible from the trail, including two high passes to the west of Raven Creek: Steamroller Pass at the head of Clear Creek, and Paradise Pass at the head of Paradise Creek. Both are high and rugged, with difficult descents to the west.

Flooding and trail/bridge damage is frequent north of the pass; it's best to call the Eagle River Nature Center, (907) 694-2108, or Chugach State Park (see Contact above) to check on conditions before setting out on the traverse.

Looking up Eagle River from The Perch, about 4 miles from the Eagle River Nature Center on the Crow Pass Trail. Black bears are commonly seen along this stretch of the river.
WILL KOEPPEN

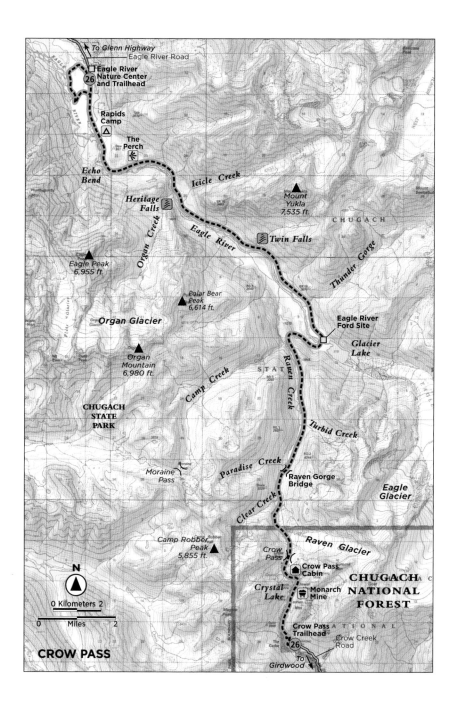

To Glenn Highway
Eagle River Road

Eagle River
Nature Center
and Trailhead
26

Rapids
Camp

The
Perch

Echo
Bend

Icicle Creek

Heritage
Falls

Organ Creek

Eagle River

Twin Falls

Mount
Yukla
7,535 ft.

CHUGACH

Thunder Gorge

Eagle Peak
6,955 ft.

Polar Bear
Peak
6,614 ft.

Organ Glacier

Organ
Mountain
6,980 ft.

Camp Creek

Raven Creek

Eagle River
Ford Site

Glacier
Lake

STATE

CHUGACH
STATE
PARK

Turbid Creek

Moraine
Pass

Paradise Creek

Raven Gorge
Bridge

Eagle
Glacier

Clear Creek

Camp Robber
Peak
5,855 ft.

Raven Glacier

Crow
Pass

Crow Pass
Cabin

CHUGACH
NATIONAL
FOREST

Crystal
Lake

Monarch
Mine

N

0 Kilometers 2

Miles
0   2

Crow Pass
Trailhead

Crow Creek
Road

26

To
Girdwood

CROW PASS

TIDBIT

If hiking the 24-mile traverse bring plenty of layers, food/water, and other safety equipment, as weather and conditions can change rapidly.

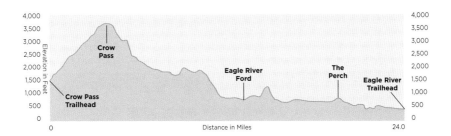

MILES AND DIRECTIONS

From Crow Pass		From Eagle River
0.0	Begin/end at the Crow Pass Trailhead.	24.0
1.7	Pass the remains of the Monarch Mine.	22.3
3.0	Reach the Forest Service's Crow Pass Cabin.	21.0
3.5	View Raven Glacier from Crow Pass.	20.5
5.5	Wade Clear Creek.	18.5
6.0	Cross the bridge over Raven Gorge.	18.0
7.5	Cross a footbridge over Turbid Creek.	16.5
12.0	Ford Eagle River.	12.0
13.0	Pass Thunder Gorge.	11.0
15.5	Arrive at Twin Falls.	8.5
19.0	Pass Heritage Falls.	5.0
20.0	Arrive at The Perch.	4.0
21.0	Reach Echo Bend.	3.0
24.0	End/begin at the Eagle River Trailhead.	0.0

Trailhead is behind the Eagle River Nature Center

Shorter hikes: The hike to the ruins of the Monarch Mine, 1.7 miles one way, involves 1,000 feet of climbing and leads to beautiful alpine country.

CHUGACH STATE PARK SOUTH

CHUGACH STATE PARK, the wild park right out of Anchorage's back door, is the third largest state park in the country, smaller only than the western Alaska's Wood-Tikchik State Park and California's Anza-Borrego Desert State Park. From coast to lush forest to mountain peak and glacier, Chugach's half a million acres stretch over 60 miles of the western end of the Chugach Mountains, possibly America's least-known major mountain range. The park includes fifteen major watersheds, seventy lakes, fifty glaciers, and thirteen peaks over 7,000 feet, not a mean feat considering that the western boundary is just above sea level. Chugach is a hiking wonderland, featuring hundreds of miles of trails and routes through incredible mountains.

The most comprehensive park map, the Imus Geographics map, is a good introduction to all Chugach has to offer. It is perfectly adequate for trail hiking, but definitely pick up the USGS topographic maps if you take to the high ridges and cross-country routes—the Imus map isn't detailed enough for serious route finding.

The southern part of the park takes in the mountains along Turnagain Arm and above the Anchorage Bowl (the basin where the city is located). The trip descriptions here and in the following section on the northern part of the park are given in order from south to north.

27. BIRD RIDGE

WHY GO?
One of the first trails to melt in the spring, combined with significant elevation, make it a great trail to get in hiking shape at the beginning of the season.

THE RUNDOWN

Distance: About 1 mile one way to alpine views; 2.5 miles one way to Peak 3,505; 6.5 miles one way to Bird Ridge Overlook

Special features: A very steep trail; fine views of Turnagain Arm

Location: 25 miles south of downtown Anchorage

Difficulty: Strenuous to very strenuous

Trail type: Developed trail, a route beyond

Total elevation gain: 3,450 feet to Peak 3,505

Best season: Mid-Apr to mid-Oct

Fees/permits: Parking fee or state parks pass

Maps: USGS Seward D-7 (NW) and Anchorage A-7; Imus Geographics *Chugach State Park*

Contact: Chugach State Park, 18620 Seward Hwy., Anchorage, Alaska 99516; 907-345-5014; http://dnr.alaska.gov/parks/

FINDING THE TRAILHEAD

The prominent parking area and trailhead, 25 miles south of downtown Anchorage, is on the north side of the Seward Highway at Mile 102.1, 0.9 mile east of the Indian Creek Bridge and 0.6 mile west of the Bird Creek Bridge.

WHAT TO SEE
The hike up Bird Ridge, the ridge between Indian and Bird Creeks, offers a chance to see the Anchorage area's first mountain wildflowers of the year; the ridge is steep and south-facing, so the snow melts early in spring. The sweeping views of alpine mountains, green valleys, and shimmering Turnagain Arm from the ridge are about as good as scenery gets.

Locals use the Bird Ridge Trail as a tune-up hike early in the year. It's an extremely steep trail, so consider taking a staff or ski poles, and be ready for sore quads the next day if this is your first hike of the year. If snowfields still linger on the ridge, there is usually a trail of packed snow to follow. The ridge is exposed and usually windy, so even if the weather is good at the trailhead, pack a hat, gloves, and warm and windproof clothing.

A hiker's silhouette in hemlocks on Bird Ridge, with Penguin Peak visible in the background.
JUSTIN WHOLEY

A hiker climbs the Bird Ridge Trail, a steep ascent for the 2.5 miles to the summit at 3,505 feet.
HAGEPHOTO

To begin the hike, follow the paved trail out of the parking lot. After about 0.2 mile of pavement and elevated boardwalk, turn left, uphill, at the restroom. Climb about 0.1 mile to a maintenance road. Turn right and continue about another 0.1 mile, until you reach a point where you can see into the next valley, Bird Creek. Look for the ridge trail cutting uphill to the left.

The trail climbs steeply. At roughly 1,000 feet in elevation, it leaves the spruce forest and opens to views of Turnagain Arm and the Bird Creek valley. After another stretch of climbing, the trail breaks out into the rocks and boulders of the alpine ridge.

The first high point with a 180-degree view is Peak 3,505, about 2.5 miles from the trailhead. Looking west, the valley of Indian Creek appears (see the Indian Valley hike), with the powerline heading over Powerline Pass toward the Glen Alps Trailhead in the distance. Looking east yields a view up the valley of Penguin Creek, and south are Turnagain Arm and the Kenai Mountains. To the north lies a jumble of wild peaks in the heart of the Chugach Mountains.

For a much longer ridge run, keep walking to the Bird Ridge Overlook, at an elevation of 4,650 feet and about 4 miles beyond Peak 3,505. The peak overlooks the east fork of upper Ship Creek.

The sweeping views of alpine mountains, green valleys, and shimmering Turnagain Arm from the ridge are worth the climb.
MOLLIE FOSTER

TIDBIT

With a steep route that climbs to an exposed ridge, bring extra layers, trekking poles, and be prepared for sore legs the follow day if this is the first big hike of the year.

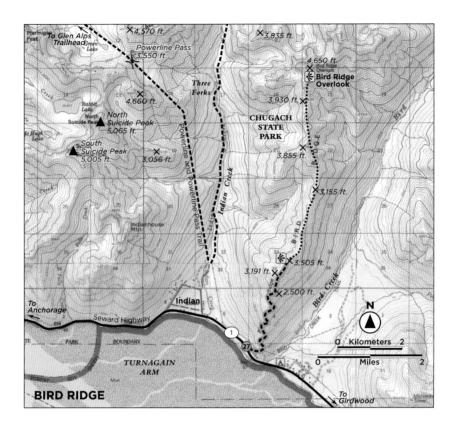

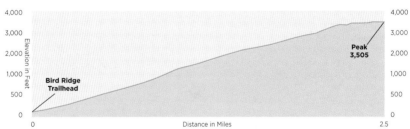

MILES AND DIRECTIONS

- **0.0** Begin at trailhead.
- **0.2** Turn left, uphill at the restroom.
- **0.3** Climb to a maintenance road; turn right.
- **0.5** Continue on the ridge trail cutting uphill to the left.
- **2.5** A 180-degree view at Peak 3,505.

28. FALLS CREEK

WHY GO?

A short, steep route traveling through a narrow valley, and climbing to outstanding views of Turnagain Arm.

THE RUNDOWN

Distances: Falls Lake: 2.5 miles one way. South Suicide Peak: 4.5 miles one way

Special features: Alpine scenery, wildlife, cross-country hiking from the end of the trail, and Chugach Range ridges and peaks

Location: 21 miles south of Anchorage

Difficulty: Very strenuous.

Trail type: A steep, less-developed trail/route

Total elevation gain: Falls Lake, 2,900 feet. South Suicide Peak, 5,000 feet

Best season: Late June to mid-Sept

Fees/permits: None

Maps: USGS Seward D-7 (NW) and Anchorage A-7; Imus Geographics *Chugach State Park*

Contact: Chugach State Park, 18620 Seward Hwy., Anchorage, Alaska 99516; 907-345-5014; http://dnr.alaska.gov/parks/

FINDING THE TRAILHEAD

Drive about 21 miles south of downtown Anchorage on the Seward Highway; the trailhead is on the north side of the highway at Mile 115.7, 1 mile east of the Windy Corner Trailhead for the Turnagain Arm Trail and 2.7 miles west of Indian Creek. Look for the highway turnout by the pretty, cascading creek.

WHAT TO SEE

A steep hike to a high tundra basin, the Falls Creek Trail threads its way up a narrow valley into the region of some of the highest peaks along Turnagain Arm. Wildflowers, wild mountains, Dall sheep, and the headwater tarn known locally as Falls Lake are all highlights of a visit to the Falls Creek drainage. In late summer the berries come out: blueberries, cranberries, crowberries, watermelon berries, salmonberries, and the poisonous baneberry. Two huge peaks—Indianhouse Mountain (4,350 feet) and South Suicide Peak (5,005 feet)—loom above the basin. Allow a good portion of a long summer day for this seemingly short hike; the trail is rough, steep, and slow, and you'll want to linger and enjoy the beauty of the place once you've expended the energy it takes to get here.

The trail is steep and brushy, especially in the alder zone, which begins about a mile into the hike. There are two potentially confusing spots in the first 0.5 mile. Take a switchback to the right where a left fork stays low along the creek, and a bit higher, take the path to the left in a small rocky opening.

At about 1.5 miles and 2,000 feet in elevation, the small sparkling stream jumps in short falls and cascades down the mountainside through pretty wildflower meadows. At about two miles, after crossing the east fork of the creek, the path climbs the ridge between the forks and disappears. From here, head left, cross-country, into the upper basin clearly visible to the west.

In another 0.5 mile the high tundra valley takes a sharp turn to the east to its headwaters in Falls Lake, a good destination at 2.5 miles and just below 3,000 feet in elevation. The best views are on the ridgeline to the north, another 0.5 mile and an 800-foot climb away. A flat area a little east of a direct line to South Suicide Peak overlooks the Indian Creek valley; bearing west of the peak leads to views down Rainbow Creek. The trip to the top of South Suicide is nontechnical but very challenging, with a one-way distance of about 4.5 miles, an elevation gain of almost 5,000 feet, and some steep talus near the top.

Most people day-hike Falls Creek, but there are good campsites in the upper basin, if you're planning on an overnight.

Shorter hikes: Any hike into Falls Creek is a steep hike. Hiking the 1.5 miles to the first wildflower meadows is a good half-day trip with a 2,000-foot elevation gain.

A woman walks across a snowfield that marks the edge of treeline on the steep but rewarding hike to views of Turnagain Arm and the Suicide Peaks. WILLIE DALTON

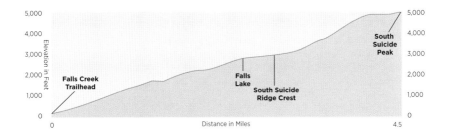

MILES AND DIRECTIONS

0.0 Begin at the trailhead.

1.5 Hike through sections of meadows and cascades.

2.5 Arrive at Falls Lake.

3.0 Reach the South Suicide ridge crest.

4.5 Summit South Suicide Peak.

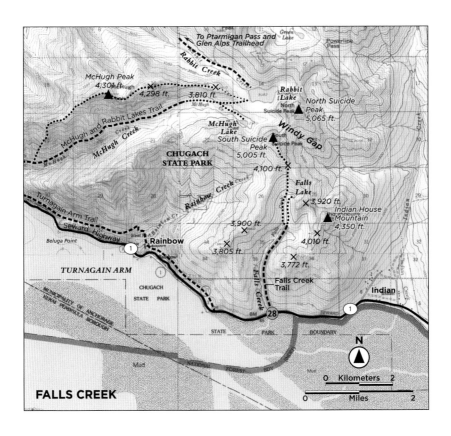

FALLS CREEK

29. MCHUGH AND RABBIT LAKES

WHY GO?

This trail winds through forest, meadow and into alpine tundra with wonderful views, lakes, and prominent peaks in McHugh Creek Valley.

THE RUNDOWN

Distance: 6.5 miles one way

Special features: Alpine tundra, mountain lakes, access to cross-country hiking

Location: 15 miles south of Anchorage

Difficulty: Strenuous

Trail type: More-developed trail for the first mile; less-developed trail to the upper valley; a route beyond

Total elevation gain: About 3,200 feet in and 200 feet out

Best season: Mid-June through Sept

Fees/permits: Parking fee or state parks pass

Maps: USGS Anchorage A-7 and A-8 (SE); Imus Geographics *Chugach State Park*

Contact: Chugach State Park, 18620 Seward Hwy., Anchorage, Alaska 99516; 907-345-5014; http://dnr.alaska.gov/parks/

FINDING THE TRAILHEAD

Drive to the McHugh Creek State Wayside 15 miles south of Anchorage, at Mile 111.9 of the Seward Highway. From the north, the picnic area is around a sharp bend in the road and is not visible until you're there. The Mile 112 marker on the northeast side of the road is a warning the picnic area is coming up. The trailhead is at the end of the upper parking lot; pass up a right fork that leads to the midlevel parking area.

The road is too steep for large vehicles or vehicles with trailers, so park these in the lower parking area just off the highway. Also, the wayside gate closes at 9 p.m., so if you plan on being out late or overnight, park in the lower area.

WHAT TO SEE

The McHugh Trail leads through forest, meadow, and brush into alpine tundra and lake country below the craggy Suicide Peaks. Great views, two lakes, and McHugh Creek's alpine basin are the highlights of the hike. Moose, Dall sheep, grouse, ptarmigan, and bears frequent this wild valley.

Take the Turnagain Arm Trail out of the upper McHugh parking area, and at the T in 0.1 mile, turn left toward Potter Creek. In another 0.2 mile, turn right, uphill, onto the signed McHugh/Rabbit Lakes Trail. About a mile from the trailhead, at the end of a series of switchbacks, a short, steep side path leads to the top of Table Rock, elevation 1,083 feet, an outcrop with sweeping views of Turnagain Arm, Cook Inlet, and the Kenai Peninsula. On a sunny day this is a popular picnic and sunbathing spot.

Past Table Rock, the trail curls into the McHugh drainage, joining the steep sidehill far above the creek. On the right in another few minutes is another open outcrop, this time with a good view of the McHugh valley and the arm. About 2 miles into the hike, just beyond the last switchbacks in the trees, another steep side trail peels off to the left (north), leading to the McHugh Peak ridgeline and eventually, about 2.5 miles from the main trail, to McHugh Peak, elevation 4,301 feet.

Most of the climb on the McHugh Trail is in the first 3 miles. By 4.5 miles the trail opens into a pretty alpine valley with scattered, low-growing mountain hemlock and willows and countless tiny blueberry and crowberry bushes. Camping is good here and near the lakes.

Near the head of the valley, where enormous glacial boulders lie scattered across the landscape, stay on the lower path to find McHugh Lake. Climb over the low ridge to the northeast, a glacial moraine, to find the much larger Rabbit Lake, at the head of the Rabbit Creek valley. North and South Suicide Peaks rise in dark cliffs above the lakes, with the aptly named Windy Gap between them.

A backpacker prepares breakfast while camping beneath the Suicide Peaks at Rabbit Lake in Chugach State Park. HAGEPHOTO

Rabbit (left) and McHugh Lakes (right) rimmed by mountains and passes on a September day. WILL KOEPPEN

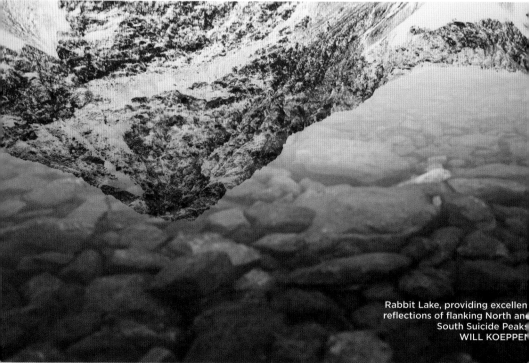

Rabbit Lake, providing excellent reflections of flanking North and South Suicide Peaks WILL KOEPPEN

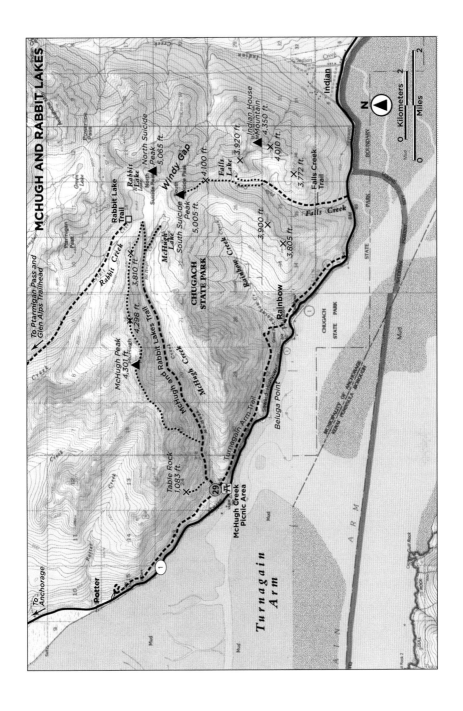

MCHUGH AND RABBIT LAKES

Potter

To Anchorage

To Ptarmigan Pass and
Glen Alps Trailhead

Rabbit Creek

Ptarmigan
Peak

Green
Lake

Rabbit Lake
Trail

Rabbit
Lake

North Suicide
Peak
5,065 ft.

North
Suicide Peak

Windy Gap

4,100 ft.

Falls
Lake

3,920 ft.

Indian House
Mountain
4,350 ft.

Indian

4,010 ft.

3,772 ft.

Falls Creek
Trail

Falls Creek

South Suicide
Peak
5,005 ft.

McHugh
Lake

3,900 ft.

Rainbow
Creek

3,805 ft.

CHUGACH
STATE PARK

Rainbow

STATE   PARK

BOUNDARY

3,810 ft.

McHugh Peak
4,301 ft.

4,298 ft.

McHugh and Rabbit Lakes Trail

McHugh Creek

1

CHUGACH
STATE
PARK

MUNICIPALITY OF ANCHORAGE
KENAI PENINSULA BOROUGH

Mud

Table Rock
1,083 ft.

29

McHugh Creek
Picnic Area

Turnagain Arm Trail

Seward Highway

Beluga Point

1

T u r n a g a i n
A r m

Mud

Mud

Mud

T U R N A G A I N   A R M

Mud

Gull Rock

TO ROCK

N

0   Kilometers   2

0   Miles   2

MILES AND DIRECTIONS

0.0   Begin at the trailhead.

1.0   A side path leads to Table Rock.

4.5   The trail opens into the upper McHugh Creek valley.

6.0   The routes divide to Rabbit and McHugh Lakes.

6.5   Arrive at either of the lakes.

McHugh Peak Ridgeline. From the low moraine between McHugh and Rabbit Lakes, hike west onto the McHugh Peak ridgeline. Travel out the ridge a short way for the view, and then backtrack to the trail for the trip out. Alternatively, for a much more difficult trip out, hike all the way back to the trailhead via the ridge, dropping down to the trail at Mile 2 via the rough track you passed on the way in.

McHugh to Rabbit Lakes Traverse. For a thru-hike option, hike a 10.8-mile traverse from McHugh Creek Trailhead to Rabbit Lake Trailhead.

Shorter hikes: Table Rock, an outcrop with a view, is 1 mile one way and an 800-foot climb.

30. TURNAGAIN ARM TRAIL

WHY GO?

The trail leads across a steep southwest slope that receives lots of spring sunshine, so the trail is one of the earliest near Anchorage to open as the landscape melts. There are numerous route options on Turnagain Arm trail from short interpretive loops to longer thru-hike options.

THE RUNDOWN

Distances: 1.9 to 9.4 miles; 4 trailheads split the 9.4-mile trail into 3 sections

Special features: Forest and coastal scenery, good early- and late-season hikes

Location: 12 miles south of downtown Anchorage

Difficulty: Easy to moderate, depending on the section hiked

Trail type: More developed.

Total elevation gain: About 200 to 800 feet, depending on the section hiked, or up to 1,400 feet for the entire trail

Best season: Mid-Apr through Oct

Fees/permits: Parking fee or state parks pass at Potter and McHugh; no fee at Rainbow or Windy Corner

Maps: USGS Anchorage A-8 (SE), Seward D-8 (NE), and Seward D-7 (NE and NW); Imus Geographics *Chugach State Park*; and Alaska State Parks brochure Turnagain Arm Trail

Contact: Chugach State Park, 18620 Seward Hwy., Anchorage, Alaska 99516; 907-345-5014; http://dnr.alaska.gov/parks/

FINDING THE TRAILHEAD

All four trailheads are just a few miles south of Anchorage on the Seward Highway. The nearest to Anchorage, the Potter Creek Trailhead, is just south of the south end of Potter's Marsh, at Seward Highway Mile 115.1, 0.1 mile south of Chugach State Park headquarters. Turn east into the parking area.

The other three trailheads, from northwest to southeast, are the McHugh Creek State Wayside, Mile 111.9; Rainbow, Mile 108.4; and Windy Corner, Mile 106.7. All are on the north, or mountain, side of the highway.

Rainbow and Windy are immediately off the highway. The McHugh trailheads are up the steep picnic-area road; the road is too steep for large vehicles or vehicles with trailers, so park these in the lower parking area just off the highway. To hike to the southeast toward Rainbow, take the right fork in the road and begin the trip from the midlevel parking area. To hike northwest toward Potter, pass the right fork in the road and continue straight ahead into the upper parking area.

WHAT TO SEE

The Turnagain Arm Trail leads across a steep southwest slope that receives lots of spring sunshine, so the trail is one of the earliest near Anchorage to open as things begin to thaw. Winding along the slope above the arm, the hike follows the route of a wagon road used to supply railroad-construction camps when crews were building this section of the Alaska Railroad from 1915 to 1918. The hike offers great views of Turnagain Arm, the Kenai Mountains, and the Chugach Range. The grade of the trail is gentle overall, but there are steep sections near each of the trailheads.

Spruce grouse, songbirds, moose, and even the occasional bear frequent the trail. In late summer look in the water below for beluga whales, the small white whales that swim up the arm to feed when salmon are running. The weather here is usually mild, but there is nearly always a wind. Fires are prohibited, and the trail is closed to mountain bikes.

Potter Creek–McHugh Creek. The section between Potter and McHugh is the most developed and most traveled section of the trail; it is a great trail for families and beginning hikers. Mainly a forest hike, this section does have one good viewpoint on a rock outcrop about 2 miles from Potter.

About Mile 3, 0.3 mile west of McHugh, the trail intersects the McHugh/Rabbit Lakes Trail. At McHugh short feeder trails connect the Turnagain Arm Trail with the picnic area. The west feeder trail leads to the upper parking lot, and the east feeder trail leads to the midlevel lot.

McHugh Creek–Rainbow. The McHugh–Rainbow section is the longest and steepest section of the trail, with a high point of 900 feet near Rainbow. Starting the hike from McHugh avoids the steep climb from Rainbow, the steepest on the trail. Crossing McHugh Creek on a bridge, the trail passes scree, rocky slopes, rock ledges, and patches of forest on the way to Rainbow. About 1.8 miles east of McHugh, a steep side trail descends to Beluga Point at Seward Highway Mile 110.2.

Rainbow–Windy Corner. The trail between Rainbow and Windy is rocky and open, with stands of small aspen trees and some of the best views along the trail. At 1.9 miles, this is the shortest section of the trail. Dall sheep use the rocky area above the highway at Windy Corner, so look for sheep as you walk the few hundred yards closest to Windy.

Panoramic views along the Turnagain Arm Trail with vistas of Turnagain Arm, the Kenai Mountains, and the Chugach Range. The trail is an old wagon route that used to supply railroad-construction camps when crews were building this section of the Alaska Railroad from 1915 to 1918. MOLLIE FOSTER

There are plenty of viewpoints along the trail, for scanning the landscape for all types of activity. Look for the bore tide, a wall of water up to 5 feet high traveling as much as 10 mph, up the arm on the incoming tide. Turnagain Arm and Knik Arm of Cook Inlet are the only places with regularly occurring bore tides in the United States. MOLLIE FOSTER

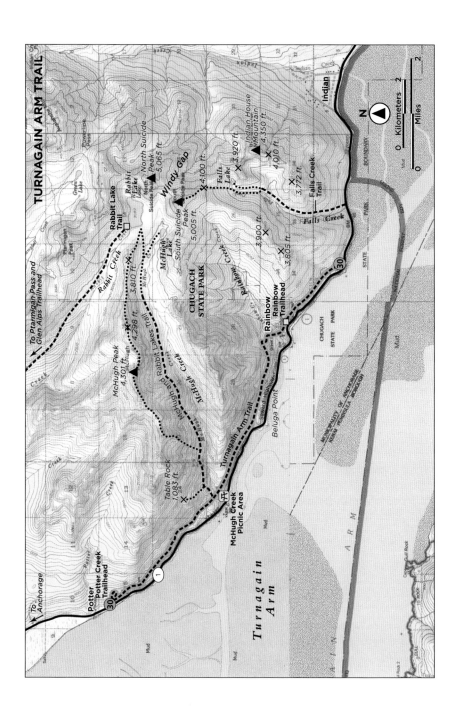

MILES AND DIRECTIONS

From Potter		From Windy Corner
0.0	Begin/end at the Potter Creek Trailhead.	9.4
3.3	Reach the trail junction to the McHugh Creek State Wayside.	6.1
7.5	Arrive/begin at the Rainbow Trailhead.	1.9
9.4	End/begin at the Windy Corner Trailhead.	0.0

Shorter hikes: The first 0.4 mile of the hike from Potter Creek is a graded interpretive trail with natural-history information panels. You can turn this short walk into about a 1-mile loop by traveling one way on the connecting trail just upslope of the interpretive trail.

At McHugh an accessible trail leads 0.1 mile one way from the McHugh Creek Picnic Area's upper parking lot to two ocean overlooks. These are good viewpoints for spotting the Turnagain Arm bore tide, a wall of water up to 5 feet high traveling as much as 10 mph up the arm on the incoming tide. Turnagain Arm and Knik Arm of Cook Inlet are the only places in the United States with bore tides; the 30-foot tidal range and the shape and length of the arm contribute to the generation of the tidal bore. Look for the bore tide at McHugh Creek about an hour after the predicted Anchorage low tide.

31. **FLATTOP MOUNTAIN**

WHY GO?

Perhaps one of the most popular trails in the summer for good reasons: close to town, numerous options for a variety of hiking abilities with access to alpine tundra, spectacular views of mountains, Cook Inlet, and the city.

THE RUNDOWN

Distances: Flattop Trail: 1.5 miles one way. Blueberry Loop Trail: a 1-mile loop. Anchorage Overlook Trail: 0.1 mile one way.

Special features: Awesome views, an accessible trail, and the most visited mountaintop in Alaska. The last pitch of the climb to Flattop is a bit rough and requires some care.

Location: In the Glen Alps area above south Anchorage.

Difficulty: Flattop: moderate; short but steep. Blueberry Loop and Anchorage Overlook: easy.

Trail type: Flattop: generally more developed; less developed on the

final pitch. Blueberry Loop: more developed. Anchorage Overlook: accessible.

Total elevation gain: Flattop: 1,350 feet. Blueberry Loop: 400 feet. Anchorage Overlook: 50 feet.

Best season: June through Sept.

Fees/permits: Parking fee or state parks pass.

Maps: USGS Anchorage A-8 (SE); Imus Geographics *Chugach State Park.*

Contact: Chugach State Park, 18620 Seward Hwy., Anchorage, Alaska 99516; 907-345-5014; http://dnr.alaska.gov/parks/.

FINDING THE TRAILHEAD

Drive about 7 miles south of downtown Anchorage on the New Seward Highway, and exit east toward the Chugach Mountains on O'Malley Road. Continue about 4 miles on O'Malley, and take a right onto Hillside Drive, just before O'Malley takes a sharp turn to the left. In another mile, turn uphill (left) off Hillside Drive onto Upper Huffman Road, and drive 0.7 mile to a three-way intersection. Here, go right onto Toilsome Hill Drive. Follow Toilsome Hill steeply uphill, just under 2 more miles, to the Glen Alps parking area and trailhead on the left.

WHAT TO SEE

On summer weekends and evenings after work, scores of Anchorage residents visit the Glen Alps entrance to Chugach State Park for short walks, berry picking, or the hike to the top of Flattop. The trail to Flattop, a high, level summit in the first tier of peaks in the Chugach Mountains, is a very popular hike to great views of mountains, ocean, and Alaska's largest city. An Anchorage outdoor tradition, begun by the Alaska Mountaineering Club, is to spend the nights of the summer and winter solstices on the summit.

Just because Flattop is close to the city, don't think that the usual mountain precautions don't apply. Decent boots with good traction and foul-weather clothing are musts, and a staff or ski pole is a good idea for the steep descent immediately off the summit. This pitch below the peak, on the rocky northwest ridge, is steep and a bit exposed, and requires some care, especially on the descent. Be careful not to roll loose rocks down onto hikers below you. If there is still snow on this pitch, it can be dangerous without an ice ax.

To start, follow the switchback trail on the southeast (mountain) side of the parking area. The first intersection with the Blueberry Loop Trail is just ahead. Blueberry Knoll is the nearby tundra knob, and Flattop is the rocky peak beyond.

In the saddle behind Blueberry Knoll, the Flattop Trail leads to the south (Rabbit Creek) side of the ridge, and the Blueberry Loop peels off west, back toward the parking area. The Flattop Trail then climbs in switchbacks to the base of the peak, to the beginning of the final, steep pitch.

The top invites a bit of wandering to see the view from all possible angles. Rock outcrops offer shelter for getting out of the wind for your picnic lunch or snack. Experienced hikers can continue out on the ridge to the southeast on the route to Peak 2 and Peak 3. When you're ready to head back to the trailhead, look for the post marking the route down, and take it slowly and cautiously.

Blueberry Loop Trail. The loop trail around Blueberry Knoll, elevation 2,700 feet, involves much less climbing, so is a better trip for families and casual hikers. There are good views here too, as well as some decent blueberry bushes.

Anchorage Overlook Trail. The overlook trail leads from the north end of the parking area to a viewpoint overlooking Anchorage and Cook Inlet. Two short paths, one paved and one gravel, climb gently to the overlook, at 2,258 feet in elevation.

All three trails are closed to bicycles.

> **TIDBIT**
> Even though the trail is close to the city, you still need to bring proper hiking gear, plenty of water, and be prepared for sudden changes in weather.

Hikers on the ridge that connects Flattop Mountain Peak 2, Peak 3, and Flaketop to Ptarmigan Pass in Chugach State Park. The 4-mile traverse is a route suitable for experienced hikers and trail runners. HAGEPHOTO

The Blueberry Hill saddle; continuing uphill will lead to the top of Flattop mountain, or staying on the loop trail will circle back to the trailhead. WILL KOEPPEN

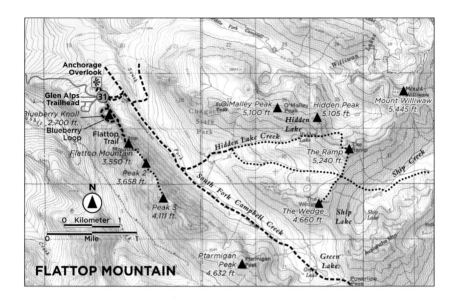

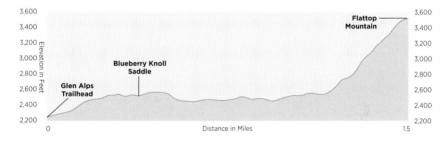

SOUTHCENTRAL'S BERRY CROP

Glen Alps and other Southcentral trails are good places to stock up on wild berries in August and September. Blueberries, raspberries, and salmonberries are local favorites. Watermelon berries make a tasty trail snack, and berry lovers also gather currants, nagoonberries, rose hips, crowberries, and low-bush and highbush cranberries. The musky scent of the red-leafed highbush cranberry is the smell of the Southcentral woods in fall.

The rest of the crop—bearberry, timber berry, mountain ash, elderberry, Devil's club, soapberry, and a few others—vary in edibility and are better admired than eaten. Baneberry, a common red berry, is extremely poisonous; it also comes in a striking white form known as porcelain berry.

Most of the common berries are red or orange. The berries' riot of color, mixed with the lush green of late summer, makes berry time a colorful season to be out on the trail.

32. SHIP LAKE PASS

WHY GO?

Ship Lake Pass is a wonderful day hike for various hiking abilities, with easy access to alpine country, and plenty of options to extend to overnight traverse options.

THE RUNDOWN

Distance: 6 miles one way

Special features: High alpine scenery, stream crossings

Location: In the Glen Alps area of south Anchorage

Difficulty: Moderate

Trail type: More-developed trail to the South Fork Campbell Creek crossing; less-developed trail/route beyond

Total elevation gain: 1,800 feet to the pass

Best season: June through Sept

Fees/permits: Parking fee or state parks pass

Maps: USGS Anchorage A-8 (SE) and Anchorage A-7; Imus Geographics *Chugach State Park*

Contact: Chugach State Park, 18620 Seward Hwy., Anchorage, Alaska 99516; 907-345-5014; http://dnr.alaska.gov/parks/

FINDING THE TRAILHEAD

Drive about 7 miles south of downtown Anchorage on the New Seward Highway, and exit east toward the Chugach Mountains on O'Malley Road. Continue about 4 miles on O'Malley, and take a right onto Hillside Drive, just before O'Malley takes a sharp turn to the left. In another mile, turn uphill (left) off Hillside Drive onto Upper Huffman Road, and drive 0.7 mile to a three-way intersection. Here, go right onto Toilsome Hill Drive. Follow Toilsome Hill steeply uphill, just under 2 more miles, to the Glen Alps parking area and trailhead on the left.

WHAT TO SEE

Three-quarters of Chugach State Park is above tree line, and this hike from Glen Alps is a fine way to sample the park's alpine country. The trip is good all summer, but fall is probably its finest season, when the gnarled mountain hemlocks are green, the blueberry and bearberry have turned fiery red, and the willows, birches, and mountain ash have gone gold.

Take one of the two parallel trails from the Glen Alps parking area to the Power-line Trail. They both begin just to the left of the route leading to Flattop Mountain. The trail to the left is a foot trail, and the one on the right is open to mountain bikes, as is the Powerline Trail. (An option for a quicker trip to Ship Lake Pass is to bike the first 2.5 miles. However, on Ship Lake Pass bikes are not allowed beyond that point.)

The Powerline Trail is just what it sounds like: an access road along the powerline that runs up South Fork Campbell Creek over, you guessed it, Powerline Pass. Turn right (southeast) when you intersect the trail. There is a good view of the route at this point; Ship Lake Pass is at the head of the large tributary valley that runs north of the South Fork valley immediately below you.

The junction with the trail toward Ship Lake Pass and Hidden Lake, about 2.5 miles from Glen Alps, is signed and obvious. Leave your bike here if you've ridden it this far, and turn east onto the trail, and cross a new footbridge crossing the South Fork. Just beyond the crossing, the trail narrows to an eroded footpath that climbs through mountain hemlock into alpine tundra.

In another mile, well above the South Fork valley now, the trails to Ship Lake Pass and Hidden Lake divide at an unmarked junction by Hidden Lake Creek. To head for the pass, fork right across the creek; intermittent, beaten paths wind up both sides of the sparkling alpine stream that flows out of the pass. (Hidden Lake, a small, concealed tarn in a rock-strewn bowl below 5,105-foot Hidden Peak, is about 1.5 miles up the trail that leads straight ahead at the crossing.)

The path toward Ship Lake Pass (4,050 feet) eventually peters out, but the route is obvious in the open tundra. Finding your way up the broad valley to the pass is easy, wandering where you will along the creek or higher up the slope. At the pass, linger a while over the views of Ship Lake and the wild Chugach Mountains. For an even better view, take a side trip to The Wedge (4,660 feet) to the right (south) of the pass or The Ramp (5,240 feet) to the left (north). Each peak is a bit less than a mile from the pass. The Wedge is the easier hike, as it's a lower peak and the route has better footing. The summit of The Ramp is up a steep scree slope from Ship Lake Pass; the climb is easier following the ridgeline from Hidden Lake.

Dall sheep are common in the higher country. Also look for Alaska's "torrent ducks" (harlequin ducks) navigating the foaming streams like expert kayakers. There is good camping near the creek that flows out of Ship Lake Pass, but bring a stove and fuel, as no fires are allowed, and there isn't any wood anyway. Use caution traveling in early summer, when snow may linger near the pass. Slipping on steep, hardpacked snow can lead to an uncontrolled slide, and late-season avalanches are possible under the right conditions.

A hiker climbs a slope on Ship Lake Pass Trail. The route is a fine example of the easy access to alpine country in Chugach State Park.
MOLLIE FOSTER

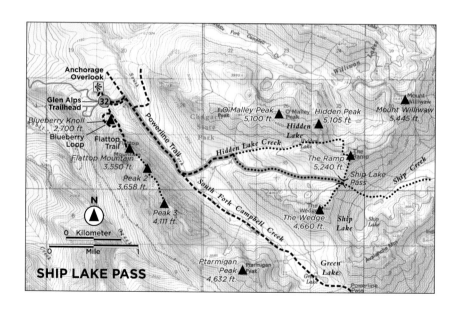

SHIP LAKE PASS

MILES AND DIRECTIONS

0.0   Begin at the Glen Alps Trailhead.

0.5   Turn right onto the Powerline Trail.

2.5   Bear left onto the Hidden Lake/Ship Lake Pass Trail and cross footbridge at South Fork Campbell Creek.

3.5   Cross Hidden Lake Creek and head east toward Ship Lake Pass.

6.0   Reach Ship Lake Pass.

The Glen Alps–Indian Valley Traverse. Linking the Ship Lake Pass hike with the Indian Valley hike makes a fine, mostly alpine, moderately strenuous two-pass traverse of about 16 miles. From Ship Lake Pass descend steeply to the southeast to Ship Lake and the west fork of Ship Creek, crossing the creek at any convenient spot. Curl around the toe of the slope between the west and middle forks of Ship Creek, join the main route along the middle fork of Ship Creek about a mile north of Indian Pass, and follow it south as it becomes the Indian Valley Trail, ending at the trailhead at Indian, accessed from Mile 103.1 of the Seward Highway south of Anchorage. The route is relatively obvious on the Imus map and the Anchorage A-7 and A-8 topos.

Shorter hikes: For an easy walk from Glen Alps, take the Powerline Trail, which hikers share with mountain bikers, up to 5 miles one way up the South Fork Campbell Creek valley.

TIDBIT

Ride a bike for the first 2.5 miles on Powerline Pass trail to connect with Ship Lake Pass trailhead. You'll have to park it at the trailhead, as bikes are not allowed on Ship Lake Pass.

Also, if hiking in autumn, be alert for moose during the rut (mating season).

33. WILLIWAW LAKES

WHY GO?

A trail with options for day hikes or multiday adventures, through alpine tundra and a series of lakes, only a short drive from downtown Anchorage.

THE RUNDOWN

Distance: 5.5 or more miles one way

Special features: Alpine tundra, wildlife, a series of lakes, and several great side trips

Location: In the Glen Alps area of south Anchorage

Difficulty: Moderate

Trail type: More-developed trail the first 2 miles; less-developed trail the next 2 miles; an alpine route beyond

Total elevation gain: 600 feet in, 200 feet out to the lower lake

Best season: June through Sept

Fees/permits: Parking fee or state parks pass

Maps: USGS Anchorage A-8 (SE, NE) and A-7; Imus Geographics *Chugach State Park*

Contact: Chugach State Park, 18620 Seward Hwy., Anchorage, Alaska 99516; 907-345-5014; http://dnr.alaska.gov/parks/

FINDING THE TRAILHEAD

Drive about 7 miles south of downtown Anchorage on the New Seward Highway, and exit east toward the Chugach Mountains on O'Malley Road. Continue about 4 miles on O'Malley, and take a right onto Hillside Drive, just before O'Malley takes a sharp turn to the left. In another mile, turn uphill (left) off Hillside Drive onto Upper Huffman Road, and drive 0.7 mile to a three-way intersection. Here, go right onto Toilsome Hill Drive. Follow Toilsome Hill steeply uphill, just under 2 more miles, to the Glen Alps parking area and trailhead on the left.

WHAT TO SEE

Middle Fork Campbell Creek flows through a jewel of an alpine valley, so close to the heart of Anchorage that it's possible to do a long wilderness day hike among Dall sheep and alpine flowers and still get back to the city in time for evening entertainment. Bands of sheep roam the valley and the nearby ridges, and Williwaw Lakes, a series of shallow alpine lakes, lie in crystalline beauty below craggy 5,445-foot Mount Williwaw.

There are two ways to get to the Williwaw Lakes Trail: from Prospect Heights Trailhead, the starting point for the Middle Fork Loop and Wolverine Peak hikes, or, a mile shorter, less of a climb, and the hike described here, from Glen Alps.

From the Glen Alps parking area, take one of the two parallel trails to the left of the route leading to Flattop Mountain. The trail to the left is for foot traffic only, and the one on the right is open to mountain bikes. Hike about 0.5 mile and turn right onto the Powerline Trail, continue 0.1 mile, and turn left onto the Middle Fork Loop Trail. Descend the trail, cross the bridge over South Fork Campbell Creek, and in another 0.1 mile, stay left on the main trail at the junction with the route to The Ballpark.

From here, it's about another mile to the junction of the Middle Fork Loop Trail with the Williwaw Lakes Trail. As you near the junction, look down over the city of Anchorage, with its miniature skyscrapers and subdivisions. Mount Susitna, the Sleeping Lady, and farther away, the snowy Aleutian Range form the backdrop.

At the junction, turn right onto the Williwaw Lakes Trail. The trail follows the Middle Fork valley and rounds a bend to the east, where striking, triangular Mount Williwaw comes into view. The hike weaves through stunted mountain hemlock and then, in the last mile below the lower lakes, emerges into alpine tundra. The trail grows fainter but the route is obvious. The first large lake, sometimes simply called Williwaw Lake, is at 2,600 feet in elevation, and the chain of lakes tops out at 3,250 feet, the farthest a bit over a mile away. There is good camping at the lakes—just don't forget the camp stove, and the bear canister.

A hiker under a rainbow on the Williwaw Lakes Trail in Chugach State Park. The trail leads 5 miles to the first in a series of alpine lakes nestled beneath the towering 5,000-foot Chugach Mountains.
HAGEPHOTO

The well-traveled trail through "The Ballpark" seen from the top of Little O'Malley. This way takes longer than it first appears.
WILL KOEPPEN

Black Lake. From the lower lake, take a side trip to Black Lake, in a hanging valley about a mile to the southwest and 300 feet above the Middle Fork valley. Simply climb up toward the obvious drainage on the mountainside above the lower lake.

The Ballpark–Williwaw Lakes Trail. For new scenery on the trip to Williwaw, try the route (no developed trail) via The Ballpark, Deep Lake, and Black Lake. Travel though a big, flat expanse of rocky tundra, close to Deep Lake and The Ballpark. Near Black Lake, cross a 3,700-foot pass with sections of loose boulders and talus. This route, a bit over 4 miles long, stays above tree line the entire trip. You'll need a map and compass, especially in marginal weather.

Mount Williwaw. The challenging route to the summit of Mount Williwaw, the peak atop the vertical wall above the lakes, starts up the drainage to the right (south) of the peak, and then turns north to ascend either a very steep gully or the south ridge, where there is one unavoidable section of free climbing with considerable exposure. It's a grand summit for experienced backcountry scramblers, and proper equipment (including ice axe) in early summer months, is a good idea.

Long Lake Loop. Another trip, best done as a 2-to-3-day backpack trip but possible as a very long day trip, links the valleys of Middle and North Fork Campbell Creek through the pass above the highest of the Williwaw Lakes. This 18-mile jaunt is a gem of a hike that passes nearly a dozen alpine lakes and ponds; the largest is mile-long Long Lake, near the head of the north fork.

The trip is best hiked from the Prospect Heights Trailhead. From Williwaw Lakes, cross the obvious pass left of Mount Williwaw to Long Lake and the north fork valley, follow the north fork downstream, pick your route toward Near Point (climbing to the 2,750-foot pass southeast of the point is the shortest), and intersect the Wolverine Bowl Trail for the hike back to Prospect Heights. Bring a topo map and your route-finding skills for this one.

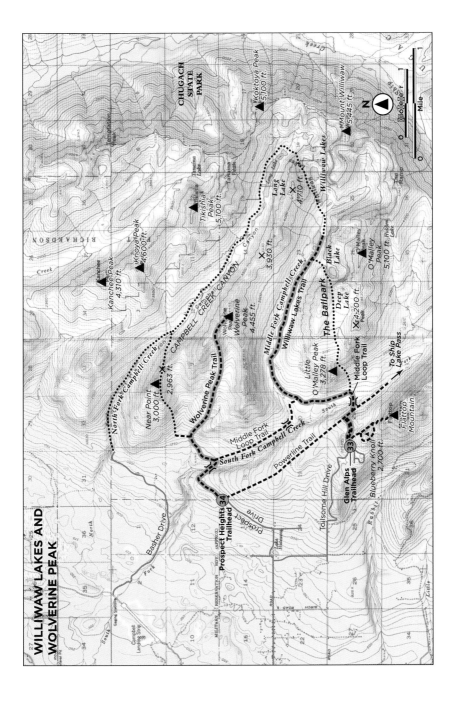

WILLIWAW LAKES AND WOLVERINE PEAK

A hiker travels by the lakes on the Williwaw Lakes Trail in Chugach State Park. At a half-million acres, Chugach State Park in Anchorage's backyard is the nation's third-largest state park. HAGEPHOTO

Shorter hikes: A stroll out the Powerline Trail, down to South Fork Campbell Creek, and out the subalpine trail to the Middle Fork Campbell Creek Bridge, makes a fine shorter or family hike.

MILES AND DIRECTIONS

0.0   Begin at the Glen Alps Trailhead.

0.5   Turn right onto the Powerline Trail.

0.6   Turn left onto the Middle Fork Loop Trail.

0.8   Cross the bridge over South Fork Campbell Creek.

2.0   Turn right onto the Williwaw Lakes Trail.

5.5   Arrive at the lower Williwaw Lakes.

34. WOLVERINE PEAK

WHY GO?

A maintained trail close to town with access to tundra and alpine with spectacular views of Chugach Mountains, Campbell Creek, and the Cook Inlet.

THE RUNDOWN See map on page 145.

Distance: 5.5 miles one way

Special features: Great views of Anchorage, the Chugach Mountains, and Campbell Creek

Location: Prospect Heights Trailhead above Anchorage

Difficulty: Strenuous

Trail type: More-developed trail for 2 miles; a less-developed but well-traveled trail/route beyond

Total elevation gain: 3,500 feet in, 100 feet out

Best season: June through Sept

Fees/permits: Parking fee or state parks pass

Maps: USGS Anchorage A-8 (NE) and A-7 (NW); Imus Geographics *Chugach State Park*

Contact: Chugach State Park, 18620 Seward Hwy., Anchorage, Alaska 99516; 907-345-5014; http://dnr.alaska.gov/parks/

FINDING THE TRAILHEAD

 Drive about 7 miles south of downtown Anchorage on the New Seward Highway and exit east, toward the mountains, on O'Malley Road. Continue about 4 miles and follow a sharp left curve in the road; just beyond the curve, take an immediate right onto Upper O'Malley Road.

In about 0.5 mile turn left at the T intersection onto Prospect Drive. In another mile bear left where Prospect intersects Sidorof Lane, and continue 0.1 mile to the Prospect Heights parking area on the right. The trail begins at the far end of the parking area.

WHAT TO SEE

Wolverine Peak, the prominent triangular peak at the intersection of two alpine ridges above south Anchorage, is a well-known local landmark. The peak offers a fine overlook of the upper valleys of North and Middle Fork Campbell Creek and a view of some of Chugach State Park's rugged inner peaks. The peak got its name from wolverine tracks once found on the summit ridge.

This trip is so close to town, that many people do it after work on long summer days. The first 2 miles of the trail, an old homestead road along the lower slopes of the Chugach Mountains, is open to mountain bikes; it's possible to ride the first 2 miles and hike the rest of the way.

From the trailhead, bear left onto the Powerline Trail in 0.1 mile and continue to the bridge across South Fork Campbell Creek, about a mile from the parking area. Climb a switchback and pass the junction with the Middle Fork Loop Trail at 1.3 miles. Just beyond a small stream, at about Mile 2 and 1,300 feet in elevation, take the narrower trail to the right, the Wolverine Peak Trail, and follow it uphill through the thickest part of the Chugach brush zone.

At about 2.5 miles, a flat patch of tundra with a view to the west makes a nice rest stop or a destination for a shorter hike. If continuing to the peak, climb to the ridge to the right, leaving the brush behind, and follow the crest as it curves left and up to intersect Wolverine's northwest summit ridge. A few snow patches linger near the summit into the early summer, but the route and the peak generally melt off early. The wild view to the east is the big payoff for the climb, and the view isn't bad toward Anchorage and Cook Inlet, either.

Shorter hikes: Hike out to the end of the old homestead road, at a small knob below Near Point, about 2.5 miles one way. The summit of Near Point is another 1.5 miles on a less-developed trail/route. The hike to the first patch of tundra on the Wolverine Peak Trail, about 2.5 miles one way, is a shorter trip with a view.

Wolverine Peak offers a fine overlook of the upper valleys of North and Middle Fork Campbell Creek and a view of some of Chugach State Park's rugged inner peaks. The peak got its name from wolverine tracks once found on the summit ridge. MOLLIE FOSTER

About 2.5 miles from Wolverine Peak Trailhead, a flat patch of tundra with views of Anchorage and Cook Inlet to the west, makes a nice rest stop, or a destination for a shorter hike.
MOLLIE FOSTER

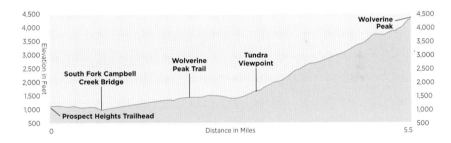

MILES AND DIRECTIONS

0.0   Begin at Prospect Heights Trailhead.

0.8   Cross the bridge at South Fork Campbell Creek.

1.3   Pass the Middle Fork Loop Trail junction.

2.0   Take the Wolverine Peak Trail.

2.5   Take a rest at the tundra viewpoint.

5.5   Reach Wolverine Peak.

CHUGACH STATE PARK NORTH

THE NORTHERN SECTION OF Chugach State Park stretches north of Anchorage from Eagle River to the Knik River. The Eagle River and Eklutna River/Lake valleys reach far back into the Chugach, providing access into the wild heart of the park.

Chugach State Park in Anchorage's backyard is the nation's third-largest state park, smaller only than western Alaska's Wood-Tikchik State Park and California's Anza-Borrego Desert State Park. From coast to lush forest to mountain peak and glacier, Chugach's half-million acres stretch over 60 miles of the western end of the Chugach Mountains. The park includes fifteen major watersheds, seventy lakes, fifty glaciers, and thirteen peaks over 7,000 feet. Chugach is a hiking wonderland, featuring hundreds of miles of trails and routes through incredible mountains.

The most comprehensive park map, the Imus Geographics map, is a good introduction to all Chugach has to offer. It is adequate for trail hiking, but be sure to pick up the USGS topographic maps for the high ridges and cross-country routes—the Imus map isn't detailed enough for serious route finding.

The trip descriptions here, as in the previous section on the southern part of the park, are given in order from south to north.

35. SOUTH FORK EAGLE RIVER

WHY GO?

The trailhead starts just below tree line and quickly climbs into alpine, by two backcountry lakes, with options for a day hike, or longer overnight trips.

THE RUNDOWN

Distance: Eagle and Symphony Lakes: 5.5 miles one way

Special features: Alpine and mountain scenery, many great side trips

Location: 8 miles southeast of Eagle River

Difficulty: Moderate to Eagle and Symphony Lakes; strenuous to very strenuous beyond

Trail type: The lakes: less developed, with some boulder hopping in the last mile. Beyond: routes and cross-country

Total elevation gain: About 1,000 feet in and 200 feet out to the lakes

Best season: Mid-June through Sept

Fees/permits: None

Maps: USGS Anchorage A-7 (NW, NE); Imus Geographics *Chugach State Park*

Contact: Chugach State Park, 18620 Seward Hwy., Anchorage, Alaska 99516; (907) 345-5014; http://dnr.alaska.gov/parks/

FINDING THE TRAILHEAD

Take the Eagle River Loop/Hiland Road exit off the Glenn Highway, a mile south of Eagle River and 11 miles north of downtown Anchorage. Go east, toward the mountains, and turn right in 0.2 mile at the traffic light at Hiland Road. Continue 7.3 miles on Hiland Road and turn right at a Chugach State Park sign on South Creek Road. In another 0.3 mile turn right onto West River Drive, and 0.1 mile farther turn left into the trailhead parking area.

WHAT TO SEE

The trail up South Fork Eagle River is a relatively painless way to get into the wild and beautiful alpine country of Chugach State Park. The high-elevation trailhead, just below tree line at 1,900 feet, is a good start; the trail leads to Symphony and Eagle Lakes, good destinations for most hikers, and also provides access to several fine cross-country routes higher in the Chugach.

The trailhead is on the edge of a subalpine subdivision with a short summer and a long avalanche season. For about the first mile, the trail stays in sight of subdivision homes as it traverses the slope west of South Fork Eagle River; this section of the trail is routed high on the west side of the valley to avoid private land in the valley bottom. The last groves of spruce forest quickly yield to subalpine patches of willow and dwarf birch and densely clustered mountain hemlocks; listen for magpies and golden-crowned sparrows as you hike this section.

At 2 miles, the trail descends to the valley bottom and crosses South Fork Eagle River on a bridge. East of the bridge, hanging above the south fork, an alpine side valley (locally named Hanging Valley for obvious reasons) seems to beg for exploration, and it is a good cross-country hike; see below.

The trail to the lakes continues up the east side of the valley, through some wet or muddy patches, for roughly 2.5 more miles to a small bridge across the Eagle Lake outlet stream. The trail leads onto a massive medial moraine (a rock pile that forms between two lobes of a glacier), which fills the strip of land between the lakes. It's boulder-hopping time; cairns mark a route up the moraine toward a high point between Eagle and Symphony Lakes.

Check out the strange, partially completed, abandoned cabin on the spine of the moraine, and take in the view of Eagle and Symphony Lakes, their valleys, and Cantata and Triangle Peaks above. Beyond the cabin, the rough trail continues a bit farther out the long ridge between the lakes. There are a few campsites on the ridge and by the lakes; Symphony Lake, a clear-water lake, has better drinking water, while Eagle Lake is silty with glacial runoff.

At 2 miles, the trail descends to the valley and crosses the south fork of Eagle River on a bridge. The river crossing is a nice turnaround for short day trips.
MOLLIE FOSTER

The high-elevation trailhead, just below tree line at 1,900 feet, is a good start; the trail leads to Symphony and Eagle Lakes, and provides access to several fine cross-country routes higher in the Chugach. JUSTIN WHOLEY

A sled dog explores the South Fork Eagle River Trail on a sunny August evening. MOLLIE FOSTER

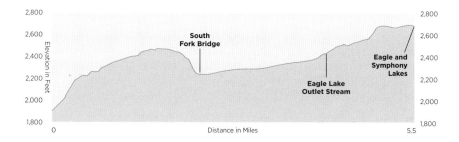

MILES AND DIRECTIONS

0.0   Begin at the trailhead.

2.0   Cross the South Fork Eagle River Bridge.

4.5   Cross the bridge over the Eagle Lake outlet stream.

5.5   The trail ends between Eagle and Symphony Lakes.

Other hikes: Rendezvous Peak Ridge. A hiker-beaten track peels off uphill and west a few minutes beyond the trailhead, leading to a saddle (Hunter Pass) at 2,850 feet in elevation on the ridge between the South Fork Eagle River and Ship Creek. To the north, it's a bit over 2 miles to Rendezvous Peak, where it's possible to descend to Arctic Valley Ski Area and Arctic Valley Road. To the south from the saddle, you can hike the ridge, up and down its many bumps and saddles, all the way to Symphony Lake if you've got the energy. An alternate way to gain the ridge if you want to hike it to the south is to climb to the saddle at 3,150 feet in elevation above the south fork trail just before it descends to the river, a bit less than 2 miles from the trailhead.

Hanging Valley. Once across the South Fork Eagle River Bridge at Mile 2, continue east on the trail until it turns south toward Eagle Lake; follow a fainter path east and then take a right fork up the slope into Hanging Valley. A hiker-beaten path continues up-valley on the south side of the creek.

From the valley floor, two fine destinations present themselves: Tarn 3,405 in the rugged cirque at the head of the southern fork of the creek, about 3 miles up the valley; and Point 5,137, locally known as Eagle River Overlook, a long, strenuous hike to the ridgeline to the east, and as the name implies, with great views into the valley of Eagle River. The route to the tarn is obvious on the topo map. For Eagle River Overlook, hike about 2 miles up Hanging Valley and climb from the valley floor up the steep, open slope to the northeast; at the top, in a broad saddle at 4,050 feet in elevation, turn right (east), continue up a broad slope to the eastern crest, and then turn north to the summit of Point 5,137. The overlook is about a 4-mile one-way jaunt up Hanging Valley, or 6 miles one way from the trailhead; the route is shown on the Imus map.

Beyond Eagle Lake. The trailless Eagle Lake valley stretches back to the falls below Flute Glacier, providing strenuous access to the glacier and to the very demanding route to the top of Eagle Peak. The valley above Eagle Lake is a wonderful place to explore on skis in winter.

Beyond Symphony Lake. From the end of the trail above Symphony Lake, it's possible to hike south, cross-country, higher into the Symphony valley to its several headwater tarns. One steep but beautiful route climbs a small ridge between Tarn 3,431 and Tarn 3,595 to a broad plateau to the southwest. The crest of the plateau forms the divide between South Fork Eagle River and North Fork Ship Creek, one of the wildest valleys anywhere in the park. The divide requires about 2.5 miles and 2,000 feet of climbing beyond Symphony Lake. Triangle Peak, 5,450 feet in elevation and one of the few relatively straightforward summits in this part of the park, lies along the ridgeline to the southeast, about 1.5 miles away.

Shorter hikes: Hike as far as the South Fork Bridge, 2 miles one way, for a shorter day trip with alpine views, a pretty stream, and berry picking in season.

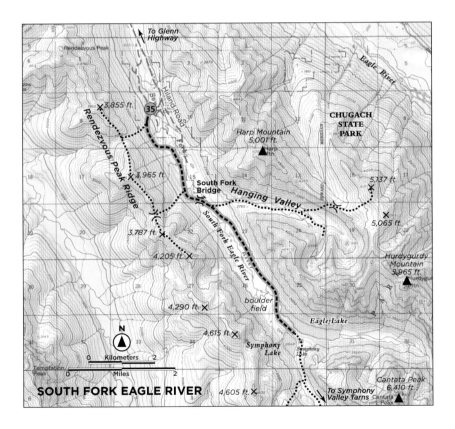

36. EAGLE RIVER VALLEY

WHY GO?

The Eagle River Valley includes a range of hiking routes, directly behind the Eagle River Nature Center: miles of hiking trails with interpretive loops or overnight treks up to 24 miles.

THE RUNDOWN

Special features: A deep valley, birding and wildlife watching, a wide variety of trails, an interpretive trail, a fee cabin and yurts, good backcountry camping, and one of Southcentral Alaska's classic alpine traverses.

Location: 12 miles southeast of Eagle River.

Trail type: Rodak Nature Trail: accessible. Other trails near the nature center: more developed. Beyond the nature center area: less developed.

Best season: Lower valley trails: May through Oct. Upper valley: late May through early Oct. Traverse: mid-June through Sept.

Fees/permits: Nature center membership or parking permit (state parks pass not valid).

Maps: USGS Anchorage A-7 (NE), Anchorage A-6; Imus Geographics *Chugach State Park*; Alaska State Parks leaflet Historic Iditarod/Crow Pass Trail.

Contact: Eagle River Nature Center, 32750 Eagle River Rd., Eagle River, AK 99577; (907) 694-2108; www.ernc.org.

KEY TRAILS, DISTANCES, DIFFICULTIES, AND ELEVATION GAINS:

Rodak Nature Trail: An interpretive loop near the center. 0.75-mile loop, easy, 100 feet

Albert Loop Trail: A loop trail to Eagle River and back. 3-mile loop, easy, 100 feet

Dew Mound Trail: Valley trail linking moraines, streams, and Dew Lake. Four loops, 1 to 6 miles round trip, easy to moderate, 100 to 400 feet

Crow Pass Trail, Eagle River Valley: Scenic valley trail with good camping. About 12 miles one way, easy to moderate, 500 feet

Crow Pass traverse: Eagle River-Girdwood Alpine Trail over Crow Pass. 24-mile killer day hike or 2-to-4-day traverse, strenuous, 3,100 feet southbound/2,000 feet northbound

FINDING THE TRAILHEAD

Take the Eagle River exit off Glenn Highway, 13 miles north of Anchorage. Turn east; turn right onto Eagle River Road, and drive 12 miles to the end of the road at the Eagle River Nature Center. The trailhead for all the trails is behind the nature center.

WHAT TO SEE

Eagle River Valley has so much going for it: miles and miles of hiking trails, a gorgeous, wildlife-rich setting, and the best nature center in Alaska. The valley and its trails have a colorful past. The Crow Pass Trail between Eagle River and Girdwood is part of the historic Iditarod Trail, the famous gold-rush-era trail between Seward, Iditarod, and Nome, and this segment crossed the highest summit on the historic trail. Further back in time, the valley lay under a wall of ice 4,000 feet thick at the height of glaciation a few thousand years back; the classic U-shape of the valley and the remnant ice hanging from some of the peaks are hints of its icy past.

Moose, black bear, and grizzly frequent the valley, and there is a large Dall sheep population on the high ridges and in the upper reaches of the valley, with a permit-only sheep-hunting season in August and September. And, with as many as fifty species of wildflowers, good mushroom hunting, waterfalls, side canyons to explore, and challenging mountaineering for experienced climbers, there is plenty to keep you busy here.

Hiking, scenery, and wildlife are the main events, but the private, nonprofit Eagle River Nature Center has a lot more to offer: natural history exhibits, a small bookstore, trail maps and information, and programs focused on everything from bears, beavers, berries, birds, and butterflies to galaxies, glaciers, and GPS receivers to "hunts" for mushrooms, orchids, and owls. For younger outdoor lovers, the center sponsors school and junior naturalist programs. The center is open Wednesday through Sunday from May through September, 10 a.m. to 5 p.m.; it's also open Friday through Sunday the rest of the year. The trails, however, are always open, except for the occasional flooding and bear-safety closure.

The center rents three popular overnight shelters: a cabin and three yurts. All are within 2 miles of the trailhead, making them much more easily accessible than, for example, the Forest Service's backcountry cabins on the Kenai Peninsula. Center volunteers keep the shelters supplied with firewood. The cabin and the Rapids Camp Yurt are located off the Crow Pass Trail, about 1.3 miles and 1.7 miles from the center, respectively, and the River Yurt is off the Albert Loop Trail, about 1.5 miles from the center. Contact the center or check the website for reservation information.

Head for the back of the nature center to start your hike.

Rodak Nature Trail. The 0.75-mile Rodak Trail forks right at a signed junction about a hundred yards down the Crow Pass Trail and loops back to the trail 0.3 mile farther out. Interpretive signs along the Rodak explain glacial geology, forest ecology, the salmon life cycle, the northern seasons, and beaver ecology. The trail loops past two large viewing decks built over the open landscape of ponds and wet meadows, which the local beavers have created here by damming the spring-fed stream that flows through this section of the valley. (The springs that feed the stream flow out of a rocky glacial moraine a mile up the valley.) From either of the decks, enjoy the great views of the valley, and watch for beavers, water ouzels, eagles, and waterfowl.

Albert Loop Trail. To take the Albert Loop, follow the Crow Pass Trail for 0.7 mile through a bottomland forest of spruce, birch, and cottonwood, turning right at the Four Corners Trail junction. In a few minutes, cross the long bridge-and-boardwalk structure over a large beaver-dammed pond; this is the same spring stream the two Rodak Trail viewing decks overlook. Next, at an intersection with the trail to the River Yurt, the Albert Loop bears right. The trail straight ahead leads out onto the gravel beds along the course of Eagle River; you'll also have a few more chances to wander out onto the riverbed farther along the loop.

Eventually the trail bears away from the river, crossing several small streams before winding back to the Rodak Trail and the nature center. A late summer and fall salmon run up the largest of these streams usually attracts a grizzly or two, so expect the Albert Loop to be at least partially closed by later in July. The trail may also be occasionally flooded, courtesy of the local beavers.

Dew Mound Trail. The Dew Mound Trail parallels the Crow Pass Trail up the valley as far as Echo Bend (Mile 3 of the Crow Pass Trail), weaving its way through a rough topography of moraines and other glacial features and passing small but pretty Dew Lake. The Dew Mound Trail connects with the Crow Pass Trail in five places, creating four loops of different lengths: about a mile via Four Corners, 3 miles via the Mountain Meadows Trail, 4 miles via Rapids Camp, and 6 miles via Dew Lake and Echo Bend. To access the Yukla Yurt, hike 2 miles on the Iditarod Trail from the Nature Center.

Crow Pass Trail. The trail up Eagle River meanders along the valley floor for 11 miles to the head of the valley before climbing toward Crow Pass. Especially in the upper part of the valley, it may be rough and slow in places, so take your time and enjoy the scenery. Peaks rise to 7,000 feet above the valley, and the many vertical mountain walls, hanging valleys, glaciers, and waterfalls make this a Yosemite without the big crowds.

There are good campsites practically everywhere, in the forest and on the river's gravel bars. The river is glacial, so it's heavy with silt after the glacier begins to melt in the early-summer heat; clear water options are to carry water from the nearest side stream, find a small side channel on the river with clearer water, or let a pot of river water partially settle out before using it. Don't forget to boil or filter all drinking water.

Fires are allowed only in the fire grates at several of the more popular campsites, but save the wood and bring a stove. It's not a great idea to camp near the fire grates, as there may be lingering food odors that can attract bears. There is a healthy population of both black and grizzly bears in the area, so use good bear-country practices when hiking and camping.

Twelve miles up the valley is a marked ford site, the safest crossing for hikers heading for Crow Pass. The ford is normally passable, but after periods of rain or glacier melt during hot weather, it may be more difficult or unsafe. The crossing is wide and the water is cold, so an extra pair of shoes and socks is a good idea.

The glacier lake at the head of the valley is about 0.3 mile upstream (southeast) from the ford site, accessible from either side of the river. There is no trail to the lake, but the walking is easy through the cottonwoods along the river's wide gravel bar.

A hiker enjoys the view on a loop trail in the Eagle River Valley. Choose from 0.75 mile to 6-mile loops, or combine trails to make a longer adventure.
MOLLIE FOSTER

A sled dog crosses one of the many bridges along the loop trails in the Eagle River Valley. Dogs must be leashed on the Rodak and Albert Loop Trails and around all built facilities.
MOLLIE FOSTER

The Eagle River Valley includes hiking loops ranging from 0.75 mile to 6 miles, directly behind the Eagle River Nature Center.
MOLLIE FOSTER

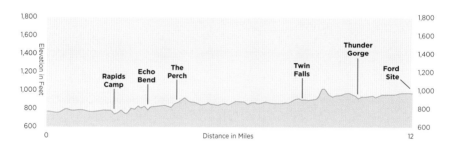

MILES AND DIRECTIONS

Crow Pass Trail, Eagle River Valley

0.0	Begin at the trailhead behind the Eagle River Nature Center.
0.1	Pass the first Rodak Nature Trail/Albert Loop junction.
0.3	Reach the second Rodak Nature Trail junction.
0.7	Pass the Albert Loop Trail junction at Four Corners.
1.7	Climb a short hill to Rapids Camp.

3.0	Reach Echo Bend.
4.0	Take in the view at The Perch.
5.0	Reach the Heritage Falls viewpoint.
5.2	Cross Icicle Creek.
8.5	Reach Twin Falls.
11.0	Cross the stream at the mouth of Thunder Gorge.
12.0	Cross Eagle River at the ford site (12 miles to Crow Pass Trailhead; see the Crow Pass hike).
12.3	Arrive at Glacier Lake (head of Eagle River Valley).

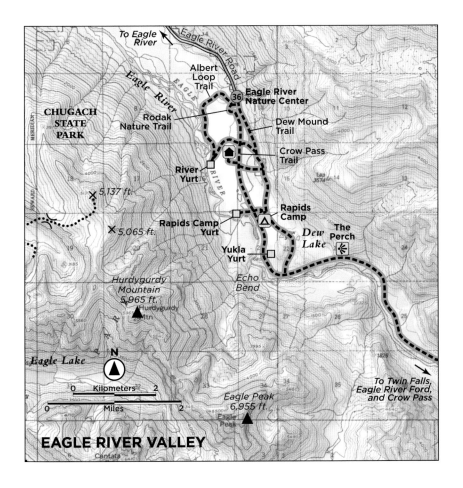

Crow Pass Traverse. The 24-mile trip over Crow Pass is usually hiked in the opposite direction, from the Crow Creek Trailhead outside Girdwood to the nature center. Some Crow Pass aficionados, however, like the hike from Eagle River to Girdwood, as the trip builds up to the highlight of Crow Pass more gradually. Come prepared for stormy weather, and be prepared to be amazed no matter which way you walk it. See the Crow Pass hike.

Day hikes galore: The most popular shorter hikes are the Rodak and Albert Loop trails and the out-and-back hike to Four Corners on the Crow Pass Trail (0.7 mile one way). These trails and the nature center are great for kids. A bit longer are the 3- and 4-mile loops on the Dew Mound Trail and out-and-back hikes on the Crow Pass Trail to Rapids Camp, where a side trail descends to the bank of the river's rocky canyon, and Echo Bend, a forested flat by the river (1.7 miles and 3 miles one way, respectively).

For a longer day hike, try the Dew Mound–Dew Lake–Echo Bend loop (6 miles); or out-and-back Crow Pass Trail hikes to The Perch (4 miles one way), a rocky outcrop with a great view far up the valley, Heritage Falls (5 miles one way), a pretty waterfall across the river from the trail, or, for a good long day on the trail, Twin Falls (8.5 miles one way), a double waterfall plunging into the valley from a side canyon.

Fishing: There are a few Dolly Varden in the river, but the fishing isn't the best in this cloudy glacial water.

THE EAGLE RIVER NATURE CENTER

Once upon a time it was a biker bar, but when Alaska State Parks took over the log cabin at the end of Eagle River Road in the early 1980s, it morphed into the Eagle River Visitor Center. For a while it was a well-funded, year-round state park visitor center, but in the early 1990s, when the bottom dropped out of the parks budget, the center lost 90 percent of its funding, falling back to a skeleton operation with just enough cash and volunteers to keep the doors open during the summer.

In the late 1990s, a small group of former visitor center volunteers set up a nonprofit group and took over the center, renaming it the Eagle River Nature Center. A few years and a few dozen membership drives, sponsor campaigns, and fundraising events later, the center was on its feet with a small paid staff, a year-round operation, an amazing variety of programs, and an ambitious trail agenda. The center staff and volunteers have upgraded the front-country trails, and have a cabin and three yurts (dome-shaped fabric-and-frame structures) for overnighters.

Now, with more than a thousand members and two to three dozen volunteers at work at any one time, the ERNC ranks high on a very short list of the best-loved institutions in Southcentral Alaska.

37. MOUNT BALDY AND BLACKTAIL ROCKS

WHY GO?

A popular trail for hearty families with spectacular views of the Knik Arm, Denali, and peaks in Chugach State Park.

THE RUNDOWN

Distances: Mount Baldy: 2.0 miles one way. Blacktail Rocks: 3.5 miles

Special features: Access from Eagle River, alpine tundra and peaks, several trip options.

Location: About 4 miles from downtown Eagle River.

Difficulty: Moderate to strenuous

Trail type: Less developed, a route beyond.

Total elevation gain: Mount Baldy: 1,600 feet. Blacktail Rocks: 2,700 feet.

Best season: June through Sept.

Fees/permits: None.

Maps: USGS Anchorage B-7 (NW, SW, SE); Imus Geographics *Chugach State Park.*

Contact: Chugach State Park, 18620 Seward Hwy., Anchorage, Alaska 99516; (907) 345-5014; http://dnr.alaska.gov/parks/.

FINDING THE TRAILHEAD

From downtown Eagle River, follow Eagle River Loop Road east from the Old Glenn Highway; the Old Glenn is Eagle River's "main street." Climb about a mile, to a point where the road levels off and begins a sweeping curve to the south, and turn left onto Skyline Drive. Follow Skyline uphill through several switchbacks and name changes, staying with the obvious main road a total of about 2.5 miles to the end of the pavement in a gravel parking area. The rough trail begins in the northeast corner of the parking area, pass the gate and head uphill. For the official Mount Baldy Trailhead, continue straight, past the big sign and follow as the trail curves through switchbacks.

WHAT TO SEE

This trail is popular, and for good reasons. The access from Eagle River is tough to match. The route used to be on private property, until the Municipality of Anchorage purchased the first section of trail (less than a mile), with Chugach State Park owned land beyond.

Follow the obvious route, past the upper gate and big trailhead sign. The hard-packed dirt trail climbs switchbacks for the first 0.25 mile. The trail links with another junction, follow the rough trail uphill. Watch your footing on the climb, but in particular, on your route down, as this rough trail is currently in a "hike at your own risk" design.

After 2 miles, the trail climbs to Mount Baldy, at 3,281 feet, from which an alpine route opens to the east toward Blacktail Rocks. The Blacktails, a common destination, are about 3.5 miles from the parking area.

Other hikes: From Skyline Drive there are two basic options for a cross-country traverse to the Ptarmigan Valley Trailhead: a low traverse of about 9 miles and 1,800 feet of elevation gain, and a high traverse of roughly 12 miles and 3,500 feet of gain. (Both involve map-reading, terrain-reading, and route-finding skills.)

For the low traverse, bear north from a low point west of Blacktail Rocks, dropping into Ptarmigan Valley and picking up the trail near its end or near the junction of the east and west forks of Little Peters Creek. For the high traverse, curl around from Blacktail Rocks through the saddle to the northeast and ascend Roundtop, then descend west via the route described above and pick up the trail along the creek.

At the summit of Mount Baldy, 3,281 feet, hikers are rewarded with gorgeous views of the wild peaks of the Chugach State Park. At a half-million acres, Chugach State Park in Anchorage's backyard is the nation's third-largest state park.
MOLLIE FOSTER

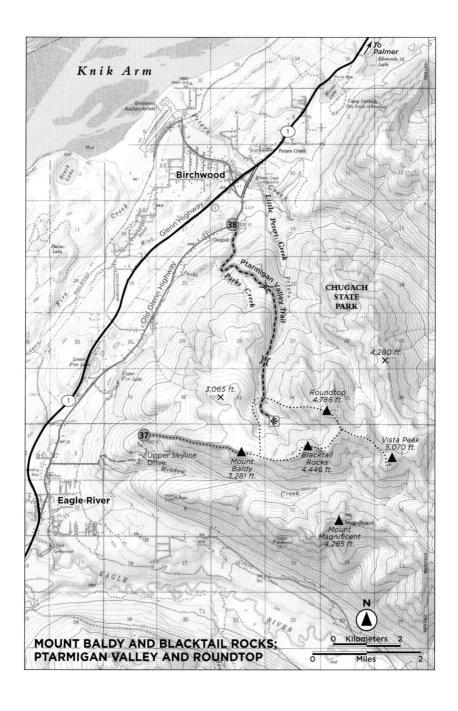

MOUNT BALDY AND BLACKTAIL ROCKS;
PTARMIGAN VALLEY AND ROUNDTOP

A hiker descends the Mount Baldy Trail on a summer evening. Watch your footing on the route down, as this rough trail is a "hike at your own risk" design. MOLLIE FOSTER

MILES AND DIRECTIONS

0.0   Start at Mount Baldy Trailhead.

0.25 Trail transitions from switchbacks to steeper grade.

2.0   Arrive at Mount Baldy summit.

3.5   Reach Blacktail Rocks summit.

TIDBIT

Bring trekking poles, especially if you have sensitive joints.

38. PTARMIGAN VALLEY AND ROUNDTOP

WHY GO?

A trail climbing through boreal forest and into alpine tundra, with a variety of route options at the top, and a stone's throw from Eagle River and Chugiak.

THE RUNDOWN See map on page 165.

Distances: Ptarmigan Valley: 5 miles one way

Special features: Alpine tundra and peaks, several trip options

Location: 15 miles north of downtown Anchorage, above Eagle River and Chugiak

Difficulty: Moderate to Ptarmigan Valley; strenuous beyond

Trail type: More developed lower; alpine routes above

Total elevation gain: Ptarmigan Valley: 2,300 feet in, 200 feet out. Roundtop: 4,300 feet in, 200 feet out

Best season: June through Sept

Fees/permits: None

Maps: USGS Anchorage B-7 (NW, SW, SE); Imus Geographics *Chugach State Park*

Contact: Chugach State Park, 18620 Seward Hwy., Anchorage, Alaska 99516; (907) 345-5014; http://dnr.alaska.gov/parks/

FINDING THE TRAILHEAD

 Take the North Birchwood exit off the Glenn Highway, 21 miles north of downtown Anchorage, and turn east, toward the mountains. At 0.3 mile turn right (south) onto the Old Glenn Highway. Continue about 0.5 mile and turn left (east) into the signed Ptarmigan Valley Trail parking area.

WHAT TO SEE

Rising high above the traffic and strip malls of Eagle River, the peaks of the western front of the Chugach Mountains are one of the most spectacular suburban playgrounds on the planet. The Ptarmigan Valley Trail climbs into the northwestern reaches of this high peaks country, taking in boreal forest and subalpine shrub zones on the way, each of which is a lush riot of green by midsummer. With alpine tundra and peaks higher up, this hike covers the entire personality of the Chugach "front" range. If you plan on sticking to the Ptarmigan Valley Trail, you likely won't need a detailed map, but if your agenda calls for ridge running or peak bagging, be sure you have a topomap, a compass, and decent weather for the trip. There's good alpine camping in Ptarmigan Valley too.

The superwide trail, initially runs under a spruce/birch canopy, followed by a spell in the subalpine brush zone; you're in prime moose habitat here. About a mile from the trailhead, a narrow side path leads to small Parks Creek to the right. About ten minutes later, the trail splits, with the drier summer trail leading left.

At about 2.5 miles the trail passes through a gap at about 1,600 feet in elevation, complete with a view of the high country ahead. It then descends slightly to join a closed road, formerly a homestead road, in the valley of Little Peters Creek. After crossing to the east side of the creek, the hike opens into alpine tundra at about Mile 4.

The trail crosses the east fork of Little Peters Creek in about another 0.3 mile; before the crossing, look up and left (east) for a clean slope running down from Roundtop (4,786 feet). This is the most direct route to the summit. Working your way around a few patches of brush below and then staying as much as possible on the crown of the slope, you'll eventually strike Roundtop's well-defined west/northwest rib, from which it's a straightforward grunt to the broad, open peak.

If Roundtop isn't enough, proceed southeast to a saddle in roughly half a mile, and from there choose between Blacktail Rocks (4,446 feet) to the southwest or the more challenging Vista Peak (5,070 feet) to the southeast. Blacktail Rocks (also known locally as "Blacktails," "Black Tail Rocks," and "Blacktail Ptarmigan Rocks") is a row of rocky peaks a bit more than half a mile from the saddle; all of the points on the crest have a fine view into the valleys of Meadow Creek and Eagle River. Vista, another 1.5 miles or so beyond the saddle, is the first really imposing peak to the east along this Chugach ridgeline. Going up the west side involves a steep, loose-rock scramble; curling around to the south slope offers an easier ascent.

The panoramas from these three summits are outstanding, but the Ptarmigan Valley Trail, minus the peak bagging, leads to a fine destination in its own right. Just continue following the trail past the crossing of the east fork of Little Peters Creek, climbing to trail's end on the broad alpine slope between the two main forks of the creek, about 5 miles from the trailhead. The view is fine, and you might find some alpine blueberries to have for dessert after lunch.

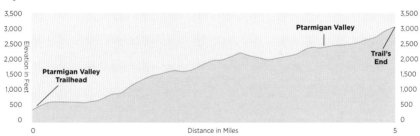

MILES AND DIRECTIONS

0.0   Begin at the Ptarmigan Valley Trailhead.
2.5   The trail descends to the Little Peters Creek valley.
3.5   Cross the Little Peters Creek Bridge.
4.0   Arrive at Ptarmigan Valley.
4.3   Cross the east fork of Little Peters Creek.
5.0   Climb the alpine slope to the trail's end.

39. TWIN PEAKS TRAIL

WHY GO?

This trail includes day hikes to longer ridgeline options with spectacular views of Eklutna Lake, the Mat Valley, and the tallest group of peaks in Chugach State Park.

THE RUNDOWN

Distances: Twin Peaks Trail: 2.5 miles one way. East Twin Pass: 4 miles one way

Special features: Alpine meadows and peaks, abundant Dall sheep

Location: In the Eklutna Lake area, 35 miles north of Anchorage

Difficulty: Moderate to the end of the Twin Peaks Trail; strenuous to East Twin Pass and beyond

Trail type: Twin Peaks Trail: more developed. East Twin Pass: route/cross-country

Total elevation gain: Twin Peaks Trail: 1,800 feet. East Twin Pass: 3,600 feet in and 100 feet out

Best season: Mid-June through Sept

Fees/permits: Parking fee or state parks pass

Maps: USGS Anchorage B-6 (NW); Imus Geographics *Chugach State Park*; Alaska State Parks brochure Eklutna Lake

Contact: Chugach State Park, 18620 Seward Hwy., Anchorage, Alaska 99516; (907) 345-5014; http://dnr.alaska.gov/parks/

FINDING THE TRAILHEAD

Take the Eklutna exit off the Glenn Highway, 26 miles north of Anchorage and 16 miles south of Palmer. Exit east, follow the access road as it curves to the south for about 0.4 mile, and turn left (east) onto the Eklutna Lake Road. Follow it about 10 miles to the recreation area at Eklutna Lake. Trailhead parking is at the end of the road, past the turnoffs for the campground and picnic area. The trailhead is on the northeast side of the parking area.

From the trailhead, walk across the Twin Peaks Creek Bridge, and turn left at the Twin Peaks/Eklutna Lakeside Trail junction in 100 feet.

WHAT TO SEE

Mountain slopes bursting with wildflowers, bright creeks tumbling over rocky streambeds, bands of Dall sheep grazing in high meadows, and golden eagles riding the air currents above—this is what the country around Twin Peaks is all about. The 2.5-mile Twin Peaks Trail, an old roadway that's closed to motor vehicles and bicycles, is the hiker's highway into the alpine terrain below the craggy summits of Twin Peaks. The maintained trail ends at a fine viewpoint, and several unmaintained hiking routes branch off from there.

East Twin Pass, 1.5 miles beyond the end of the trail and a full-day round-trip hike, is a gap on the prominent ridge to the north at 4,450 feet in elevation. Twin Peaks, west of the pass on the same ridge, are rugged, crumbling masses of rock that are difficult and dangerous to climb, so the pass and the walk-up peaks nearby are the best longer hiking trips in this part of the park.

From the trailhead, the Twin Peaks Trail climbs via switchbacks through mixed forest and brush. A bench with a view of Eklutna Lake and Bold Peak is about 1.5 miles from the trailhead. A mile beyond, the old roadway ends at about 2,700 feet in elevation, with views of Twin Peaks and the green alpine slopes below East Twin. Look for sheep on these slopes; large bands of ewes and lambs use the area all summer, and there may be a few, usually solitary, rams nearby as well.

For a half-day hike, the end of the Twin Peaks Trail might be it, but if you've got more time and energy, there is much more to do from here. For East Twin Pass and the slopes below East Twin Peak, follow the steep hiker's path that angles down from the end of the maintained trail, crossing Twin Peaks Creek (also called Thachkatnu Creek) below. Once across the creek, the path divides. One fork meanders northwest onto the slopes below East Twin Peak, a fine place to spend some time lounging and looking for sheep and wildflowers. For the pass, follow the path leading northeast, or right, after you ascend out of the creek bottom.

After crossing a tributary creek entering from the left, or northwest, pick out East Twin Pass on the main ridge at the top of the gully directly ahead. The path peters out, but you can see where you're going the rest of the way; the direct route to the pass crosses a major sheep trail or two in the final climb.

To the north of East Twin Pass are the massif of Pioneer Peak, the Matanuska River, and the town of Palmer. Hiking up to the peaks on either side of the pass nets even better views, and possibly a chance to look down on Dall sheep! Peak 5,050 to the northwest has the best view of the Mat Valley, and rocky Peak 5,150 to the southeast looks east toward Bold, Bashful, and Baleful Peaks, the highest group of summits in Chugach State Park. Eklutna Lake isn't visible until farther out the ridge to the southeast, on 5,450-foot Pepper Peak.

Retracing your steps down from the pass is the easiest way to head back to the trailhead, but, if you've got the topo map and the weather is clear enough to see where you're going, consider a longer return via either of two loop routes. First, heading northwest by way of Peak 5,050, stay on the ridge until you drop into a saddle at 4,850 feet in elevation below the east face of East Twin Peak; then descend the smooth slopes to the south, staying west of the gully leading down from the saddle. A little more than a mile from the saddle, you'll reach the edge of the cut of Twin Peaks Creek again; find the path down to the creek crossing, and rejoin the Twin Peaks Trail on the other side.

For the second loop option, head southeast from East Twin Pass to Pepper Peak, and join the steep but straightforward ridge route that drops off the peak to the southeast, rejoining the Twin Peaks Trail in about 2 miles, at the Mile 1.5 vista point, after losing about 3,500 feet of elevation.

There's one more possibility: Climb steeply to the southeast from the end of the Twin Peaks Trail, reaching the point of the ridge southeast of Pepper Peak in about a mile and roughly 800 feet of elevation gain. Spend a while here taking in the spectacular view of Eklutna Lake, the Eklutna valley, and the dark, sharp peaks around the head of the lake.

Most people day-hike the Twin Peaks area. There are possible campsites along the forks of Twin Peaks Creek beyond the end of the maintained trail, but flat spots are at a premium.

A hiker on the trail near Pepper Peak, with the jagged summits of West and East Twin Peaks in the background.
MOLLIE FOSTER

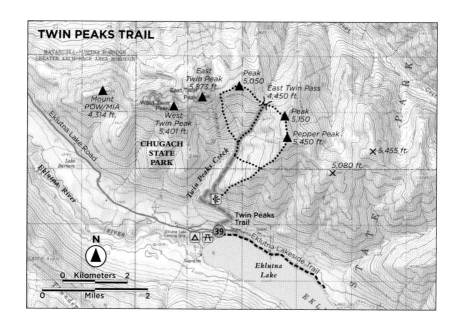

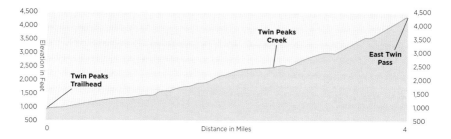

MILES AND DIRECTIONS

0.0 Begin at the trailhead.

1.5 A vista of Eklutna Lake and Bold Peak opens up.

2.5 The Twin Peaks Trail ends.

4.0 Reach East Twin Pass.

A hiker enjoys the bench with a view of Eklutna Lake and Bold Peak, 1.5 miles from the trailhead. Twin Peaks Trail, is a hiker's highway into the alpine terrain below the craggy summits of Twin Peaks.
MOLLIE FOSTER

Shorter hikes: It's still a fairly steep haul, but the hike to the first full view of Eklutna Lake, about 1.5 miles from the trailhead with an 1,100-foot elevation gain, makes a decent shorter hike.

40. BOLD RIDGE TRAIL

WHY GO?

Alpine wildflowers, views of the gorgeous 7-mile-long Eklutna Lake, and one of the top panoramic views anywhere in Chugach State Park.

THE RUNDOWN

Distances: Bold Ridge Overlook: 3.5 miles one way. Head of Bold Valley: 4 miles one way

Hike or bike to the Bold Ridge Trailhead, an additional 5 miles one way, on the Eklutna Lakeside Trail

Special features: Alpine tundra; massive, glacially carved Bold Peak; views of Eklutna Lake and Glacier. Bike rentals for the Eklutna Lakeside Trail are available near the trailhead

Location: In the Eklutna Lake area, 35 miles north of Anchorage

Difficulty: Bold Valley: strenuous. Bold Ridge Overlook: very strenuous

Trail type: More-developed trail for the first 2.5 miles; a route beyond

Total elevation gain: Bold Ridge Overlook: 3,600 feet. Head of Bold Valley: 2,800 feet

Best season: Late June through Sept

Fees/permits: Parking fee or state parks pass

Maps: USGS Anchorage B-6; Imus Geographics *Chugach State Park*; Alaska State Parks brochure Eklutna Lake

Contact: Chugach State Park, 18620 Seward Hwy., Anchorage, Alaska 99516; (907) 345-5014; http://dnr.alaska.gov/parks/

FINDING THE TRAILHEAD

Take the Eklutna exit off the Glenn Highway, 26 miles north of Anchorage and 16 miles south of Palmer. Exit east, follow the access road as it curves to the south for about 0.4 mile, and turn left (east) onto the Eklutna Lake Road. Follow it about 10 miles to the recreation area at Eklutna Lake. Trailhead parking is at the end of the road, past the turnoffs for the campground and picnic area. Begin the trip from the trailhead on the northeast side of the parking area.

Cross the Twin Peaks Creek Bridge, turn right in 100 feet onto the Eklutna Lakeside Trail, and hike or bike 5 miles to the Bold Ridge Trailhead; the trailhead is on the left side of the Lakeside Trail just beyond the Bold Creek Bridge.

WHAT TO SEE

Mountain wildflowers, great views of milky-blue Eklutna Lake and massive Bold Peak, and one of the best panoramas anywhere in Chugach State Park lie only a few miles (albeit steep miles) up the Bold Ridge Trail.

If you mountain-bike the 5 miles of the Eklutna Lakeside Trail to the Bold Ridge Trailhead instead of walking it, you'll cut about 3 hours off the round-trip, making a reasonable day hike feasible. The Lakeside Trail is a graded gravel roadway and an easy mountain bike trip. The trail is closed to cars and trucks at all times but is open to all-terrain vehicles from Sunday to Wednesday each week, so if you want to be sure of a quiet hike or bike along the lake, do the trip between Thursday and Saturday. You'll have to leave your bike near the Bold Ridge Trailhead; the Bold Ridge Trail is suitable for and open only to foot traffic. Bringing a bike chain and lock is a good move for security and peace of mind.

An overnight option other than backpacking is the Yuditnu Creek Cabin (reservation and fee required). The cabin is about 3 miles out the Lakeside Trail and 2 miles north of the Bold Ridge Trailhead. For cabin information and reservations use the Alaska State Parks website (see "Contact" above) or call the Department of Natural Resources Public Information Center in Anchorage at (907) 269-8400.

The stiff uphill hike to Bold Ridge follows a steep, abandoned road for the first 2.5 miles. The roadway climbs through aspen, birch, and brushy slopes, gaining about 2,500 feet of elevation and ending on a tundra point, Knob 3,400. The route divides on the knob: The lower path to the southeast leads to the head of Bold Valley and the glacial rubble at the base of Bold Peak; the higher path, to the south, climbs Bold Peak's northwest ridge and leads to the overlook point.

Bold Valley. A camp in the valley is a good base for exploring the area, including the convoluted, rocky geography of the head of the valley. Bold Creek flows only a short distance out of the moraine before disappearing underground for about a mile, so choose a campsite with water in mind. A stiff climb leads to some fine ridge running on either side of the valley. Hunter Creek Pass, the 4,850-foot notch to the left (north) of Bold Peak's glacial rubble, offers a view and a route into Hunter Creek, a wild, rarely visited valley.

Bold Ridge Overlook. The higher route from Knob 3,400 leads up another 1,000 feet in a little over a mile to the overlook point on Bold Ridge. The path may disappear, but the route is easy enough to follow; just hike up to the ridge and follow it toward Bold Peak until the view bowls you over, and you've found the overlook, at an elevation of 4,456 feet. The vertical face of 7,522-foot Bold Peak looks close enough to reach out and touch. Eklutna Lake, River, and Glacier are spread out below, and rugged, dark peaks hog the skyline to the south; all in all, not bad for a day hike.

Shorter hikes: Knob 3,400 at Miles 2.5 is a good shorter destination with good views of Eklutna Lake and Bold Peak.

A group of Dall sheep on a ridge in the Bold Valley in Chugach State Park. Camping in the valley provides a nice basecamp for exploring the area, and steep climbing routes can connect to spectacular ridgeline hiking.
CARL BATTREALL

The Bold Ridge Trail includes mountain wildflowers, great views of milky-blue Eklutna Lake, and 7,522-foot Bold Peak. The route has one of the best panoramas anywhere in Chugach State Park, only a few (steep) miles from the trailhead
CARL BATTREALL

TIDBIT

Biking the 5 miles of the Eklutna Lakeside Trail to the Bold Ridge Trailhead will cut about 3 hours off the round-trip, rather than walking to the trailhead.

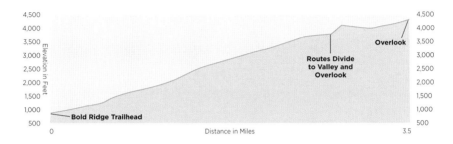

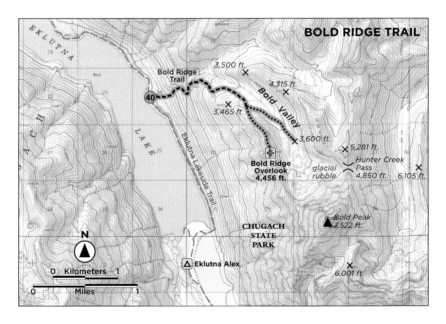

MATANUSKA AND SUSITNA VALLEYS

NORTH OF ANCHORAGE ARE the Matanuska and Susitna Rivers, by far the two largest of Cook Inlet's rivers. The Talkeetna Mountains, north of the Matanuska and east of the Susitna, are a rugged range with a few hiking trails, mainly in the Little Susitna River–Hatcher Pass area. Farther north, off the Parks Highway in the main Susitna watershed, is fine hiking country in Denali State Park.

Besides the hikes described here, there are several routes into the Talkeetnas off the Glenn Highway northeast of Palmer; most combine all-terrain-vehicle and foot trails and cross-country hiking, with a few decent game trails thrown in for good measure. Motorized traffic, however, is a major problem for hikers in the area, which can be an ATV zoo on summer weekends and during hunting season. The area is essentially all state land, none of it state park, and the State of Alaska has made little to no effort to accommodate hikers.

There is some fine country for longer trips farther back in the Talkeetnas, however, if you're willing to look past the ATV damage and are more or less self-sufficient at route finding; try Kings River/Young Creek at Glenn Highway Mile 66.7, Purinton Creek/Boulder Creek/Chitna Pass at Mile 89, Pinochle Creek/Hicks Creek at Mile 99.7, or Squaw Creek/Belanger Pass at Mile 123.3. Options for getting into the backcountry as painlessly as possible are to do your trip midweek, grit your teeth and hustle out beyond the ATV day users as quickly as possible, or ride a mountain bike partway. Be sure to plan your trip on topographic maps before heading out.

41. PIONEER RIDGE

WHY GO?

A strenuous hike climbing to the highest point accessible by a trail with stunning views of Knik Glacier, Matanuska Valley, and the Chugach Mountains.

THE RUNDOWN

Distance: 4.5 miles one way

Special features: Great views, high-country access

Location: 40 miles north of Anchorage

Difficulty: Very strenuous

Trail type: More-developed trail lower; an alpine route above, marked with fiberglass stakes

Total elevation gain: 5,100 feet

Best season: Late June through Sept

Fees/permits: Parking fee or borough parks pass

Maps: USGS Anchorage C-6 (SE) and B-6; Imus Geographics *Chugach State Park*

Contact: Matanuska-Susitna Borough, 350 East Dahlia Ave., Palmer, AK 99645; (907) 745-9690; www.matsugov.us

FINDING THE TRAILHEAD

 Turn east from the Glenn Highway onto the Old Glenn Highway, 12 miles south of Palmer and 30 miles north of Anchorage. Drive about 8.5 miles to Knik River Road, which continues straight ahead on the south side of the Knik River as the Old Glenn curves north to cross a bridge over the river. Take Knik River Road about 4 miles to the marked trailhead on the right.

WHAT TO SEE

A long, steady, uphill hike, the Pioneer Ridge Trail climbs to a spectacular view of Knik Glacier, and higher up, of the Matanuska Valley, Pioneer Peak, and the Chugach Range. The 5,300-foot shoulder of Pioneer Peak is the highest point hikers can reach on a trail in Southcentral Alaska. The peak is nearly vertical on the north, or Palmer, side, but this hike follows the seldom seen east side of the mountain, where a steep but passable feeder ridge leads up to the peak's shoulder.

With few flat places to recoup your energy, expect a slow hike; breaking a mile an hour is a good pace going up. Plan on a full summer day and pack food and water accordingly. Camping is possible in the high country, with some water available from snow and snowmelt ponds around 5,000 feet in elevation, but carrying a full pack up this trail requires a lot of stamina.

Above tree line the trail is marked intermittently with orange or red fiberglass stakes. Higher up the ridge, the trail is not obvious on the ground, so pay attention to the route; clouds and mist often obscure the higher elevations and could make finding your way down difficult if the weather gets too thick.

A few picnic tables along the trail lend an oddly civilized touch to the trip. If you're feeling fatigued as you near the top, it might help (or it might not) to know that Colony High School Junior ROTCers carried the materials for the tables up the trail on their backs.

On a sunny day the view of the Knik Glacier and the Chugach at about 2 miles is incredible. Look for Mounts Palmer, Gannett, Goode, and even Marcus Baker, the highest point in the Chugach Mountains, on the skyline. Pioneer Peak is not visible until higher up the trail.

At 4,600 feet, voilà! Another unlikely picnic table appears, just right for a rest in a really scenic spot before the final 700-foot climb. The view here includes the ridge and both of Pioneer Peak's summits. Don't turn around here, though; the last push to Pioneer Ridge is worth the effort. Once you top out on the ridge, views of the steep country around Goat Creek open up, and the ridgeline leading west toward Pioneer Peak makes a good walk if you haven't had enough yet. (The "goats" of Goat Creek are actually Dall sheep.)

Pioneer Peak itself is just inside the boundary of Chugach State Park. The south summit (6,350 feet) is still about 2 miles and another 1,000-foot elevation gain away; the climb is a bit rough and circuitous, but experienced hiker/scramblers can manage it. To get to the north, slightly higher summit (6,398 feet), however, means crossing a steep, dangerous gap between the peaks and requires mountaineering experience and gear.

The ridgeline leading from the shoulder to the southeast curls around Goat Creek and ties in with other ridges that really hardy hikers can follow into the Eklutna Lake valley, connecting with the Twin Peaks or Bold Ridge Trails. Check the topo for this ridge-running route; it's a very long trip and an extremely challenging one, even for experienced long-distance ramblers.

Look for raptors, nesting migratory birds, arctic ground squirrels, and Dall sheep on the Pioneer Ridge hike, and be alert for moose and bears. Also beware of stinging nettle on and near the trail in brushy sections.

A hiker climbs the ridge above Knik River on a late June day. In the distance the Knik Glacier descends into the valley.
NATHANIEL WILDER

The south summit of Pioneer Peak close to the end of the ridge trail. At 6,350 feet, the summit is non-technical but for experienced (and brave) hikers only.
WILL KOEPPEN

A hiker descends Pioneer Ridge above the Knik River on a late June day.
NATHANIEL WILDER

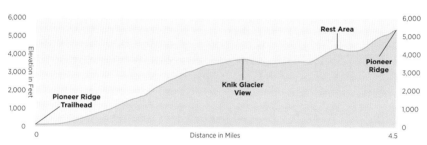

MILES AND DIRECTIONS

0.0   Begin at the marked trailhead.

2.0   Pass the brush line and enter open, high-elevation country.

3.7   Take a well-earned break at 4,600 feet.

4.5   Meet the ridge crest at 5,300 feet elevation.

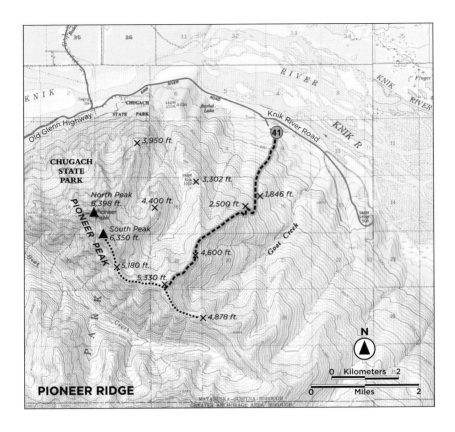

PIONEER RIDGE

TIDBIT

Bring plenty of water, layers, and a windbreaker if you plan on hiking to the ridgeline. Trekking poles are a good idea too, especially with sensitive joints.

Shorter hikes: Take the trail about 2.5 miles to the first viewpoint of Knik Glacier, still a demanding hike that climbs about 2,000 feet.

42. LAZY MOUNTAIN AND MATANUSKA PEAK

WHY GO?

Two routes climbing into alpine ridges and peaks with views of the Chugach and Talkeetna Mountain ranges, Pioneer Peak, and the Matanuska River in the valley below.

THE RUNDOWN

Distances: Lazy Mountain Trail: 2.5 miles one way (allow at least 4 hours round-trip). Matanuska Peak Trail: 6 miles one way (allow at least 10 hours round-trip)

Special features: High ridges and peaks, fine views, wildflower meadows

Location: 4 miles east of Palmer

Difficulty: Lazy Mountain Trail: strenuous. Matanuska Peak Trail: strenuous to very strenuous

Trail type: Less-developed, steep trails/routes. The Matanuska Peak Trail is brushy lower, and rocky and difficult near the peak

Total elevation gain: Lazy Mountain Trail: about 3,000 feet. Matanuska Peak Trail: about 2,000 feet to McRoberts Creek basin and 5,800 feet to Matanuska Peak

Best season: Lazy Mountain: mid-May through Sept. Matanuska Peak: mid-June through mid-Sept

Fees/permits: Parking fee or borough parks pass

Maps: USGS Anchorage C-6 (SE)

Contact: Matanuska-Susitna Borough, 350 East Dahlia Ave., Palmer, AK 99645; (907) 745-9690; www.matsugov.us

FINDING THE TRAILHEAD

Lazy Mountain Trail. Drive to Palmer on the Glenn Highway and turn right (east) onto West Arctic Avenue/Old Glenn Highway at Mile 42.1; the intersection is the second traffic light in Palmer as you drive north from Anchorage. Follow Arctic Avenue east, toward the mountains, about 2.3 miles through town and across the Matanuska River Bridge, then curving south, to Clark-Wolverine Road.

Turn left (east) and follow Clark-Wolverine Road 0.7 mile to Huntley Road. Turn right onto Huntley, following a sign for the Lazy Mountain Recreation Area, and in another mile, bear right at a fork in the road. Then drive downhill 0.2 mile into the parking area. The parking area and trailhead are a day-use area only.

Views of the inner Chugach Mountains, from the 6,119-foot summit of Matanuska Peak. JUSTIN WHOLEY

Only 6 miles from the trailhead, enjoy panoramic views of the jagged peaks in the Chugach surrounding Matanuska Peak. JUSTIN WHOLEY

A nice spot to break for lunch, along the Matanuska Peak Trail. JUSTIN WHOLEY

Matanuska Peak Trail. Follow the Lazy Mountain Trailhead directions as far as Clark-Wolverine Road. Continue south 0.4 mile on the Old Glenn Highway to Smith Road, and turn left (east). Follow Smith Road due east 1.5 miles to the T inter-section, and drive straight through the intersection into the trailhead parking area.

WHAT TO SEE

Lazy Mountain (3,720 feet) and Matanuska Peak (6,119 feet) are the prominent peaks east of Palmer. Lazy Mountain is the rounded peak nearer town, and Mat Peak is the tall, stately peak behind it. A trail leads to each summit, and it's possible to connect the two trails for a very long high-country adventure just a stone's throw from Palmer.

These trails are a bit rough. Lazy Mountain is extremely steep in places and can be very slick when wet. The lower 2.5 miles of the Mat Peak Trail are thick with tall grasses and cow parsnip by late summer, and if the vegetation is wet even with dew, you'll be soaked to the neck if you don't have rain gear on. Watch for cow parsnip and stinging nettle on both trails; long pants are a good idea.

The Mat Peak Trail (and the Lazy Mountain Trail, if you hike off-trail) leads into the alpine basin of McRoberts Creek, a good day or overnight destination if you're not up for the stiff climb to the Mat Peak summit. Allow at least 10 hours for the entire trip if you climb the peak.

Lazy Mountain. The wide, graded trail that begins at the end of the parking lot is the Morgan Horse Trail, which leads about 1.5 miles south to the Matanuska Peak Trail. To head for Lazy Mountain, instead take the narrow footpath that begins on the uphill side of the lot at the far (northeast) end. Immediately out of the parking area, take the well-traveled trail fork to the right.

The climb is nearly unrelenting, and part of it is steep in the extreme. The first bump with a view, at about 1.5 miles and 2,500 feet in elevation, is a good destination—there is even a picnic table for relaxing and having lunch.

The peak is still a mile and three more bumps away. The grade moderates and the views improve as the trail climbs into low-growing alpine vegetation. The very top is narrow and rocky with a drop-off on both sides, so be careful, especially with any children who have managed to make it this far. The view at the top is terrific: Matanuska Peak rises off the ridge to the east, the Matanuska River below separates the Chugach and Talkeetna Mountains, and Pioneer Peak dominates the view to the south across the Knik River.

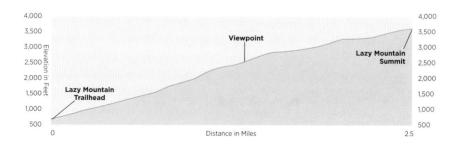

MILES AND DIRECTIONS

0.0   Start your hike at the Lazy Mountain Trailhead.

1.5   Reach a viewpoint at 2,500 feet elevation.

2.5   Attain the summit of Lazy Mountain.

McRoberts Creek and Matanuska Peak. From the Mat Peak Trailhead, follow the narrow lane that serves as the beginning of the trail. In 0.1 mile it intersects the Morgan Horse Trail, and at 0.3 mile, just as you're starting to climb the first hill on the lane, take the trail to the left; look for a hiker sign on a birch tree about 20 feet off the lane. The climbing begins for real at this intersection. In another 0.1 mile bear left and uphill as the trail splits. In another 0.4 mile, in a grassy aspen flat, Mat Peak is clearly visible ahead.

At about 2.5 miles the trail crosses a small perennial stream that flows down from the Lazy Mountain ridgeline. Once out of this draw, tall meadow vegetation is less of a problem, and soon it's forgotten as you ramble along on a well-beaten alpine path in the McRoberts Creek basin. From the basin to the peak, the route is marked with fiberglass stakes.

At about 3 miles, a route to the left, or north, leads toward Lazy Mountain. In another mile, on an alpine flat above McRoberts Creek, is another picnic table. This spot, 4 miles from the trailhead, is a good destination. Beyond the table, the route crosses a gulch and begins the steep climb to the peak, still about 3,000 feet above. Scree and loose rock on the summit ridge make for slow going, and the final pitch, which ascends a steep boulder field, requires a reasonable amount of caution.

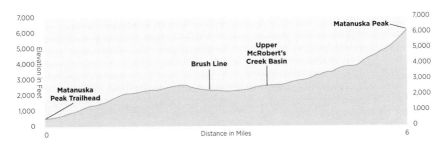

MILES AND DIRECTIONS

0.0   Start at the Matanuska Peak Trailhead.

0.9   Reach an opening with a view of Matanuska Peak.

2.5   Cross an unnamed stream and emerge into alpine terrain.

3.0   Pass the junction with a route to the left (northwest) toward Lazy Mountain.

6.0   Reach the peak and savor the view.

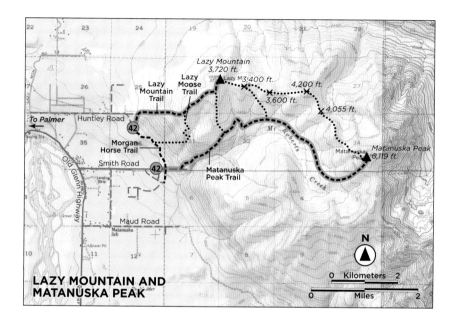

LAZY MOUNTAIN AND MATANUSKA PEAK

From the peak, there is a great view west and south back to Palmer and the Matanuska River, but the real draw is the vista east into the mountain kingdom of the inner Chugach, undoubtedly one of the wildest views on earth within 10 miles of an espresso shop.

Loop trips: If you're up for a killer hike, try the very long loop, about 13 miles and 7,400 feet of elevation gain, connecting the two trails via the ridge between Lazy Mountain and Matanuska Peak. Pick the route up or down Mat Peak carefully; the safest section of the mountain just below the peak is the south/southwest side, requiring a traverse to get to or from the ridge that connects to Lazy Mountain, which trends northeast from Mat Peak.

A second loop possibility is the route between Lazy Mountain and Mile 3 of the Mat Peak Trail, approximately a 9-mile round-trip. For an even shorter loop, about 7 miles, take the south ridge of Lazy Mountain about a mile downhill to Mile 1.5 of the Mat Peak Trail.

To complete any of these loop trips without a shuttle, take the Morgan Horse Trail between the two trailheads, adding about 1.5 miles to the trip.

> **TIDBIT**
>
> An easier approach, although a bit longer, is the Lazy Moose trail, which avoids the steep, eroded sections, and connects with the original Lazy Mountain trail about halfway up.

43. WEST BUTTE

WHY GO?

A trail the whole family can enjoy, climbing to the summit of a prominent bluff with panoramic views at the top.

THE RUNDOWN

Distance: 1.5 miles one way

Special features: Butte with mountain and river views, wildflower meadows

Location: 6.5 miles southeast of Palmer

Difficulty: Moderate to difficult

Trail type: Developed

Total elevation gain: About 650 feet

Best season: mid-May through Sept

Fees/permits: Parking fee or borough parks pass

Maps: USGS Anchorage C-6 (SE)

Contact: Matanuska-Susitna Borough, 350 East Dahlia Ave., Palmer, AK 99645; (907) 745-9690; www.matsugov.us

FINDING THE TRAILHEAD

 From Palmer, head southeast on the Old Glenn Highway, 5.5 miles from Palmer. Take a right on Bodenburg Loop, continue 0.5 mile, turn left on Mothershead Circle, proceed about 400 feet to the trailhead parking on the right. The trailhead is 300 feet further along Mothershead Circle.

WHAT TO SEE

A trail suitable for most hiking abilities, with spectacular views at the top, 1.5 miles from the trailhead. The route for the West Butte Trail travels along the west side of Bodenburg Butte. From the start, the first mile is moderate climbing, following a wide gravel path winding through old growth forest and alder. Around the 1-mile mark at the top of a hill, is a bench to rest and take in the vista of the Matanuska River below and the Talkeetna Mountains to the northwest. Here the route transitions to more difficult, as it climbs the west side of the Butte. Climbing above tree line, the trail is a mix of a narrow path and stairs, then winds around a steep western slope. On the crest of the west side of the butte, the trail winds along grassy slopes toward the summit to the east. The last 0.5 mile of the route can be difficult, hike it at your own pace. At the top, enjoy fantastic views of the Talkeetna and Chugach Mountains, Matanuska and Knik River valleys, and the Knik Glacier.

At the top, keep an eye out for wildflowers blanketing the rolling meadow landscape.

Bicycles and horses are allowed on the first mile of the gravel trail, but not beyond.

Two hikers wave to a sea plane flying by the Brodenburg Butte on a clear afternoon, with Pioneer Peak in the background. WILLIE DALTON

A family rests on the granite summit of the Brodenburg Butte on a clear summer evening, with Pioneer Peak visible in the background. WILLIE DALTON

TIDBIT

Bring your binoculars for this hike, and scan the surrounding area from the summit.

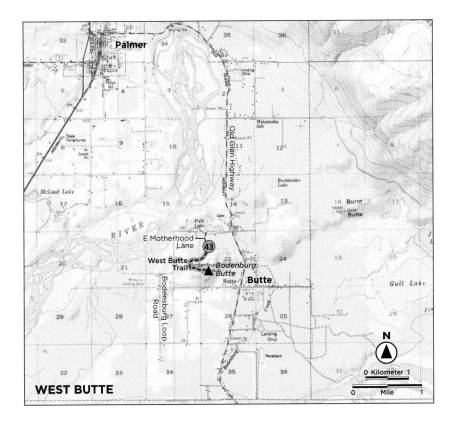

WEST BUTTE

44. MINT GLACIER VALLEY

WHY GO?

Mint Glacier Valley Trail includes access to a mountain and glacier landscape, with further routes for mountaineering options from the higher points on the trail.

THE RUNDOWN

Distance: 8 miles one way.

Special features: A rugged mountain and glacier landscape, mountaineering access.

Location: 16 miles north of Palmer.

Difficulty: Strenuous.

Trail type: More-developed trail lower; a well-beaten route above.

Total elevation gain: 2,500 feet.

Best season: July through mid-Sept.

Fees/permits: Parking fee or state parks pass.

Maps: USGS Anchorage D-6.

Contact: Alaska State Parks, Mat-Su/Copper Basin Area, Finger Lake, Mile 0.7 Bogard Road, 7278 East Bogard Rd., Wasilla, AK 99654; (907) 745-3975; http://dnr.alaska.gov/parks/.

FINDING THE TRAILHEAD

Drive north of Palmer on the Glenn Highway to Fishhook-Willow Road, which is about 1.4 miles north of the intersection of the Glenn and West Arctic Avenue in Palmer, the second and last traffic light in Palmer as you drive north from Anchorage. Turn west toward Hatcher Pass, and drive about 14 miles to the Gold Mint Trailhead parking area on the right, just before the road curves sharply uphill to the left.

WHAT TO SEE

Following the valley of the upper Little Susitna River, the Gold Mint Trail leads to the river's headwaters in the high basin below the Mint Glacier, an awesome landscape of waterfalls and serrated peaks. The area is popular with mountaineers, and there is good off-trail hiking as well. The Mint Valley is the big attraction of this hike;

there are really no great intermediate destinations on the Little Su, although the river and distant mountain views about 4 miles from the trailhead may be appealing if your agenda calls for a less demanding hike.

The lower portion of the trail cuts through alder thickets with limited views. The first good view is about 1.5 miles from the trailhead, in a meadow on a low hill. At about 2.5 miles, a bit east of the double drainage that enters the Little Su from the south, the trail passes directly across the river from the site of the Lonesome Mine. The mine, worked in the 1930s, was unique for the area in that it produced more silver than gold. Avalanches and fires have finished off most of the mine structures. The USGS map shows the trail crossing the river to the area of the mine, but it now stays on the north side of the river.

At about 3.5 miles, the trail turns the corner to the north, with a distant view of the peaks, glaciers, and waterfalls at the head of the valley. The trail deteriorates as it leads north, and at 4 miles or so, it joins the bank of the foaming, boulder-strewn stream. There are a few possible campsites in this stretch.

At about 7 miles and 3,000 feet in elevation, the trail reaches the end of the Little Su's broad valley. The track becomes fainter as it climbs toward the Mint Valley; follow rock cairns through the rocky tundra. A second route curls around the left side of the steep dome ahead, but stay right, in sight of the steep course of the river, for the most direct route to the upper basin.

The high basin, elevation 4,300 feet, is starkly beautiful, with dark spires, boulder slides, and remnant glaciers all around. A good destination from the basin is the high pass to the north, locally known as Backdoor Gap, which lies not quite a mile and about 1,200 feet of elevation gain above the basin; it overlooks the Pennyroyal Glacier and more of the Talkeetna range.

Good campsites are limited in the lower valley, but there is decent camping in the upper basin. Weather is always a consideration this high in the Talkeetnas, so be prepared to wait out a storm if you want to be assured of a chance to explore the high country. You could easily spend several days exploring here.

The Mint Hut, a Mountaineering Club of Alaska hut, is located to the east of the trail in the upper basin. The hut was built and is maintained with volunteer labor and membership dues, so the club requests that hut users be or become members. Contact the club for information; go to www.mtnclubak.org/ or write to MCA at PO Box 243561, Anchorage, AK 99524. The club also sponsors classes, hikes, and climbs, and holds monthly meetings in Anchorage with hiking and mountaineering programs.

A hiker passes the Mint Hut, located about 8 miles near the end of the designated trail, in the upper basin. The hut is maintained with volunteer labor and membership dues, so the club requests that hut users be or become members.
For more information, visit: www.mtnclubak.org.
HAGEPHOTO

The Little Susitna River with gorgeous jagged peaks of the Talkeetna Mountains in the background
ALASKA STATE PARK

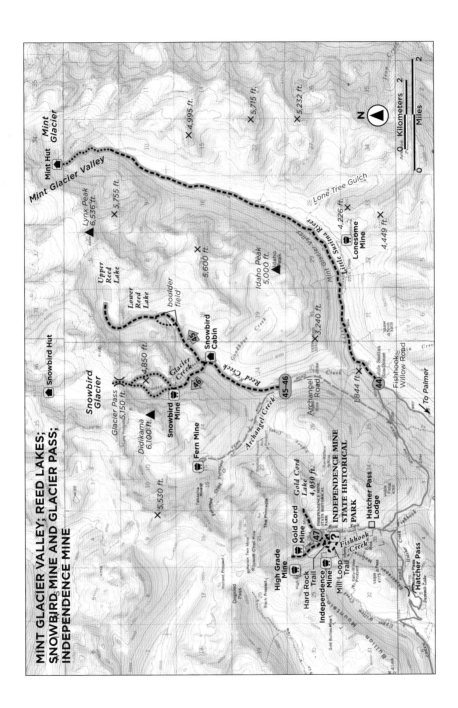

MINT GLACIER VALLEY; REED LAKES; SNOWBIRD MINE AND GLACIER PASS; INDEPENDENCE MINE

The 8-mile Mint Glacier Valley Trail leads to a high glacial valley in the Talkeetna Mountains. The area is popular with mountaineers, with good off-trail hiking opportunities. ALASKA STATE PARKS

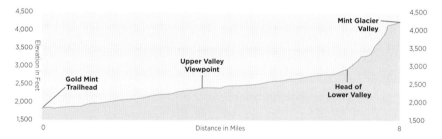

MILES AND DIRECTIONS

0.0   Start at the Gold Mint Trailhead.

1.5   Take in the view from a meadow in the lower valley.

3.5   The view of the head of the Little Susitna River opens to the north.

7.0   Arrive at the head of the lower valley.

8.0   Enter the Mint Glacier Valley.

TIDBIT

The Mint Hut, is located to the east of the trail in the upper basin. The hut is maintained with volunteer labor and membership dues, so the club requests that hut users be or become members. For more information, visit: www.mtnclubak.org.

45. **REED LAKES**

WHY GO?

The trail provides wonderful access for day hikes or overnight treks into jagged granite peaks, rock walls, glaciers, and lakes in the heart of the Talkeetna Mountains.

THE RUNDOWN See map on page 195.

Distances: Lower Reed Lake: 3 miles one way. Upper Reed Lake: 4 miles one way

Special features: Glacial lakes, rugged mountains, rock-climbing areas

Location: 19 miles north of Palmer.

Difficulty: Moderate

Trail type: More-developed trail for the first 1.5 miles; a well-beaten route the rest of the way

Total elevation gain: 1,300 feet to the lower lake, 1,800 to the upper lake

Best season: July to mid-Sept

Fees/permits: None

Maps: USGS Anchorage D-6

Contact: Alaska State Parks, Mat-Su/Copper Basin Area, Finger Lake, Mile 0.7 Bogard Road, 7278 East Bogard Rd., Wasilla, AK 99654; (907) 745-3975; http://dnr.alaska.gov/parks/

FINDING THE TRAILHEAD

Drive north of Palmer on the Glenn Highway to Fishhook-Willow Road, which is about 1.4 miles north of the intersection of the Glenn and West Arctic Avenue in Palmer, the second and last traffic light in Palmer as you drive north from Anchorage. Turn west toward Hatcher Pass, and, after about 14 miles, pass the Gold Mint Trailhead, and follow a sharp left curve where the road begins to climb steeply. Continue about 0.8 mile to Archangel Road and turn right; take this road about 2.3 miles to the trailhead on the right, 0.2 mile beyond the bridge over Archangel Creek. Going is slow on the rough road, but the scenery is spectacular.

WHAT TO SEE

An annual pilgrimage for many Anchorage and Mat–Su hikers, the Reed Lakes Trail leads into the heart of the Talkeetna Mountains, a land of jagged granite peaks, rock walls, blocky boulders, glaciers, and cirque lakes. The trail makes a great long day hike, but there are plenty of good campsites near the lakes and on the benches above them. Rock climbers use the trail to get to good climbing areas.

Look for alpine wildflowers, tundra-nesting birds, arctic ground squirrels, and marmots, and if energy allows, scramble up to the ridges and peaks near the lakes.

The trail is wide and easy for the first 1.5 miles, following an old road to the site of Snowbird Mine Village, but is much rougher beyond, including a section of boulder hopping to get into the upper valley of Reed Creek. Just past the Snowbird Cabin, a dilapidated remnant of the Snowbird village, the trail forks; to the left is the Snowbird Mine Trail. Continue straight ahead for Reed Lakes. Just beyond, the trail crosses Glacier and Reed Creeks to the east side of the valley. Both creeks are bridged.

Beyond the crossing, the trail climbs switchbacks toward the upper valley of Reed Creek. At the top of the pitch, the trail more or less disappears as it crosses a massive field of granite boulders that chokes the narrow valley. This boulder hop is challenging for the older, the younger, and the canine. A less-challenging option is to cross the valley at the lower section of the boulder field to a hiker's path on the other side, thereby avoiding some of the bouldering. In either case, the trail eventually ends up on the west side of the creek and emerges into the upper valley, with its alpine meadows and meandering, pooling stream.

The east side of the upper Reed valley is one big boulder slide, and azure Lower Reed Lake lies near the end of the slide, at 3,750 feet in elevation. Upstream, the creek pours over two rock ledges. Around the bend to the right, 500 feet higher and a mile farther, is the upper lake, which lies at the head of the drainage below Lynx Peak (6,536 feet). There's good cross-country hiking and scrambling above the upper lake toward the Kashwitna River drainage to the north and the Little Susitna River (see the Mint Glacier Valley hike) to the southeast.

The portion of trail climbing to Upper Reed Lake at 4,250 feet. WILL KOEPPEN

Above tree line, the Reed Lakes
Trail provides ample opportunities
to leave the beaten path and create
your own adventure.
WILL KOEPPEN

The trail makes a great long
day hike, but there are plenty
of campsites near the lakes
to make it an overnight trip.
HAGEPHOTO

The trail is closed to motor vehicles, but the first 1.5 miles are open to and suitable for mountain bikes. This is a popular trail on good summer weekends.

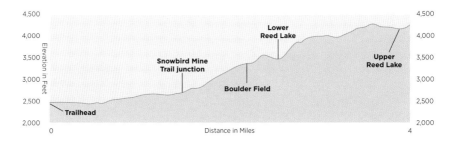

MILES AND DIRECTIONS

0.0   Begin at the trailhead.

1.5   Intersect the Snowbird Mine Trail (see Snowbird Mine and Glacier Pass hike).

2.5   Enter the upper Reed Creek valley.

3.0   Arrive at Lower Reed Lake.

4.0   Reach the end of the beaten path at Upper Reed Lake.

Shorter hikes: Hike about 2 miles to a lower valley view, 2.5 miles into the upper valley with its pretty stream, or 3 miles to Lower Reed Lake. Two miles on the trail is about the limit for smaller children because of the boulder field.

TIDBIT

At the upper valley of Reed Creek, the trail dissolves as it crosses a huge field of granite boulders through the narrow valley. This section can be difficult for the occasional hiker, and there's another, less challenging option: cross the valley at the lower section of the boulder field to a hiker's path on the other side.

46. SNOWBIRD MINE AND GLACIER PASS

WHY GO?

A trail traveling by mining ruins, mountain scenery, and a glacier, off Archangel Road.

THE RUNDOWN See map on page 195.

Distances: Snowbird Mine: 2.5 miles one way. Glacier Pass: 4 miles one way

Special features: Mining ruins, Talkeetna Mountains scenery, and a remnant mountain glacier

Location: 19 miles north of Palmer

Difficulty: Moderate to the Snowbird Mine; strenuous to Glacier Pass

Trail type: More-developed trail below; less-developed trail to the Snowbird Mine; a route/cross-country hike from the mine to Glacier Pass

Total elevation gain: Snowbird Mine: 1,500 feet. Glacier Pass: 2,700 feet

Best season: July through Sept

Fees/permits: None

Maps: USGS Anchorage D-6

Contact: Alaska State Parks, Mat-Su/Copper Basin Area, Finger Lake, Mile 0.7 Bogard Road, 7278 East Bogard Rd., Wasilla, AK 99654; (907) 745-3975; http://dnr.alaska.gov/parks/

FINDING THE TRAILHEAD

Drive north of Palmer on the Glenn Highway to Fishhook-Willow Road, which is about 1.4 miles north of the intersection of the Glenn and West Arctic Avenue in Palmer, the second and last traffic light in Palmer as you drive north from Anchorage. Turn west toward Hatcher Pass, and after about 14 miles, pass the Gold Mint Trailhead, and follow a sharp left curve where the road begins to climb steeply. Continue about 0.8 mile to Archangel Road and turn right; take this road about 2.3 miles to the trailhead on the right, 0.2 mile beyond the bridge over Archangel Creek. Going is slow on the rough road, but the scenery is spectacular.

WHAT TO SEE

The Snowbird Mine Trail climbs into the high country of the Talkeetnas to the ruins of the Snowbird Mine, and a route continues up Glacier Creek to Glacier Pass and the Snowbird Glacier, which fills the high basin north of the pass. The granite peaks, alpine wildflowers, mine ruins, and glacier make this a diverse and beautiful hike.

Take the Reed Lakes Trail 1.5 miles to the Snowbird Cabin, the last dilapidated remnant of the Snowbird Mine Village. Turn left, uphill, at the Y in the trail just past the cabin. A steep path follows cable lines that run between the village and the mine, located in Glacier Creek's hanging valley.

Pass the old cable towers on the first level of the hanging valley, and climb to the next level to see more of the ruins. The Snowbird's ore came from the mountainside to the west. The mine was prospected in the 1920s, developed in the 1940s, and closed in 1950.

The Glacier Creek valley above the mine is magical: A small, bubbling mountain brook flows through alpine meadows, with granite boulders lying around in giant heaps. Glacier Pass is directly above to the north, but the granite dome ahead, at 4,850 feet in elevation, blocks the view. The hike to the pass is essentially a cross-country trip, so carry a map and compass—don't forget that the weather can change and visibility can disappear quickly at this elevation.

A hiker on the Snowbird Mine and Glacier Pass Trail, a route traveling into high alpine in the Talkeetna Mountains.
MIKE RECORDS

The most-traveled route is to the left of the dome, ascending the creek, but either side will do. Taking the route to the right allows you to pass by the pretty tarn in the basin east of the creek. In either direction getting onto the pass ridge as soon as possible yields the easiest walking. Allow two or more hours for the one-way trip from the mine to the pass; although it's only about 1.5 miles, it's slow going.

Glacier Pass, at 5,150 feet in elevation, looks out over the Snowbird Glacier to the north. The glacier, about a square mile in size, survives in a north-facing basin protected from the sun by high peaks like Didikama (6,100 feet). In late summer, when all the snow is melted and you can see the surface of the glacier, it is relatively safe to venture out onto the ice, but be wary of a few crevasses and holes. The meltwater cuts channels all along the surface and then drops in free fall down several deep holes in the ice. To be safe, stay off the steeper ice slopes unless you've brought crampons. There's plenty of exploring and scrambling to be done on the slopes and peaks around the glacier.

American Alpine Club has a Snowbird Hut on the northeast side of the glacier. The hut is free, open to the public, and managed on an open basis so it cannot be reserved.

MILES AND DIRECTIONS

- **0.0** Begin at the trailhead.
- **1.5** Turn left at the Snowbird Mine/Reed Lakes Trail junction.
- **2.5** Arrive at the Snowbird Mine.
- **4.0** Hike to Glacier Pass.

Shorter hikes: The steep, 2.5-mile hike to the Snowbird Mine is a great trip into the alpine world of the Talkeetnas.

47. INDEPENDENCE MINE

WHY GO?

Hiking trails suitable for all hiking abilities, in picturesque Independence Mine State Historical Park.

THE RUNDOWN See map on page 195.

Distances: The Hard Rock Trail, 0.5 mile one way, an easy walking tour through a partially restored mining camp. The Gold Cord Lake Trail, 0.5 mile one way, a hike to an alpine lake

Special features: Mining history, alpine tundra, and the rugged Talkeetna Mountains. Independence Mine is on the National Register of Historic Places. Pets allowed on leash only in the mine area

Location: 20 miles north of Palmer

Difficulty: Hard Rock Trail: easy. Gold Cord Lake Trail: moderate

Trail type: Hard Rock Trail: more developed. Gold Cord Lake: less developed

Total elevation gain: Hard Rock Trail: 100 feet. Gold Cord Lake: 600 feet each

Best season: Mid-June through Sept

Fees/permits: Day-use fee or Alaska State Parks pass; fee for optional guided walking tour

Maps: USGS Anchorage D-7, Alaska State Parks brochure Independence Mine State Historical Park

Contact: Alaska State Parks, Mat-Su/Copper Basin Area, Finger Lake, Mile 0.7 Bogard Road, 7278 East Bogard Rd., Wasilla, AK 99654; (907) 745-3975; http://dnr.alaska.gov/parks/

FINDING THE TRAILHEAD

 Drive north of Palmer on the Glenn Highway to Fishhook-Willow Road, which is about 1.4 miles north of the intersection of the Glenn and West Arctic Avenue in Palmer, the second and last traffic light in Palmer as you drive north from Anchorage. Turn west toward Hatcher Pass and drive 17 miles to Gold Cord Road; the last 3 miles beyond the Gold Mint Trailhead, are fairly steep. At Gold Cord Road continue straight ahead as the road over Hatcher Pass bears left. Continue past the Hatcher Pass Lodge to the park entrance station; then drive another mile and park in the parking area adjacent to the visitor center.

WHAT TO SEE

Independence Mine State Historical Park commemorates the Alaska-Pacific Consolidated Mining Company gold mines near Hatcher Pass, the second-richest lode (vein) mines in Alaska's history. The park's trails are all alpine hikes, beginning at

3,500 feet in elevation. There are many acres of alpine tundra to explore, and wild-flowers are out in force by late June or early July.

The Independence Mine walking tour begins at the visitor center, which is housed in the restored mine manager's residence. Inside, check out the displays about the mine's most prosperous days in the late 1930s and early 1940s. Outside, an accessible walkway with interpretive signs leads to several camp buildings, including bunkhouses, a warehouse, the commissary, the assay office, and the mess hall.

Hard Rock and Mill Loop Trails. Beyond the first cluster of buildings in the restored mining camp, the Hard Rock Trail winds at an easy grade up to the mine's shops, mill complex, and the tunnel portal that carried water down to the processing area. The trail connects with Mill Loop Trail, combining both for a 0.5 mile interpretive loop altogether.

Gold Cord Lake Trail. The hike to Gold Cord Lake (4,050 feet in elevation) starts below the visitor center parking area, at the road-closure gate on Gold Cord Road. A small sign marks the trail, which leads to the northeast toward an obvious, high basin. The trail climbs gently across the high tundra. The small holes all around are the burrows of arctic ground squirrels.

Most of the climb to the lake happens in the last, very steep 0.1 mile. At the lake, which may hold ice well into the summer, a waterfall slides down a rock face to the north, and the Chugach Mountains rise far above civilization to the southeast.

A bird's eye view of the historic mine buildings within Independence Mine State Historical Park. ALASKA STATE PARKS

The Powerhouse historic mine building within Independence Mine State Historical Park. Take care around the collapsing buildings and mine structures.
ALASKA STATE PARKS

TIDBIT

The visitor center is typically open from mid-June to mid-September. Take care around the collapsing buildings and mine structures, and please don't disturb the privately owned Gold Cord and High Grade Mine buildings.

TALKEETNA

THE HISTORIC TOWN OF Talkeetna, is where three rivers—the Talkeetna, Chulitna, and Susitna—combine to make up the Big Susitna drainage. The word "Talkeetna" loosely means "river of plenty" and a short walk from downtown Main Street offers views of the river, and on a clear day, Denali and the massive Alaska Range.

48. TALKEETNA LAKES PARK

WHY GO?

More than 1,000 acres of untouched forest and lakes with about 8 miles of trails for hiking, fishing, mountain biking, and non-motorized boating.

THE RUNDOWN

Special features: Freshwater lakes surrounded by forests of spruce, cottonwood, and birch

Location: 2.5 miles south of downtown Talkeetna

Difficulty: Easy to Moderate

Trail type: Developed

Total elevation gain: Less than 200 feet

Best season: May-Oct

Fees/permits: Parking fee or borough parks pass

Maps: USGS Talkeetna B-1

Contact: Matanuska-Susitna Borough, 350 East Dahlia Ave., Palmer, AK 99645; (907) 745-9690; www.matsugov.us

KEY DISTANCES AND DIFFICULTIES:

X Lake Loop: 3.3 miles one way, easy to moderate

Mink Loop: 0.75 miles one way, easy

Martin Loop: 2 miles one way, easy to moderate

Otter Loop: 1.9 miles one way, easy to moderate

Ermine Loop: 0.18 miles one way, easy

FINDING THE TRAILHEAD

From downtown Talkeetna, drive south about 2 miles, and turn east onto Comsat Road. Turn right at the first intersection into the main parking lot. A wooden sign indicates the entrance to the park, and the trailhead is obvious from there.

WHAT TO SEE

Talkeetna Lakes Park includes approximately 8 miles of multiuse trails winding through more than 1,000 acres of dense forest, within walking distance of the historic town of Talkeetna. The trails travel through vast forest of spruce, cottonwood, and birch, and by beautiful freshwater lakes. This area is the only park in the Matanuska Susitna Borough that comprises both water and land recreational opportunities. The park is a wilderness getaway, providing a serene setting for hiking, running, fishing,

canoeing, and mountain biking on the trails in the summer months. More than 200 acres of the park include lakes, the four named ones are X, Y, Z, and Tigger.

If planning an adventure to Talkeetna Lakes Park, consider adding a water activity to the mix. The area is well known for the quiet, peaceful lake scene. Bringing a canoe, stand-up paddleboard, or packraft would add another element to your outdoor experience. The main entrance to the park is the trailhead off Comsat Road. From there, follow the small access road west to X Lake, drop off your boat, and park back at the trailhead. Another access point is on the north side of Y Lake by way of a steel trail south of Comsat Road. The third access is on the south side of the park, with a walk-in trail from Whigmi Road, connecting to southwest side of Tigger Lake, which has a dock and put-in location.

In the middle of the summer, the mosquitoes are difficult to ignore. Plan (and pack) for encountering persistent bugs, and hope for a light breeze.

A walk in Talkeetna Lakes Park providing excellent reflections of trees, kayakers, stand up paddle boarders, on a clear autumn evening.
WILLIE DALTON

TIDBIT

In addition to hiking, plan a water adventure in one of the numerous beautiful lakes within the park. Also, be sure to leave enough time to check out the charming, quaint town of Talkeetna.

DENALI STATE PARK

DENALI STATE PARK, encompassing more than 300,000 acres, is a recreational paradise with accessible hiking, fishing, and camping between the Talkeetna Mountains and the Alaska Range. The prominent borders on the east side of the park are Curry and Kesugi Ridges, a 35-mile-long alpine ridge, and a world-class multi-day overnight backpacking adventure (see Kesugi Ridge). Denali State Park provides some of the best views in the state of Denali and the Alaska Range, from pullouts on the side of the highway, to the two hikes described below.

49. BYERS LAKE

WHY GO?

A hike for all activity levels with minimal elevation gain and views of Byers Lake and the Alaska Range on clear days.

THE RUNDOWN

Distance: A 4.8-mile loop

Special features: Wildlife, backcountry campsites, fishing, fee cabins; adjacent to road-accessible Byers Lake Campground

Location: About halfway between Talkeetna and Cantwell

Difficulty: Easy

Trail type: More developed

Total elevation gain: Less than 100 feet

Best season: Late May through Sept

Fees/permits: None

Maps: USGS Talkeetna C-1 (trail not shown); Alaska Natural History Association *Denali State Park Map and Guide*

Contact: Alaska State Parks, Mat-Su/Copper Basin Area, Finger Lake, Mile 0.7 Bogard Road, 7278 East Bogard Rd., Wasilla, AK 99654; (907) 745-3975; http://dnr.alaska.gov/parks/

FINDING THE TRAILHEAD

The trailhead is in the Byers Lake Campground in Denali State Park, Mile 147 of the Parks Highway, about 14 miles north of the Chulitna River Bridge and 17 miles south of the Little Coal Creek Trailhead. Turn east off the Parks Highway onto the campground road and drive 0.6 mile to the boat-launch parking area on the right. Park here, walk toward the lake and the boat launch, and, to hike the trail clockwise as described here, bear left on the trail along the lake.

If you're headed to walk-in Cabin #2 or choose a short out-and-back trip along the west side of the lake, park in the picnic area 0.3 mile from the highway on the right side of the campground road. Start the hike on the closed road behind the road barrier at the end of the parking area.

WHAT TO SEE

The easy hike around Byers Lake makes a good day trip, but there is also a walk-in fee cabin, Cabin #2, and a backcountry camping area, the Lakeshore Camp, for overnighters. Day hiking the lake while staying in the Byers Lake Campground or in the fee cabin on the campground road (Cabin #1) is a good option too. For cabin reservations, go through the state parks website, check with the Mat-Su parks office (see "Contact" above), or contact the Department of Natural Resources

Public Information Center, 550 West 7th Ave., Suite 1260, Anchorage, AK 99501; (907) 269-8400; http://dnr.alaska.gov/parks/cabins/.

The trail is near campground-style civilization, but it's wilder than you might imagine. Look for nesting swans and their young (called cygnets) and the beavers that have set up housekeeping near the lake. You can pick blueberries and cranberries in season, enjoy wildflowers like wild iris, dogwood, twinflower, and spirea, and lounge on the lake's small sand beaches when the water level is lower. By mid-August the pungent smell of highbush cranberries, Southcentral Alaska's musky odor of fall, is in the air. Check out the bridges on the trail: a long, springy suspension bridge over the inlet stream and a massive gabion-piling bridge over the outlet stream.

Hiking the trail clockwise, the junction with the Cascade Trail is about 1.5 miles from the boat launch and trailhead. A 0.3-mile side trip to the east on the Cascade Trail leads to a foaming, 100-foot cascade on a creek that drops from the alpine ridge above. Another two-plus very steep miles up this trail takes you to Mini-Skinny Lake, the first lake on Kesugi Ridge. The ridge is a fine alpine area with many small peaks and tarns; see the Kesugi Ridge hike.

At about 2 miles, Lakeshore Camp offers a half-dozen tent sites, picnic tables, outhouses, and a food cache for bear safety, and the park is planning to put in a kitchen shelter. The trail continues south along the eastern shoreline of the lake to the outlet stream, crosses the massive bridge, and then turns north along the west side of the lake. In less than a mile, it joins a closed road; Cabin #2 is 0.2 mile away to the east. Heading north, the picnic area and the boat launch are just a short stroll away.

Shorter hikes: Hike just over a mile one way to the east to the suspension bridge over Byers Creek. From the picnic area, accessible via a spur off the campground entrance road, stroll about 0.5 mile south to the cabin or just over a mile to the lake's outlet stream.

Fishing: There are rainbow trout, grayling, Dolly Varden, and a small population of lake trout in Byers Lake, but fishing is better from a boat than from the shoreline. No gasoline-powered boats are allowed on the lake, and the area is closed to all salmon fishing.

MILES AND DIRECTIONS

Clockwise		Counterclockwise
0.0	The trail begins and ends at the boat launch.	4.8
1.2	Arrive at the inlet stream bridge.	3.6
1.5	Intersect the Cascade Trail.	3.3
2.0	Camping is available at Lakeshore Camp.	2.8
3.5	Arrive at the outlet stream bridge.	1.3
4.4	Meet the trail to Cabin #2 (0.2 mile to cabin).	0.4
4.6	Arrive at the picnic area.	0.2
4.8	The trail ends/begins at the boat launch.	0.0

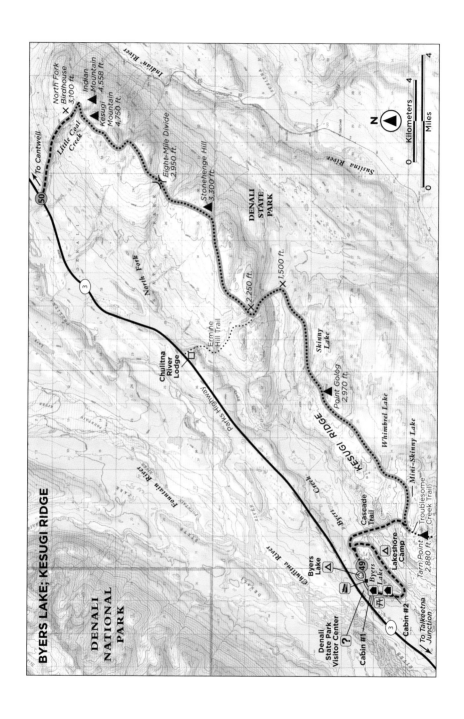

BYERS LAKE; KESUGI RIDGE

DENALI
NATIONAL
PARK

DENALI
STATE
PARK

To Cantwell

North Fork
Birdhouse
3,100 ft.

Indian
Mountain
4,558 ft.

Kesugi
Mountain
4,750 ft.

Little Coal Creek

Indian River

Eight-Mile Divide
2,950 ft.

Stonehenge Hill
3,300 ft.

2,250 ft.

1,500 ft.

Ermine
Hill Trail

North Fork

Chulitna
River
Lodge

Parks Highway

Fountain River

Chulitna River

Point Golog
2,970 ft.

Skinny
Lake

KESUGI RIDGE

Whimbrel Lake

Mini-Skinny Lake

Cascade
Trail

Byers
Creek

Byers
Lake

Lakeshore
Camp

Tarn Point
2,880 ft.

Troublesome
Creek Trail

Denali State Park
Visitor Center

Cabin #1

Cabin #2

Byers
Lake

To Talkeetna
Junction

Susitna River

N

Kilometers   4

Miles   4

50. **KESUGI RIDGE**

WHY GO?

A trail with a wide variety of choices for overnight treks traveling along a ridge, with some of the best views of Denali and the Alaska Range in the state.

THE RUNDOWN See map on page 214.

Distance: 27.5-mile traverse

Special features: High, wild country; ridge rambling; views of Denali and the Alaska Range

Location: About halfway between Talkeetna and Cantwell

Difficulty: Very strenuous

Trail type: A more-developed trail up to the ridge; a marked route along the ridge

Total elevation gain: 5,400 feet north to south; 6,000 feet south to north

Best season: Late June through mid-Sept

Fees/permits: None

Maps: USGS Talkeetna Mountains D-6 and C-6 and Talkeetna C-1 (trail not shown); Alaska Natural History Association *Denali State Park Map and Guide*. Bring the USGS maps and copy the route from maps posted in the park

Contact: Alaska State Parks, Mat-Su/Copper Basin Area, Finger Lake, Mile 0.7 Bogard Road, 7278 East Bogard Rd., Wasilla, AK 99654; (907) 745-3975; http://dnr.alaska.gov/parks/

FINDING THE TRAILHEAD

The Little Coal Creek Trailhead, the north trailhead, is located in Denali State Park at Mile 164 of the Parks Highway, about 17 miles north of Byers Lake Campground and about 4.5 miles south of the north boundary of the park. Turn east onto the marked access road to the trailhead.

The south trailhead is in the Byers Lake Campground, located at Parks Highway Mile 147, 17 miles south of Little Coal Creek and about 14 miles north of the Chulitna River Bridge. Turn east off the Parks Highway onto the campground road and drive 0.6 mile to the boat-launch parking area on the right. Park here, walk toward the lake and the boat launch, and bear left on the trail along the lake.

WHAT TO SEE

Kesugi Ridge, a long alpine ridge across the Chulitna River basin from the Alaska Range and Denali, is a fine 2-to-4-day backpack. It can be done in two days, but plan on three or four or even more to make the most of the trip. It's a glorious 20-plus miles of alpine hiking in "real Sound of Music country," as one of the park bulletin boards used to say.

Many Alaskans think of this as the Curry Ridge hike, but Curry is the next ridge to the south. Kesugi, 2,500 to 4,700 feet in elevation, is a big raised block of earth between the Chulitna and Susitna Rivers, thrust into the sky by the same faulting that produced the Alaska Range and Denali. Kesugi means "the ancient one" in the Dena'ina Athabaskan language, a fitting combination with the meaning of Denali, "the high one."

The hike is challenging. Besides the climb to the ridge, there are several ups and downs of hundreds of feet while on the ridge route. Above tree line, the hike is a marked route, sometimes a beaten path across the tundra and sometimes just a series of cairns to follow. Don't start without the topo maps. Trail brochures and overview maps can be found online at http://dnr.alaska.gov/parks/aktrails/explore/trailmapguide.htm, while topo maps are still your best bet.

Lousy weather, cold winds, and bad visibility are common. Try the traverse only if you are confident of your route-finding ability, your gear, and your ability to deal with alpine weather. Otherwise, sampling the high country on an out-and-back hike from either trailhead is a good option.

It's much faster and easier to tree line from Little Coal Creek than from Byers Lake. The Ermine Hill Trail, which descends from the Kesugi route to the Parks

A hiker climbs with views of Denali and the Alaska Range on the Kesugi Ridge Trail on a clear September day. The 27.5-mile trail connects the Little Coal Creek and Byers Lake trailheads.
HAGEPHOTO

On the Kesugi Ridge Trail, getting above treeline is relatively quick, with views of tundra covering the mountainsides in the high country. WILLIE DALTON

Denali, 20,310 feet, on a clear summer day as seen from Kesugi Ridge. Kesugi Ridge is a big raised block of earth between the Chulitna and Susitna Rivers, thrust into the sky by the same faulting that produced the Alaska Range and Denali. YNEZ SLAYMAKER

Highway at Mile 156.5, is a bad-weather bail-off trail about halfway along the hike, or an alternate access route to the ridge.

There are plenty of water sources along the trail to filter for drinking, with the exception of a 5-mile stretch, just north of the Ermine Hill Trail.

MILES AND DIRECTIONS

From Little Coal Creek		From Byers Lake
0.0	Begin/end at the trailhead.	27.5
3.0	The North Fork Birdhouse, about 3 miles in and 3,100 feet elevation, an expanse of rolling alpine tundra with sweeping views and great wildflowers. Camping here and hiking to the highest section of Kesugi Ridge (Indian Mountain, 4,558 feet; Kesugi Mountain, 4,750 feet) makes a challenging trip; a map posted at the North Fork crossing shows the easiest routes to the peaks. The ridge route stays lower, on a 3,000-foot bench below the higher peaks.	24.5
4.0	The trail's high point, about 3,500 feet.	23.5
7.5	North Fork Byers Creek crossing, about 2,900 feet.	20.0
8.0	Eight-Mile Divide, 2,950 feet, where the trail joins the Susitna/Chulitna River divide.	19.5
10.0	Stonehenge Hill, a high point littered with bedroom-size chunks of granite, at 3,300 feet. Ten-Mile Tarn is just to the west.	17.5
13.5	Junction with the Ermine Hill Trail, the bad-weather escape route, in a 2,250-foot saddle. It's about 3 miles to the Parks Highway.	14.0
15.0	A forested valley bottom, the low point of the ridge route at about 1,500 feet. The path here is brushy and steep. Make plenty of noise to dissuade bears.	12.5
17.5	Skinny Lake, 2,100 feet, in a narrow basin set among long, low granite ridges, protected enough to shelter a few spruce trees. The lake attracts many campers.	10.0
19.0	Point Golog, 2,970 feet, a rocky point with a panoramic view, completely encircled by alpine lakes and ponds.	8.5
22.0	Whimbrel Hill, 2,500 feet, a good birding spot. Swampy Whimbrel Lake is below to the east.	5.5
23.5	Mini-Skinny Lake, 2,700 feet. Good camping, and a good hike from Byers Lake.	4.0
24.0	Trail junction, about 2,500 feet. To the left, or south, is scenic Tarn Point (2,880 feet, about 0.8 mile) and the Troublesome Creek Trailhead (12 miles). (See information on the Troublesome Creek Trail below under "Other hikes.") Turn right (north) for the extremely steep trail down toward the Byers Lake Trailhead.	3.5
26.0	The Cascades, a foaming white-water drop of 100 feet in the creek that drains Whimbrel Lake.	1.5
27.5	End/begin at the Byers Lake Trailhead.	0.0

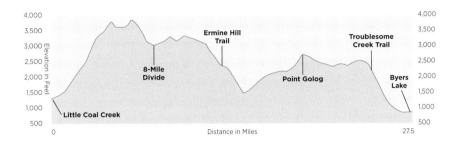

Other hikes: Hike between Little Coal Creek and the Upper Troublesome Creek Trailhead, Mile 137.6 of the Parks Highway, for a 37-mile traverse, or between Troublesome and Byers Lake, a 15-mile traverse. Troublesome-Byers is less of an alpine hike and therefore can be a marginal-weather substitute for Kesugi Ridge. The Upper Troublesome Creek Trail, though, is troublesome because bears typically feed on salmon in the creek from roughly mid-July to early September; be on your best bear-country behavior if you hike Troublesome. At the time of this writing, the trail is in great condition, but be aware that seasonal trail closures are always a possibility.

Shorter hikes: The hike from Little Coal Creek to tree line (about 2 miles one way) or to the North Fork Birdhouse (3 miles one way) samples the high country, and the Birdhouse make a good short backpack. Mini-Skinny Lake, 4 miles from the Byers Lake side, is a fine long day hike or overnighter.

For a much shorter hike, try the Chulitna Confluence Trail, 1.2 miles one way and easy, beginning at the Lower Troublesome Creek Trailhead, directly across from the Upper Troublesome Creek Trailhead at Parks Highway Mile 137.6.

TIDBIT

Lousy weather, cold winds, and bad visibility are common. Try the traverse only if you are confident of your route-finding ability, your gear, and your ability to deal with alpine weather. Otherwise, sampling the high country on an out-and-back hike from either trailhead is a good option.

A kayaker paddles Byers Lake with 20,310-foot tall Denali in the background, as viewed along the Byers Lake trail. The loop is a great trail for families and hikers of various abilities.
MOLLIE FOSTER

DENALI NATIONAL PARK AND PRESERVE

DENALI NATIONAL PARK AND PRESERVE is a 150-mile swath of parkland along the Alaska Range, between the Nenana River and the Kichatna Mountains. Spilling well over the range to the north, the park also includes major rivers—the Teklanika, Toklat, and Kantishna—that drain north into the Yukon River basin. The Outer Range in the northeast, the Kantishna Hills in the north-central, and a huge expanse of boreal forest in the northwest part of the park complete the geography. Altogether, the park/preserve covers about 6 million acres, the size of about three Yellowstone National Parks.

Denali the peak is the anchor of Denali the park; it is the tallest mountain in North America, at 20,310 feet. Relatively few people get to the top of the mountain, but many more sample the backcountry north of the peak, where hikers enjoy alpine mountains, swift rivers, wildflowers, and wildlife.

The park is accessible via the Parks Highway, 240 miles north of Anchorage and 120 miles south of Fairbanks. The 90-mile park road, which parallels the north side of the Alaska Range, gives hikers a rare degree of easy access to Alaska's mountain wilderness. Most Denali visitors travel at least part of the park road. Denali's road corridor is the most intensively visited and managed park area in the state.

There are few developed trails in the backcountry. A few shorter trails explore the front country near the park entrance and a few points along the road corridor, but most hiking in the park involves cross-country travel in the backcountry.

Introduce yourself to Denali by checking out the park website at www.nps.gov/dena, and by reading the park newspaper, Denali Alpenglow. The website describes hiking in the park, transportation into the park's interior, campgrounds and reservations, backcountry permits, and park fees.

The National Geographic map Denali National Park and Preserve is good for orientation, planning, and hiking the park entrance trails, but USGS topographic maps are necessary for backcountry hiking.

THE PARK INTERIOR

There are literally hundreds of cross-country hiking possibilities in the interior of the park, accessible either by day hiking or by backpacking. No guidebook can begin to do justice to all the places you can explore, and that approach would conflict with park policy; park managers do not recommend specific hikes, hoping that as a result, hikers will spread out over the landscape in small parties, leaving the land relatively unscarred for future visitors. What follows here, then, is a trip-planning guide for day hikers and backpackers who want to visit Denali's interior.

THE PARK ROAD

From approximately Memorial Day to mid-September, most access into the park past Savage River, Mile 15 on the park road, is by park bus, for a fee. There are shuttle buses for day visitors and camper buses for overnight visitors with campground reservations or backcountry camping permits. Check out the options on the website listed.

In April the park road is usually opened in stages, the schedule depending on the winter snowpack and spring weather. Until the shuttle buses begin running, some stretches of the road are open to private vehicles. Check with the park on conditions at the time—the road situation changes from day to day in April and early May. In mid-September the park opens the road to private vehicles by lottery; apply to the park in May for a September permit.

DAY HIKING FROM THE PARK ROAD

There are no permit requirements for day hikers, and there are several options for day hiking in the interior of the park. Either pick out a hike yourself from maps and information on the website or at the Backcountry Information Center, or join one of the Discovery Hikes. "Disco" hikes are daily, moderate to strenuous, ranger-led day hikes to different backcountry destinations. Register one to two days in advance; special shuttle buses for Disco hikers depart the Wilderness Access Center each morning. There is a significant fee for the bus ticket.

The park also usually offers guided walks in the park interior at the Eielson Visitor Center and on trails in the park entrance area.

Unguided day hikers can take a shuttle bus into the park, go hiking, and return to the park entrance area by bus later the same day. Alternatively, camp at one of the campgrounds on the park road, take a shuttle bus to your hike, and return to your campground by bus that evening. You can also bike the park road, camp in a campground, and take day hikes by catching a shuttle bus to and from the hike. Visit the Park's website on cycling for more details.

Backpacking in Denali's backcountry: This involves a slug of logistics at the park's Backcountry Information Center. Park managers have carved the backcountry into management units and established a permit system with quotas for overnight visitors, all part of the effort to keep the hordes of visitors from loving the park's fragile tundra to death.

Backpackers have to get in touch with the terrain in Denali's trailless backcountry, following streambeds and ridgelines, practicing route-finding skills, and crossing unbridged streams safely. For more information, see the introductory section, "Hiking in Alaska," or visit the park's Web page, www.nps.gov/dena, and choose the "Plan Your Visit" tab. Reading over the information on the backcountry page of the website is handy homework to do before you arrive at the park. The site includes a Backcountry Camping Guide, a map of the backcountry units, and a detailed list of considerations for trips into the backcountry.

When you're planning your trip from home, the best approach is to study several options and don't get your heart set on one favorite route; chances are you'll have to adjust your expectations when you get to the Backcountry Desk and apply for your permit, which you have to do in person.

GETTING A BACKCOUNTRY PERMIT

Head for the Backcountry Information Center to get started; the park estimates it will take about an hour to go through the process and walk away with your permit. You plan your own trip, using the information at the desk and advice from staff. NPS issues permits in person only, with no advance reservations. You can buy USGS topo maps for your hike at the Backcountry Information Center.

The steps for getting a permit are as follows:

1. Plan your itinerary. Check the quota board to see which units are open. Then, to choose among them, look over the unit descriptions and the topographic maps that show the unit topography and boundaries. For a multiday trip, you may have to change units during your hike, so check out the units adjacent to your top choices too.
2. Watch a video about visiting Denali's backcountry.
3. Attend a safety talk, where you will receive your permit and the park-provided bear-resistant food container(s) that are required for your trip.
4. Copy the backcountry unit boundaries and any closure areas near where you'll be hiking onto your topo maps.
5. Buy a ticket for the camper bus in the Wilderness Access Center and get ready to go.

You might be a bit frazzled by your permit experience, but persevere; there's some great backcountry out there once you actually make it into the park.

51. **TRIPLE LAKES TRAIL**

WHY GO?

This trail travels by forest, creeks, and lakes, and climbs into subalpine with panoramic views of the river valleys below.

THE RUNDOWN

Distances: 9 miles one way. (plus 0.5 mile on connecting trail to Denali Visitor Center)

Special features: Lakes, creeks, forest, ridge walking in subalpine with panoramic views

Location: Trail leads from Denali Visitor Center near park entrance

Difficulty: Strenuous

Trail type: Developed

Total elevation gain: 1,100 feet

Best season: May through mid-Sept

Fees/permits: National park entrance fee, or National Parks Pass

Maps: USGS Healy C-4; Denali National Park and Preserve *Alpenglow*; National Geographic *Denali National Park and Preserve*

Contact: Denali National Park and Preserve, PO Box 9, Denali Park, AK 99755; (907) 683-9532; www.nps.gov/dena

---

FINDING THE TRAILHEAD

The main access is at the Denali Visitor Center, Mile 1.5 of the Denali Park Road, via 0.5 mile of the McKinley Station Trail to the northern trailhead. The south trailhead leads from a limited parking area on the north side of the Nenana River Bridge, approximately Mile 231.5 of the George Parks Highway.

WHAT TO SEE

Triple Lakes Trail connects boreal forest to subalpine lakes, climbing to ridgeline with views of the glacially-carved river valleys and mountain ranges to the east and west. The trail leads directly to the first lake (the lake names are in order from south to north), with options to hike down for the second and third lakes, or continue on the main trail. This 9-mile thru-hike has two trailhead options, starting from the main Denali Visitor Center, or the southern trailhead off the George Parks Highway.

The trail is an easily accessible, maintained trail with gorgeous views, fishing, and opportunities for viewing wildlife. This trail has options for all hiking abilities, most hikers can walk the first few miles of the trail for an out-and-back hike from either end, or for those looking for a bigger challenge, can traverse the entire 9 miles.

The northern route beginning from the visitor center, is a mellow approach with bridge crossings and winding through boreal forest before climbing the switchback sections of the trail a few hundred feet in elevation. From the Denali visitor center, begin with the McKinley Station Trail for about 0.5 mile, until the trailhead begins, before crossing Hines Creek. Cross the bridge, and continue on the trail intersecting with a suspension bridge over Riley Creek. From here the trail winds through the boreal forest, a carpet of mosses and lichen cover the forest floor, as the trail skirts next to the glacially-fed creek. After a few miles, the trail climbs uphill through switchbacks and at the top, views of the Yanert River Valley to the east and Riley Creek Valley to the west, Mount Fellows (an old volcanic core), and additional peaks standing higher than 10,000 feet in the Eastern Alaska Range.

The southern trailhead begins from the shoulder of the highway at Mile 231.5, just north of the Nenana River Bridge on the west side of the road, there's a small parking area leading to the marked trail. The trail immediately climbs through the forest, crossing the railroad tracks and continuing uphill to gorgeous vistas to the south of the Nenana River.

The trail leads uphill winding through boreal forest to a railroad crossing (be sure to look both ways, it is active). Switchbacks continue and at the top, a breathtaking view of the Nenana River Valley to the south, and Yanert River Valley to the southeast. This trail is one of the first areas where the spring pasque flowers grow after the snow melts. Later in summer, wildflowers of all shapes, colors, and sizes can be viewed along the trail. After 1.2 miles, the trail leads to the eastern shore of the first lake, beavers have been known to frequent the area. The trail winds through forest and within a mile there's a fork in the trail, with an option to hike downhill to the second lake, or continue on the main trail above.

Triple Lakes Trail is a favorite among locals, and for a good reason: a diverse range of terrain, on a maintained trail with gorgeous vistas. The trail offers many perks in the summer months, wildflowers dot the trail: pasque, bluebells, fireweed, prickly rose, jacob's ladder, raspberries, and blueberries in the alpine. The lakes are prime habitat for wildlife: beavers frequent the area, moose feed on the grasses underwater, and waterfowl and swans can be viewed along the trail. Fishing for arctic grayling in the lakes is also popular. If a day trip isn't long enough, backcountry camping is an option here too.

The first lake, about 1.2 miles fro
the south trailhead, with a glass
reflection of the fall foliage on th
surrounding mountai
MOLLIE FOSTE

A view of the Yanert River
Valley from the Triple Lakes
Trail, a 9-mile thru-hike from
the Denali Visitor Center to the
Parks Highway.
MOLLIE FOSTER

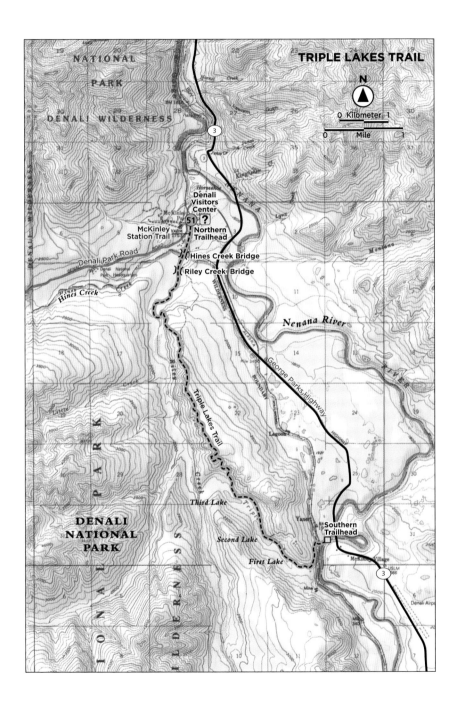

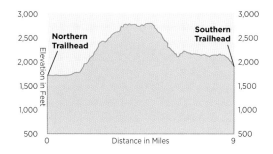

MILES AND DIRECTIONS

Denali Visitor Center		George Parks Highway
0.0	Northern trailhead	9.0
1.7	Switchbacks begin	7.3
2.5	Trail leads to alpine	6.5
4.0	Trail travels below treeline	5.0
4.6	View of 2 lakes	4.4
5.5	Spur trail leading to third lake	3.5
7.2	Split to second lake	1.8
7.8	Trail travels by the first lake	1.2
9.0	Southern trailhead	0.0

Shorter hikes: The Oxbow Trail is across the highway from the southern trailhead for Triple Lakes. The maintained trail is flat, with rooty sections along the designated route. The Oxbow Trail is a 1.6-mile loop through the boreal forest with beautiful views of the Nenana River.

TIDBIT

If hiking the 9-mile hike-through traverse, there's a shuttle from the Denali Visitor Center to The Village (in either direction), to make it a round trip.

52. **MOUNT HEALY TRAIL**

WHY GO?

A trail winding through forest and climbing into subalpine with access to ridgetop hiking, and potential views of Denali.

THE RUNDOWN

Distances: 2.7 miles one way

Special features: Spruce forest, subalpine, panoramic views of surrounding peaks

Location: Trail leads from Denali Visitor Center near park entrance

Difficulty: Strenuous

Trail type: Lower trail developed, a route beyond

Total elevation gain: 1,700 feet

Best season: June through mid-Sept

Fees/permits: National park entrance fee, or National Parks Pass

Maps: USGS Healy C-4; Denali National Park and Preserve *Alpenglow*; National Geographic *Denali National Park and Preserve*

Contact: Denali National Park and Preserve, PO Box 9, Denali Park, AK 99755; (907) 683-9532; www.nps.gov/dena

FINDING THE TRAILHEAD

Park at the Denali National Park Visitor Center, at Mile 1.5 of the Denali Park Road. Start walking from the visitor center via the Taiga Trail 0.5 mile to the official Mount Healy Trailhead.

WHAT TO SEE

The hike up Mount Healy, the ridge overlooking the entrance to Denali National Park, provides access to ridgeline hiking on one of the steepest designated hiking trails near the border of the national park. At the overlook, hikers are rewarded with sweeping panoramic views of the Alaska Range, the Yanert River Valley to the east, and the entrance area in the valley below.

Hikers use the Mount Healy Overlook Trail as an accessible path to ridgeline hiking, with endless options at the top for experienced adventurers. The overlook is exposed, and typically windy, so bring appropriate gear, even if it's warm at the trailhead.

To begin the hike from the Denali Visitor Center, connect first with the Taiga Trail, a flat, gravel path. After crossing a bridge over a small creek, about 0.5 mile from the visitor center, is the junction, and trailhead for Mount Healy Overlook Trail. Follow the sign, and turn left (west) to follow the maintained hard-packed trail. From here, the trail continues at a gradual grade, through tall deciduous vegetation with Mount Healy straight ahead. About 1 mile past the junction on the left, are two benches, and a nice resting point, or turnaround point, with a beautiful views of mountains in the Alaska Range.

Soon after the bench spot, the route starts to switchback, and continues to climb at a steeper grade as it winds along the mountainside. As the trail curves uphill, be sure to keep your head up, and look for views at the switchbacks of the expansive valley and mountain peaks. The hard-packed gravel path continues uphill, with stone steps intermittent along the trail. As you gain views of face of the mountain, and the open valley to the south, the overlook point is just ahead. Cresting the ridge, take in beautiful views of the expansive valleys and jagged peaks of the Alaska Range and the entrance to the 6-million-acre park.

From here, experienced hikers may want to continue along the ridgeline, with the true summit of Mount Healy, an additional 1,500 feet of climbing.

As the Mount Healy Trail wir
uphill, keep your head up, and lc
for views of the expansive valley a
mountain pea
MOLLIE FOST

The view from the 3,500-foot overlook along Mount Healy Trail. Hikers are rewarded with sweeping panoramic views of the Alaska Range, the Yanert River Valley to the east, and the entrance area in the valley below.
MOLLIE FOSTER

Hikers use the Mount Healy Overlook Trail as an accessible path to ridgeline hiking, with endless options at the top for experienced adventurers. This is the only entrance area trail in the national park with opportunities to view 20,310-feet tall Denali.
MOLLIE FOSTER

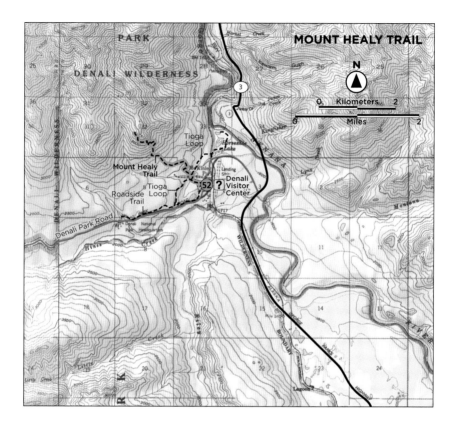

TIDBIT

Stick to the trail on the switchbacks, and avoid the temptation to take the shortcut, as it leads to erosion on the trail.

53. **SAVAGE RIVER VALLEY**

WHY GO?

Two trail options, providing routes for all hiking abilities in a gorgeous river valley.

THE RUNDOWN

Distances: Savage River Loop: 2-mile loop. Savage Alpine Trail: 4 miles one way

Special features: Wide, braided river valley, alpine terrain

Location: 15 miles into Denali National Park

Difficulty: Easy to Strenuous

Trail type: Developed

Total elevation gain: Savage River Loop: Negligible. Savage Alpine Trail: 1,500 feet

Best season: June to mid-Sept

Fees/permits: National park entrance fee, or National Parks Pass

Maps: USGS Healy C-5; Denali National Park and Preserve *Alpenglow*; National Geographic *Denali National Park and Preserve*

Contact: Denali National Park and Preserve, PO Box 9, Denali Park, AK 99755; (907) 683-9532; www.nps.gov/dena

FINDING THE TRAILHEAD

Both trails are about 15 miles into Denali National Park.

Savage River Loop. Take the courtesy shuttle from the entrance area stops, the main access points via the Wilderness Access Center or Denali Visitor Center, to Savage River area trailheads. Another option is to drive a private vehicle to Mile 15 to the limited parking area, and the turnaround point for all private vehicles on the road. Savage River Loop trailheads are on both sides of the Savage River.

Savage Alpine Trail. The western trailhead access is behind the parking area on the east side of the river at Mile 15. The eastern trailhead is at Mile 12.8 near Savage River Campground, park at the Mountain Vista day use area, which typically has more open parking than the Mile 15 trailhead. The trailhead is on the opposite side (north) of the Park Road from the parking area.

WHAT TO SEE

Savage River Loop and Savage Alpine Trail are accessible trails in the expansive Savage River Valley, about 15 miles into Denali National Park. Savage River Loop is a shorter, two-mile loop, and Savage Alpine Trail is a 4-mile, one-way thru-hike route.

**SAVAGE ALPINE TRAIL/
SAVAGE RIVER LOOP**

Both trails have similar views to the south, but from different vantage points. It's possible to connect the two trails, for about a total of 6 miles, traveling in either direction, with courtesy shuttle transportation to make a round trip.

Savage River Loop. The 2-mile loop trail begins on either side of the Savage River, with a bridge over the river, a common turnaround point, about 1 mile from the trailhead. The trail is a wide gravel path to start, and transitions to a hard-packed dirt trail later on. The trail is popular and well traveled, so expect to pass by other hikers, especially on a day with nice weather.

The 2-mile loop sticks close to the Savage River for a majority of the trail, with a few areas where it rises a few dozen feet above the level of the water. From the trail, enjoy the river scene, while taking in the view of the Savage River Valley (in both directions) and scan Mount Margaret (to the west) for Dall sheep.

Hiking off trail is permitted, however it is best for experienced hikers, as the canyon is steep, and can be easy to lose your footing on a backcountry route. It is best to travel within your hiking ability.

A hiker takes in the view at a ridge on the Savage Alpine Trail, a 4-mile thru-hike trail near Savage River, 15 miles into Denali National Park.
MOLLIE FOSTER

A view to the north of Savage River, the area has two trail options, a 2-mile loop or a 4-mile thru-hike route into alpine, 15 miles into Denali National Park.
MOLLIE FOSTER

Savage Alpine Trail. This 4-mile trail, has two trailheads, one behind the parking area at Savage River, on the east side of the river, and the other near Savage River Campground, about Mile 13 of the Denali Park Road. The more common route direction is from the Savage River Campground (park at the Mountain Vista day use area) to Savage River, where hikers can use the courtesy shuttle back to their vehicles, or the park entrance.

From the Mile 13 trailhead, the wide gravel path stays parallel to a small creek for a little more than a mile. From this side, the trail climbs gradually, and almost to the halfway point, the route switchbacks as the grade increases. The trail continues above treeline, with sweeping panoramic views of the Savage River Valley, and 20,310-feet tall Denali, weather permitting. Scan the mountainside for Dall sheep and other wildlife, always being alert and keeping a safe distance from any encounters. Closer to the west trailhead, the trail starts to descend into the Savage River Valley, with picturesque views as the route travels down to the parking area. If you parked your car at Savage River Campground, catch a courtesy shuttle or walk, about 2 miles to the east and the parking area.

TIDBIT

Take the courtesy Savage River shuttle, which typically run on the hour in one direction, as there is limited parking at the trailheads. Check the up-to-date shuttle bus schedule, before heading out on the trail.

FAIRBANKS

FAIRBANKS, ALASKA'S LARGEST INTERIOR city, is better known for rivers and winter trails than for summer hiking. The best backcountry hiking in the region is in the Chena River State Recreation Area to the east (Granite Tors, Angel Rocks, and Chena Dome) and on the rolling bareback ridges of the Steese National Conservation Area and White Mountains National Recreation Area north of town (off the Steese and Elliott Highways, Pinnell Mountain and Summit Trail).

54. CREAMER'S FIELD

WHY GO?

One of the top areas in the north for viewing migrating birds, with walking trails suitable for all activity levels.

THE RUNDOWN

Distances: Seasonal Wetland Trail: 0.7 mile one way. Boreal Forest Trail: a 2-mile loop. Farm Road Trail: 0.8 mile one way

Special features: Birding, interpretive trails, guided walks, a visitor center, and a piece of Fairbanks history

Location: On College Road in Fairbanks

Difficulty: Easy

Trail type: Seasonal Wetland Trail: accessible. Boreal Forest and Farm Road Trails: more-developed

Total elevation gain: Essentially none

Best season: Mid-Apr through Sep

Fees/permits: None

Maps: Trail maps are available at the trailhead kiosk and the Farmhouse Visitor Center

Contact: Creamer's Field Refuge, Alaska Department of Fish and Game, 1300 College Rd., Fairbanks, AK 99701; (907) 459-7307; www.creamersfield.org/

FINDING THE TRAILHEAD

Creamer's Field is located at 1300 College Road in Fairbanks, about halfway between University Avenue and the Steese Highway, just east of the Tanana Valley Fairgrounds. From University Avenue and College Road, drive east on College Road about 2 miles, past the Fairgrounds, to the traffic light at Danby Street. Turn left (north) and follow the road around the Alaska Fish and Game regional headquarters to the refuge.

From the Steese, drive to College Road, turn west and continue about 1.6 miles to the access road to Creamer's, which from this direction is about 0.1 mile east of the traffic light at Danby Street.

Creamer's is on the city's Red Line bus route.

WHAT TO SEE

Creamer's Field offers short hikes in the heart of Fairbanks, good migratory-bird viewing in spring and fall, and a chance to explore a sample of the forests and wetlands of Interior Alaska. Creamer's is a historic dairy that operated until 1966 (see sidebar below). The Creamer's buildings are on the National Register of Historic

Places, and the old farmhouse has been renovated as the refuge's visitor center. The center is open from June 1 to September 1; naturalists lead walks on the trails several times a week in season. Pick up a trail guide and checklists at the center, and don't forget your binoculars. The center and the Seasonal Wetland Trail are wheelchair accessible.

A local nonprofit group, the Friends of Creamer's Refuge (907-452-5162), co-operates with the Alaska Department of Fish and Game on education programs on the refuge, such as staffing the visitor center, leading nature walks, and organizing special events.

In spring and fall Creamer's attracts great flocks of migratory birds such as geese, ducks, cranes, and plovers, which stop to rest and feed here on their long journeys between their summer and winter grounds. Some of the birds, including a large group of young sandhill cranes, remain on the refuge all summer. The first of the migratory birds, usually Canada geese, arrive in mid-April. The height of the north-ward spring migration is from mid-April to mid-May, and mid-August to mid-September is the height of the fall migration to the south. There are sometimes as many as 2,000 cranes and 2,000 geese resting and eating at Creamer's.

Pets are allowed only on leashes or under voice control. To avoid disturbing nest-ing and resting birds, please don't wander off the trails into the fields.

A sandhill crane dances to attract attention at Creamer's Field in Fairbanks.
ALEXANDER LEE

The Creamer's buildings are on the National Register of Historic Places, and the old farmhouse has been renovated as the refuge's visitor center. The center is open from June 1 to September 1.
ALEXANDER LEE

THE CREAMER FAMILY'S DAIRY

The dairy history of Creamer's Field goes back to Alaska's Gold-Rush era. Just after the turn of the twentieth century, a couple named Belle and Charles Hinckley took a sternwheeler up the Yukon and Tanana Rivers to the new town of Fairbanks with three cows and an idea: starting a dairy on the gold-rush frontier. On the way up the river, they made friends with Charlie and Anna Creamer, another couple on their way to Fairbanks. Years later, in 1928, the Creamers took over the Hinckley dairy—with a name like Creamer (pronounced like it's spelled), what could have been more natural? Dairying in the subarctic had its challenges, like feeding the cows over the long winter (answer: grow three tons of hay and grain per cow) and keeping the milk from freezing in the delivery truck (a woodstove did the trick).

The natural meadows next to the dairy had apparently always attracted migrating birds, but when the Creamers turned the meadows into grain fields and pasture, the birds probably couldn't believe their luck. In spring and fall they could take a break from migrating and eat their fill of the leftover oats and barley in the fields. The return of the geese to Creamer's has marked the coming of spring in Fairbanks for many years, and when the dairy folded in 1966, the community pitched in to help the Alaska Department of Fish and Game buy the fields to protect them as bird habitat.

And how do the birds fare now that the cows and the Creamers are gone? Refuge staff and volunteers grow and spread barley for them, farmed more or less organically, and recently built a large pond to attract more birds into the fields. The birds still seem to like it at Creamer's.

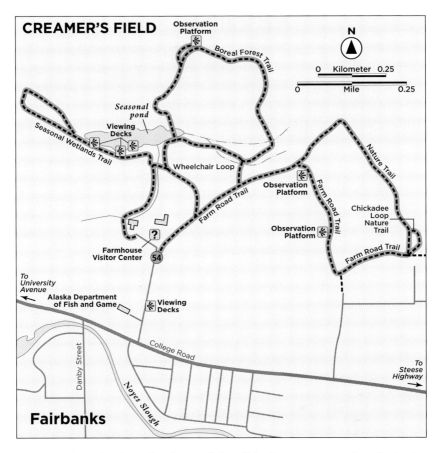

Seasonal Wetland Trail. This graded trail leads to a group of small viewing decks overlooking a seasonal wetland. Interpretive panels focus on the wetland and its seasonal wildlife.

Boreal Forest Trail. This trail, a 2-mile loop that splits off from the Seasonal Wetland Trail about 0.2 mile from the visitor center, meanders through a lowland forest typical of Alaska's Interior, with white and black spruce, tamarack, paper birch, balsam poplar, aspen, and some tree-size willows. A short side trail leads to a viewing tower overlooking a section of the refuge.

Farm Road Trail. The Farm Road Trail, no surprise, is a dirt road that winds through fields and patches of forest; look and listen for migratory waterfowl.

TIDBIT

The first of the migratory birds, usually Canada geese, arrive in mid-April. The height of the northward spring migration is from mid-April to mid-May, and mid-August to mid-September is the height of the fall migration to the south.

55. GRANITE TORS

WHY GO?

A 15-mile, or 2-mile loop trail, with access to massive tors in the alpine with vistas of the Alaska Range and Chena River Valley.

THE RUNDOWN

Distance: A 15-mile, or 2-mile loop

Special features: Great views, scenic granite outcrops, a rock-climbing area for experienced climbers, and a trail shelter. Limited water on the trail

Location: 45 miles east of Fairbanks in the Chena River State Recreation Area

Difficulty: Strenuous

Trail type: More developed at lower elevations; less developed in the high country

Total elevation gain: About 2,700 feet

Best season: June through Sept

Fees/permits: Parking fee or state parks pass

Maps: USGS Big Delta D-5; Alaska State Parks leaflet *Granite Tors Trail*

Contact: Alaska State Parks, Northern Area, 3700 Airport Way, Fairbanks, AK 99709; (907) 451-2695; http://dnr.alaska.gov/parks/

FINDING THE TRAILHEAD

From Airport Way and the Steese Highway in Fairbanks, drive about 5 miles north on the Steese to Chena Hot Springs Road. Turn east and drive 39 miles to the Tors Trail Campground. Turn left into the campground and park in the day-use area by the river. Walk along the gravel path to the south, past the bulletin board, back out to the main road, and cross the bridge over the river to the west. Cross the Chena Road cautiously to the trailhead on the south side of the road.

WHAT TO SEE

The Granite Tors are granite towers, pinnacles, and slabs that crown Munson Ridge, the alpine ridge at the head of Rock Creek, southwest of the Chena River. (A tor is a large, isolated outcrop of rock.) Tors formed millions of years ago when molten rock pushed upward and cooled before it reached the earth's surface. The surrounding earth slowly eroded, exposing the less erodible rock pinnacles. There are scattered tors west of the Plain of Monuments, including the Lizard's Eye, a tor with a round, eyelike opening near the top.

The trail, which loops completely around the Rock Creek drainage, is a rare breed in Alaska: a loop trail that returns exactly to its starting point. The east and west forks of the trail divide about 0.3 mile from the trailhead. For hikers looking for a shorter outing, there's a 2-mile loop option, see map. There is a primitive, emergency trail shelter (no reservation, no fee, first-come, first-served) at the eastern edge of the alpine area on the hike, about 7 miles from the trailhead on the East Trail. The trail is open to foot traffic only.

If you're walking the entire loop, the East Trail is the better place to start. There is one very steep section of the trail a mile below the Lizard's Eye, and it's downhill if you start from the east. About 5 miles of the trail is alpine, marked with rock cairns and wooden tripods. Watch the weather; it can change from sunny, T-shirt-and-shorts weather to cold, blowing rain and fog quickly, making the route across the high country somewhat difficult to follow. The tors invite exploring, but they can be dangerous climbing for inexperienced and unequipped parties, so stay within the limits of your skills and experience.

If you don't want to hike the entire loop, you have plenty of options. Knob 2,211 has a good view of the alpine ridge and the distant tors; it's a 4-mile one-way hike on the East Trail. The North Tors are 6 miles one way via the East Trail, and the Lizard's Eye is 5 miles one way via the West Trail. For a shorter walk, head a mile or so up either fork of the trail. The East Trail crosses Rock Creek and threads through lush spruce/birch forest, passing the edge of a beaver pond. The West Trail runs along a continuous boardwalk through black spruce wetlands before it begins climbing.

Hiking near one of the massive tors, along the 15-mile Granite Tors Trail.
JUSTIN WHOLEY

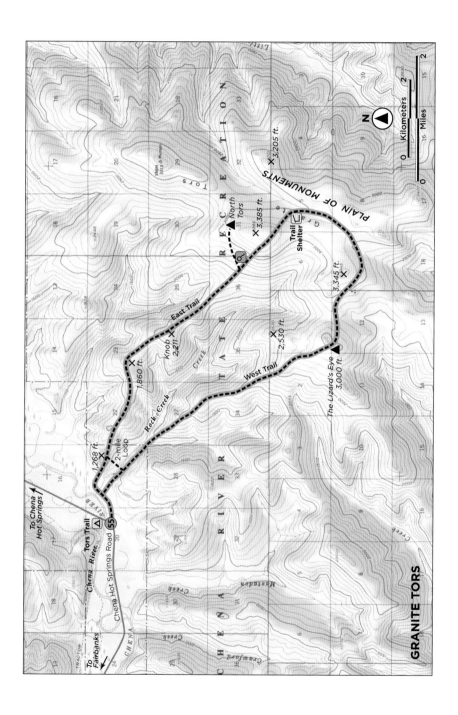

GRANITE TORS

The Plain of Monuments is a short trek off the Granite Tors Trail. The tors are granite towers, pinnacles, and slabs that crown Munson Ridge, the alpine ridge at the head of Rock Creek, southwest of the Chena River.
JUSTIN WHOLEY

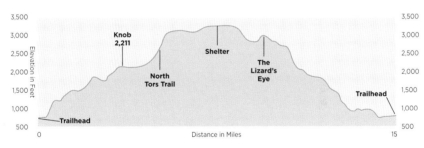

MILES AND DIRECTIONS

Starting East of Rock Creek		Starting West of Rock Creek
0.0	Begin/end at the trailhead.	15.0
4.0	Take in the view from Knob 2,211.	11.0
7.0	Arrive at the trail shelter on the eastern edge of the alpine area.	8.0
8.0	Reach the Plain of Monuments.	7.0
10.0	Hike to The Lizard's Eye.	5.0
15.0	Return to/begin at the trailhead.	0.0

56. ANGEL ROCKS

WHY GO?

A trail winding through aspen, spruce, and granite outcrops, with options for a longer traverse to Chena Hot Springs.

THE RUNDOWN

Distance: Angel Rocks: 1.7 miles one way or a 4-mile loop. Angel Rocks–Chena Hot Springs traverse: 8.3 miles

Special features: Angel Rocks: granite outcrops, good views, and rock climbing for experienced climbers. Traverse: an alpine ridge run and a trail shelter

Location: 55 miles east of Fairbanks in the Chena River State Recreation Area

Difficulty: Angel Rocks: moderate. Traverse: strenuous

Trail type: More developed lower on the Angel Rocks Trail and Chena Hot Springs trails; less developed near Angel Rocks; a route across the alpine tops

Total elevation gain: Angel Rocks: 750 feet. Traverse: about 2,000 feet

Best season: June through Sept

Fees/permits: Angel Rocks Trailhead: parking fee or state parks pass

Maps: USGS Circle A-5, Alaska State Parks leaflet *Angel Rocks Trail*, and the *Chena Hot Springs Trail* leaflet

Contact: Alaska State Parks, Northern Area, 3700 Airport Way, Fairbanks, AK 99709; (907) 451-2695; http://dnr.alaska.gov/parks/

FINDING THE TRAILHEAD

From Airport Way and the Steese Highway in Fairbanks, drive about 5 miles north on the Steese to Chena Hot Springs Road. Turn east and drive just short of 49 miles to the Angel Rocks Trailhead on the right, just before the Mile 49 bridge over the Chena River. Chena Hot Springs, the other end of the traverse, is at the end of the Chena Road, 7.5 miles beyond the Angel Rocks Trailhead.

WHAT TO SEE

The granite Angel Rocks shoot up out of the forest on the hillside above the Chena River, offering plenty of cracks and crevices to explore and good views to enjoy. The area around the rocks is a pleasant scene of granite, aspen, and spruce.

It's a steep, somewhat rough trail, but this is a much easier hike to see a tor landscape than the hike to the Granite Tors. Keep an eye on the kids, though; there are some steep drops here, and the trail that loops through the rocks and back down to the river is steep and rough.

For a longer hike, try the traverse to Chena Hot Springs across the 2,800-foot alpine ridge east of Angel Rocks. You'll need to shuttle a car or bicycle to the hot springs or arrange for a ride back to the trailhead. Between Angel Rocks and the Chena Hot Springs trails, the route is unimproved except for scattered rock cairns that mark the way. Be sure to take a topographic map, compass, warm clothes, and rain gear, and be prepared to turn back if bad weather moves in and the visibility deteriorates.

The Angel Rocks Trail is open to foot traffic only, and open fires are prohibited.

Angel Rocks: The trail first parallels the North Fork of the Chena, and then forks right and begins to climb, reaching a small outcrop with a view of the granite towers in about a mile. The path skirts several of the rocks, with side trails leading to good views. (Be careful of the exposure, and don't try climbing unless you're equipped and experienced.)

A dramatic tor on the Angel Rocks Trail. A tor is a large, isolated outcrop of rock.
JUSTIN WHOLEY

The trail levels off and splits behind the rocks, at about 1,750 feet in elevation. Take a left to explore the upper rocks. The right fork leads up to one more granite tower, to the ridge above, and, eventually, to Chena Hot Springs. For the shortest return to the trailhead, explore around the rocks and then retrace your steps from the trail junction back down the hill.

Alternatively, follow the left fork through the rocks and continue steeply down to the valley bottom. Then turn south along a small slough and follow it back to the main trail. Taking the left fork adds about 0.5 mile to the hike.

Angel Rocks–Chena Hot Springs: From the trail junction behind Angel Rocks, follow the trail up the ridge to the last granite tower. Above the tower the trail becomes rougher. Cairns lead into a forested saddle, at which point the route of travel changes from southeast to east. Follow this rough route and some cairns across the saddle and up to the 2,800-foot summit, the high point of the hike. The route continues east along this alpine ridge crest; savor the views of the Alaska Range and the nearby peaks of the Tanana Hills if it's a clear day. Look east to Far Mountain, at 4,694 feet the highest peak in the area, and west to Chena Dome, at 4,421 feet.

A bit over a mile from the first point on the alpine ridge, at the last rocky alpine bump, the route turns northeast through brush and small trees toward Point 2,644. After a few more bumps, the route drops into a forested saddle at 2,450 feet in elevation and picks up the Overlook Trail from Chena Hot Springs. The trail shelter (no reservation, no fee, first-come, first-served) is in the saddle, about 100 feet to the right (east) of the trail. If the snow is gone, the only nearby water is an intermittent spring about 0.4 mile north on the trail.

Continue down the Overlook Trail, meeting the primitive trail to Bear Paw Butte at 6.7 miles. Stay right at the Bear Paw junction for the shortest way to the hot springs. At about 7.5 miles, take a left onto the Hillside Cutoff. (The main trail may be wet below, and the cutoff is higher and drier.) At about 8.1 miles the cutoff trail dead-ends into a dirt road. Take the road to the right, about 0.2 mile to the bottom of the hill and onto the resort grounds.

Welcome to Chena Hot Springs (www.chenahotsprings.com; 907-451-8104 or 800-478-4681). Break out the swimsuit and head for the spring-fed hot pool, tubs, and spas. Besides the usual lodge amenities, including rooms, meals, and a bar, there is a three-dimensional relief model inside that shows the route you've just hiked.

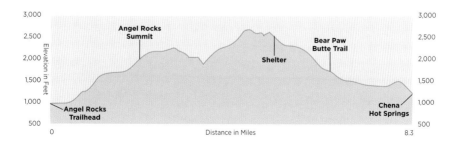

MILES AND DIRECTIONS

0.0   Begin at the Angel Rocks Trailhead.

1.7   Reach the Angel Rocks summit.

3.5   Pass the traverse's high point at 2,800 feet elevation.

5.0   Reach the trail shelter in the saddle below the ridge crest.

6.7   Intersect the Bear Paw Butte Trail.

8.3   Reach Chena Hot Springs.

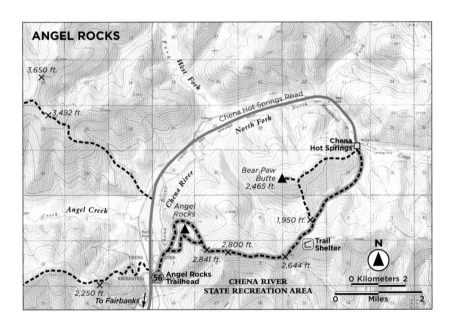

Shorter hikes: Besides the hike to Angel Rocks, Chena Hot Springs has an easy trail system for short walks. Stay on the higher trails like the Hillside Cutoff, the Ridge Trail, and the Overlook Trail; the lower trails in the Spring Creek valley are cross-country ski trails and can be very wet and muddy in summer.

57. CHENA DOME

WHY GO?

A strenuous trail into alpine country, with wildflowers, berries, and spectacular views in Chena River State Recreation Area.

THE RUNDOWN

Distance: A 30-mile loop

Special features: Alpine rambling, great views, and wildflowers

Location: 55 miles east of Fairbanks in the Chena River State Recreation Area

Difficulty: Very strenuous

Trail type: An alpine route with occasional cairns

Total elevation gain: About 8,300 feet

Best season: June through Sept, water availability is best in June

Fees/permits: None

Maps: USGS Circle A-5 and A-6, Big Delta D-5 (route not shown); Alaska State Parks leaflet *Chena Dome Trail*

Contact: Alaska State Parks, Northern Area, 3700 Airport Way, Fairbanks, AK 99709; (907) 451-2695; http://dnr.alaska.gov/parks/

FINDING THE TRAILHEAD

From Airport Way and the Steese Highway in Fairbanks, drive about 5 miles north on the Steese to Chena Hot Springs Road and turn east. Continue about 49 miles to the south trailhead and 50.5 miles to the north trailhead. Both trailheads are on the left (west) side of the road, beyond (north of) the Angel Rocks Trailhead and the Mile 49 bridge over the Chena River.

The park recommends starting the hike from the north trailhead, at Mile 50.5, and this guidebook agrees 100 percent.

WHAT TO SEE

A hike for true animals, the Chena Dome Trail loops around the Angel Creek watershed on an alpine ridgeline with views that go on forever. About 3 miles of developed trail lead to the ridgeline from either trailhead, and from there the hike is an alpine route marked with rock cairns and mileage posts. To follow this route, especially in inclement weather with low visibility, map-reading and route-finding skills are essential.

June and July are the flower months on this hike; August is the berry month. Look for migratory birds like plovers and surfbirds nesting on the tundra, and for resident ptarmigan. Stay alert for bears, especially in the wooded saddles where visibility is limited. The trail is open to bicycling and horseback riding but isn't really suitable for either beyond tree line. Open fires are prohibited; there isn't much wood anyway.

If you start from the north trailhead, you will spread out the total amount of climbing (a whopping 8,300 feet) more evenly over the whole hike. Hiking the south side involves an incredible amount of climbing and dipping between peaks and saddles, and starting there means doing most of the climbing in the first half of the hike, when your pack is heaviest.

The route is very steep in places and, especially on the south side, somewhat difficult to follow in spots. A topo map, the state parks leaflet, and a compass are required gear. Carry a good tent, decent rain gear, warm clothes, and extra food; if the weather turns, it can be very nasty on the exposed ridge.

Water is scarce in the high country, so the best advice is to carry as much as possible and replenish at every opportunity. Many of the low saddles on the hike hold water in small tundra ponds either early in the summer or after heavy rain. The most reliable water appears to be snowbanks and pools about Mile 12 and tundra ponds and a gully that may hold snow just past Mile 20. Taking the hike before the summer solstice is probably the best advice for finding ample water. There is a trail shelter at Mile 17 (no reservation, no fee, first-come, first-served), but there is no reliable water nearby.

A hiker takes a break as the route enters alpine terrain on the Chena Dome Trail.
JUSTIN WHOLEY

A mile marker on the 30-mile Chena Dome loop, traversing alpine ridges around the Angel Creek watershed. ALASKA STATE PARKS

Other possible hikes from the north trailhead: Point 3,700. A long, out-and-back day hike to the 3,700-foot ridge with the first panoramic view of the route and the Angel Creek drainage, 4.5 miles one way with 2,700 feet of climbing.

Chena Dome: An out-and-back killer day hike or overnight to Chena Dome, 10 miles one way, with limited water. It takes 5,000 feet of climbing to get there, but the ridge walking is superb.

Shorter hikes: From the north trailhead, hike 1 mile one way to the first viewpoint or 3 miles one way to the rocky viewpoint at tree line.

> **TIDBIT**
>
> Start your hike from the north trailhead, so climbing the 8,300 feet in elevation gain is spread out more evenly over the whole hike. Carry as much water as possible, and refill at every chance, as there are not many sources, especially in a dry year.

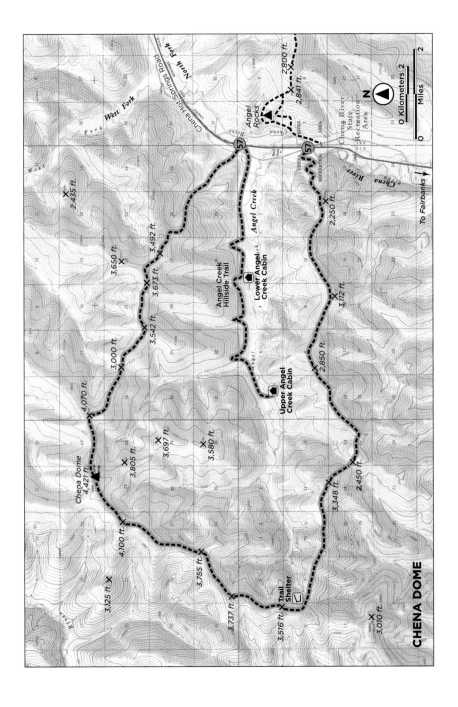

CHENA DOME

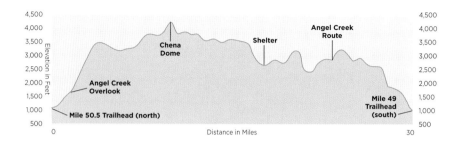

MILES AND DIRECTIONS

0.0   Start hike at the Mile 50.5 trailhead to hike counterclockwise.

1.0   Angel Creek valley viewpoint.

3.0   A rock outcrop with a fine view at tree line.

4.5   The ridgeline at 3,700 feet; views of the entire route open up, with Chena Dome straight ahead.

7.0   A low saddle, possible water in small pools.

8.5   Wreckage from a military plane crash in the 1950s, a possible spring below.

10.0 Chena Dome, 4,421 feet, the hike's high point, with a radio relay station on top. Look south to the Alaska Range and northwest to the White Mountains; all around are the Tanana Hills. After the route drops off the peak, ridge-rambling heaven begins—for the next 6 miles, it's a nearly flat ridge run.

17.0 The trail shelter, located in a wooded, 2,750-foot saddle. The trail completes its curl around the upper end of Angel Creek here and strikes out to the east. Beyond the cabin, it's peaks and saddles for the next 8 miles or so, with some major ups and downs. A bulldozer scar from fire suppression work during the raging wildfire season of 2004 runs across part of this section of the route.

21.0 Change in direction. The trail turns northeast across a low, wooded saddle and regains the high ridge on the other side. This part of the route may be a bit difficult to follow, especially in bad weather.

22.5 A marked route off the ridge from a saddle at 2,850 feet elevation into the Angel Creek valley, a bad-weather bail-off route. There is a fee cabin in the valley bottom, and a mucky ATV trail leads from there out to the main road.

27.0 A rocky opening at 2,250 feet elevation. Rock cairns mark the trail as it drops off the ridge to the northeast, beginning its descent in switchbacks to the south trailhead.

30.0 The south trailhead, Mile 49 of Chena Hot Springs Road.

58. PINNELL MOUNTAIN

WHY GO?

This trail travels along a ridgeline, with spectacular panoramic views, wildlife, and wildflowers, and one of the top longer hikes in the region.

THE RUNDOWN

Distance: A 27.3-mile traverse

Special features: High tundra hiking, wildflowers, panoramic views, two trail shelters with water catchment systems

Location: 100 miles northeast of Fairbanks in the Steese National Conservation Area

Difficulty: Strenuous

Trail type: More-developed trail lower; a marked route with sections of constructed trail higher

Total elevation gain: 5,500 feet westbound, 6,000 feet eastbound

Best season: June to mid-Sept

Fees/permits: None

Maps: USGS Circle B-3, B-4, C-3, and C-4; BLM brochure *Pinnell Mountain National Recreation Trail*

Contact: Bureau of Land Management, Northern Field Office, 222 University Ave., Fairbanks, AK 99709; (800) 437-7021; www.blm.gov/ak/

FINDING THE TRAILHEAD

From the intersection at Airport Way, drive 11 miles north of Fairbanks on the Steese Expressway to the intersection of the Steese and Elliot Highways. Turn east onto the Steese (signed as Alaska Route 6). Twelvemile Summit, the west trailhead, is another 75 miles from the intersection, and Eagle Summit, the east trailhead and the recommended starting point, is 96 miles away.

The Steese is a partially paved state highway with limited services, so start the trip with a full gas tank and a good spare tire. There are campgrounds along the road, and there is a small emergency shelter at Eagle Summit.

WHAT TO SEE

The premier long hike in the Fairbanks area, the Pinnell Mountain Trail is a National Recreation Trail for good reason. It traverses the highest ridge in the area, so it offers nearly continuous panoramic views as well as wildlife and wildflowers. This is the highest of the Fairbanks area's ridge trails, ranging between 3,000 and 5,000 feet in elevation.

Migratory birds like lesser golden-plovers, Lapland longspurs, northern wheatear, and surfbirds nest in the high tundra along the trail, and alpine wildflowers put on a show in June and July—look for lousewort, moss campion, mountain avens, alpine azalea, forget-me-not, oxytrope, frigid shooting star, roseroot, Parry's wallflower, and windflower, to name some of the species that carpet the miles of tundra. Plenty of open slopes make it easy to scan for wildlife; hikers sometimes spot wolves, bears, caribou, or wolverines from the trail. Marmots, pikas, and ptarmigan are common. The ridge the trail traverses is made up of a complex stew of ancient rocks, some of them among the oldest in Alaska. One of the rock groupings here is the Birch Creek Schist, the source of the gold that led to the European settlement of this part of the state.

The trail near Eagle Summit is a good place to see the midnight sun a few days before and after the summer solstice, which usually falls on June 21. The sun skims but doesn't dip below the horizon from this vantage point.

There are developed trail approaches at each end of the hike, stretches of boardwalk across swampy areas, and bench-cut switchbacks in some steep areas, but the Pinnell Trail is mainly a route marked with cairns and mileposts. The trail's first 8 miles or so are in excellent shape, and though it's a bit rougher beyond, it's still adequately marked.

Bring along topo maps, the BLM brochure, a compass, foul weather gear, and warm clothing. These high ridges catch a lot of weather, and high winds, rain, and snow can hit anytime. Clouds and fog can obscure the trail markers, so be prepared for route finding with map and compass. In the event of really bad weather, there are several hikeable ridges that lead back down south to the Steese Highway; they are relatively obvious on the topo map. The quickest route down into the trees is from the North Fork Shelter, Mile 17.5, along a southeast-trending ridge that leads to a mining road on the North Fork of Birch Creek, which you can follow out to the Steese.

The Ptarmigan Creek Shelter at Mile 10 and the North Fork Shelter at Mile 17.5, both small, enclosed log shelters, are available for overnighting and ducking out of the weather on a no-fee, first-come, first-served basis. They have no source of heat, but they do have water courtesy of catchment systems. Please cook outside the shelters to disperse food odors so animals won't be attracted to them, and don't leave anything, especially food, in the shelters. There are good campsites along the ridge too, particularly in lower saddles that offer some protection from the weather. There is no firewood, so don't forget the camp stove, and by all means remember the bug dope.

By midsummer, water near the trail may be scarce except for the catchments at the two shelters; be sure to fill up there. The best bets for surface water are low saddles (from seeps, snowmelt pools, and tundra ponds), and north-facing slopes (from snow patches). The section of the trail that crosses a low saddle at about Mile 20, at the bottom of the climb to Table Mountain, passes within 0.3 mile or so of an upper tributary stream of the North Fork of Birch Creek. Following the stream downhill is probably the best bet for finding running water in the dry part of the year.

In other places you may have to descend a long way to find water. Carry as much as possible and refill at every opportunity. Boil or filter all water, including the shelter catchment water, and to protect water quality as much as possible, dispose of wash water and human waste below and well away from any possible water source.

A backpacker on the 27-mile Pinnell Mountain traverse. The trail travels along a high ridgeline, with spectacular panoramic views, wildlife, wildflowers, and is one of the longer hikes in the region. BUREAU OF LAND MANAGEMENT

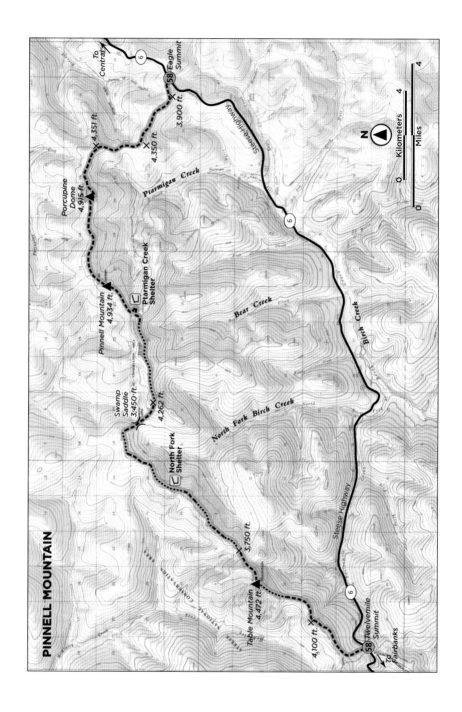

PINNELL MOUNTAIN

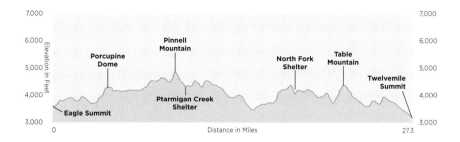

MILES AND DIRECTIONS

0.0   Begin at the Eagle Summit Trailhead.

4.0   Climb to Peak 4,351.

6.0   Pass below the summit of Porcupine Dome.

9.0   Reach Pinnell Mountain (4,934 feet).

10.0 The Ptarmigan Creek Trail Shelter is available for overnighting.

14.5 Descend to Swamp Saddle (3,450 feet).

17.5 The North Fork Trail Shelter is also available for overnighting.

22.0 Summit Table Mountain (4,472 feet).

27.3 End the hike at the Twelvemile Summit Trailhead.

Shorter hikes: Eagle Summit is the higher trailhead, so the views get better faster from there. Some possible destinations from each end:

From Twelvemile Summit

Point 4,100: a bit over 2 miles one way and a 1,000-foot climb. The summit is a short off-trail climb.

Table Mountain (4,472 feet): 5 miles one way and a 1,700-foot climb.

From Eagle Summit

Point 3,900: The first hill above the trailhead, 0.5 mile one way and a 300-foot climb.

Peak 4,350: 2.5 miles one way and a 700-foot climb. At about Mile 2, where the trail curls around the ridge below the peak, climb away from the trail to the southwest to the summit.

Peak 4,351: 4 miles one way and a 1,000-foot climb.

TIDBIT

From both trailheads, the first 8 miles or so are in fairly good shape, but beyond the rougher route may only be marked with cairns and mileposts. Bring adequate maps, compass, and route-finding skills. Also, carry as much water as possible, and refill at every chance, as there are not many sources, especially in a dry year.

59. SUMMIT TRAIL

WHY GO?

This is one of a few trails in the White Mountains Recreation Area with a dry route for hiking in the summer. The most popular route is the first 3.5 miles from Wickersham Dome Trailhead to the Wickersham Dome.

THE RUNDOWN

Distance: Wickersham Dome: 3.5 miles one way. Beaver Creek: 20 miles one way

Special features: Alpine tundra and views, Beaver Creek (a national wild river), and a trail shelter

Location: 40 miles northwest of Fairbanks in the White Mountains National Recreation Area

Difficulty: Wickersham Dome: moderate. Beaver Creek: strenuous

Trail type: More developed

Total elevation gain: Wickersham Dome: about 900 feet in and 100 feet out. Beaver Creek: about 1,800 feet in and 2,700 feet out

Best season: June through Sept

Fees/permits: None

Maps: USGS Livengood A-3, B-2, B-3; Bureau of Land Management leaflet *Summit Trail*; BLM *White Mountains National Recreation Area* Winter Trails Map

Contact: Bureau of Land Management, Northern Field Office, 222 University Ave., Fairbanks, AK 99709; (800) 437-7021; https://www.blm.gov/alaska

FINDING THE TRAILHEAD

From the intersection at Airport Way, drive 11 miles north of Fairbanks on the Steese Expressway to the intersection of the Steese and Elliott Highways. Continue north, straight ahead, on the Elliott Highway (signed as Alaska Route 2) another 28 miles to the Wickersham Dome Trailhead on the right.

WHAT TO SEE

The Summit Trail is one of the few trails in the White Mountains National Recreation Area dry enough for summer hiking; the area is better known and more popular for its extensive system of winter trails and cabins. The trail follows a fairly dry ridgeline to Wickersham Dome and beyond, eventually descending to Beaver Creek, a hike of 20 miles one way. The shorter trip to the north side of Wickersham Dome leads to distant views of the White Mountains, the rugged peaks in the heart of the recreation area. In season, there is good berry picking along the trail. The trail is closed to motorized use.

Wickersham Dome: Take the trail out of the north end of the parking area, the left side as you face away from the highway. (Another trail, the Wickersham Creek Trail, begins straight ahead, bearing east.) The Summit Trail climbs gradually through sparse spruce and brushy dwarf birch, reaching a 2,660-foot alpine knob in about a mile. After crossing a wet, forested saddle on boardwalk, pass by the Ski Loop Trail junction at about 2 miles. The ski trail leads back to the Wickersham Creek Trail, but it is usually deep in water and muck in the summer.

Above tree line again on the slope of Wickersham Dome, find a summer blueberry and wildflower bonanza, with tiny gardens of alpine azaleas and other flowers. There is a communication tower on the top of the dome; the high points on the north side, however, afford good views minus the signs of humanity. At the high point on this section of the trail, roughly 2,900 feet in elevation, head off-trail to the west for the best views, to one of the small knobs that rise 200 feet or so above the elevation of the trail.

Beaver Creek: A strenuous trip of 20 miles one way, the hike to Beaver Creek climbs and descends along the ridge beyond Wickersham Dome. There are few sources of water other than Beaver Creek, so plan to carry plenty with you.

The trail is planked across most of the wet-tundra areas on the hike. The Summit Trail Shelter, about Mile 8, is a no-fee, first-come, first-served shelter with a rain catchment system for water. (Be sure to treat the water just as you would surface water). The trail reaches its high point, 3,100 feet, about Mile 10, and at Mile 13 begins the long descent to the creek. The last 2 miles of the hike are on the Wickersham Creek Trail. The hike ends at Beaver Creek, a national wild river, about 4 miles above the "Big Bend" in the creek where it turns sharply around the flank of the White Mountains.

The Borealis-LeFevre Cabin is across Beaver Creek from the end of the trail. The creek, though, may be uncrossable at higher water levels. Early-summer high water usually subsides by mid-June. Look up or down the creek for the best crossing spot for the water level. It's possible to make a loop by returning on the Wickersham Creek Trail, but it is usually a wet, muddy hike.

The Summit Trail is one of the few trails in the White Mountains National Recreation Area dry enough for summer hiking. The shorter trip to Wickersham Dome leads to distant views of the White Mountains and the rugged peaks in the heart of the recreation area.
RYAN DELANEY/BLM

A moderate hike of 7 miles on the Wickersham Creek and Trail Creek Trails, leads to Lee's Cabin. The cabin has a nice view, and is a comfortable place to spend the night.
RYAN DELANEY/BLM

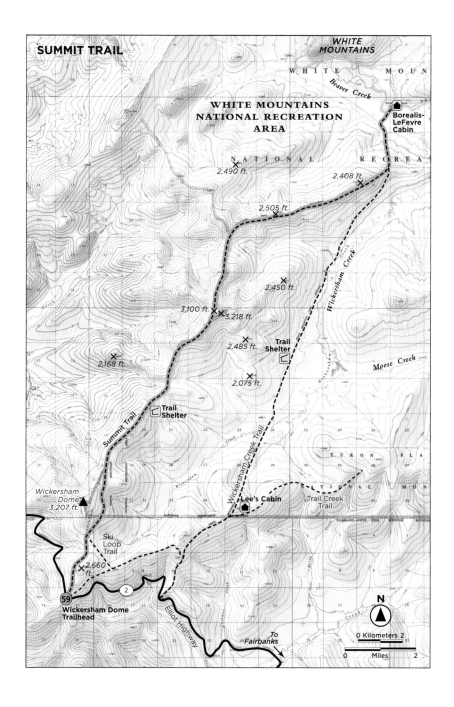

SUMMIT TRAIL

WHITE
MOUNTAINS

WHITE MOUNTAINS
NATIONAL RECREATION
AREA

Beaver Creek

Borealis-
LeFevre
Cabin

N A T I O N A L   R E C R E A

× 2,490 ft.

× 2,408 ft.

× 2,505 ft.

× 2,450 ft.

Wickersham Creek

3,100 ft. × × 3,218 ft.

× 2,168 ft.

× 2,485 ft.

Trail
Shelter

Moose Creek

× 2,075 ft.

Summit Trail

Trail
Shelter

Y U K O N   F L A

Wickersham Creek Trail

Wickersham
Dome
3,207 ft. ▲

Lee's Cabin

Trail Creek
Trail

N A T I O N A L   M O N

Ski
Loop
Trail

FAIRBANKS-NORTH STAR BOROUGH   BOUNDARY

× 2,660
ft.

2

59

Wickersham Dome
Trailhead

Elliot Highway

To
Fairbanks

N

0 Kilometers 2

0   Miles   2

MILES AND DIRECTIONS

0.0 Set off from the Wickersham Dome Trailhead.

1.0 Reach Point 2,660.

2.0 Pass by the junction with the Ski Loop Trail.

3.5 Reach the north side of Wickersham Dome.

8.0 The Summit Trail Shelter is available if the weather is inclement.

10.0 Reach the trail's high point at 3,100 feet.

18.0 Join the Wickersham Creek Trail for the last 2 miles of the hike.

20.0 The trail ends at Beaver Creek.

Lee's Cabin: An easy/moderate hike of 7 miles one way on the Wickersham Creek and Trail Creek Trails leads to Lee's Cabin, another BLM fee cabin. The Wickersham Creek Trail leaves the east end of the Wickersham Dome parking area. Follow it 6 miles to the intersection with the Trail Creek Trail and take the latter trail another mile to the cabin. These trails are open to all-terrain vehicles, but are hikeable to Lee's Cabin. Though this hike isn't particularly scenic, the cabin has a nice view and is a comfortable place to spend the night. As with the Summit shelter, there is no surface water, but there is a rain catchment supply that should be boiled or filtered before using.

For more information on the cabins and the shelter mentioned here, go to the BLM website (see "Contact" above). For reservations for the Borealis-LeFevre Cabin or Lee's Cabin, apply in person at the BLM Public Room in Fairbanks or call BLM and pay by credit card (also see "Contact" above).

TIDBIT
The first 1.5 miles of the trail can be a mix of maintained and non-maintained (swampy), prepare accordingly.

DELTA JUNCTION

MOST PEOPLE KNOW IT as the official end of the Alaska Highway, Historical Mile 1422, as it joins the Richardson Highway on the route to Fairbanks. It has also known as "Bison City" as in the 1920s about twenty bison were transplanted to the area from Montana, and now there is a herd of a couple hundred remaining. About 15 miles north of town is a 600-acre recreation area with hiking trails worth visiting.

60. QUARTZ LAKE STATE RECREATION TRAILS

WHY GO?

A 600-acre recreation area popular for hiking trails, lakes, fishing, swimming, and camping.

THE RUNDOWN

Special features: Hiking trails, lakes, campsites with day-use areas, and scenic views

Location: 10 miles north of Delta Junction

Trail type: Less developed to developed

Best season: June through Sept

Fees/permits: Parking fee or state parks pass

Maps: USGS Big Delta A-4, *Alaska State Parks Quartz Lake State Recreation Area*

Contact: Alaska State Parks, Northern Area, 3700 Airport Way, Fairbanks, AK 99709; (907) 451-2695; http://dnr.alaska.gov/parks/

KEY DISTANCES, DIFFICULTIES, AND TOTAL ELEVATION GAINS:
Quartz Lake Loop Trail: 1.8 mile one way, easy to moderate, 350 feet

Lost Lake Trail: 1.3 miles, easy, 200 feet

Bluff Point Trail: 3-mile loop, easy, 200 feet

Walk About Trail: 1 mile, easy, 300 feet

Bert Mountain Trail: 1.7 mile, moderate, 850 feet

FINDING THE TRAILHEAD

Quartz Lake State Recreation Area is 10 miles north of Delta Junction. Drive north on the Richardson Highway, at Mile 277.8, head east on the Quartz Lake Access Road. Continue about 3 miles until you reach the recreation site.

WHAT TO SEE

Quartz Lake State Recreation Area includes a variety of recreation options within the 600-acre property, only 10 miles from Delta Junction. The area is known for hiking trails, fishing, boating, swimming, and camping. The five hiking trails offer easy access for the whole family to enjoy a stroll in the wild environment.

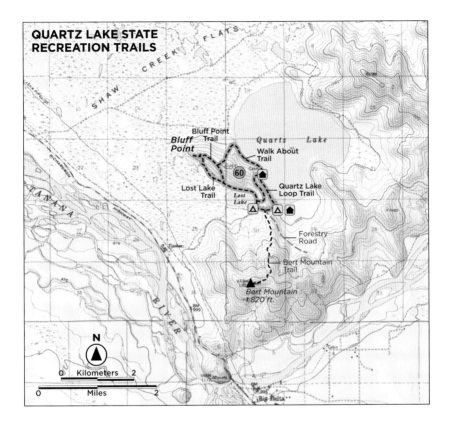

TIDBIT

Consider spending more than a day at Quartz Lake, and check out camping or the public use cabins in the area.

Bluff Point Trail overlook, a 3-mile loop, with Moose Pond and Bert Mountain in the background. Quartz Lake is a 600-acre recreation area popular for hiking trails, lakes, fishing, swimming, and camping.
JUSTIN WHOLEY

One popular route is Quartz Lake Loop Trail, hiking from Quartz Lake Campground to the Glatfelder Cabin, and the most maintained section of trail. Another section is hiking Lost Lake Trail to Bluff Point, and looping with Bluff Point Trail back to the trailhead. At Mile 1.3 of Lost Lake Trail, look for the moose pond, a destination with fantastic opportunities for viewing moose, swans, geese, and ducks (bears and beavers roam as well). Besides the hiking trails, fishing is a prime draw to Quartz Lake Recreation Area. It is one of the most accessible fishing in all of Interior Alaska. Quartz Lake is stocked every year with more than 300,000 rainbow trout and coho salmon, with more than 34,000 fish harvested annually.

WRANGELL–ST. ELIAS NATIONAL PARK AND PRESERVE

WRANGELL–ST. ELIAS NATIONAL PARK AND PRESERVE is the biggest national park in the United States, at 13.2 million acres, or about the size of six Yellowstones. The park/preserve straddles the wild corner of the state where four world-class mountain ranges meet: Wrangell, St. Elias, Chugach, and Alaska ranges. It's a land of fire (volcanoes) and ice (mountain and valley glaciers), lying at the heart of one of the earth's largest internationally protected areas, an Indiana-size swath of country that takes in three Canadian parks and the U.S.'s Glacier Bay National Park and Preserve in addition to Wrangell–St. Elias. The park and neighboring Kluane National Park in the Yukon Territory contain ten of North America's fifteen highest peaks.

Only two roads lead into Wrangell–St. Elias: the McCarthy and Nabesna roads, in the central and northern sections of the park/preserve, respectively. The most easily accessible hiking is off these two roads; Root Glacier and Stairway Icefall and Bonanza Ridge are in the McCarthy Road area, and Caribou Creek, Trail and Lost Creeks, and Skookum Volcano are off the Nabesna Road.

Make your first stop the park visitor center, located at Mile 106.8 of the Richardson Highway near Copper Center, about 10 miles south of Glennallen. The park also has information stations at Mile 59 of the McCarthy Road, in Kennecott, and at Slana, on the Glenn Highway/Tok Cutoff at the intersection with the Nabesna Road.

Most of the park/preserve is remote and accessible only by air; for a brief description of the fly-in backcountry, see the park entry in "Off the Beaten Path" at the end of this book. There are also several other hiking possibilities out of the McCarthy area and from the Nabesna Road; ask at one of the park stations or check the website www.nps.gov/wrst for more information.

McCarthy and Kennecott The tiny, isolated neighboring settlements of McCarthy and Kennecott, the park gateway towns in the Chitina River area, have lately become something of a tourist attraction. To sum it up, McCarthy has most of the services and Kennecott has most of the visible history. Kennecott is a historic mining settlement, a company town set up in 1911 to mine and mill the high-grade copper deposits on Bonanza Ridge, above the Kennicott River to the east (see Bonanza

Ridge). (Yes, there are two spellings of the name, after the Alaska explorer Robert Kennicott: "Kennicott" for the river, glacier, and valley; and the originally misspelled "Kennecott" for the mines and the mining company, and for the settlement as well.)

Kennecott died out in the 1930s, but it's now a designated National Historic Landmark, and the National Park Service is working to stabilize and restore many of the structures in the settlement. To learn more, take the self-guided walking tour or a guided interpretive walk. Stop in at the park's Kennecott Visitor Center for information.

Driving to McCarthy and Kennecott is a commitment. From the park visitor center in Copper Center, it's about 55 miles via the Richardson and Edgerton Highways to Chitina and the Copper River. (Say it Chit' na, and be sure to fill your tank there; it's the last gas on the drive.) Then, east of the Copper River Bridge, the pavement ends and the rough, dusty 60 miles of the McCarthy Road begin. Allow about 2.5 hours for this last leg of the trip. There is also private van service to McCarthy; check with the park for details (907-822-5234; www.nps.gov/wrst).

The road ends on the west bank of the Kennicott River, in the middle of a large block of private land; this is not your typical national park entrance. The river is the end of the line for private-visitor vehicles. From there, walk or bike across the Kennicott River Bridge and continue 5 road miles east and north to Kennecott or 1 road mile east and south to McCarthy. A mountain bike comes in very handy on the restricted dirt roads of McCarthy and Kennecott. You can rent a bike at the private campground about 0.5 mile from the end of the road; check with the park before you visit to be sure rentals are available. The only free day-use parking is at the small NPS visitor information station about 0.8 mile from the end of the road; you can fill your water bottles here too. For the hikes described here, the best plan is to camp at one of the private campgrounds near the end of the road, leave your vehicle there, and bike or take a shuttle to Kennecott.

Besides the campgrounds, overnight options include lodges, B&Bs, and a hostel; the park has all the information. You can also backpack camp in a semi-developed area on the trail to the Root Glacier, about 1.5 miles out the main trail from Kennecott (see Root Glacier and Stairway Icefall).

61. ROOT GLACIER AND STAIRWAY ICEFALL

WHY GO?

A trail with both short and longer overnight options and easy access from a historic mining town to the Root Glacier.

THE RUNDOWN

Distances: About 2 miles one way to the snout of the Root Glacier; 4 miles one way to the Stairway Icefall viewpoint

Special features: Historic Kennecott, the Root Glacier, the Stairway Icefall, and views of the Wrangell Mountains. Root Glacier is a good family trip

Location: Kennecott

Difficulty: Lower trail: easy. Upper trail: moderate

Trail type: Lower trail: more developed. Upper trail: less developed, infrequently maintained

Total elevation gain: Root Glacier spur trail: 200 feet. Stairway Icefall viewpoint: 1,000 feet

Best season: June through mid-Sept

Fees/permits: None

Maps: USGS McCarthy C-6 and B-6; National Geographic *Wrangell–St. Elias National Park and Preserve*

Contact: Wrangell–St. Elias National Park and Preserve, Mile 106.8 Richardson Highway, PO Box 439, Copper Center, AK 99573; (907) 822-5234; www.nps.gov/wrst

FINDING THE TRAILHEAD

The hike begins in the historic settlement of Kennecott, 5 miles east and north of the end of the McCarthy Road (see McCarthy and Kennecott). From the end of the road, walk or bike across the Kennicott River Bridge and continue 0.5 mile on a restricted road to the McCarthy/Kennecott junction. Turn left (north) and continue about 4.5 miles into Kennecott; the trail begins at the north end of the settlement. You can also catch a ride to Kennecott on one of the approximately hourly shuttle vans (fee charged), either from the east side of the bridge or in McCarthy, which is about 0.5 mile south from the McCarthy/Kennecott junction.

WHAT TO SEE

Hike north along the main road through Kennecott, passing the road/trail to Bonanza Ridge about 0.3 mile past the last of the Kennecott buildings (see the Bonanza Ridge hike). Beyond, the road narrows to a foot trail paralleling the rubble-strewn Kennicott Glacier. From here, look out on Donoho Peak, the peak that separates the Root and Kennicott Glaciers, and if it's a clear day, the snowy mass of Mount Blackburn (16,390 feet), one of the park's signature volcanic peaks, beyond and left of Donoho.

Jumbo Creek, at a bit over a mile, flows down a steep, narrow bed and disappears under the glacier. In another 0.2 mile, a signed spur trail leads about 0.3 mile down to the snout of the glacier. In summer the lower portion of the glacier is relatively safe to walk on, but ice conditions can change from year to year; crampons may be necessary. For adventurous hikers looking for a longer trip, crossing the glacier on crampons puts you within striking distance of the Donoho Peak ridge. Guided glacier trips leave Kennecott daily.

Near the spur trail is a partially developed hike-in camping area, with tent sites, an outhouse, and bear-proof food-storage boxes, all within about 0.2 mile of the trail junction. If you camp at one of the sites, please use a camp stove and store food and anything with an odor in the bear-proof boxes; park personnel are especially concerned about avoiding bear-human conflicts here. The nearest water is Jumbo Creek.

Hikers travel the short trail to the edge of the Root Glacier. Just beyond the trail junction for Root Glacier, it's 0.3 mile to the glacier, or 2.5 miles to the Stairway Icefall viewpoint.
MOLLIE FOSTER

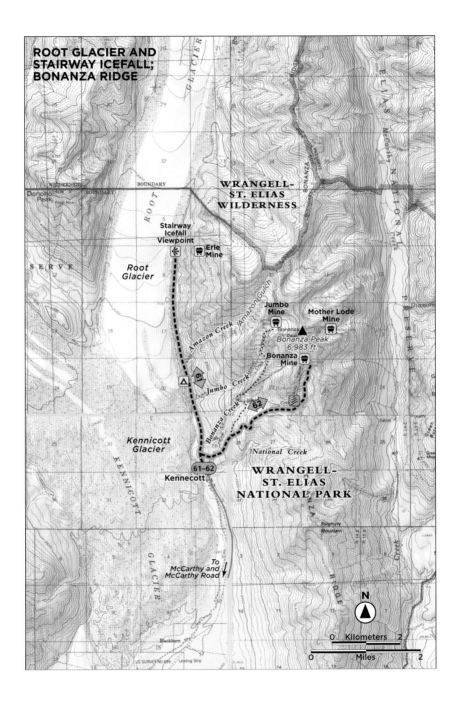

ROOT GLACIER AND
STAIRWAY ICEFALL;
BONANZA RIDGE

WRANGELL-
ST. ELIAS
WILDERNESS

Stairway
Icefall
Viewpoint

Erie
Mine

Root
Glacier

SERVE

Jumbo
Mine

Mother Lode
Mine

Bonanza

Bonanza Peak
6,983 ft.

Bonanza
Mine

9

62

Jumbo Creek

Bonanza Creek

Amazon Creek

Amazon Gulch

Kennicott
Glacier

National Creek

61–62

Kennecott

WRANGELL-
ST. ELIAS
NATIONAL PARK

Porphyry
Mountain

To
McCarthy and
McCarthy Road

N

0   Kilometers   2

0   Miles   2

Beyond the glacier spur trail, the main trail narrows and winds through low brush on its way north. The final section follows the crumbling edge of the Root Glacier's steep-sided lateral moraine. The viewpoint at the end of the trail, however, is worth the effort. In the distance the Stairway Icefall plunges 5,000 feet from the heights of the Wrangell Mountains down to the glacier. Look for an old cable line stretching up the steep talus slope and cliffs to the east, toward the site of the Erie Mine, one of the mines that fed the Kennecott mill.

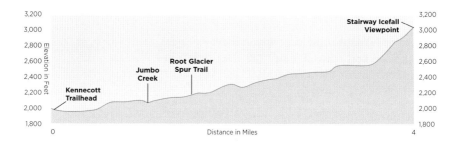

MILES AND DIRECTIONS

0.0   Begin at the Kennecott Trailhead.

0.3   Pass the Bonanza Mine Trail/Road.

0.4   Cross Bonanza Creek.

1.3   Pass the Jumbo Creek backcountry camping area.

1.5   Meet the Root Glacier spur trail (0.3 mile to glacier).

4.0   Climb to the Stairway Icefall viewpoint.

62. BONANZA RIDGE

WHY GO?

This trail is a great way to climb into alpine scenery, rich with mining history, and spectacular views of the surrounding mountain peaks, accessible from Kennecott.

THE RUNDOWN See map on page 273.

Distance: 4.5 miles one way

Special features: Alpine scenery, geology, mining history

Location: Above Kennecott

Difficulty: Very strenuous

Trail type: More-developed trail/closed road; rougher paths explore the area above the mine

Total elevation gain: About 4,000 feet

Best season: Mid-June to mid-Sept

Fees/permits: None

Maps: USGS McCarthy B-6, B-5, and C-5; National Geographic Wrangell–St. Elias National Park and Preserve

Contact: Wrangell–St. Elias National Park and Preserve, Mile 106.8 Richardson Highway, PO Box 439, Copper Center, AK 99573; (907) 822-5234; www.nps.gov/wrst

FINDING THE TRAILHEAD

The hike begins in the historic settlement of Kennecott, 5 miles east and north of the end of the McCarthy Road (see McCarthy and Kennecott). From the end of the road, walk or bike across the Kennicott River Bridge and continue 0.5 mile on the restricted road to the McCarthy/Kennecott junction. Turn left (north) and continue about 4.5 miles on the road into Kennecott; the trail begins at the north end of the settlement. You can also catch a ride to Kennecott on one of the approximately hourly shuttle vans (fee charged), either from the east side of the bridge or in McCarthy, which is about 0.5 mile south of the McCarthy/Kennecott junction.

WHAT TO SEE

The Bonanza hike leads high into the Wrangell Mountains to the Bonanza Mine, one of the four copper mines that fed the ore concentration mill in Kennecott during the town's heyday. Just above the remains of the mine, Bonanza Ridge (about 6,000 feet in elevation) is a fine place for gaping at rugged peaks and ridges marching off into the distance and for checking out the striking blue-green rock outcrops that made Bonanza Ridge one of North America's richest copper deposits.

First, the big picture: Kennecott company miners dug out the high-grade copper ore of Bonanza Ridge at four mines: the Bonanza, Jumbo, Mother Lode, and Erie Mines. Cable cars carried the ore off the ridge and into the valley, where workers processed it in the Kennecott mill. Then the ore went into rail cars for a trip down the Copper River and Northwestern Railway to the port at Cordova. From Cordova, ships carried it to the Lower 48 for smelting and sale.

The trail runs along the old wagon road to the mine, more or less following the route of the cable tramway for the ore cars, but with many curves and switchbacks to lessen the grade for the wagons and now, conveniently, for you, the hiker. To find the old wagon road, first hike north out of Kennecott, and about 0.3 mile past the last of the town's historic structures. Turn sharply right at the sign, onto an obvious four-wheel-drive road, there's also a bathroom stop. At the top of the first switchback turn left following the road up the hill. If you reach the top of the mill building, you missed the turn.

Head steeply uphill past several private driveways and cabins, and after the better part of an hour of climbing, as the road bends sharply right in an unusual level spot, pass a partially cleared route to the left that leads to the Jumbo Mine, one of the other Kennecott mines. The Jumbo route, which also follows an old wagon road, is densely overgrown in alder at lower elevations and cow parsnip and tall grasses higher up. If you're up for a brushy, adventurous hike, take the 3-mile one-way trip to the mine and a nearby cirque and rock glacier, but don't expect to have time to get to the Bonanza the same day.

About 0.5 mile above the Jumbo Mine intersection, the Bonanza Trail emerges from the mountain brush zone to views of the high country ahead and the Jumbo Mine to the north. Just above, continue straight ahead at the intersection with a private road. In about another mile, at a bend in the trail, pass one of the cable tram stations and look downhill to another station, called an angle station, where the route of the cable line changed direction and ran down National Creek toward Kennecott.

Near the top of Bonanza Falls, a small creek spills over a rock ledge to the right of the trail; this stream is the only water source on the hike. Strewn all over the area are abandoned mining equipment and lumber from long-collapsed buildings, and the Bonanza Mine is clearly visible high on the ridge above. Beyond this point the most direct trail is foot-worn through scree and rubble, although the wagon road continues uphill in long switchbacks.

It's only when you close in on the standing structures left from the mine—perched on the side of a steep bowl just below the Bonanza Ridge crest—that you can see what a massive undertaking it was. The mine consisted of bunkhouses, a tram terminal, warehouses, and generally just a stunning amount of lumber construction.

For a more natural climax to the hike, climb carefully to the crest of the ridge for a great 180-degree view into the wild mountains at the heart of the park.

The terrain isn't great for camping, so a day trip to Bonanza is preferable for most hikers. If you do the hike on a warm midsummer day, be sure to slap on the sunscreen and carry plenty of water; the alpine section of the hike faces south and west and can heat up considerably on a sunny day.

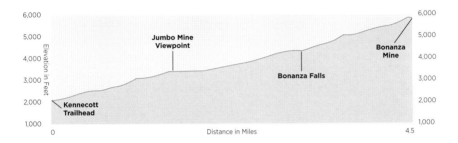

MILES AND DIRECTIONS

0.0 Begin at the Kennecott Trailhead.

0.3 Turn right at the Root Glacier/Bonanza junction.

0.4 Turn left at the top of the first switch-back.

1.5 Pass the Jumbo Mine Trail/Route.

2.0 Take in the Jumbo Mine view.

3.0 Pass a historic tram station.

3.5 Reach Bonanza Falls.

4.5 Arrive at the Bonanza Mine.

TIDBIT

There's loads of mining history on this trail, but resist the temptation to clamber around in the building remains. Everything having to do with the mines is protected, and federal law prohibits taking any "souvenirs," so please leave it all in place.

63. CARIBOU CREEK

WHY GO?

A developed lower trail with easy access to alpine, to connect with ridges for longer, overnight treks in the Mentasta Mountains.

THE RUNDOWN

Distance: 3 miles to brush line plus an additional 1.5 steep off-trail miles to the Mentasta divide

Special features: A relatively easy trip into alpine country; fantastic views on the high ridges

Location: 19 miles east of Slana, off the Nabesna Road

Difficulty: Moderate to strenuous

Trail type: Less-developed trail to brush line; route to cross-country beyond

Total elevation gain: About 800 feet on the trail to brush line;

an additional 2,200 feet off-trail to the Mentasta divide

Best season: Mid-June to mid-Sept

Fees/permits: None

Maps: USGS Nabesna C-5, National Geographic Wrangell–St. Elias National Park and Preserve

Contact: Wrangell–St. Elias National Park and Preserve, Slana Ranger Station, Mile 0.5 Nabesna Road, PO Box 885, Slana, AK 99586; (907) 822-7401; www.nps.gov/wrst

FINDING THE TRAILHEAD

Drive 19.5 miles east on the Nabesna Road from the Glenn Highway/Tok Cutoff and park in a large, signed parking area on the left (north) side of the road. Walk 0.3 mile east on the road to the signed trailhead on the left.

WHAT TO SEE

A relatively simple hike on an old all-terrain-vehicle track, the Caribou Creek Trail leads into alpine country about as painlessly as possible, and from there the choices are yours. The rugged, high valley above the end of the trail invites exploration, and a few steep but nontechnical routes lead up the ridges on either side of the creek. You can also hike all the way to the summit ridge of the Mentasta Mountains, at the head of the drainage. The view is spectacular from the divide, particularly to the east toward Noyes Mountain, and the ridge rambling is fine, if steep in places, for several miles east and west along the ridgeline.

Doing the summit ridge is a long, hard day hike, so if you want more than a brief taste of the high country, plan on an overnight. The track ends at a primitive cabin, you must reserve the cabin in advance, but it is free. The low-brush tundra bench one level up the drainage from the cabin is a good tenting option; higher up, the valley is so steep that spots flat enough for a tent are few and far between.

At roughly 1.5 miles from the Nabesna Road, the trail passes a hunting camp in the forest, and soon after it crosses the small rocky stream and breaks out into a meadow with a view of the mountains ahead. Continuing up the west side of the creek, the track climbs among willow and dwarf birch, leaving the spruce forest behind. At one point it follows a rocky, secondary stream channel for a short distance; don't cross the creek here, but hike on another ten to fifteen minutes to an obvious crossing. On the east side of the creek, the trail ends at the cabin.

From the tundra bench just up the drainage from the cabin, you can climb obvious feeder ridges to the east and west to reach the 5,000-plus-foot ridgelines on either side of the creek. Point 5,620 to the east is a good if steep destination, or for an even more ambitious hike, you can circle around the head of the watershed and take in the summit ridge.

If you decide to head up the drainage into the high alpine valley, stay on the right (east) side of the creek, climbing and sidehilling your way up-valley. About a mile up, look for an inviting, gently sloping ramp angling northeast toward the Mentasta divide. This is a good if not exactly easy route to the summit ridge; you'll end up on the divide in the northeast corner of Section 25 (T. 10N, R. 10E) on the topo map.

For any of these higher, off-trail jaunts, be sure to study the map and the terrain and choose your route carefully (bring the USGS quad; the scale of the National Geographic map is less than ideal for cross-country mountain rambles). Many of the slopes in the neighborhood are steep and rocky enough to be a bit dangerous, especially on the descent or if the weather prevents good visibility.

The 3-mile Caribou Creek Trail is a hike on an old all-terrain-vehicle track, leading into alpine country about as easy as it gets, with endless options for tundra walking from there.
JASON REPPERT

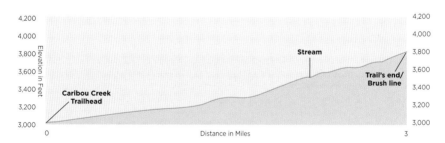

MILES AND DIRECTIONS

0.0   Begin at the trailhead.

2.0   Cross a small rocky stream.

3.0   Reach the end of the trail at brush line and a small, primitive cabin.

64. TRAIL AND LOST CREEKS

WHY GO?

A trail for day hikes, or longer loop routes, climbing into alpine country through a 6,000-foot pass in the Mentasta Mountains.

THE RUNDOWN

Distance: About 21 miles, plus a bit less than 2 miles of road walking between the two trailheads

Special features: Alpine meadows and canyons, a 6,000-foot pass, Dall sheep. The hike is an undeveloped route following creek beds, ATV tracks, and game trails; map-reading and route-finding skills are essential

Location: 30 miles east of Slana, off the Nabesna Road

Difficulty: Very strenuous

Trail type: Lower half: a route. Upper half: cross-country

Total elevation gain: About 2,900 feet

Best season: July to mid-Sept

Fees/permits: None

Maps: USGS Nabesna C-5; National Geographic Wrangell-St. Elias National Park and Preserve

Contact: Wrangell–St. Elias National Park and Preserve, Slana Ranger Station, Mile 0.5 Nabesna Road, PO Box 885, Slana, AK 99586; (907) 822-7401; www.nps.gov/wrst

FINDING THE TRAILHEAD

The trailhead for Trail Creek, the jumping-off point for the hike as described here, is about 29 miles east on the Nabesna Road from the Glenn Highway/ Tok Cutoff (see the Nabesna Road). The Lost Creek parking area is 31 miles east of the Glenn, 0.1 mile east of Lost Creek, on the north side of the road.

WHAT TO SEE

This high-country hike connects Trail and Lost Creeks over an unnamed 6,000-foot pass in the spectacular alpine country of the Mentasta Mountains. The trip follows the valleys of the two creeks, looping around a striking, unnamed, brown-and-white-layered mountain visible north of the Nabesna Road. The scenic highlights are craggy Noyes Mountain (8,147 feet) on the crest of the range; an ice-cored, rubble-covered valley near the pass; and miles of side valleys and ridges on either side of the pass. It's a challenging but rewarding hike; you could easily spend several extra days exploring the country on either side of the pass, rambling through the wild domain of hundreds of Dall sheep. Besides sheep, you might see moose and bear on the trip. Stop and check out a bear-resistant food container at the Slana Ranger Station.

Camping is good almost anywhere on the lower stretches of the creeks. Of the upper valleys, camping is better on upper Trail Creek. Lost Creek's upper basin, on the east side of the pass, is probably the best high-elevation camping. Trail Creek is more of a valley hike, and Lost Creek more of a canyon hike.

The lower sections of the hike follow the gravel streambeds of the two creeks, occasionally following all-terrain-vehicle tracks and game trails. Where the creeks swing over against their banks, you can cross the creek or climb up the bank into the forest. Creek levels vary significantly here, depending on snowmelt and recent rains.

Other trails: About 2 miles from the road, a well-traveled ATV trail leads east to Big Grayling Lake and to a hiking route to Soda Lake (10 miles one way from the Lost Creek parking area) and more of the Mentasta Mountain high country. Ask for a trip sheet at the Slana station or at the park visitor center in Copper Center.

MILES AND DIRECTIONS

0.0   Start at the Trail Creek Trailhead.

2.0   Trail Creek's valley begins to narrow in the Mentasta foothills. Below, the easiest walking is on the west side, but above, the east side is easier.

This 21-mile high-country hike connects Trail and Lost Creeks over an unnamed 6,000-foot pass in the spectacular alpine country of the Mentasta Mountains. WRANGELL-ST. ELIAS NATIONAL PARK & PRESERVE

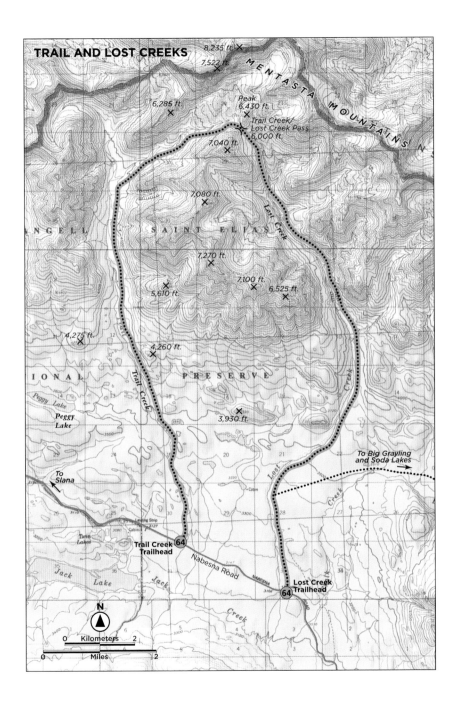

TRAIL AND LOST CREEKS

8,235 ft. ✕
7,522 ft. ✕

MENTASTA MOUNTAINS

6,285 ft. ✕

Peak
6,430 ft. ✕

Trail Creek/
Lost Creek Pass
6,000 ft. ✕

7,040 ft. ✕

7,080 ft. ✕

Lost Creek

ANGELL   SAINT   ELIAS

7,270 ft. ✕

5,610 ft. ✕

7,100 ft. ✕   6,525 ft. ✕

4,275 ft. ✕

4,260 ft. ✕

Trail Creek

IONAL   PRESERVE

Peggy Lake

Peggy
Lake

3,930 ft. ✕

Creek

To Big Grayling
and Soda Lakes →

To
Slana

Lost Creek

Trail Creek
Trailhead (64)

Landing Strip

Tune
Lakes

Nabesna Road

Lost Creek
Trailhead (64)

Jack Lake

Jack

Creek

N
▲

0   Kilometers   2

0   Miles   2

3.5 An obvious rimrock point, Point 4,260, is above to the right. Turning a corner, the hike passes the last large grove of spruce trees at about 3,800 feet elevation.

5.5 The easiest route climbs up to and crosses a tundra bench east of the creek on ATV tracks and game trails. Willow and dwarf birch brush gradually disappear as the hike gains elevation. Stay high at least until you reach the pass fork.

7.0 The fork of Trail Creek that leads to the pass flows in from the right, or east. Consult your topographic map to be sure you're heading up the correct fork. Before you reach the pass fork, you'll pass a running stream issuing out of a slot canyon on the right (east). Beyond is a flat stretch of tundra; the next valley to the north, a large, obvious valley, is the pass fork. To get there, either follow Trail Creek to the confluence or cut across to the northeast, taking a higher, shorter route across the tundra with a few ups and downs.

9.0 The pass fork narrows and enters a dry rock-rubble canyon, curving right (south) toward the pass. Follow the canyon from here if you've taken the high route this far.

10.0 The stream narrows to a slot; climb around (left is best) if you can't get through. Above the slot is a rocky bowl, with the pass above to the right. Once in the pass, hike up Peak 6,430 for the best view.

11.0 Lost Creek's upper canyon cascades down 600 vertical feet over the next 0.5 mile. The canyon is passable, but it could be an impossible route at high water, requiring a difficult hike around it.

11.5 At the bottom of the canyon, at a confluence with a stream entering from the east, aufeis (shelf ice) may linger in the stream bottom well into the summer. Below the upper canyon, the best traveling is on the left (east) side of the stream all the way to the trailhead. There are places just below that require climbing, wading the creek, or picking your way along the left bank at lower water levels.

14.0 Lost Creek's impassable lower canyon. Climb about 200 feet to the alpine bench on the east side and pick up a good animal trail across the top. The route eventually drops back to the creek below the canyon.

15–21 At the bottom of the lower canyon, the Lost Creek valley widens and spruce forest reappears. Follow the creek's gravel bed, either crossing it or following moose trails on the bank where necessary, to the hike's end at the Nabesna Road.

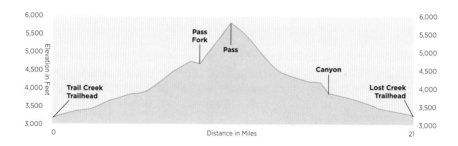

65. SKOOKUM VOLCANO

WHY GO?
Skookum Volcano Trail travels into the alpine, with stunning volcanic geology, and options for longer, high country adventures.

THE RUNDOWN

Distances: Volcano Canyon Trail: 1.5 miles one way. Theresa Dome pass: 2.5 miles one way

Special features: Alpine hiking, stream crossings, striking volcanic geology, Dall sheep, optional hikes into the higher country beyond the end of the trail

Location: 36 miles east of Slana on the Nabesna Road

Difficulty: Trail hike: moderate. Pass hike: strenuous

Trail type: Less-developed trail into the canyon; a route/cross-country beyond

Total elevation gain: Trail's end: 900 feet. Theresa Dome pass: 1,900 feet

Best season: Late June to mid-Sept

Fees/permits: None

Maps: USGS Nabesna B-5; National Geographic *Wrangell–St. Elias National Park and Preserve*

Contact: Wrangell–St. Elias National Park and Preserve, Slana Ranger Station, Mile 0.5 Nabesna Road, PO Box 885, Slana, AK 99586; (907) 822-7401; www.nps. gov/wrst

FINDING THE TRAILHEAD
The marked trailhead is in a pullout on the south side of the Nabesna Road, about 36 miles east of the Glenn Highway/Tok Cutoff. (For information about the Nabesna Road, see page 215.) It's possible to return to the road via a cross-country loop east and north from the pass below Theresa Dome; the loop route reaches the road in a small pullout about 1.4 miles east of the Skookum Trailhead.

WHAT TO SEE
The Skookum Volcano Trail is a short hop into the domain of an extinct volcano, a mountain that roared to life between two million and three million years ago, but (luckily for hikers) has been dormant in more recent times. Water and frost has carved out a hiking route into the volcano, yielding a glimpse of what the inner life of the more recently active volcanoes in the Wrangell Mountains must be like.

The trail begins in the forest just northeast of an unnamed small creek, following the course of the creek south toward the mountains. It joins the creek's gravel bed in less than a mile and enters the canyon at tree line, at about 3,400 feet in elevation.

Below a major fork in the stream, hop over the creek, and follow up the left fork. Shortly afterwards the marked trail ends, at about 1.5 miles from the trailhead.

To reach the pass behind Theresa Dome, the obvious dome to the left, continue up the left fork another mile, climbing steeply in places, aiming for the west edge of the massive cliffs ahead. Take two more left forks in the stream drainage to stay on the most direct line to the pass, elevation 4,850 feet.

From the pass, you can return the way you came, with the advantage of seeing Skookum's volcanic scenery again, or you can keep going east, dropping into the obvious drainage that curves north and loops back to the Nabesna Road. The loop route is fairly obvious, but there is no trail and no marking. Stay in the rocky creek bed to avoid the thickest of the brush. Once on the road, you're about 1.4 miles southeast of the starting point. Both the out-and-back hike and the loop are about 5 miles total distance off the road; the road walk back to the trailhead makes the loop a bit longer.

Another possible cross-country destination is the western alpine shoulder of Theresa Dome, elevation about 4,200 feet. To get there, leave the trail about a mile from the trailhead, crossing the creek from west to east when you're above the trees and near the mouth of the volcano canyon, and then climb up the long, green slope

Skookum Volcano Trail travels into the alpine, with stunning volcanic geology, and options for longer, high country adventures. Pictured is a backcountry, multiday route that explores the colorful geology of the Wrangell Mountains and provides exceptional views of the Mentasta Mountains.
WRANGELL-ST. ELIAS NATIONAL PARK & PRESERVE

toward the dome to the east. The view from the shoulder is worth the effort, and it's even better if you keep climbing to the top of the dome (5,400 feet). You can also hike up the dome from the pass.

The area is a geological fantasyland. Massive, flat-lying lava flows form cliffs to the west and south of the main canyon. Theresa Dome is a cinder cone that still has its original shape. Light-colored volcanic ash forms strange, curlicue towers above the pass. Harder bumps of rock (andesite dikes) protrude from deep layers of ash, and huge pyroclastic boulders—volcanic bombs welded together out of chunks of rock—are strewn along the streambed of the canyon.

In the animal realm, look for Dall sheep, bears, arctic ground squirrels, and pikas.

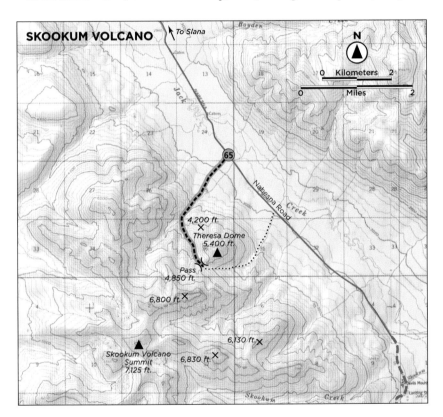

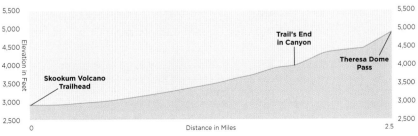

GLENNALLEN TO VALDEZ

THIS PART OF THE state takes in the Copper River Valley minus Wrangell–St. Elias National Park, a section of the Chugach Mountains, and eastern Prince William Sound at Valdez. It is unfortunately one of the least hiker-friendly sections of the state on the road system.

Valdez, in particular, is in an incredible mountain and fjord setting but has only very limited hiking. A local group has restored a section of the historic Valdez Trail along the Richardson Highway through Keystone Canyon, and Alaska State Parks has built a primitive, 11-mile one-way trail from the west edge of Valdez to Shoup Bay, a state marine park featuring Shoup Glacier, two fee cabins, a camping area, and wildlife galore. Shoup Bay is a fine destination, but it's much better reached by kayak or other watercraft than by backpacking the primitive trail.

66. TONSINA RIVER

WHY GO?

A short, easy trail suitable for most hiking abilities, with spectacular vistas of the Chugach Mountains and Tonsina River from a panoramic overlook.

THE RUNDOWN

Distance: 1.5 mile one way

Special features: A surprisingly scenic spot; a good short hiking break on the long drive to McCarthy

Location: 45 miles southeast of Glennallen

Difficulty: Easy

Trail type: Developed

Total elevation gain: None in, 200 feet out

Best season: July through Oct

Fees/permits: None

Maps: USGS Valdez C-3 (trail not shown)

Contact: Bureau of Land Management, Glennallen Field Office, Glenn Highway Mile 186.5, PO Box 147, Glennallen, AK 99588; (907) 822-3217; https://www.blm.gov/alaska

FINDING THE TRAILHEAD

 Drive about 32 miles south of Glennallen or 86 miles north of Valdez on the Richardson Highway and turn east onto the Edgerton Highway, the road to Chitina and McCarthy. The trailhead is 12.3 miles east on the Edgerton, in a small pullout on the south side of the road. The trail sign and register are barely visible from the highway, so the trailhead is easy to miss; coming from the west, watch for Milepost 12 and then be prepared to pull off the highway 0.3 mile beyond.

WHAT TO SEE

The Tonsina River Trail is a short, pleasant forest walk that ends on a bluff overlooking the Tonsina River. The Tonsina flows east into Prince William Sound by way of the Copper River, which it joins a few miles below. The main event of the hike is the striking view from the bluff, which combines the river far below with the alpine ridges of the Chugach Mountains far above to the south.

The change in vegetation as you reach the dry, sandy river bluff is also dramatic, as the spruce-cottonwood forest suddenly yields to aspen, grasses, and sagebrush. Look and listen for hawks along the bluff, and look across the main stem of the river for the channel that some industrious beavers have turned into a small lake.

The forest is low and protected, so it can be mosquito-infested in midsummer, but the bluff is often breezy and relatively bug-free. The small red berries of soapberry, one of the common shrubs along the trail, are a favorite food of bears. Also in the red/orange forest-fruit department, look for rose hips, timber berries, and highbush cranberries if you do the hike in late summer or fall.

TIDBIT

Plan on hiking this 3-mile round-trip trail to split up a long drive (which is common in this portion of the state).

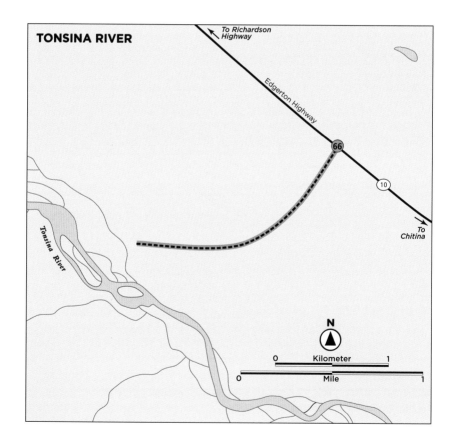

67. WORTHINGTON GLACIER

WHY GO?

A short trail with 1,200 feet in elevation and options for more adventurous hikers, with stunning views of the Worthington Glacier.

THE RUNDOWN

Distance: 1 mile one way

Special features: Worthington Glacier. The hike is a bit exposed and potentially dangerous in places on the narrow ridge. Day use only

Location: 33 miles north of Valdez

Difficulty: Moderate to Strenuous

Trail type: Less-developed trail/route

Total elevation gain: 1,200 feet

Best season: Late June through mid-Sept

Fees/permits: None

Maps: USGS Valdez A-5 (trail not shown)

Contact: Alaska State Parks, Kenai/PWS Area Office, PO Box 1247, Soldotna, AK 99669; (907) 262-5581; http://dnr.alaska.gov/parks/

FINDING THE TRAILHEAD

 The Worthington Glacier State Recreation Site is immediately off the Richardson Highway, about 33 miles north of Valdez and 2.7 miles north of Thompson Pass. Turn west into the recreation area. A 0.4-mile access road leads to the parking area.

WHAT TO SEE

Another of Alaska's fine crop of drive-up glaciers, Worthington has the distinction of being 3 miles down the road from the state's snowiest weather-recording station, Thompson Pass, where 81 feet fell in the winter of 1952–1953. As you might guess from the setting, this is a popular recreation site, especially on clear days.

The glacier falls 4 miles from its source to the terminus at the lake below the recreation site's viewing shelter. The dam that created the lake is a terminal moraine, a mass of rock and gravel that accumulates at the toe of a glacier; the Worthington moraine is less than one hundred years old. Like most of Alaska's glaciers, the

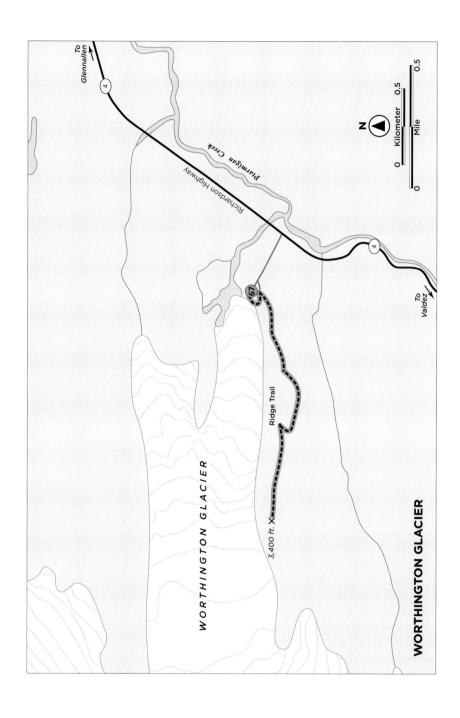

To Glennallen

4

Ptarmigan Creek

Richardson Highway

4

To Valdez

67

Ridge Trail

3,400 ft. X

WORTHINGTON GLACIER

N

Kilometer 0.5

0

Mile 0.5

0

WORTHINGTON GLACIER

A hiker walks near Worthington Glacier, the official trail is 1 mile one-way with 1,200 feet elevation, and provides numerous options for adventurers looking for off trail hiking.
CRAIG BRANDT

A view from the Worthington Glacier Trail, which is easily accessible from the Richardson Highway, and a popular way to split up a long drive.
ERICA WATSON

Worthington Glacier is in retreat, but not as dramatically as many others. All that snowfall helps.

To get a better look, follow a short, paved, accessible interpretive trail, which leads to a viewing platform looking out on the toe of the glacier. The trail also loops back along the lake, adding up in total to about 0.5 mile.

Hikers looking for more of a challenge, head to the Ridge Trail, which leaves from the west end of the parking area. From here, the main Ridge Trail climbs steeply with the glacier's lateral moraine to the left (south), yielding a spectacular view of the glacier and the country around it.

The trail continues climbing through an alder forest with switchbacks. Follow the ridge for 0.25 miles, then follow as the trail veers left into a brush thicket and into a large valley west of the ridge. Follow the well-marked route, rather than the old trail along the crumbling cliff ridge.

On the way up the Ridge Trail, you'll walk through sloping wildflower meadows where columbine, valerian, and geranium bloom in red, white, and blue at summer's height. The contrast between the blue ice in the valley to the north and the green alpine meadows and small mountain brook in the valley to the south could hardly be more striking. Continue following the trail as it travels through tundra, and to the right, reconnects with the ridge to the turnaround point. Look for stunning views of the Worthington Glacier from this point.

This is a more difficult hike than you might expect for only a 2-mile round-trip; good knees, boots with decent traction, and a staff or ski pole are all highly recommended, and this is not a hike for smaller children. In a few places on the foot-wide trail, there is considerable exposure, with steep, hardpacked scree slopes on one or both sides, not exactly an ideal place for people who don't care for heights. A fall from some points on the moraine could be serious.

TIDBIT

Plan on hiking this 2-mile round-trip trail to split up a long drive (which is common in this portion of the state).

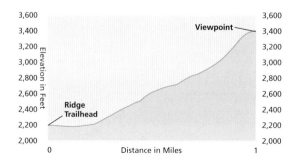

CORDOVA

CORDOVA, IN EASTERN PRINCE William Sound, is accessible only by state ferry or air and, unlike many other scenic Alaska coastal towns, isn't yet a major industrial-tourism destination. The 48-mile Copper River Highway east of Cordova is the road to a fine vacation of hiking, backpacking, camping, fishing, and wildlife watching. Bring your best rain gear—eastern Prince William Sound can be extremely wet.

Cordova is well known for its shorebird festival the first week of May each year. The Copper River delta, the largest wetland on North America's entire Pacific Coast, attracts the largest shorebird gathering anywhere in the Americas in the spring, and the bird life in general is spectacular from spring to fall.

For other hikes not described in detail here, try the Heney Ridge Trail, 5 miles out Whitshed Road on Hartney Bay, which climbs 3.5 miles to outstanding views from a point on Heney Ridge. The Childs Glacier Trail, accessible by boat (due to Million Dollar Bridge closure), at Mile 48 of the Copper River Highway in the Childs Glacier Recreation Area, leads 1 mile to a view of the Childs Glacier and the Copper River, one of the most stunning sights in Alaska.

68. POWER CREEK AND CRATER LAKE

WHY GO?

This trail system travels by rain forest, glacial valleys, alpine ridges, and lakes. Go on a day hike or plan an overnight trek; the diversity of the landscape on this chain of trails is among some of the best.

THE RUNDOWN

Distances: Crater Lake: 2.4 miles one way. Power Creek Cabin: 4.2 miles one way. Mount Eyak ridge traverse: 12 miles between the Power Creek and Crater Lake trailheads

Special features: Scenery, alpine rambling, a fee cabin, and a trail shelter. Anyone tackling the ridge traverse should be experienced in route finding

Location: The 2 trailheads are 2 and 7 miles northeast of Cordova

Difficulty: Crater Lake and Power Creek: moderate. Traverse: strenuous

Trail type: Crater Lake and Power Creek: more-developed trail. Traverse: a ridgetop route

Total elevation gain: Crater Lake: 1,500 feet. Power Creek: 700 feet. Traverse: about 3,000 feet

Best season: Late June through Sept

Fees/permits: Fee for cabin use

Maps: USGS Cordova C-5 (trails not shown); Forest Service leaflets Crater Lake Trail and Power Creek Trail; National Geographic Prince William Sound East

Contact: Chugach National Forest, Cordova Ranger District, 612 Second Street, PO Box 280, Cordova, AK 99574; (907) 424-7661; www.fs.usda.gov/chugach/

FINDING THE TRAILHEAD

Both trailheads are on Power Creek Road, the extension of Cordova's Lake Avenue. From First Avenue and Browning in downtown Cordova, drive 0.2 mile and take a hard left onto 2nd Ave. Drive another 0.1 mile to the second right, which is Lake Avenue; Lake is the street with a small, shingled church on the southwest corner.

Turn right (east) onto Lake Avenue and continue past the city airstrip and floatplane base, a total of about 2 miles from downtown, to the city-owned

Skater's Cabin. For the Crater Lake Trailhead, park on the right side of the road by the cabin, and walk across the road to the signed trailhead.

For the Power Creek Trail, keep driving past Skater's Cabin, about another 5.5 miles, to the trailhead at the end of the road.

WHAT TO SEE

The Power/Crater Trail system leads into spectacular country, traversing rain forest, the glacial Power Creek valley, mountain meadows, and alpine Mount Eyak ridge and Crater Lake. You can day-hike or camp at Crater Lake, day-hike up Power Creek, rent the Power Creek Cabin for an overnight hike, or spend two or more days on the Eyak traverse. The diversity of terrain and vegetation on these hikes is outstanding.

Crater Lake Trail. This 2.4-mile hike begins as a climb through dripping western hemlock forest above Eyak Lake—keep an eye out for blueberries, black slugs, and blue-ribbon-worthy skunk cabbage. At about a mile, a short side trail leads to an overlook of the lake and the surrounding country.

At Crater Lake, wildflower meadows, rocky promontories, and gravel beaches make a pretty setting for a ramble along the shoreline. There are a few protected campsites near the lake. A steep hiking route up the ridge to the southwest and south leads to the top of Mount Eyak. (There is a city-maintained trail to the peak from the south.)

The Mount Eyak ridge route to Power Creek cuts away from the lake and heads north along the ridge. The traverse may be a bit easier beginning on the Power Creek side, as from that direction the longest climb is on a developed trail instead of the steep, sometimes slick route above Crater Lake.

Power Creek Trail. There aren't any dull moments at the beginning of the 4.2-mile Power Creek hike. A deep gorge encloses thundering Ohman Falls (not "oh, man"; it's named after a hydropower pioneer named Oscar Ohman). Smaller, snow-fed waterfalls slide down the valley walls as the trail cuts through a jungle of salmonberry and ferns. Above the falls, the trail runs through a broad basin known locally as Surprise Valley, with its wide, braided stream and sandbars.

The trail cuts into the rock ledge at the west edge of the valley as it passes a series of beaver dams, ponds, and lodges. Look for major beaver architecture and nesting waterfowl, swans included, along this section of the creek. At 2.3 miles the hike reaches the Alice Smith Cutoff to Mount Eyak ridge and the traverse to Crater Lake.

The Power Creek Trail ends at the cabin, a big cedar shelter with a rain catchment barrel—there is no surface water close by. (Remember to boil or filter the barrel water just as you would surface water.) Try counting all the waterfalls on the steep mountain slopes on both sides of the valley. The cabin is available through the Forest Service's reservation-and-fee system (www.reserveusa.com or 877-444-6777).

Young hikers take a break overlooking Orca Inlet on the Mount Eyak Ridge. This trail system allows options for hikes ranging from 2.4 miles one way, to a 12-mile traverse of Mount Eyak Ridge. CHELSEA HAISMA

MILES AND DIRECTIONS

0.0   Start from the Power Creek Trailhead.

1.0   Pass Ohman Falls.

2.3   The hike reaches the Alice Smith Cutoff.

4.2   The trail ends at Power Creek Cabin.

Mount Eyak Ridge Traverse. The 12-mile traverse makes a great 2-to-3-day backpack, but you'll need a map and compass and route-finding experience for the trip. The weather and visibility in Prince William Sound's mountains are subject to change on about ten seconds' notice, and the cairns that mark the route along the ridge may be very difficult to follow when clouds close in. In good weather, though, the views are simply amazing.

From Mile 2.3 of the Power Creek Trail, take the Alice Smith Cutoff west and up about 1,200 feet to the ridgetop, passing through a mossy, bouldery forest, steep

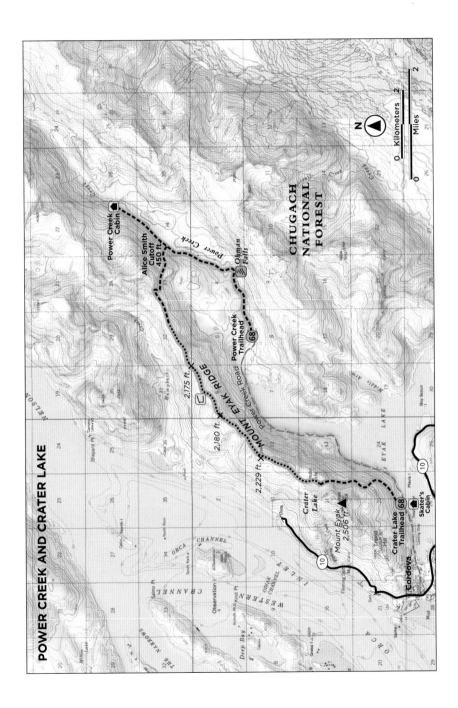

POWER CREEK AND CRATER LAKE

Power Creek Cabin

Alice Smith
Cutoff
450 ft

Power Creek

Ohman
Falls

Power Creek
Trailhead
68

CHUGACH
NATIONAL
FOREST

2,175 ft.

MOUNT EYAK RIDGE

2,180 ft.

2,229 ft.

Power Creek Road

EYAK LAKE

Crater
Lake

Mount Eyak
2,506 ft.

Crater Lake
Trailhead 68

Skater's
Cabin

10

Cordova

N

0   1   2   Kilometers
0   1   2   Miles

brush patches, and subalpine stands of mountain hemlock. The trail first touches the ridgeline at about 1,700 feet in elevation. Look north across a high lake basin to Snyder Mountain, elevation 3,432 feet, and scan the area for mountain goats.

A bare but enclosed shelter (no reservation, no fee) sits on the north side of the ridge at about 1,900 feet in elevation, a bit more than 2 miles out the ridge. There are snow patches and runoff for water nearby, though these may dwindle by late summer. In about another 3 miles, the route begins to drop steeply into the Crater Lake basin; take care to find the right route before descending. Just above the lake, find the Crater Lake Trail and hike the 2.4 miles to the trailhead.

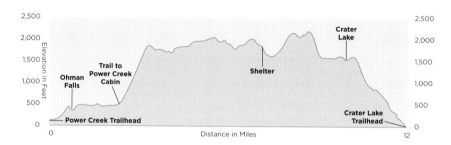

MILES AND DIRECTIONS

- **0.0** Start from the Power Creek Trailhead.
- **1.0** Pass Ohman Falls.
- **2.3** Turn left (west) at the Alice Smith Cutoff.
- **4.3** Climb to Mount Eyak ridge.
- **6.5** Reach the trail shelter on the ridge.
- **9.6** Descend to Crater Lake.
- **12.0** Arrive at Crater Lake Trailhead.

Shorter hikes: The 1-mile hike, one way, to Ohman Falls on the Power Creek Trail is the best easy hike on this trail system.

Fishing: There are stocked rainbow trout in Crater Lake.

69. SHERIDAN MOUNTAIN TRAIL

WHY GO?

A challenging trail traveling through forests near streams and waterfalls with spectacular views of Sheridan and Sherman Glaciers.

THE RUNDOWN

Distances: 2.9 miles one way

Special features: Spruce-hemlock forest, following a stream, waterfalls, and a scenic alpine basin

Location: 18 miles east of Cordova.

Difficulty: Difficult

Trail type: Developed

Total elevation gain: About 2,300 feet

Best season: May through Oct

Fees/permits: None

Maps: USGS Cordova C-4; Forest Service leaflet McKinley Lake–Pipeline Lakes Trail System; National Geographic Prince William Sound East

Contact: Chugach National Forest, Cordova Ranger District, 612 Second Street, PO Box 280, Cordova, AK 99574; (907) 424-7661; www.fs.usda.gov/chugach/

FINDING THE TRAILHEAD

 Drive east on the Copper River Highway to Mile 13.7. Turn north on Sheridan Glacier Road, and follow the main road 4.3 miles to the end, and look for trailhead sign.

WHAT TO SEE

The Sheridan Mountain Trail starts in a spruce-hemlock forest, winding along a stream with plenty of places to stop and enjoy the vistas including waterfalls along the route. The first stretch of trail includes intermittent boardwalks crossing the wet, Muskeg vegetation that is common to the temperate rainforest in the Cordova region. This trail is moderately steep in difficulty starting at 200 feet in elevation until 0.35 mile, where the route begins climbing traveling through dense forest canopy and open rocky chutes, providing intermittent glimpses of the expansive Copper River Delta. At Mile 1.5, the trail crosses a bridge over a large stream, and a nice option for a rest stop to enjoy and watch the powerful waterway tumble through a boulder streambed.

From Mile 1.6 to 1.9 the route climbs, traveling by timber and shrub vegetation, then opens to a small alpine basin. The trail continues to open, and follow the rock cairns for another mile, to the top of the ridge with spectacular vistas of Sheridan and Sherman Glaciers, and the infamous Copper River Delta. The Copper River Delta is one of the ten largest rivers by volume, and one of the most productive wetlands on the Pacific Coast of the United States.

Take in the sights from the top, because on a day with good visibility, you'll want to spent some time taking in the stunning views.

MILES AND DIRECTIONS

- **0.0** Begin at the Sheridan Mountain Trailhead.
- **0.3** Route starts climbing.
- **1.5** Cross a bridge over a large stream.
- **1.9** Opens to small alpine basin.
- **2.9** Top of the ridge.

SHERIDAN GLACIER TRAIL

A hiker climbs along the 2.9-mile
Sheridan Mountain Trail,
showcasing spectacular
views of Sheridan and Sherman
Glaciers from the ridge.
MIKE AUSMAN

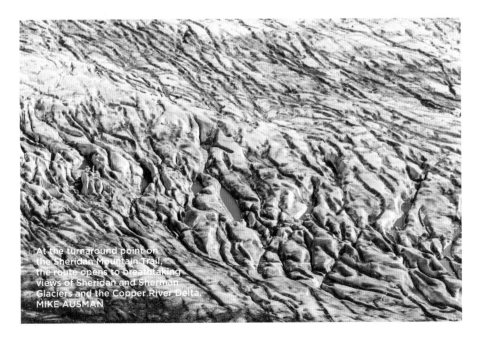

At the turnaround point on
the Sheridan Mountain Trail,
the route opens to breathtaking
views of Sheridan and Sherman
Glaciers and the Copper River Delta.
MIKE AUSMAN

70. McKINLEY LAKE

WHY GO?

A maintained trail traveling by lakes with spawning salmon (and other fish), a historic mine, and two cabins.

THE RUNDOWN

Distances: 2.4 miles one way

Special features: Fishing, spawning salmon, a historic mine, and 2 fee cabins

Location: 21 miles east of Cordova

Difficulty: Easy

Trail type: More developed

Total elevation gain: About 60 feet

Best season: May through Oct

Fees/permits: Fee for cabin use

Maps: USGS Cordova B-4; Forest Service leaflet *McKinley Lake–Pipeline Lakes Trail System*; National Geographic *Prince William Sound East*

Contact: Chugach National Forest, Cordova Ranger District, 612 Second Street, PO Box 280, Cordova, AK 99574; (907) 424-7661; www.fs.usda.gov/chugach/

FINDING THE TRAILHEAD

The McKinley Lake Trailhead is on the north side of the Copper River Highway, about 21.6 miles east of Cordova.

WHAT TO SEE

The McKinley Lake hike can be a wet one, but if you want to spend the night, there is a dry cabin waiting for you at the lake. There is also a cabin just off the road, only 250 feet from the trailhead; both are available through the Forest Service reservation-and-fee system (www.reserveusa.com or 877-444-6777). Campsites are very limited.

The trail meets the shoreline of McKinley Lake in just two places: the southern lobe of the lake at Mile 1, and the cove at the upper end of the lake by the McKinley Lake Cabin. The cabin is nestled into the woods just above the lake. This end of the lake is full of spawning red salmon by late July, and bears may be nearby looking for a fish dinner.

Beyond the cabin is all that's left of the Lucky Strike Mine, which must have been named before the results were in. Though over 100 claims were staked and about $200,000 spent on development, the mine yielded only sixteen ounces of gold and nine ounces of silver. Rusting machinery, pipe, tram track, and a collapsed tunnel are the most obvious evidence of the mine. Faint paths branch back into the forest where the mine once operated, but take care while exploring around the shafts, and don't drink any water from the mine area—it may be contaminated with heavy metals.

Like several of Cordova's hikes, this trail is improved with boardwalk and log corduroy across wet sections. Here and on other Cordova trails, the Forest Service has covered wood surfaces with fishing net recycled from Cordova's fishing fleet for better traction.

An alternate route to or from McKinley Lake is the Pipeline Lakes Trail, which is *very* wet and a mile longer than the McKinley Lake Trail. This hike isn't recommended without rubber boots and a real passion for the venerable Alaska sport of muskeg slogging. If any of the trail markers are down, the route may be a bit difficult to follow in a place or two, so keep an eye on where you are on the topographic maps you've brought with you. There is a bit of history here too: the lakes were a source of water for the trains that ran from Cordova to the Kennecott Copper Mine on the Copper River and Northwestern Railway from 1911 to 1938.

An aerial view of McKinley Lake. The easy 2.4-mile trail travels by lakes with spawning salmon, a historic mine, and two cabins. MIKE AUSMAN

MILES AND DIRECTIONS

0.0   Begin at the McKinley Lake Trailhead.

0.1   Pass McKinley Trail Cabin.

1.0   Arrive at the south end of McKinley Lake.

1.2   Intersect the Pipeline Lakes Trail.

2.2   Arrive at McKinley Lake Cabin.

2.4   Reach the Lucky Strike Mine.

Fishing: McKinley Lake supports salmon, cutthroat trout, and Dolly Varden. The outlet stream, a 0.5-mile bushwhack from the trail, offers the best fishing. Red salmon cruise up the stream in late June and early July, and there is a silver-salmon run in September.

TIDBIT
Remember your rain gear for this adventure.

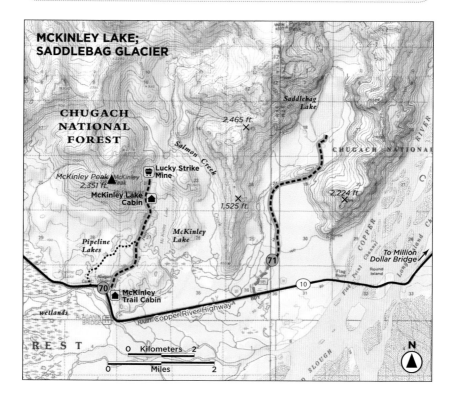

71. SADDLEBAG GLACIER

WHY GO?

This trail provides easy access to a gorgeous lake (with floating ice), mountains and jagged peaks, waterfalls, and a glacier.

THE RUNDOWN See map on page 306.

Distance: 3 miles one way

Special features: Rain forest and Saddlebag Glacier

Location: 25 miles east of Cordova

Difficulty: Easy

Trail type: More developed

Total elevation gain: 200 feet in

Best season: May through Oct

Fees/permits: None

Maps: USGS Cordova B-3 and B-4 (trail not shown), Forest Service leaflet *Saddlebag Glacier Trail*; National Geographic *Prince William Sound East*

Contact: Chugach National Forest, Cordova Ranger District, 612 Second Street, PO Box 280, Cordova, AK 99574; (907) 424-7661; www.fs.usda.gov/chugach/

FINDING THE TRAILHEAD

 Drive 24.8 miles east of Cordova on the Copper River Highway and turn north onto an unpaved forest road. Continue about a mile to the trailhead.

WHAT TO SEE

The locals call this trail Cordova's Portage Glacier (see the Portage Pass hike) without the RVs, visitor center, or crowds. The mass of Saddlebag Glacier's blue ice in the distance, the beautiful lake with its floating ice, green mountainsides, waterfalls, and jagged peaks make a spectacular view at the end of this easy half-day hike.

The first half of the Saddlebag Trail winds through Sitka-spruce rain forest, with mosses hanging thickly from tree branches, bright green lichen on tree trunks, knee-high ferns, and a sea of devil's club. The second half of the hike is grassy and brushy with alder and cottonwood. Remember to sing to those potential bears in the woods.

The tread is relatively dry (for Cordova, of course), so some mountain bikers use the trail. The trail ends on a gravel beach with a great view of the valley and the glacier; be sure to scan the high slopes for mountain goats. It's possible to camp here at lower water levels.

Shorter hikes: Hike a mile or so out the trail to get a taste of Cordova's rain forest.

A reflection on Saddlebag Lake, a highlight and turnaround point on the 3-mile one-way trail. MIKE AUSMAN

Packrafters paddle on Saddlebag Lake, a beautiful lake with floating ice, green mountainsides, waterfalls, and jagged peaks, make it a spectacular view at the end of this easy 3-mile one-way hike. MIKE AUSMAN

The 3-mile Dan Moller trail parallels the Kowee Creek, climbing out of the forest and into high country with mountain views along the way to the historic Dan Moller Cabin.
MOLLIE FOSTER

SKAGWAY

SKAGWAY, A SMALL TOWN at the head of Alaska's Inside Passage, has always been a tourist town, beginning with the Klondike gold rush of 1898. It's easily the most pedestrian-friendly town in the state; all the local trails are easily accessible for travelers without cars. Skagway is accessible by road from the Yukon and British Columbia, by ferry from Haines, or by air.

72. LAUGHTON GLACIER

WHY GO?

A trail only accessible by railroad, traveling by a cabin, and ending with a spectacular view of the Laughton Glacier.

THE RUNDOWN

Distance: Laughton Glacier Cabin: 1.5 miles one way. Laughton Glacier: 2.5 miles one way

Special features: Laughton Glacier, subalpine fir forest, a fee cabin. The trailhead is a flag stop on the White Pass & Yukon Route Railroad, not accessible by road

Location: 14 miles north of Skagway on the WP&YR Railroad

Difficulty: Easy to the cabin, moderate to the glacier

Trail type: More-developed trail to the cabin; a route

following Laughton Creek to the glacier

Total elevation gain: 200 feet to the cabin and 1,000 feet to the glacier

Best season: Mid-June to mid-Sept

Fees/permits: Fee for cabin use

Maps: USGS Skagway C-1 (SE); Skagway Trail Map

Contact: Skagway Convention & Visitors Bureau, Broadway/ 2nd Ave. PO Box 1029, Skagway, AK 99840; (888) 762-1898; www.skagway.com

FINDING THE TRAILHEAD

The trailhead is the Laughton Glacier Flag Stop at White Pass & Yukon Route Railroad Mile 14; there is no road access. The train depot is on 2nd Ave. in downtown Skagway, just east of Broadway and the National Park Service visitor center. All flag stops should be ticketed at least a day in advance. Check with the WP&YR for a current schedule and fares (www.whitepassrailroad.com or 800-343-7373).

WHAT TO SEE

The sight at the end of this trip is breathtaking: a five-fingered ice fall spilling out of a riot of jagged, dark peaks onto the flat ice of the Laughton Glacier. The glacier flows off the Sawtooth Range into a cold, north-facing valley in the upper watershed of the Skagway River, and it's a relatively simple hike to see it. The trip follows the roaring river through a band of sweetly aromatic subalpine fir forest for 1.5 miles to the Forest Service fee cabin at Laughton Glacier. This upper valley, known as Warm Pass Valley, was the route of a historic gold-rush trail to Atlin, British Columbia.

The hiking route to the glacier turns up the north-facing Laughton Creek valley. Beginning as a well-beaten path from the cabin, it crosses the glacier's rocky outwash plain, staying close to the west bank of the creek. The path grows fainter as you go, but the route is obvious enough and a few rock cairns mark the way. In about a mile the route peters out as it reaches a huge boulder pile in front of the rocky face of the glacier, where murky streams pour out into the daylight from under the ice. Don't approach any overhanging ice, and travel onto the glacier at your own risk.

To see more, climb around the boulder field to the right (west) and hike farther along the margin of the ice. It's about another mile to the end of the valley, in a glacier-filled basin below the five crevassed, whipped-cream fingers of nearly vertical ice. Look back down the valley to see the neat "trim line" along the edge of the forest that the glacier left behind in its recent retreat.

There are a few tent sites in the trees near the cabin, near the river and Laughton Creek. For reservations, go to www.reserveusa.com or call (877) 444-6777.

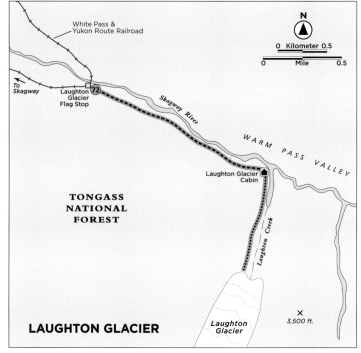

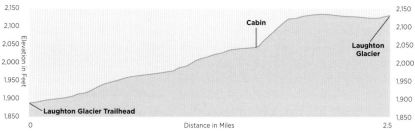

Denver Glacier: The Denver Glacier Trailhead is a WP&YR flag stop, at Mile 6. This is a rougher hike, 3.5 miles one way, to the moraine below the Denver Glacier. The Forest Service fee cabin is a renovated railroad car at the trailhead.

73. CHILKOOT PASS

WHY GO?

One of the longest trail traverses in Southeast Alaska, this trail travels through a variety of terrain, rich with history.

THE RUNDOWN

Distance: A 33-mile traverse

Special features: Forests, streams, lakes, alpine country, and a hike that's dripping with history. The north trailhead, Lake Bennett, is not on a road; access is by train or foot. No firearms allowed and pets are strongly discouraged. Canada Customs requires post-hike check-in at Fraser, British Columbia, or Whitehorse, Yukon

Location: Northwest of Skagway

Difficulty: Strenuous

Trail type: More developed, with some steep boulder-hopping on the Golden Stairs

Total elevation gain: About 4,500 feet from Dyea to Bennett, the usual direction, or about 2,500 feet from Bennett to Dyea

Best season: Late June to mid-Sept

Fees/permits: Permit and fee required; see below for details

Maps: USGS Skagway C-1 (SW, NW) and Canadian topo maps White Pass (104 M/11), Homan Lake (104 M/14), and Tutshi Lake (104 M/15). Most hikers use the National Park Service's *A Hiker's Guide to the Chilkoot Trail* or National Geographic's *Chilkoot Trail*

Contact: Klondike Gold Rush National Historical Park, 2nd and Broadway, PO Box 517, Skagway, AK 99840; (907) 983-9200; www.nps.gov/klgo. Permits through Parks Canada, (800) 661-0486 or (867) 667-3910 winter; www.pc.gc.ca/chilkoot

FINDING THE TRAILHEAD

 The Dyea and the Log Cabin trailheads are road-accessible, while Lake Bennett, at the north end of the trail, is accessible only by train or foot. Commercial shuttle vans run between Skagway and the Dyea and Log Cabin trailheads, and there is bus service to and from Log Cabin. Bennett is a stop on the White Pass & Yukon Route Railroad, which runs to and from Skagway; for schedules and fares, see www.whitepassrailroad.com or call (800) 343-7373. Check the park website or contact park personnel for up-to-date transportation options, as they are subject to change from year to year.

Dyea: From the NPS visitor center in lower downtown Skagway, drive about 2 miles north on State Street/Klondike Highway to Dyea Road. Turn left and continue about 7 miles to the trailhead on the right side of the road, just before the Taiya River Bridge. Trailhead parking is located on the side road to the Dyea Ranger Station and Campground, about 0.5 mile before (south of) the trailhead.

Log Cabin: Drive 27 miles north of Skagway on the Klondike Highway, about 5 miles north of the Canadian Customs station at Fraser. The parking area is on the left (west) side of the highway. You can end your trip by hiking out to Log Cabin via the Log Cabin Cutoff Trail (Mile 29.3 of the Chilkoot Trail) and the right-of-way along the railroad tracks, a total of about 6 miles from the Chilkoot Trail to Log Cabin.

Lake Bennett: The Bennett train depot is around the east side of the lake at the Canadian end of the Chilkoot Trail.

WHAT TO SEE

An outdoor museum, a beautiful hike, and the only long trail traverse in Southeast Alaska, the Chilkoot Trail attracts hikers from all over the world. The hike is amazingly diverse, taking in coastal and interior forests, a large river, a snowy mountain basin, rocky country above tree line, sparkling alpine streams, and huge lakes.

Large numbers of hikers, designated campsites, cooking shelters, and ranger stations make this not exactly a wilderness hike, but there are compensations: a chance to meet hikers from all over the country and the world, and the experience of hiking through a landscape littered with artifacts from the gold rush, for starters. (Please leave all artifacts in place and take only photos for your memories.) If you want to avoid the biggest crowds, do the trip outside the peak season, which most years is from mid-July to mid-August.

If you think there are a lot of hikers on the trail now, you should have been there during the winter of 1897–1898. The Coast Range peaks rang with the voices of thousands of gold stampeders that winter as they plodded back and forth over Chilkoot Pass, shuttling the "ton of goods" that it would take to survive a year of prospecting in the Yukon. The Chilkoot was one of two trails, and the more popular of the two, that connected the Pacific with the navigable headwaters of the Yukon River.

The "historically correct" direction is south to north, from Dyea to Lake Bennett, the direction the stampeders took. However, the hike is equally fine from north to south, and even a little easier starting at either Bennett or Log Cabin.

This is Alaska's most regulated hike. There are fifty permits issued per day for crossing Chilkoot Pass, forty-two available by reservation and eight saved for walk-ins. You'll need to check in at the trail center the day before you hope to start if you want a walk-in slot. See "Contact" above for information and reservations.

Camping is in designated areas only. Each camp includes a toilet, several tent sites, and a pole or cache for hanging food out of reach of bears. Most camps also have small cooking and warming shelters. Please build fires only in the stoves in the shelters; cook in the shelters or at least 300 feet from any campsite; and hang or cache your food when not cooking or eating. Keeping bears from developing a taste for human food is a big concern here, so be on your best bear-country behavior. Bring a good tent; sleeping in the shelters isn't allowed.

The hike may seem tame with all these amenities, but the weather in the high country can be just as nasty and unforgiving as anywhere else in Alaska. Between Sheep Camp and Deep Lake is a long, difficult 10 miles of alpine hiking. Bring plenty of warm layers and rain gear; you'll likely be very happy you did.

Dyea to Sheep Camp: The lower part of the trail follows the Taiya River valley through coastal forest. Finnegan's Point, the site of a short-lived toll road during the gold rush, is the first designated camp on the trail. The Canyon City shelter and camp is in a cottonwood flat by the river at 7.5 miles; the historic townsite of Canyon City is about 0.5 mile beyond the camp and across the river. Not much is left of this "city" that grew up at the mouth of the Taiya River canyon as the lower terminal of a cable tram used to haul supplies over the pass.

Beyond Canyon City the trail climbs above the river, which crashes over boulders through a deep canyon below. Above the canyon, Pleasant Camp is, well, pleasant, and definitely not as crowded as Sheep Camp, the next designated camp on the trail.

Sheep Camp is in the last mile of forest before the subalpine and alpine section of the hike begins. Most hikers camp here because it's the last camp before the pass, and the next day is a long hike to Happy Camp or Deep Lake, the next designated camps on the hike. A ranger station and the historic townsite are about 0.5 mile up the trail from the camping area.

Sheep Camp to Lake Lindeman: The mountain wonderland begins above Sheep Camp. Waterfalls tumble down sheer granite faces, and splintered cotton-woods along the trail serve as a reminder of the 1898 snow slide that killed about sixty gold stampeders. Above tree line the climb up Long Hill leads to The Scales, where tram operators weighed their loads before hoisting them over the pass. The tram towers and piles of cable and equipment at The Scales are the most concentrated group of artifacts on the trail.

From The Scales, it's a steep boulder-field climb up the Golden Stairs (the trail consisted of steps carved in snow in the winter of 1897–1898). At the top, enjoy the great view back down the Taiya River valley. A few minutes more, and you're across the pass and in sight of the Parks Canada warden's cabin. Welcome to Canada.

Snow stays near the pass and in the Crater Lake basin north of the pass well into the summer, feeding the valley of lakes and cascading streams to the north that is arguably the scenic highlight of the hike. Happy Camp, 4 miles beyond the pass, is still on the edge of the alpine zone; the next camp in the trees is Deep Lake, another 2.5 miles past Happy Camp. Those 2.5 miles aren't the fast downhill romp you might imagine; the trail climbs and then winds down the ridge east of Long Lake over that distance. Below Deep Lake the Chilkoot descends to forested Lake Lindeman along a sheer-walled gorge carved by the lake's outlet stream.

Lindeman to Bennett: Lindeman is a place to stay awhile and explore. There are two camping areas, a Parks Canada field camp, an interpretive tent, and a gold-rush cemetery here, not to mention loons on the lake and, in good budget years, warden-led hikes to the site of the stampeders' 1898 winter city.

Leaving Lindeman, the trail follows a granite, piney ridge to Bare Loon Lake (campsite, no shelter). In another 0.3 mile the spur trail to the railroad tracks and Log Cabin forks right. The final miles of the hike to Lake Bennett are soft and sandy. Lindeman Rapids, not far off the trail between the lakes, claimed several stampeders' outfits and a few lives in the spring of 1898.

The historic church at Bennett is the only gold-rush-era building still standing anywhere along the trail. The train depot, the end of the trail, is just around the corner of the lake to the east.

The Chilkoot Trail on the way from Skagway to Finnegan's Point includes a mix of terrain, from wide gravel tracks to long boardwalks over swamps. The Chilkoot Pass is a 3-to-5-day traverse through the Coast Mountains, from Alaska into Canada, following the route of the Klondike gold rush of 1898. WILL KOEPPEN

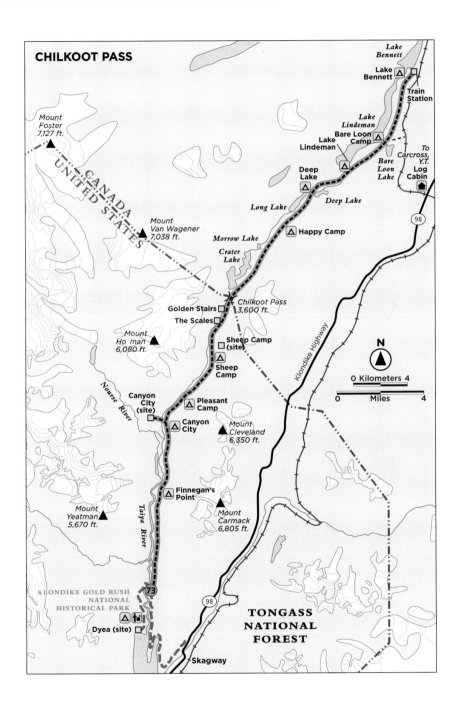

CHILKOOT PASS

Lake Bennett
Lake Bennett
Train Station

Mount Foster 7,127 ft.

CANADA
UNITED STATES

Lake Lindeman
Bare Loon Camp
Lake Lindeman

To Carcross, Y.T.
Log Cabin

Deep Lake
Deep Lake

Bare Loon Lake

Long Lake

98

Mount Van Wagener 7,038 ft.

Morrow Lake

Happy Camp

Crater Lake

Chilkoot Pass 3,600 ft.

Golden Stairs
The Scales

Mount Ho man 6,080 ft.

Sheep Camp (site)

Sheep Camp

Klondike Highway

N

0 Kilometers 4
0 Miles 4

Nourse River

Canyon City (site)

Pleasant Camp

Canyon City

Mount Cleveland 6,350 ft.

Finnegan's Point

Mount Yeatman 5,670 ft.

Taiya River

Mount Carmack 6,805 ft.

KLONDIKE GOLD RUSH
NATIONAL
HISTORICAL PARK

73

Dyea (site)

98

TONGASS
NATIONAL
FOREST

Skagway

Chilkoot Pass at 3,600 feet, on the border between Alaska and Canada. HALEY JOHNSTON

MILES AND DIRECTIONS

0.0 Begin at the trailhead.

5.0 Finnegan's Point* is the first designated camp on the trail.

7.5 The Canyon City* shelter and camp is in a cottonwood flat.

10.5 Arrive at Pleasant Camp*.

11.5 Sheep Camp* is the last camp before the pass.

12.0 Arrive at the Sheep Camp ranger station/historic site.

16.0 Climb to The Scales.

16.5 Cross Chilkoot Pass.

20.5 Happy Camp* is still on the edge of the alpine zone.

23.0 Deep Lake* offers forest camping.

26.0 The trail descends to Lake Lindeman*.

29.0 Bare Loon Lake* offers a campsite but no shelter.

29.3 The Log Cabin Cutoff Trail forks right.

33.0 The hike ends at Lake Bennett*.

*Designated camp areas

DOING THE KLONDIKE OUTDOORS

The great Klondike gold rush through Chilkoot Pass materialized out of nowhere in 1897 and vanished into history by 1899. The vivid stories in the stampeders' diaries, however, reveal the rush as one of the most amazing two-plus years the North has ever seen. Many of the best stories that have come down to us today tell of the amazing outdoor adventures the stampeders shared and of the wild, pristine country they traversed on their way to the gold diggings.

More than a century later, you can still see and do much of what they experienced. At the top of the list is backpacking the Chilkoot Trail. On the easier side, take a National Park Service–led walking tour of the Dyea townsite, the long-defunct town at the foot of the trail, or do the same in the history-tourism town of Skagway, which was the jumping-off point for an alternate route to the Klondike through White Pass.

Across the border in the Yukon Territory, the short hike to Whitehorse Rapids, just outside the town of Whitehorse, leads to a stretch of raging river that tore apart many stampeders' boats, not to mention their dreams. Plus, you can canoe the river to Carmacks or Dawson, paddling through Lake LaBarge, the scene of Robert Service's famous poem "The Cremation of Sam McGee," and floating past the remains of a few grounded and beached steamboats from the gold-rush days.

74. DEWEY LAKES

WHY GO?

A trail with day hike and overnight options by lakes, within walking distance of downtown Skagway.

THE RUNDOWN

Distances: 0.6 to 4.2 miles one way

Special features: Lakes, alpine country, and a trail shelter at Upper Dewey Lake

Location: Above downtown Skagway

Difficulty: Lower Dewey Lake: easy if a bit steep. Upper Dewey Lake and Devil's Punch Bowl: strenuous

Trail type: Lower lake: more developed. Upper lakes: less developed, very steep in places

Total elevation gain: Lower Dewey Lake: 500 feet. Upper Dewey Lake: 3,100 feet. Devil's Punch Bowl: 3,700 feet

Best season: Lower lake: mid-May through early Oct. Upper lakes: mid-June to mid-Sept

Fees/permits: None

Maps: USGS Skagway B-1 (NW); Skagway Trail Map

Contact: Skagway Convention & Visitors Bureau, Broadway/2nd Ave. PO Box 1029, Skagway, AK 99840; (888) 762-1898; www.skagway.com

FINDING THE TRAILHEAD

In downtown Skagway follow 2nd Ave. east three blocks from the National Park Service visitor center. If driving, park on the street or in the lot east of the railroad station on 2nd Ave. On foot, turn left along the railroad siding just before 2nd Ave. crosses the tracks. In 0.1 mile cut across the tracks (watch for trains!) to the trailhead.

WHAT TO SEE

There are two Dewey Lakes, and they are very different places. Lower Dewey Lake lies in the trees 500 feet above downtown Skagway, and the hike is easy if a bit steep. Upper Dewey Lake, in a subalpine basin at 3,097 feet in elevation, is a long, very steep haul up the mountain slope above the lower lake. Devil's Punch Bowl is an icy lake in an alpine cirque a little less than a mile above and south of Upper Dewey Lake.

From the trailhead, follow marked switchbacks about 0.5 mile up to a trail junction; the trail to Sturgill's Landing and the south leg of the 2-mile loop trail around Lower Dewey Lake forks right here. If your objective is Upper Dewey Lake or Devil's Punch Bowl, turn left at the intersection, and in another 0.2 mile, pass a spur trail to the lower lake and another fork to the loop trail to the right. Then turn right in 0.1 mile at the marked junction for Upper Dewey Lake, where the trail to Icy Lake and Upper Reid Falls bears left.

Lower Dewey Lake: The lower lake, long and narrow, lies in a slot in the bench above the city. The loop trail winds about 2 miles around the lake, leading to several pleasant picnic sites.

Upper Dewey Lake: The trail to the upper lake climbs very steeply along the course of cascading Dewey Creek. The grade eases to a "normal" trail climb about a third of the way up, and there are some wet, eroded sections beyond. Just below the lake, the forest opens into subalpine stands of mountain hemlock and subalpine fir, and the trail crosses the creek on a footbridge.

The lake is just below tree line in a classic cirque, or glacial basin, below steep, rocky slopes and peaks. The trail shelter is a log cabin, and there are campsites on

he lower Dewey Lake, long and narrow,
cludes a loop trail 2 miles around the lake,
ading to several pleasant picnic sites.
ACHEL DEEHAN

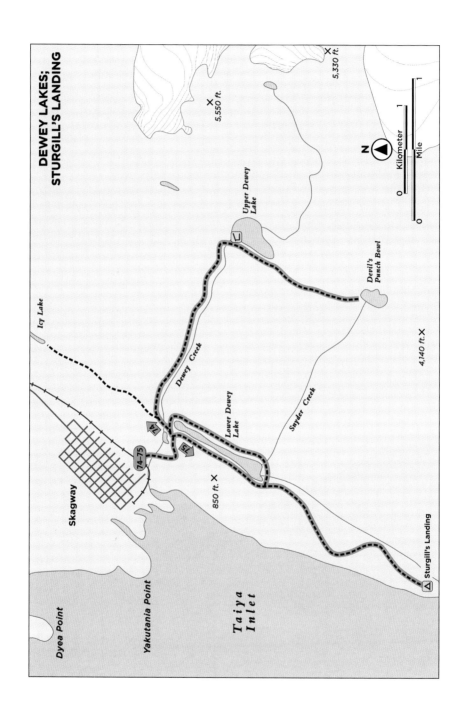

DEWEY LAKES;
STURGILL'S LANDING

Dyea Point

Skagway

Yakutania Point

Icy Lake

74–75

74

75

850 ft. X

Lower Dewey
Lake

Dewey Creek

Upper Dewey
Lake

Devil's
Punch Bowl

Snyder Creek

4,140 ft. X

X
5,550 ft.

X
5,330 ft.

N

Kilometer
0   1

Mile
0   1

T a i y a
I n l e t

Sturgill's Landing

the lake. Bring a stove if you plan to camp near the lake; there's little firewood here. Hiking around the lake is easy and scenic, and there is a good side trip up into the basin above the lake. Sheer rock walls rim the basin, and a waterfall tumbles down from above.

Devil's Punch Bowl: A less-developed trail/route leads from Upper Dewey Lake to Devil's Punch Bowl; bear right about 100 feet beyond the Upper Dewey Cabin to find it. Marked with rock cairns, the path leads through stunted mountain hemlocks, boulders, and alpine tundra across the ridge to the south to Devil's Punch Bowl. The lake's shoreline is rugged and not too inviting for camping.

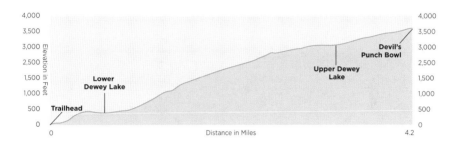

MILES AND DIRECTIONS

0.0   Begin at the trailhead.

0.5   Arrive at the Lower Dewey Lake Loop/Sturgill's Landing junction.

0.7   The trail to Icy Lake and Reid Falls bears left.

3.0   Reach Upper Dewey Lake.

4.2   Arrive at Devil's Punch Bowl, an icy lake in an alpine cirque.

Fishing: There are a few small trout in Lower Dewey Lake.

TIDBIT

The best views on the entire hike are from the high point on the trail to Devil's Punch Bowl.

75. STURGILL'S LANDING

WHY GO?

A moderate trail traveling by a lake, with views of mountains and glaciers ending at a woodcutter's camp.

THE RUNDOWN See map on page 322.

Distance: 3.5 miles one way

Special features: Coastal scenery and wildlife, a large lake, and a "magic" forest

Location: Southeast of downtown Skagway

Difficulty: Moderate

Trail type: More developed to Lower Dewey Lake, less developed beyond; rocky and steep in the final stretch

Total elevation gain: 500 feet in, 500 feet out

Best season: Mid-May to early Oct

Fees/permits: None

Maps: USGS Skagway B-1 (NW); Skagway Trail Map

Contact: Skagway Convention & Visitors Bureau, Broadway/2nd Ave. PO Box 1029, Skagway, AK 99840; (888) 762-1898; www.skagway.com

FINDING THE TRAILHEAD

In downtown Skagway follow 2nd Ave. east three blocks from the National Park Service visitor center. If driving, park on the street or in the lot east of the railroad station on 2nd Ave. On foot, turn left along the railroad siding just before 2nd Ave. crosses the tracks. In 0.1 mile cut across the tracks (watch for trains!) to the trailhead.

WHAT TO SEE

Sturgill's Landing, the site of a woodcutter's camp in a small, rocky cove on Taiya Inlet, dates from Skagway's early days. The Forest Service has built a small camp and picnic area on the point above the beach, with tables, fire pits, and an outhouse. There are a very few tent spots nestled among the rocks, pines, and spruces, and a small creek empties onto the cove's log-strewn beach just to the east. The view from the beach takes in the mountains and glaciers across the fjord, and if you're lucky, you might spot a seal or two in the ocean. Also check out the miscellaneous equipment left behind from the woodcutting operation.

Follow the trail from Skagway toward Lower Dewey Lake, and turn right in 0.5 mile, at the top of the climb. Follow the west side of the Lower Dewey Lake Loop Trail to the end of the lake, about 1.5 miles from the trailhead. Continue straight ahead beyond the lake toward Sturgill's.

The trail tunnels through sections of densely clustered hemlock forest that locals call the "Magic Forest." Toward the end of the hike, the trail becomes steep, rocky, and poorly defined, but the destination is obvious. Take care with children on this final stretch. Once in sight of the cove, bear right to find the camp/picnic area.

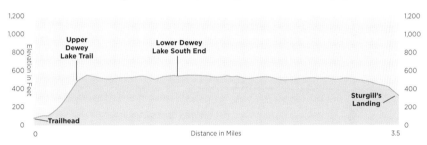

MILES AND DIRECTIONS

0.0   Begin at the trailhead.

0.5   Pass the Upper Dewey Lake Trail (see Dewey Lakes hike).

1.5   Arrive at the south end of Lower Dewey Lake.

3.5   Reach Sturgill's Landing.

Sturgill's Landing, a 3.5-mile trail, with gorgeous views of the Taiya Inlet. The trail shares the first stretch with Dewey Lake Trail, and at 0.5 mile, the routes split.
RACHEL DEEHAN

HAINES

HAINES, A SMALL TOWN in northern Southeast Alaska, is a state ferry stop, and it is also connected by road to the Alaska Highway. Haines is best known as the fall gathering place of unbelievable numbers of bald eagles in the area now protected as the Chilkat Bald Eagle Preserve. There are no national parks or forests near Haines; the small trail system here is entirely a volunteer and Alaska State Parks effort.

76. MOUNT RIPINSKY AND 7 MILE SADDLE

WHY GO?

A trail with breathtaking views of the mountains, valleys, and ocean on both sides, and one of the best high-elevation hiking trails in the area.

THE RUNDOWN

Distances: (From 7 mile trailhead) Mount Ripinsky: 3.8 miles one way. 7 Mile Saddle: 1.9 miles one way. Ripinsky–7 Mile Saddle traverse: 10 miles

Special features: An alpine ridge hike, sweeping views. Allow at least 8 to 10 hours for the day hike across the ridge

Location: The prominent mountain ridge above Haines

Difficulty: Ripinsky and 7 Mile Saddle out-and-back trips: strenuous. Traverse: very strenuous

Trail type: Young Road to 7 Mile Saddle: less developed. 7 Mile to 7 Mile Saddle: more developed

Total elevation gain: Mount Ripinsky: 3,200 feet. 7 Mile Saddle: 2,400 feet. Traverse: 4,800 feet from 7 Mile, 4,500 feet from Young Road

Best season: Late June to mid-Sept

Fees/permits: None

Maps: USGS Skagway A-2 (NE) and B-2 (SE and SW)

Contact: Alaska State Parks, Haines Ranger Station, PO Box 430, Haines, AK 99827; (907) 766-2292; http://dnr.alaska.gov/parks/

FINDING THE TRAILHEAD

Young Road Trailhead: From downtown Haines, follow 2nd Ave. uphill (north) from Second and Main Street. In 0.3 mile continue straight ahead on Young Road where the main road, now Lutak Road, angles right toward the ferry terminal. In another 0.2 mile cross Oslund Drive, continuing uphill on Young Road. In the next mile stay on Young Road, bearing left at several intersections with subdivision roads. At about 1.3 miles from Main Street, the road narrows to a rutted dirt lane and utility right-of-way. Continue 100 feet to a large parking area on the right; park here and walk 0.1 mile along the right-of-way to the trailhead on the left.

7 Mile Trailhead: Look for the trail sign and boardwalk trail at Mile 6.8 of the Haines Highway, northwest of Haines, on the north (mountain) side of the road. Park 0.1 mile west in one of the pullouts on either side of the road and walk back to the trailhead.

Shuttle distance between the trailheads is about 9 miles, so a bicycle is a reasonable shuttle vehicle; there are bikes for rent in Haines.

WHAT TO SEE

Mount Ripinsky, the peak at the top of the vertical rock wall north of Haines, is the first of a string of alpine summits in the Takshanuk Mountains, which divide the Chilkat and Chilkoot River watersheds. The hike, a ridge ramble taking in Ripinsky, Peak 3,920, and 7 Mile Saddle, is the only high-elevation trail trip near Haines. It's a beauty, with glorious views of wild peaks and valleys, ocean on two sides, and the broad, gray Chilkat River as it empties into the Pacific. This fine trail was conceived and built primarily by local volunteers.

The ridge can be heavy with snow until late June or early July. If traveling earlier, bring an ice ax and snowshoes and pay attention to avalanche danger. The route can be easy to lose in early summer snow and in bad weather, so bring your map and compass and be prepared to backtrack if necessary.

You've got options. Choose between an out-and-back hike from either of the two trailheads or, for the whole enchilada, the 10-mile traverse between the trailheads. The 7 Mile Trail is a better trail and climbs into the high country more quickly. Young Road, only a mile from downtown, provides easier access for travelers without cars.

The traverse between the two trailheads is a strenuous, very long day or overnight hike. Doing the traverse from Young Road saves about 300 feet of elevation gain, but that's not much on this hefty hike, and walking north to south from 7 Mile is a bit more scenic. By late July, water may be scarce along the top of the ridge.

Mount Ripinsky Trail (Young Road): The trail climbs through deep, dark hemlock forest into alpine country, passing the headwaters of Johnson Creek before climbing to Ripinsky's southeast summit, elevation 3,563 feet. The northwest and higher summit, 3,610 feet, is about 0.4 mile farther out the ridge.

7 Mile Saddle Trail (Haines Highway): The trail to the ridgeline is one switchback after another. Climbing steeply through a succession of lodgepole pine and birch, Sitka spruce, thickets of mountain hemlock, and subalpine meadows, the trail reaches tree line just northwest of 7 Mile Saddle. The saddle is a great day-hike destination; allow 3 to 4 hours for the round-trip and leave some time for exploring. Heather meadows and mountain hemlock groves interfinger in the saddle, and there is plenty of room for camping. Small springs west of the saddle and a pond east of the trail in the saddle supply water, but they may dry up later in summer.

Traverse: The traverse is marked intermittently with cairns and stakes, and there is a boot-worn path most of the way. From 7 Mile Saddle it's a steep climb to Peak 3,920, the high point of the hike. Coming off the peak, a section of fixed chain helps in one section of steep descent. The route then drops to a hemlock-dotted saddle about 500 feet below Peak 3,920 and soon dips to its low point, 2,850 feet, in Jones Gap. Both the saddle and gap offer possible campsites.

Between Jones Gap and Ripinsky's northwest summit, snow can obscure the path well into summer; keep in mind that it curls around to the north between the gap and the peak. You may begin meeting day hikers from Young Road when you reach Ripinsky. Southeast of the peak, pass the headwaters of Johnson Creek, another possible camp spot, and continue down the mountain to the trailhead, bearing straight ahead at the only major trail intersection, where a side trail drops steeply down to Piedad Road in Haines.

The Ripinsky-7 Mile Trail rates at least a footnote in Alaska conservation history. One of Alaska's so-called "orphan" trails (trails on unprotected, nonpark state lands), it almost became an all-terrain-vehicle destination when a promoter tried to get permission to run motorized tours up to Ripinsky. A coalition of Haines citizens, going against the tide of state lands history, pushed through a plan to protect the trail, saving this jewel of a hike that volunteers worked so hard to create.

hiker overlooks panoramic views above Haines, the wild peaks and valleys, ocean on two sides, and the broad, gray Chilkat River as it empties into the Pacific. Mount Ripinsky and 7 Mile Saddle Trails are the only high-elevation hiking routes near Haines. ANDY HEDDEN

Trail sign along the ridgeline, the 10-mile traverse of Mount Ripinsky and 7 Mile Saddle is marked intermittently with cairns and stakes, and there is a boot-worn path most of the way.
ANDY HEDDEN

MT. RIPINSKY
NORTH SUMMIT
ELEVATION 3690
SKYLINE TRAILHEAD   3.8 Mi
CITY OF HAINES   4.8 Mi.

A trail leading up 3.8 mile Mount Ripinsky, with options for a 10-mile traverse over Mount Ripinsky to 7 Mile Saddle, ending on an alpine ridge with breathtaking bird's eye views above Haines.
ANDY HEDDEN

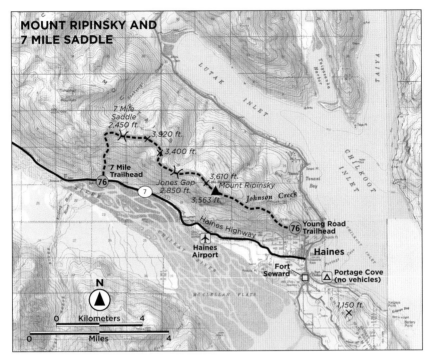

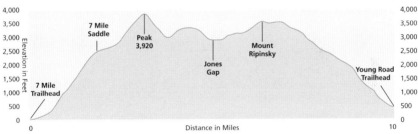

MILES AND DIRECTIONS

7 Mile		Young Road
0.0	Begin/end at the 7 Mile Trailhead.	10.0
1.9	Cross 7 Mile Saddle.	8.1
3.2	Summit Peak 3,920, the route's high point.	6.8
4.7	Descend to the route's low point at Jones Gap.	5.3
6.2	Reach Mount Ripinsky's northwest summit.	3.8
6.6	Climb to Mount Ripinsky's southeast summit.	3.4
7.5	Pass upper Johnson Creek.	2.5
10.0	Begin/end at the Young Road Trailhead.	0.0

77. MOUNT RILEY

WHY GO?

A moderate trail traveling by forest, glaciated mountains, canals, and inlets surrounding Haines, from the highest point on the Chilkat Peninsula.

THE RUNDOWN

Distances: 2.8 miles one way from Mud Bay Road, 4 miles from Beach Road, or a 7-mile traverse between the 2 trailheads

Special features: Forest hiking, summit views, a side trip to the coast

Location: 3 miles south of Haines

Difficulty: Moderate

Trail type: More developed with a few rough spots; less developed near Mount Riley's summit

Total elevation gain: 1,500 feet from Mud Bay Road; 1,600 feet from Beach Road

Best season: Late May through Sept

Fees/permits: None

Maps: USGS Skagway A-2 (NE) and A-1 (NW)

Contact: Chilkat State Park, Alaska State Parks, Haines Ranger Station, PO Box 430, Haines, AK 99827; (907) 766-2292; dnr.alaska.gov/parks/

FINDING THE TRAILHEAD

Mud Bay Road: From Main Street in downtown Haines, travel south on 3rd Avenue, which becomes Mud Bay Road as it leaves town. Jog right about 0.8 mile from Main at a sign for Chilkat State Park and continue on Mud Bay Road to the trailhead, a total of about 3 miles from Main Street. Park on the right (west) side of the road; the trail begins on the opposite side.

Beach Road: From Main Street, travel south along block on 3rd Avenue, turn left onto the Haines Highway, and follow it east and south; there's a name change to Beach Road as you reach the waterfront. Pass the Portage Cove Campground, climb a hill, and follow the road through a subdivision to the trailhead at the end of the road, a bit more than 2 miles from Main Street.

WHAT TO SEE

Mount Riley, at 1,760 feet in elevation, is the highest point on the Chilkat Peninsula. The peak, a rock outcrop in a sea of forest, offers sweeping views of Haines, Chilkat and Chilkoot Inlets, Taiya Inlet, and Lynn Canal, and the glaciated mountains all around. The Mount Riley Trail from Mud Bay Road is the shortest and most direct route to the top. The Battery Point/Riley Summit Trail from Beach Road is slightly longer, but it's also more varied and scenic.

Mount Riley Trail from Mud Bay Road: After a brief flat stretch, the trail becomes a tangle of steep switchbacks through an open forest of spruce and hemlock. Near the peak the trail reaches a marshy opening, crosses it on boardwalk, and meets the Riley Summit Trail from Beach Road. From here, it's 0.2 mile to the summit.

Mount Riley, 1,760 feet in elevation, is the highest point on the Chilkat Peninsula. The peak, a rock outcrop in a sea of forest, offers sweeping views of Haines, Chilkat and Chilkoot Inlets, Taiya Inlet, and Lynn Canal, and the glaciated mountains all around.
ANDY HEDDEN

Trail sign for Mount Riley, a moderate trail traveli
through forest, with vistas of glaciated mountains, car
and inlets surrounding Haines, from the highest point
the Chilkat Peninsu
ANDY HEDDI

MILES AND DIRECTIONS

Mount Riley from
Mud Bay Road

0.0	Begin at the southern trailhead.
1.1	Arrive at the Lily Lake spur trail.
2.6	Intersect the trail to Beach Road.
2.8	Reach the Mount Riley summit.

Riley Summit from Beach Road: The hike to Mount Riley from Beach Road passes the junction with the short trail to the coast at 0.9 mile, and then begins to climb through a dark forest dotted with huge rock outcrops. It eventually gains the ridgeline north of Mount Riley and continues to the peak. The ridgeline itself is a north-facing slope, which may hold snow well into June.

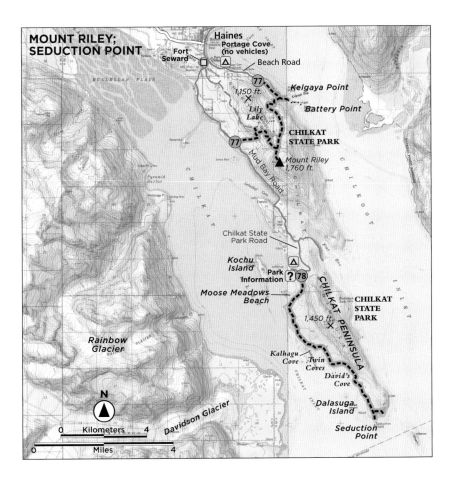

MILES AND DIRECTIONS

0.0	Begin at the northern trailhead.
0.9	Arrive at the trail junction for Kelgaya Bay.
2.2	Reach the Mount Riley ridge.
3.8	Intersect the trail to Mud Bay Road.
4.0	Reach the Mount Riley summit.

Mount Riley Traverse: The recommended starting point for the traverse is Mud Bay Road. Road distance between the two trailheads is only 5 miles, so a bicycle is a reasonable shuttle vehicle.

Lily Lake Road: This 4.5-mile hike to Mount Riley makes a good loop option for hikers without cars. Combining this hike with the trail from Beach Road forms a loop of sorts from the Fort Seward/Portage Cove area of Haines. Another option is to mountain-bike the road to the closure and hike to the summit from there.

Follow FAA Road from behind Fort Seward's Officers Row (the row of big frame houses above the square) about a mile to the road closure, and continue about 2 miles on the Lily Lake water facility road to the intersection with the Mount Riley Trail from Mud Bay Road. Take the trail about 1.5 miles to the summit.

Battery Point Trail: The hike to Kelgaya Bay is a short day or overnight trip. From the Beach Road Trailhead hike 0.9 mile to a trail junction; the right fork leads to Mount Riley and the left leads 0.1 mile to the Kelgaya Bay beach. It's another 0.2 mile to Kelgaya Point. There are campsites in the forest behind the point, but the only source of freshwater is a small creek back at the trail junction.

The developed trail ends at Kelgaya Point, but you can hike along the coast and through the forest to Battery Point, roughly another 0.6 mile. Hike around the crescent beach south of Kelgaya Point, climb into the large meadow at the far end, and follow the height of land from there through forest to the point. The rock shelf on the point offers a fine view.

Watch for scoters, harlequin ducks, and marine mammals along the coast. Earlier in summer the coastal meadows explode in bloom with shooting stars, lupine, irises, chocolate lilies, and other wildflowers.

78. SEDUCTION POINT

WHY GO?

Seduction Point is a coastal hike with chances to view a variety of marine life while traversing the tip of the Chilkat Peninsula.

THE RUNDOWN See map on page 335.

Distance: 7 miles one way

Special features: Coastal scenery, wildlife, pretty coves along the way. Avoid high tide between the 2 Twin Coves and between David's Cove and Dalasuga Point. Allow 10 hours for the round-trip hike

Location: 8 miles south of Haines

Difficulty: Easy to Kalhagu Cove; moderate to strenuous beyond

Trail type: More-developed trail to Kalhagu Cove; less-developed trail/route beyond. Between David's Cove and Dalasuga Point, the hike is a scramble over coastal boulders

Total elevation gain: Kalhagu Cove: about 150 feet in and 350 feet out. Seduction Point: 500 feet in and 700 feet out

Best season: May through mid-Oct

Fees/permits: None

Maps: USGS Skagway A-1 and A-2

Contact: Chilkat State Park, Alaska State Parks, Haines Ranger Station, PO Box 430, Haines, AK 99827; (907) 766-2292; dnr.alaska.gov/parks/

FINDING THE TRAILHEAD

 From Main Street in downtown Haines, travel south on 3rd Avenue, which becomes Mud Bay Road as it leaves town. Jog right about 0.8 mile from Main at a sign for Chilkat State Park and continue about 6 more miles to the signed gravel access road to the park. Turn right, drive 1.6 miles to a fork in the road, and bear left into the trailhead parking area.

The right fork leads to a state park campground in 0.1 mile, a homey log-cabin information station and viewing deck in 0.2 mile, and a saltwater boat launch in 0.4 mile. The boat launch is an alternate trailhead for the hike.

WHAT TO SEE

The hike follows the coastline on the west side of the Chilkat Peninsula to Seduction Point, the point of land that splits Chilkat and Chilkoot Inlets. The trip features coastal meadows, rugged points and small coves, and good bird and marine-mammal watching. If you're lucky, you might see humpback whales, orcas, sea lions, seals, or porpoises along the coast. Also look for large paper birch trees on the bluffs above the ocean; Dalasuga Point in particular has a fine grove of birches.

It's an easy, well-traveled trail as far as Kalhagu Cove, the western of the Twin Coves, and relatively easy as far as David's Cove. Beyond David's, private land and rough topography force hikers to negotiate a rough, rocky section of the coast. Check tide tables before leaving, and avoid high tide on this section and the beach section between the two Twin Coves.

From the parking area, the trail leads about a mile downhill through forest, crosses a small stream, and emerges on coastal meadows known locally as Moose Meadows. The meadows are full of wildflowers in summer, and Moose Meadows Beach is a good spot to watch for shorebirds, seabirds, and marine mammals.

You can also start the hike at the park boat launch, following the coastline (rocky, no trail) to meet the trail at Moose Meadows Beach. This is a good option early in the year when the first mile of the trail may still be icy.

Beyond Moose Meadows the trail alternates between beach and forest before a climb and descent to Kalhagu Cove through blueberry patches and deep, mossy forest. The trail emerges on the Kalhagu beach and disappears briefly; walk the beach and find the trail on the far side of the cove. Repeat this sequence at East Twin Cove.

At David's Cove an old campsite in a meadow near the bend in the cove makes a good turnaround point for a less-demanding hike. Another adventurous option is to travel off-trail, curl around the beach and begin the scramble through the jumble of rocks, boulders, outcrops, and storm-tossed logs between David's and Dalasuga Coves. The scramble can be extremely treacherous when wet; stay high to avoid the slickest rocks.

Just before reaching Dalasuga Point, look for the trail leading uphill onto a grassy bluff. Once on the bluff, bear left: The faint path on the right wanders out to a viewpoint on the bluff. The trail from here is rarely traveled and may be difficult to follow in places. In about 0.5 mile the trail splits. The right fork leads to a view from Seduction Point, and the left drops down to a campsite (carry water) in the cove east of the point.

Allow 10 hours for the round-trip day hike. There are possible campsites at most of the coves and also several small streams for collecting water, but only Moose Meadows and David's Cove have campsites near fresh water. If you're not backpacking, camping at the park campground and hiking the trail is an ideal combination; you can walk to the trailhead from your campsite.

Expect to see and hear some low-elevation air traffic on the hike.

The 7-mile Seduction Point Trail winds along coastline of the Chilkat Peninsula to Seduction Point, the point of land that splits Chilkat and Chilkoot Inlets.
ANDY HEDDEN

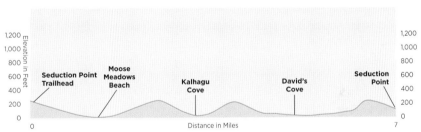

MILES AND DIRECTIONS

- **0.0** Begin at the trailhead.
- **1.2** The trail emerges on the coast at Moose Meadows.
- **3.0** Descend to Kalhagu (West Twin) Cove.
- **4.5** Reach David's Cove, an alternate turnaround point.
- **6.3** Arrive at Dalasuga Point.
- **6.8** Arrive at the junction of the paths to the viewpoint and campsite.
- **7.0** Reach Seduction Point.

Shorter hikes: The easy hike to Moose Meadows, 1.2 miles one way, makes a great short day hike, family hike, or overnight. You can also do Moose Meadows as a 2.5-mile loop by linking the trail, the coastline north of the meadows, the boat launch, and the park road.

JUNEAU

JUNEAU, ALASKA'S CAPITAL, has the most extensive trail system in Southeast. Juneau also has the most active private trail group in the state, Trail Mix (www.juneautrails.org). About 250 miles of trails radiate out from the Juneau road system across city, state, and U.S. Forest Service land; visitors could easily spend two weeks exploring the Juneau trails. Like most of Southeast, the only thing missing in Juneau is a selection of multiday backpack trips. To save yourself the cost of multiple USGS maps, buy a copy of the Alaska Natural History Association's Juneau Area Trails Guide, a large, waterproof map that covers the entire Juneau area.

At the height of the summer cruise-ship season, the near-constant flight-seeing traffic can be a problem for people seeking natural quiet in and around Juneau. The best choices for quiet trips are the ones farthest out the road to the north.

If you're traveling without a car, Perseverance Trail, Mount Juneau and Granite Creek, and Dan Moller Trail are accessible by foot or bus from downtown Juneau, and East Glacier and Nugget Creek, West Glacier, Montana Creek and Windfall Lake, and Auke Nu Trail are a short distance from the Auke Bay ferry terminal.

FROM MINING ROADS TO HIKING TRAILS

Juneau got its start as a gold-mining camp, and these days many of the trails hikers enjoy are remnants of the area's mining past. The discovery claim was on Gold Creek, the stream the Perseverance Trail follows. An Auke Bay Tlingit chief led two prospectors named Joe Juneau and Richard Harris to the find in 1880, and things escalated from there. The town was first known as Harrisburg, but Juneau won out in the long run.

Within a few years of the discovery, Juneau was a full-blown mining mecca, and many of today's trails were cleared for the first time. Perseverance, Montana Creek, Auke Nu, and Amalga began as trails, trams, and log corduroy roads to mining claims. The Nugget Creek Trail (see East Glacier and Nugget Creek) was the route of a mining trail, tram, flume, and pipeline. The Treadwell Ditch Trail (see Dan Moller Trail) is just what the name says, an old maintenance trail along a 12-mile-long ditch, dug in 1890, which captured water from several Douglas Island creeks and carried it to the enormous Treadwell Gold Mine at the south end of the island.

79. PERSEVERANCE TRAIL

WHY GO?

A wide, multiuse trail in a beautiful subalpine basin with views of mountains, streams, and waterfalls combined with historic mining ruins, all within walking distance of downtown Juneau.

THE RUNDOWN

Distance: 3 miles one way, plus about 2 miles of connecting trails

Special features: A pretty subalpine basin, wild mountain streams and waterfalls, historic mining ruins; within walking distance of downtown Juneau

Location: 1.5 miles east of downtown Juneau

Difficulty: Moderate

Trail type: More developed

Total elevation gain: About 1,000 feet on the main trail, 1,500 feet including connecting trails

Best season: Mid-May through mid-Oct

Fees/permits: None

Maps: USGS Juneau B-2 (SE) and B-1 (SW); Alaska Natural History Association Juneau Area Trails Guide

Contact: Alaska State Parks, Southeast Area, 400 Willoughby Ave., Juneau, AK 99801; (907) 465-4563; www.juneautrails.org

FINDING THE TRAILHEAD

From Egan Drive and Main Street in downtown Juneau, travel up Main Street and turn right on 6th and left on Gold. Jog right on 8th and left onto Basin Road, and follow it to the trailhead at the end of the road, about 1.5 miles from Egan and Main. The roads to the trailhead are extremely steep and narrow (one of the reasons Juneau is called "a little San Francisco"), so if you drive, drive slowly and be prepared to yield to pedestrians and other vehicles.

If you walk from downtown, add the 1.5-mile uphill hike to the quoted distances.

WHAT TO SEE

Hikers, runners, and mountain bikers all use the wide, graded, popular Perseverance Trail in the Gold Creek valley above Juneau. The valley is the site of the 1880 gold discovery that led to the founding of the city; the trail runs along the old wagon road to the Perseverance Mine, first traveled in 1889. Mountain scenery, waterfalls and cascades, and mining history are the highlights of the hike. There are not many day hikes in Alaska that combine high-country scenery with historical interest as well as Perseverance Trail does.

Two of the three biggest mines in Juneau's early days, the AJ (Alaska Juneau) and the Perseverance, operated in the valley. You can look across the valley to the AJ Mine Portal Camp in the first mile, and take a side trail farther up the valley to the edge of the AJ Glory Hole, an enormous, sheer-sided chasm (800 feet deep!) that yielded millions of dollars in gold. The Perseverance Mine was at the end of the wagon road high in the Silver Bow Basin, but avalanches and fires destroyed the mine's major structures long ago.

The first mile of the hike offers good views of Snowslide Gulch and Gold Creek's Ebner Falls. The steep trail to Mount Juneau begins across from the spur trail to the falls at Mile 1 (see the Mount Juneau and Granite Creek hike). Above Ebner Falls the old wagon road follows close by big, foaming, boulder-strewn Gold Creek, crossing it three times and its tributary Granite Creek once on the way to the Silver Bow Basin.

Hikers, runners, and mountain bikers all use the wide, popular Perseverance Trail in the Gold Creek valley above Juneau.
MOLLIE FOSTER

Just beyond the first of the four major bridges, the Red Mill Trail, a 1-mile loop, leads away to the right (south) toward the AJ Glory Hole. Not quite halfway around the loop, a spur trail splits off and, 0.4 mile and about a 200-foot elevation gain later, ends on the lip of the chasm. (There's a barrier between you and the drop-off, but keep an eye on the young ones here.) The awesome Glory Hole is the history highlight of the trail, so don't miss it.

The Granite Creek Trail (again, see the Mount Juneau and Granite Creek hike) peels off to the left (east) just beyond the bridge over the creek, about 2 miles from the trailhead. The upper junction with the Red Mill Trail is just beyond the third Gold Creek Bridge. At about 2.7 miles the mine camp spur leads very steeply uphill, in several switchbacks over about 0.2 mile, to miscellaneous mining camp remains and (even better) a grand view of Lurvey Falls and the Silver Bow Basin.

As you near the end of the maintained trail, a small bridge crosses Lurvey Creek and provides a good view of the falls above. After one last, short climb, the trail

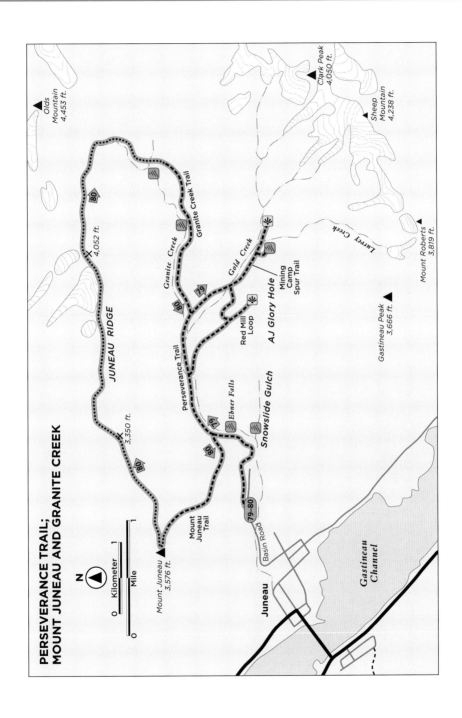

PERSEVERANCE TRAIL;
MOUNT JUNEAU AND GRANITE CREEK

N

0 Kilometer 1
0 Mile 1

Mount Juneau
3,576 ft.

JUNEAU RIDGE

3,350 ft.

4,052 ft.

80

80

80

80

Olds
Mountain
4,453 ft.

Granite Creek

Granite Creek Trail

Perseverance Trail

Mount
Juneau
Trail

79

80

80

79

Ebner Falls

Snowslide Gulch

Red Mill
Loop

AJ Glory Hole

Gold Creek

Mining
Camp
Spur Trail

Larvey Creek

Clark Peak
4,050 ft.

Sheep
Mountain
4,238 ft.

Mount Roberts
3,819 ft.

Gastineau Peak
3,666 ft.

79-80

Basin Road

Juneau

Gastineau
Channel

ends at a viewpoint of a nice set of cascades on Gold Creek. A rough, unmaintained path continues into the brush beyond the end of the developed trail, eventually leading to the high ridges above.

The Red Mill Trail, the side trail to the AJ Glory Hole, and the mining-camp spur trail are all relatively new trails built by Trail Mix, Juneau's nonprofit trail group. If you hike all the trails and see everything the Gold Creek valley has to offer, you'll end up with a hike that's just short of 8 miles.

Shorter hikes: The 1-mile, one-way hike to Ebner Falls leads to some great scenery on Gold Creek.

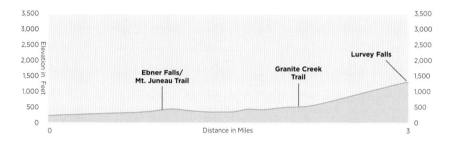

MILES AND DIRECTIONS

0.0   Begin at the trailhead.

1.0   Reach Ebner Falls and the Mount Juneau Trail.

1.5   Arrive at the lower junction of the Red Mill Trail.

2.0   The Granite Creek Trail peels off to the left.

2.3   Arrive at the upper junction of the Red Mill Trail.

2.7   Intersect the mining camp spur trail.

2.9   Enjoy the view of Lurvey Falls.

3.0   The trail ends at a viewpoint of a set of cascades on Gold Creek.

80. MOUNT JUNEAU AND GRANITE CREEK

WHY GO?

Trails with easy access from downtown Juneau, quickly climbing above treeline into alpine with spectacular views, and options for a longer loop traverse.

THE RUNDOWN See map on page 344.

Distance: Mount Juneau: 3 miles one way. Granite Creek: Up to 4.5 miles one way. Juneau Ridge–Granite Creek loop: a 12-mile loop

Special features: Alpine ridges and valleys, incredible views, wildflowers. Allow at least 10 hours for the loop hike

Location: 1.5 miles east of downtown Juneau

Difficulty: Mount Juneau: strenuous. Granite Creek: moderate to strenuous. Juneau Ridge–Granite Creek loop: very strenuous

Trail type: More-developed lower; mainly a less-developed trail/route higher. Snow lingers well into the summer

Total elevation gain: Mount Juneau: 3,000 feet. Granite Creek: 1,400 to 1,900 feet. Juneau Ridge–Granite Creek loop: 3,900 feet

Best season: Late June to mid-Sept

Fees/permits: None

Maps: USGS Juneau B-2 (SE) and B-1 (SW); Alaska Natural History Association *Juneau Area Trails Guide*

Contact: Alaska State Parks, Southeast Area, 400 Willoughby Ave., Juneau, AK 99801; (907) 465-4563; www.juneautrails.org

---

FINDING THE TRAILHEAD

 These hikes begin at the Perseverance Trailhead, the same trailhead as that for the Perseverance Trail hike. From Egan Drive and Main Street in downtown Juneau, travel up Main Street and turn right on 6th and left on Gold. Jog right on 8th and left onto Basin Road, and follow it to the trailhead at the end of the road, about 1.5 miles from Egan and Main. The roads to the trailhead are extremely steep and narrow, so if you drive, drive slowly and be prepared to yield to pedestrians and other vehicles.

If you walk from downtown, add the 1.5-mile uphill hike to the quoted distances.

WHAT TO SEE

The alpine country of Mount Juneau, Juneau Ridge, and Granite Creek is a fine hiking destination in Juneau's backyard. These hikes are all more difficult than the Perseverance Trail, with which they share a trailhead. The Mount Juneau hike, 3 miles one way, climbs a relatively short but very steep trail to the peak, at 3,576 feet in elevation, which overlooks mountains, ocean, snow, and ice. The trail up Granite Creek, about 4.5 miles one way, leads into the creek's alpine upper basin below the 4,453-foot dome of Olds Mountain. The strenuous loop route across the ridge linking Mount Juneau and Granite Creek can be 12 miles of alpine fun and beauty if you tackle it on a clear day.

If you're prepared for wind and challenging weather, consider camping in the upper basin of Granite Creek or higher on Juneau Ridge. Be sure to carry a map and compass; if the weather deteriorates, finding your way could be difficult, and the ridge loop especially could turn into a survival march on short notice.

Mount Juneau: Join the trail to Mount Juneau 1 mile out the Perseverance Trail, across from the side trail to Ebner Falls. The trail climbs steeply via switchbacks through brush and patches of Sitka spruce, leveling off about halfway to the peak as it crosses an open slope above Gold Creek and Juneau (take your time during open slope crossing). The last stage of the hike is a very steep climb up a subalpine mountainside. The steep grade and small, loose rocks present a bit of a hazard, especially coming down; a walking staff is a big help.

Just below the peak you'll notice, perhaps with some dismay, the remains of a tramline leading up to the summit. A collection of junk buildings, container vans, and tram equipment from a defunct attempt at a tourist attraction litters the mountaintop, but just walk out the ridge a bit to get away from the mess and the view is fine. Snowy mainland peaks stretch forever to the east, and the Inside Passage, Admiralty Island, and the Chilkat and Fairweather ranges lie in full view to the west, all the way to Glacier Bay.

For safety's sake, stick close to the trail on the final, steep section below the summit, especially in early summer when steep, potentially dangerous snowfields linger in places on the mountainside.

Granite Creek: The trail up Granite Creek forks left (east) about 2 miles out the Perseverance Trail, just before the Perseverance crosses the creek. Negotiate the roughest part of the trail, a steep rock pitch, just beyond the trail junction, and you're home-free except for the elevation gain. Granite Creek's lower basin is another 1.5 miles up the trail, at the top of the creek's lower cascades. Another mile of less-developed trail/route leads past another set of cascades into the pretty, wildflower-rich alpine headwater basin.

There are plenty of campsites among the rock slabs, snow patches, marmots, and heather of the two basins. From the upper basin, a climb of Olds Mountain is possible but quite a project, or you can take a jaunt into a land of alpine knobs and bowls on the way up toward Juneau Ridge to the north and west.

MILES AND DIRECTIONS

- **0.0** Set out from the Perseverance Trailhead.
- **2.0** Follow the Granite Creek Trail to the east.
- **3.5** Reach the lower basin.
- **4.5** Reach the upper basin.

Juneau Ridge-Granite Creek Loop: Taking the loop from west to east, from Mount Juneau to Granite Creek, is the recommended direction; you won't have to scramble down the steep trail off Mount Juneau, and the constant views of wild ice and mountains will keep you entertained as you stroll east on Juneau Ridge.

From Mount Juneau, it's about 4.5 miles of ridge running to the headwaters of Granite Creek and the trail/route down the creek. There is no constructed tread on the ridge, but there is a hiker-made path or rock cairn markers much of the way. Experienced ridge runners will find this ramble relatively easy, with no major ascents and descents. The views are continuously amazing. To the north are Black-erby Ridge and its high points, Cairn Peak and Observation Peak. To the south the Mount Roberts/Sheep Mountain ridge rises between Gold Creek below and Sheep Creek, in the next valley to the south.

Though the trail is narrow and can be overgrown, there are multiple viewpoints of Downtown Juneau, Gastineau Channel, and Douglas Island before climbing above treeline.
WILLIE DALTON

Near Granite Creek the route becomes less obvious. Take the lower, inner ridge off Peak 4,052, not the higher ridge toward Olds Mountain. Don't drop off the ridge until you can see the moderately sloping route into the Granite Creek basin. Starting down too soon leads to slopes too steep to descend safely.

Snow stays on the ridge well into the summer, but by early July a snow-free route has usually opened on all the steep sections. Travel early in summer may require an ice ax. Don't step out onto the cornices that overhang the north edge of the ridge.

Once in the valley of Granite Creek, follow the trails down Granite and Gold Creeks to the trailhead. Also see the Perseverance Trail hike.

After cresting treeline, prepare to take in fantastic views of Mount Roberts and the many waterfalls cascading down the mountainsides.
WILLIE DALTON

The trailhead for Mount Juneau, 1 mile up the Perseverance Trail.
MOLLIE FOSTER

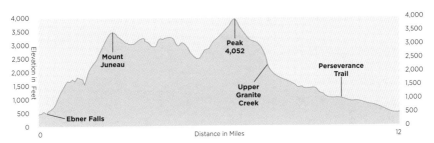

MILES AND DIRECTIONS

0.0 Start from the Perseverance Trailhead.

1.0 Turn west and uphill on the Mount Juneau Trail.

3.0 Climb to the Mount Juneau summit.

6.0 Arrive at Peak 4,052.

7.5 Reach the head of Granite Creek.

10.0 Rejoin the Perseverance Trail.

12.0 End at the Perseverance Trailhead.

81. DAN MOLLER TRAIL

WHY GO?

This boardwalk trail parallels the Kowee Creek, climbing out of the forest and into high country, with mountain views along the way to the historic Dan Moller Cabin.

THE RUNDOWN

Distance: 3 miles one way to Dan Moller Cabin

Special features: Meadows, a subalpine basin, a fee cabin, and an off-trail route to the crest of Douglas Island

Location: A mile west of Juneau on Douglas Island

Difficulty: Strenuous

Trail type: More-developed trail to the cabin; a route beyond

Total elevation gain: 1,700 feet to the cabin

Best season: Late May through Oct

Fees/permits: Fee for cabin use

Maps: USGS Juneau B-2 (SE); Alaska Natural History Association *Juneau Area Trails Guide*

Contact: Tongass National Forest, Juneau Ranger District, 8510 Mendenhall Loop Road, Juneau, AK 99801; (907) 586-8800; www.juneautrails.org

FINDING THE TRAILHEAD

From Egan Drive and 10th Street in Juneau, take the Juneau-Douglas Bridge west across Gastineau Channel and bear left at the roundabout toward 3rd Avenue. Take the first right turn onto Cordova Street, follow the left curve at the end of Cordova onto Pioneer Avenue in 0.2 mile, and find the trailhead on the right in another 0.2 mile, nestled between houses in a residential area.

Travelers without cars can take the Juneau-Douglas city bus to the corner of the Douglas Highway and Cordova Street and walk 0.4 mile to the trailhead.

WHAT TO SEE

The Dan Moller Trail, a boardwalk trail, is a good antidote for the rain-forest claustrophobia that can strike anyone who has been in Southeast too long. The hike follows the course of Kowee Creek, meandering along a string of wet meadows that come alive with wildflowers early in summer. There's a view of forests and mountains nearly everywhere except for a short stretch or two in the trees, and the trail is close enough to the creek that hikers can hear it singing away on its run to Gastineau Channel.

The hike passes the Zahn Bench viewpoint in twenty minutes or so, and shortly afterwards meets the Treadwell Ditch Trail, which you can follow as far north as Eaglecrest Ski Area. The Moller trail continues through meadow and forest, climbing into the cooler air of a mountain hemlock forest in the last 0.5 mile before the cabin.

The large cabin, popular as a ski cabin in winter, is on a cleared knoll above the creek (reservation and fee required; www.reserveusa.com or 877-444-6777). For water, take the trail behind the cabin to the creek. There aren't many spots dry and level enough for tents nearby.

The planked trail ends behind the cabin, but it's a pretty hike across wet ground up to the basin at the head of the left fork of Kowee Creek. If you want to climb high, continue a little less than a mile, with about 500 feet of elevation gain, to a saddle on the ridgeline above. This is the crest of Douglas Island, and several hikeable peaks rise to either side of the saddle, including Peak 2,850 and Mount Troy, at 3,005 feet. The view from the crest takes in Juneau, Mount Jumbo, and Admiralty Island. On a clear day this is a relatively easy way to spend some time on Juneau's fine mountaintops.

The cable towers in the upper basin are the remains of Douglas Ski Bowl, the main Juneau-area ski hill before Eaglecrest opened in the 1970s. Dan Moller was the forester who laid out the trail in the 1930s.

A hiker climbs down some of the many stairs along the 3-mile boardwalk trail to Dan Moller Cabin. Careful while hiking during wet weather, as the boardwalk can be extremely slippery.
MOLLIE FOSTER

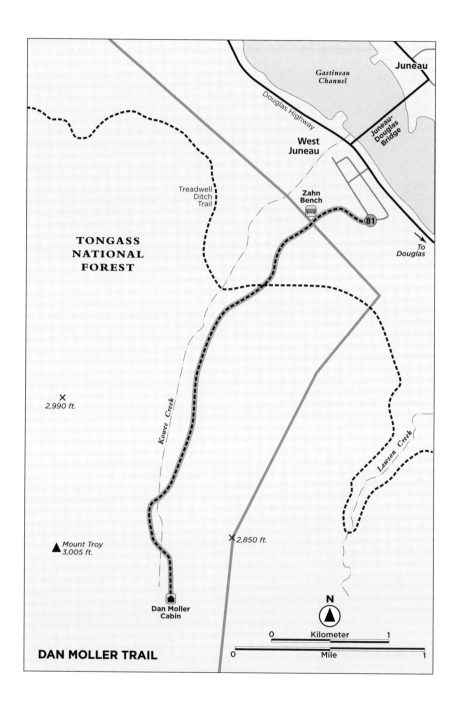

Gastineau Channel

Juneau

Douglas Highway

West Juneau

Juneau-Douglas Bridge

Treadwell Ditch Trail

Zahn Bench

81

To Douglas

TONGASS NATIONAL FOREST

× 2,990 ft.

Kowee Creek

Lawson Creek

▲ Mount Troy 3,005 ft.

× 2,850 ft.

Dan Moller Cabin

N

| 0 | Kilometer | 1 |
| 0 | Mile | 1 |

DAN MOLLER TRAIL

The route follows the Kowee Creek, and is close enough to the water that hikers can hear it singing on its run to Gastineau Channel. There are views of forests and mountains nearly everywhere, except for a short stretch or two in the trees.
MOLLIE FOSTER

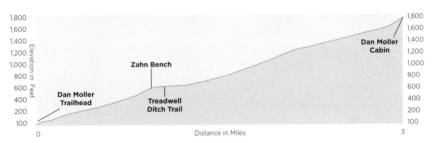

MILES AND DIRECTIONS

0.0   Begin at the trailhead.

0.6   The hike passes the Zahn Bench viewpoint.

0.8   Intersect the Treadwell Ditch Trail.

3.0   Arrive at the Dan Moller Cabin.

Shorter hikes: Take the 0.6-mile walk to the Zahn Bench, a viewpoint "for those who like a comfortable seat and a good view," as the plaque on the bench says.

82. EAST GLACIER AND NUGGET CREEK

WHY GO?

Accessible from the Visitors Center, these easy, maintained trails provide a variety of day hike options for all hiking abilities, near the Mendenhall Glacier.

THE RUNDOWN

Distances: East Glacier Trail: a 3.5-mile loop. Nugget Creek Trail: 2 miles one way. East Glacier/Nugget Creek: 7.5 miles round-trip

Special features: Alaska's southernmost road-accessible glacier, a visitor center focused on glaciers and glacial landscapes, waterfalls, and successional and old-growth forests

Location: 13 miles north of Juneau

Difficulty: Moderate

Trail type: More developed

Total elevation gain: East Glacier Trail: 600 feet.

East Glacier/Nugget Creek: 1,500 feet

Best season: Mid-May to mid-Oct

Fees/permits: Fee for visitor center entry; none for hiking

Maps: USGS Juneau B-2 (NW); Forest Service *Mendenhall Glacier* brochure; Alaska Natural History Association *Juneau Area Trails Guide*

Contact: Tongass National Forest, Mendenhall Glacier Visitor Center, Mendenhall Glacier Road, Juneau, AK 99801; (907) 789-0097; www.fs.usda.gov/tongass/

FINDING THE TRAILHEAD

These hikes begin at the Mendenhall Glacier Visitor Center outside Juneau. From downtown, drive 9 miles north on Egan Drive/Glacier Highway to the south junction with the Mendenhall Loop Road. Turn right (east) onto the Loop Road. Continue straight ahead on the Loop Road and Mendenhall Glacier Road about 3.6 miles to the visitor center. The trails begin behind the visitor center, up the main stairway from the road.

A privately owned bus line, the Glacier Express, offers regular service to the visitor center from the cruise-ship terminal in downtown Juneau.

WHAT TO SEE

The East Glacier and Nugget Creek Trails lead beyond the crowds at the Mendenhall Glacier Visitor Center into the forest and glacier landscape above the

Mendenhall Valley. The visitor center, set on a hill on the south shore of Mendenhall Lake, was the Forest Service's first-ever visitor center, built in the 1960s. The lake and glacier are the premier destination for the thousands of cruise-ship tourists who visit Juneau, but they don't venture much beyond the visitor center and the short trails just outside it, leaving the mountains above the center very quiet in comparison.

Mendenhall Glacier flows 12 miles off the Juneau Icefield, terminating on the floor of the Mendenhall Valley, the home of a Juneau bedroom community. The Mendenhall is Alaska's southernmost road-accessible glacier, not to mention the only one in a suburban setting. The glacier is the focus of the visitor center; be sure to check out the center's exhibits, and if you need a book or map, stop at the small Alaska Natural History Association shop inside.

East Glacier Trail: This 3.5-mile loop begins 0.1 mile behind the visitor center along the Trail of Time interpretive trail. It climbs the steep slope east of the visitor center, dips into the Nugget Creek valley, and circles back to the Trail of Time.

The forest of cottonwood, alder, and spruce on the lower slope is young; this area has only been out from under the ice since the 1930s. A short spur trail in the first mile leads to the AJ Waterfall, created by water that runs through a tunnel from Nugget Creek. Until the 1940s the tunnel supplied water to a hydroelectric plant for the Treadwell and AJ Mines. The AJ falls, however, are just a warm-up for the view at about 1.3 miles, where the trail overlooks roaring Nugget Creek Falls and the face of the Mendenhall Glacier. Nugget Creek Falls drops 300 feet from Nugget Creek's Lower Basin down to the level of the lake.

At about 1.5 miles the East Glacier Trail intersects the Nugget Creek Trail, which continues up Nugget Creek about 2 miles. The East Glacier Trail then climbs away from the creek, ducking into older spruce-hemlock forest not affected by the glacier in recent times. The trail passes the remains of an ore-car rail line, crosses a rock ledge, and begins a slow descent to the Trail of Time, which it meets at a small trail shelter by a bridge over Steep Creek. Follow the Trail of Time out to the trailhead on Mendenhall Glacier Road, across from the visitor center's lower parking area.

Nugget Creek Trail: The Nugget Creek Trail, 2 miles one way, begins 1.5 miles out the East Glacier loop trail and dead-ends at Vista Creek at the site of a defunct trail shelter. Camping here isn't too grand, but there is a place to pitch a tent along the creek in the trees above the shelter site.

Mainly a forest trail above the glacier's trimming influence, Nugget Creek is a pretty hike with no great destination. There is one viewpoint: a view of Bullard Mountain from a brushy draw a few minutes from trail's end. A rough route extends up the valley from Vista Creek; there are two more basins above in 4 miles of valley before it ends at the Nugget Creek Glacier.

East Glacier/Nugget Creek: For the longest possible hike here, combine the East Glacier loop with an out-and-back trip on the Nugget Creek Trail, a total of about 7.5 miles round-trip.

Hike the trails behind the Mendenhall Glacier Visitors Center for closer views of the Mendenhall Lake with the massive glacier in full view.
MOLLIE FOSTER

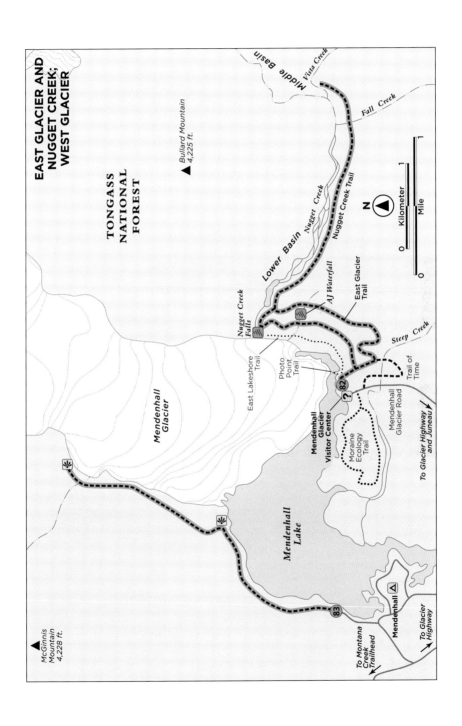

EAST GLACIER AND
NUGGET CREEK;
WEST GLACIER

TONGASS
NATIONAL
FOREST

Bullard Mountain
4,225 ft.

Middle Basin

Vista Creek

Fall Creek

Lower Basin

Nugget Creek

Nugget Creek Trail

N

Kilometer

Mile

Nugget Creek
Falls

AJ Waterfall

East Glacier
Trail

Mendenhall
Glacier

East Lakeshore
Trail

Photo
Point
Trail

Steep Creek

Trail of
Time

Mendenhall Glacier
Visitor Center

Mendenhall
Glacier Road

Moraine
Ecology
Trail

To Glacier Highway
and Juneau

Mendenhall
Lake

McGinnis
Mountain
4,228 ft.

Mendenhall

To Glacier
Highway

To Montana
Creek Trailhead

To Glacier
Highway

Shorter hikes: Photo Point Trail: This paved, accessible trail, 0.3 mile one way, leads to a rocky viewpoint above Mendenhall Lake.

East Lakeshore Trail: Branching off from the Photo Point Trail, the trail leads about 0.5 mile to the base of Nugget Creek Falls. Please avoid the lakeshore here early in summer to protect nesting birds. In these days of climate change, there's something of a Juneau beach scene along this lakeshore during the hottest days of summer.

Trail of Time: This is a 0.5-mile, self-guided trail that interprets the glacier's advances and retreats and the landscape left behind after the ice's most recent retreat. Pick up the guide pamphlet at the visitor center or at the kiosk in the parking area.

Moraine Ecology Trail: A 1.5 mile-loop, this trail begins in the lower parking area and circles across the low, forested, pond-dotted moraine in front of Mendenhall Lake.

A short spur trail in the first mile leads to the AJ Waterfall, created by water that runs through a tunnel from Nugget Creek. Until the 1940s the tunnel supplied water to a hydroelectric plant for the Treadwell and AJ Mines. MOLLIE FOSTER

83. **WEST GLACIER**

WHY GO?

A trail leading to views of a glacial lake, waterfalls, and a glacier, with options to hike beyond maintained trail to gain intimate views of the glacial ice.

THE RUNDOWN See map on page 357.

Distances: 3 miles one way

Special features: Views of blue ice and alpine peaks, access to a very strenuous route to McGinnis Mountain

Location: 13 miles north of Juneau

Difficulty: Moderate

Trail type: Mainly a more-developed trail; a rougher, partially marked route for about the last 0.4 mile

Total elevation gain: About 1,300 feet

Best season: Late May through Sept

Fees/permits: None

Maps: USGS Juneau B-2 (NW); Alaska Natural History Association *Juneau Area Trails Guide*

Contact: Tongass National Forest, Juneau Ranger District, 8510 Mendenhall Loop Rd., Juneau, AK 99801; (907) 586-8800; www .juneautrails.org

FINDING THE TRAILHEAD

From downtown Juneau, drive 9 miles north on Egan Drive/Glacier Highway to the south junction with the Mendenhall Loop Road. Turn right (east) onto the Loop Road and follow it about 3.7 miles to Montana Creek Road, including a left turn at a signed intersection for the Loop Road just over 2 miles from Egan Drive. Turn right at Montana Creek Road, and in about 0.3 mile bear right onto Skaters Cabin Road toward Mendenhall Campground. Continue about 0.7 mile, passing the campground, to the trailhead at the end of the road.

From the ferry terminal, turn onto the north side of the Mendenhall Loop Road at Glacier Highway Mile 12, drive about 2.5 miles to Montana Creek Road, turn left, and continue to the trailhead.

The city's Mendenhall Valley bus stops at the intersection of Montana Creek Road and the Loop Road. From there, it's 1 mile to the trailhead.

WHAT TO SEE

The West Glacier hike follows the west side of Mendenhall Lake and Mendenhall Glacier, mainly through brushy woods of alder and cottonwood, to several viewpoints above the valley. Last is best in this case: From the final overlook above the glacier, you get to look into the hall of the mountain king. This is a beauty of an area, but be prepared for frequent helicopter noise, as the glacier is a prime destination for flight-seeing tours.

The trail begins to climb after about a mile, crossing several tumbling mountain streams that spill off the slope of McGinnis Mountain, elevation 4,228 feet, the alpine peak west of the glacier. There are several rock outcrops with great views, and the scenery improves as the trail climbs.

The viewing bench on the rock outcrop at 1 mile is the first viewpoint. At about two miles the trail crosses an avalanche stream, a gully wiped clean of vegetation by snow slides. Above the glacier now, look out over blue ice, green forests, and snowy peaks, with the white froth of Nugget Creek Falls in the distance across the glacier.

The trail is a bit rougher over rocks as it approaches a block of bare rock at 3 miles. The obvious trail ends on this outcrop. The West Glacier overlook, however, is still

A small group of hikers are dwarfed by the massive Mendenhall Glacier. The Mendenhall is Alaska's southernmost road-accessible glacier, not to mention the only one so close to a suburban setting. MOLLIE FOSTER

around the corner, at least 1 mile away on a route marked with a few cairns. From here, the route is a mixture of overgrown vegetation and scrambling over rocks and crossing a number of (typically smaller) waterways. Follow the faint but discernible route carefully, up and then back down a rocky shoulder to a point directly above the glacier. Continue until you reach a point with your desired view, there is not a designated glacier view spot. From the bluffs, the view takes in miles of ice, dark peaks, and a dozen or so waterfalls.

Glacial ice fresh off the glacier, floats in the Mendenhall Lake, visible from the West Glacier Trail.
MOLLIE FOSTER

The 3-mile one way West Glacier Trail begins in the forest, climbing to views of Mendenhall Lake, waterfalls and the Mendenhall Glacier.
MOLLIE FOSTER

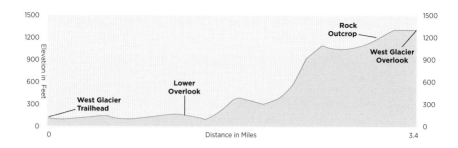

MILES AND DIRECTIONS

0.0   Begin at the trailhead.

1.0   Reach the lower overlook.

2.0   The trail crosses an avalanche stream.

3.0   A rock outcrop marks the end of the maintained trail.

The brushy forest along the trail is "successional," a forest that is pioneering the new land that emerged since the glacier's retreat in the 1930s. Eventually spruce trees will grow up and shade out the cottonwood and alder, and hemlock seedlings will sprout under the spruce canopy.

McGinnis Mountain: A rough route from the Mile 3 outcrop climbs McGinnis Mountain via a long spur ridge. The 4-mile route is strenuous, somewhat hard to find, and suitable for experienced hiker/scramblers only. The best months for heading up McGinnis are July and August.

Shorter hikes: Hike 1-mile one way to the lower viewpoint location at about 250 feet in elevation.

TIDBIT

This trail is popular for good reasons. Be prepared for large groups and helicopter noise on the trail, avoid peak times to skip the crowds.

84. MONTANA CREEK AND WINDFALL LAKE

WHY GO?

A trail leading by forest, wetlands, and a lake, with options for day hikes or overnight adventures.

THE RUNDOWN

Distances: Montana/Windfall traverse: 11 miles one way. Windfall Lake: 3.5 miles one way from the north trailhead

Special features: A creek walk, forests, wetlands, a large lake, fishing, and a fee cabin. Windfall Lake is a good family trip

Location: 15 miles north of Juneau

Difficulty: Traverse: moderate. Windfall Lake: easy

Trail type: More developed

Total elevation gain: Traverse: 700 feet. Windfall Lake: 100 feet

Best season: May through Oct

Fees/permits: Fee for cabin use

Maps: USGS Juneau B-2 (NW), B-3 (NE), and C-3 (SE); Alaska Natural History Association *Juneau Area Trails Guide*

Contact: Tongass National Forest, Juneau Ranger District, 8510 Mendenhall Loop Rd., Juneau, AK 99801; (907) 586-8800; www .juneautrails.org

FINDING THE TRAILHEAD

Montana Creek (south): About 9 miles north of Juneau on Egan Drive/ Glacier Highway, turn right (east) onto Mendenhall Loop Road. Just over 2 miles from the highway, turn left at a signed intersection for the Loop Road, and continue to Montana Creek Road, a total of about 3.7 miles from the highway. Turn right up Montana Creek Road and follow it 2 miles to the end of the road and the beginning of the hike. If traveling from the ferry terminal or other points to the north, turn east at the north junction of the Loop Road, Mile 12 of the Glacier Highway, drive 2.5 miles to Montana Creek Road, turn left, and continue to the trailhead.

Travelers without cars can take the Mendenhall Valley city bus as far as the intersection of the Loop Road and Montana Creek Road, 2 miles from the trailhead.

Windfall Lake (north): Drive about 27 miles north of Juneau on the Glacier Highway. Just south of the Herbert River Bridge, turn right onto the access road and follow it about a mile to the trailhead.

WHAT TO SEE

The trip from the Montana Creek Trailhead to Windfall Lake, the only overnight trail traverse near Juneau, features lush forest, pretty creeks, meadows and wetlands, and half-mile-long Windfall Lake. The best camping is at the northwest end of Windfall Lake, which is an easy, popular hike from the north trailhead and a good family overnight trip. There is a Forest Service fee cabin on the northeast shore of the lake (reservation and fee required; www.reserveusa.com or 877-444-6777). The trail is planked across wet sections.

Montana Creek to Windfall Lake: The first mile of the traverse is along a closed road. At this writing a horseback-riding concession operates on the old road-bed, but guided rides end at the end of the road, where the real trail begins, near the confluence of Montana and McGinnis Creeks.

Entering the forest, the path follows Montana Creek through its narrow, V-shaped valley. The trail stays close by the creek for nearly 2 miles. After crossing the creek, it leads to the low divide between Montana and Windfall Creeks in a broad, wet meadow at 850 feet foot in elevation. On the Windfall Creek side, the trail stays high above the deeply incised stream until the valley widens at about Mile 5 of the hike. There, crossing the creek on a bridge, it leads into a fantasy forest of gnarled, moss-hung spruces and ranks of tall devil's club.

The south end of Windfall Lake is an extensive wetland and a bird paradise. The cabin is around the curve of the lake from there, in its private domain just above the water. The most popular area of the lake, at the north end, is much closer to the Windfall Lake (north) trailhead, so most lake visitors begin hiking there. A planked spur trail at the north end of the lake (3 miles from the north trailhead and 8 miles from Montana Creek Road) leads 0.3 mile to the lakeshore and another 0.2 mile to the best campsites on a dry point of land between two small coves.

The 3.5-mile Windfall Lake trail travels by forest, creeks, wetlands, and a lake.
MOLLIE FOSTER

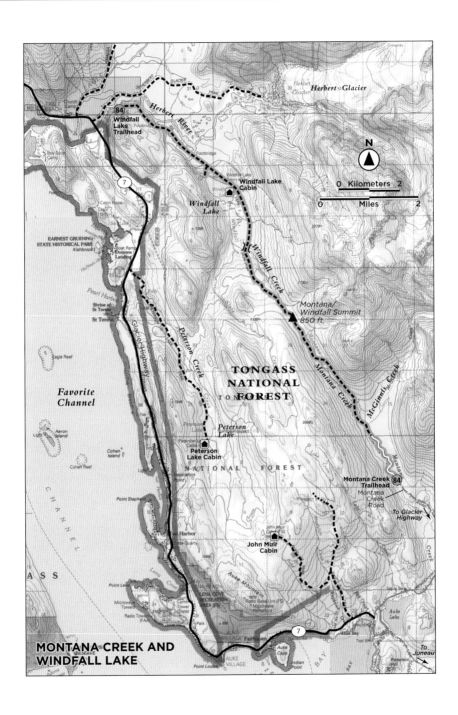

MONTANA CREEK AND WINDFALL LAKE

Below the lake, the traverse meets the Herbert River and follows the silty glacial stream to the trailhead, crossing and recrossing its south channel. Look for bald eagles along the river.

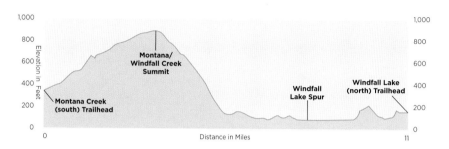

MILES AND DIRECTIONS

Montana Creek/Windfall
Lake Traverse

0.0	Begin at the Montana Creek (south) Trailhead.
1.0	The closed road ends.
3.0	Cross the upper Montana Creek Bridge.
4.0	Reach the Montana/Windfall Creek summit.
6.0	Cross the Windfall Creek Bridge.
7.5	Arrive at the Windfall Lake Cabin.
8.0	Intersect the Windfall Lake spur trail.
8.5	Cross the upper Herbert River Bridge.
11.0	End the hike at the Windfall Lake (north) Trailhead.

Windfall Lake from
North Trailhead

0.0	Begin at the trailhead.
2.5	Cross the upper Herbert River Bridge.
3.0	Arrive at the Windfall Lake spur trail.
3.5	Reach the Windfall Lake Cabin.

Fishing: The lake supports Dolly Varden and cutthroat trout and pink, silver, and red salmon during spawning runs. Windfall Creek and the Herbert River below the lake are closed to fishing in June and July to protect returning red salmon.

85. AUKE NU TRAIL

WHY GO?

A trail traveling by meadows, on boardwalks, leading to a cabin with spectacular 360-degree views of the water and mountains surrounding Auke Bay.

THE RUNDOWN

Distances: Auke Nu/John Muir Cabin: 3 miles one way

Special features: Meadows, mountain views, and a fee cabin. The area is generally too wet for comfortable tent camping

Location: Auke Bay, about 13 miles north of Juneau

Difficulty: Moderate

Trail type: Mainly more developed; the upper section of the Spaulding Meadows trail is less developed and wet

Total elevation gain: Spaulding Meadows: 1,600 feet. John Muir Cabin: 1,500 feet

Best season: May through Oct

Fees/permits: Fee for cabin use

Maps: USGS Juneau B-2 (NW) and B-3 (NE); Alaska Natural History Association *Juneau Area Trails Guide*

Contact: Tongass National Forest, Juneau Ranger District, 8510 Mendenhall Loop Rd., Juneau, AK 99801; (907) 586-8800; www.juneautrails.org

FINDING THE TRAILHEAD

Look for the trailhead on the north side of the Glacier Highway about 13 miles north of downtown Juneau, a mile east of the state ferry terminal and 0.4 mile west of the roundabout (stay on the Glacier Highway). The small trailhead parking lot is on the north side of the highway, one drive west of Seaview Avenue. The city's Mendenhall Valley bus stops at the junction.

WHAT TO SEE

The Auke Nu and Spaulding Trails share the first 0.8 mile and then divide to different destinations. The Auke Nu Trail climbs gradually toward Auke Mountain and the John Muir Cabin, which is on the crest of a 1,550-foot knob near the head of Auke Nu Creek.

Hikers can choose between a half-day hike on the Auke Nu Trail, or an overnight to the Muir cabin (reservation and fee required; www.reserveusa.com or 877-444-6777). Berry bushes grow in the neighborhood, and bears are fairly common.

The Auke Nu Trail crosses Waydelich Creek and climbs gradually on the east side of Auke Nu Creek, finally crossing the creek about 0.2 mile below the cabin. The creek is the best source of fresh water for overnighters at the cabin; be sure to filter, boil, or treat it. Juneau volunteers built this large, solid log cabin as a Juneau centennial project in 1980 and refurbished it in 2001.

The rough, primitive Spaulding trail leads to meadows on the higher ground between Waydelich and Lake Creeks, with a view of the peaks west of Mendenhall Glacier. At this writing, the condition of the Spaulding trail is rough, and for adventurous hikers interested in scrambling through bogs and meadows.

The John Muir Cabin with spectacular 360-degree views of the water and mountains surrounding Auke Bay.
MOLLIE FOSTER

A hiker walks over the dense root section of the 3-mile Auke Nu Trail. The moderate route travels through the trees with some sections of roots, boardwalks and bridges.
MOLLIE FOSTER

Full boardwalks or small sections of boardwalks are a common sight on the Auke Nu Trail.
MOLLIE FOSTER

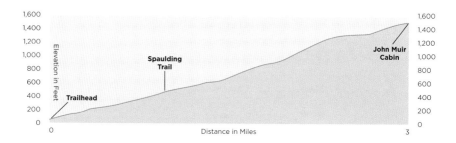

MILES AND DIRECTIONS

0.0 Begin at the trailhead.

0.8 Pass the Spaulding Trail junction.

1.0 Cross Waydelich Creek.

2.8 Cross Auke Nu Creek.

3.0 Arrive at John Muir Cabin.

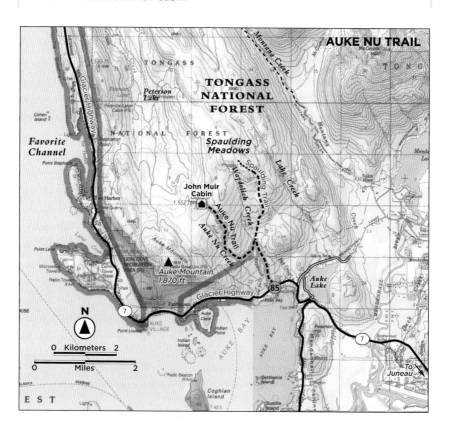

86. HERBERT GLACIER

WHY GO?

An easy walk through dense forest to views of the Herbert Glacier and outwash plain below.

THE RUNDOWN

Distance: 4 miles one way to the end of the trail below the glacier; another mile off-trail to the glacier's face

Special features: Lush forest and Herbert Glacier

Location: 27 miles north of Juneau

Difficulty: Easy on the trail; moderate to the glacier's face

Trail type: More-developed trail to the glacier's outwash plain; a route beyond

Total elevation gain: 200 feet in, 100 feet out; another 300 feet to the face of the glacier

Best season: Mid-May through Oct

Fees/permits: None

Maps: USGS Juneau C-3 (SE); Alaska Natural History Association *Juneau Area Trails Guide*

Contact: Tongass National Forest, Juneau Ranger District, 8510 Mendenhall Loop Rd., Juneau, AK 99801; (907) 586-8800; www .juneautrails.org

FINDING THE TRAILHEAD

 Drive about 27 miles north of Juneau on the Glacier Highway. The trailhead is on the right (east) side of the road, the first big parking area, north of the Herbert River Bridge.

WHAT TO SEE

Deep forest, a large river, a glacial "beach," bedrock, and blue ice make a fine setting for this 4-mile trail up the Herbert River. The maintained trail ends on the Herbert Glacier's outwash plain, with Herbert Glacier in the distance.

The lower part of the trail traverses the floor of the Herbert and Eagle River valleys, passing through a forest of Sitka spruce and, underneath the spruce, a mini forest of devil's club and ferns. The trail brushes up against the river twice in the first 1.5 miles, and then bears away from the stream and skirts a series of rocky, rolling hills.

A bush plane flies over the Herbert Glacier, at the overlook point at Mile 4 of the trail.
MOLLIE FOSTER

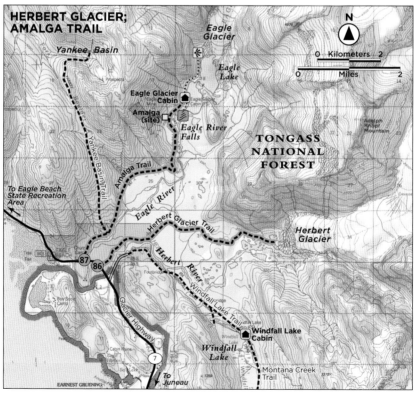

HERBERT GLACIER; AMALGA TRAIL

At about 2.5 miles the hike passes a small pond (look for ducks), and at about 3.5 miles you'll pass a beaver pond. In another 0.5 mile the trail emerges onto the open outwash plain with part of the glacier visible ahead, still about 0.5 mile away.

For folks who want a closer look, it's possible to scramble around to the river's source as it thunders out of the glacier. The least brushy route follows the river up and bears left as the river curves to the north along the face of the glacier. A detour onto the rocky moraine is necessary; don't even think about trying to cross the river. Negotiating the moraine requires a little scrambling, but the general direction of the route is obvious. The river's source is about a mile from the end of the trail. It's best to stay off the glacier unless you know what you're doing.

The sandbars and outwash in the last 0.5 mile of the trail are probably the best campsites on the hike. In this last section of the trail, be sure to look up; you might see a wild goat or two in the mountains above the glacier.

Shorter hikes: The lower trail, about the first 1.5 miles, is a pleasant forest and river walk.

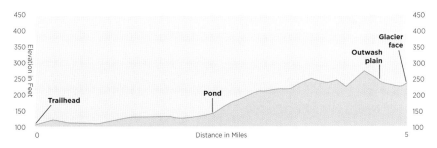

A hiker walks on the 4-mile Herbert Glacier trail, which travels through lush forest, before opening to an outwash plain, with the glacier in the distance.
MOLLIE FOSTER

87. AMALGA TRAIL

WHY GO?

A rough, challenging trail traveling through forest, ending at a cabin, with views of a glacial lake and Eagle Glacier.

THE RUNDOWN See map on page 372.

Distance: 5.6 miles one way

Special features: Eagle Lake and Glacier, a thundering waterfall, a fee cabin on the lake, and a rough, brushy spur route to an overlook of the glacier

Location: 28 miles north of Juneau

Difficulty: Strenuous

Trail type: Less developed

Total elevation gain: 500 feet in, 300 feet out

Best season: Mid-May through Oct

Fees/permits: Fee for cabin use

Maps: USGS Juneau C-3 (SE); Alaska Natural History Association *Juneau Area Trails Guide*

Contact: Tongass National Forest, Juneau Ranger District, 8510 Mendenhall Loop Rd., Juneau, AK 99801; (907) 586-8800; www.juneautrails.org

FINDING THE TRAILHEAD

 Drive about 28 miles north of Juneau on the Glacier Highway; the trailhead parking area is on the right, just across the highway bridge over the Eagle River.

WHAT TO SEE

A forest hike with ups and downs, the trail to Eagle Lake ends with a suddenly opening out on a grand view of Eagle Lake, the wild peaks and waterfalls above it, and Eagle Glacier as it twists its way down the canyon at the head of the lake. Also known as the Eagle Lake Trail, the hike follows the route of what was once a horse tramway and trail leading to the now-vanished mining settlement of Amalga, which had its heyday from about 1905 to 1927.

The overnight options are good ones; pick one of the campsites near the small, clear-running streams in the last 0.5 mile before the lake, or stay in the cabin (reservation and fee required; www.reserveusa.com or 877-444-6777). The cabin has a covered deck, and wooden table by the lakeshore, all set to maximize the view of the mountain kingdom at the head of the lake. Don't be surprised if you end up spending most of your time at the cabin simply staring at the view.

The cabin comes with a propane heater and a supply of propane, but please use it sparingly, as it costs big bucks to fly in the propane. For water, the river and lake are thick with glacial silt; the nearest clear water is about 0.2 mile back along the main trail or about 0.3 mile along the route to the glacier overlook—see more on that route below.

The trail begins in a cluster of paths connecting with the Eagle Beach State Recreation Area across Glacier Highway; if in doubt, stay on a north and east course near the river. (The Eagle Lake Trail is a good day hike for Eagle Beach campground campers.) The trail stays relatively close to the Eagle River in the first stretch, passing the intersection with the rarely maintained trail to Yankee Basin at about 1 mile. At about 1.5 miles the Eagle trail peels away from the river, and then crosses a nice stream, Boulder Creek, at about 2 miles. At this writing, the second half of the route is more of a backcountry, primitive trail through section of bogs, creeks, and mud. The hike alternates between the river and wetlands away from the river before reaching the Mile 5 stream and campsites. After a short climb the trail reaches a junction; the cabin is just ahead to the right, and the rough route leading about 2 miles to the glacier overlook takes off to the left.

From the cabin, take in the beautiful views of Eagle Lake, the wild peaks and waterfalls above, and Eagle Glacier as it twists its way down the canyon at the head of the lake.
MOLLIE FOSTER

The hike to the overlook is steep, brushy, and slow, and therefore is best done as a side trip as part of an overnight hike rather than as a day hike from the trailhead. There is a good bit of bare, sloping rock on the route, and it is extremely slick in wet weather.

A fainter trail continues past the cabin, leading about 0.3 mile to the wide, foaming, thundering Eagle River Falls, just below the point where the river emerges from the lake. Don't miss it.

In the wildlife department, look for ducks in the lake, waterfowl and kingfishers in the wetlands along the trail, and bald eagles near the river. You'll likely see plenty of black-bear scat, but the forest is thick here, so sightings are probably rare.

A bridge along the primitive Amalga Trail. Some smaller waterways on the route do not have bridge crossings. MOLLIE FOSTER

The Eagle Glacier Memorial Cabin, 5.6 miles from the trailhead. The cabin has a covered deck, and plenty of space to maximize the view of the mountain kingdom at the head of the lake.
MOLLIE FOSTER

MILES AND DIRECTIONS

0.0   Begin at the trailhead.

1.0   Pass the Yankee Basin Trail.

2.0   Cross Boulder Creek.

5.0   Pass potential campsites near a forest stream.

5.5   Intersect the glacier overlook route; bear right to the cabin.

5.6   Arrive at Eagle Glacier Cabin.

TIDBIT

At this writing, most of the second half of the trail is a nonmaintained, rough, scramble route, best for backcountry hikers ready for a challenge.

88. POINT BRIDGET

WHY GO?

A variety of short trails traveling through old-growth forest and wildflower meadows, along the coast with route options for short day hikes, or longer loop adventures.

THE RUNDOWN

Distance: Point Bridget Trail: 3.7 miles one way. Cedar Lake Trail: 2.1 miles one way. North Bridget Cove Trail: 1.8 miles one way

Special features: Wildflower meadows, old-growth forest, coastal scenery and wildlife, three fee cabins

Location: 38 miles north of Juneau

Difficulty: Easy

Trail type: More-developed trail to Blue Mussel Cabin; then a 0.1-mile hike over a stony beach to Point Bridget. Cedar Lake Trail is less developed. North Bridget Cove Trail: a route alternating through forest and beach

Total elevation gain: Cedar Lake Trail: Up to 450 feet

Best season: Apr through mid-Nov

Fees/permits: Fee for cabin use

Maps: USGS Juneau C-3 (NW) (trail not shown); Alaska State Parks brochure *Point Bridget State Park*; Alaska Natural History Association *Juneau Area Trails Guide*

Contact: Alaska State Parks, Southeast Area, 400 Willoughby Ave., Juneau, AK 99801; (907) 465-4563; www.dnr.state.ak.us/parks

FINDING THE TRAILHEAD

 The signed trailhead is about 38 miles north of Juneau on the Glacier Highway, on the left (north) side of the road.

WHAT TO SEE

A short, nearly flat hike with a lot of variety and three fee cabins for overnighters, Point Bridget is a great trip for beginning hikers and families. Both kids and adults will find plenty to do, exploring old-growth forest, wildflower meadows, stony beaches, and small creeks. In the wildlife department, the possibilities are deer, geese, rafts of sea ducks, whales, sea lions, seals, and, beginning in late July, salmon runs in Cowee Creek (and maybe bears too, so make plenty of noise on the trail, especially when the fish are running).

Cowee Meadows Cabin, at 2.3 miles, is in the meadow by Echoing Creek. The Blue Mussel Cabin, 3.6 miles from the trailhead, is on the coast just inside Point Bridget. A tiny creek runs by the cabin, and there's even a wood-fired sauna. Camping Cove Cabin is 4.4 miles from the trailhead, or via the North Bridget Cove Trail 1.8 miles (see map).

To stay any of the cabins, a reservation and fee are required; go to the Alaska State Parks website or contact the Juneau state parks office (see "Contact" above). Berm Beach, at about 2.6 miles, has tent sites back in the trees, with the nearest water from Echoing Creek, by the Cowee Meadows Cabin.

The hike begins on a boardwalk through muskeg and forest and reaches the upper end of Cowee Meadows in about 0.5 mile. Then the trail skirts the meadows on the west, just inside the forest, to the Cowee Meadows Cabin. This forest/meadow edge is a good place to look and listen for a variety of birds and other wildlife. The drier parts of the meadow put on a wildflower show in early summer, practically swimming in shooting stars, lupine, chocolate lilies, irises, and other flowers.

At Echoing Creek, behind Cowee Meadows Cabin, a 0.7-mile, less-developed trail climbs about 300 feet in elevation to Cedar Lake, a small, pretty lake set in yellow cedars. Beyond the cabin the Point Bridget Trail continues to Berm Beach and its fine wildflower meadow. The beach is rocky but holds some tide-pool treasures. A minus tide is best for exploring the intertidal zone.

At the west end of Berm Beach, the trail climbs the bluff into the forest. Just before it drops back down to the Blue Mussel Cabin, a short side trail leads to a small

View of Berners Bay from the Point Bridget Trail.
ALASKA STATE PARKS

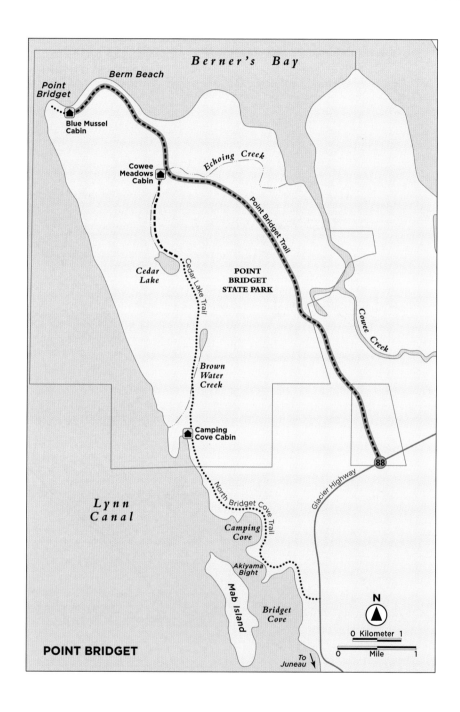

Berner's Bay

Berm Beach

Point Bridget

Blue Mussel Cabin

Cowee Meadows Cabin

Echoing Creek

Point Bridget Trail

Cedar Lake

Cedar Lake Trail

POINT BRIDGET STATE PARK

Cowee Creek

Brown Water Creek

Camping Cove Cabin

North Bridget Cove Trail

88

Glacier Highway

Lynn Canal

Camping Cove

Akiyama Bight

Mab Island

Bridget Cove

To Juneau

N

0 Kilometer 1

0 Mile 1

POINT BRIDGET

Cowee Meadow Cabin, 2.3 miles from the trailhead on the Point Bridget Trail.
ALASKA STATE PARKS

opening on the bluff with a picnic table. It's a good spot to take a break, have lunch, and look out over the ocean for sea mammals and seabirds.

Shortly after the side trail to the bluff, the main trail dips down to the beach and the cabin. A rougher trail continues out the bluff to the forest on Point Bridget, but the easiest way to get to the point is by rock-hopping 0.1 mile along the beach.

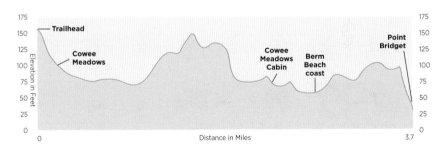

MILES AND DIRECTIONS

0.0   Begin at the signed trailhead.

0.5   Reach Cowee Meadows.

2.3   Arrive at Cowee Meadows Cabin.

2.6   Reach the coast at Berm Beach.

3.6   Arrive at Blue Mussel Cabin.

3.7   Hike along the beach to Point Bridget.

SITKA

SITKA, ALTHOUGH IT IS a significant city in Southeast, is just a small freckle of civilization on big, wild, mountainous Baranof Island. The only major Southeast community on the outer Pacific coast, Sitka is, like most towns in the region, accessible only by air or water.

The town is about as user friendly as it gets for traveling hikers. Indian River, Sitka National Historical Park, and Harbor Mountain are accessible on foot from downtown Sitka, and Gavan Hill and Starrigavan Bayis less than a mile from the ferry terminal.

For other hikes on the road system, try the Thimbleberry and Heart Lakes Trails (4 miles east of town on Sawmill Creek Road, 0.8 mile one way). For a longer trip to a viewpoint, hike the steep, strenuous trail to Mount Verstovia (Sawmill Creek Road just east of downtown, 2.5 miles one way.)

89. INDIAN RIVER

WHY GO?

This trail travels through the forest with a picturesque clearwater stream and waterfall, within walking distance of downtown Sitka.

THE RUNDOWN

Distance: 4.3 miles one way

Special features: A pretty, clearwater stream, deep forest, and a waterfall. The trailhead is within easy walking distance of downtown Sitka

Location: A mile east of downtown Sitka

Difficulty: Moderate

Trail type: More developed; the last mile is a little rougher

Total elevation gain: About 650 feet

Best season: Mid-Apr through Oct

Fees/permits: None

Maps: USGS Sitka A-4 (SW)

Contact: Tongass National Forest, Sitka Ranger District, 204 Siginaka Way, Sitka, AK 99835; (907) 747-6671; www.fs.usda.gov/tongass/

FINDING THE TRAILHEAD

Follow Sawmill Creek Road about 0.6 mile south from the intersection of Sawmill and Lake Street to Indian River Road, by the State Trooper Training Academy, on the left (north) side of the road. Follow Indian River Road about 0.5 mile to a gate; park your car here if driving. Walk straight ahead to the trailhead past the city waterworks building.

Another access to Indian River Trail is via the Sitka Cross Trail, a route connecting multiple trails from downtown Sitka.

WHAT TO SEE

Indian River is as good a low-elevation, forest-and-stream hike as there is in Southeast. The small river is a beautiful clear-water stream full of rocky riffles, deep green pools, and bouldery rapids. The hike features several crossings of forks of the river and its tributaries, all over log bridges.

The forest is the signature spruce-hemlock-cedar forest of Southeast, with cathedral-like, open, mossy pockets of giant Sitka spruce. Wood thrushes, Steller's jays, and winter wrens are common, and runs of silver, pink, and chum salmon make their way up the river in late summer and fall. Hikers sometimes spot deer and bears in the valley.

At 0.5 mile a muskeg opening on the left side of the trail provides a view up the valley to The Sisters, the alpine peaks that split the two forks of the Indian River. The trail's grade is gradual, with the steepest section in the last mile between the last river crossing and the falls. The maintained trail ends at the east fork of the river just below the falls. There are several places to camp along the trail, with established sites in the first mile, at the river forks, and at the falls.

Local bushwhackers use the trail to reach a couple of cross-country routes: to Billy Basin, to the south, which once hummed with the activity of a mine and ore mill, and to the subalpine basin about 1.5 miles up the river beyond the end of the trail.

The small river is a beautiful clear-water stream full of rocky riffles, deep green pools, and bouldery rapids. The hike features several fork crossings and tributaries, all over log bridges.
SARAH STEHN

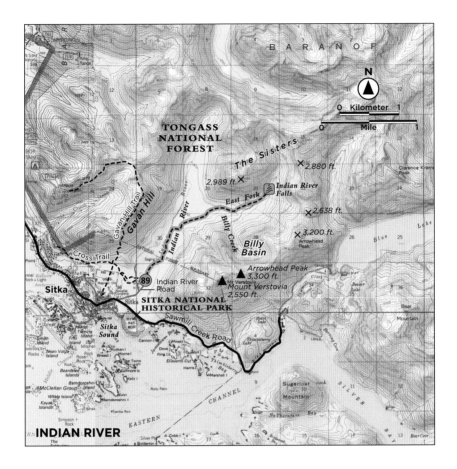

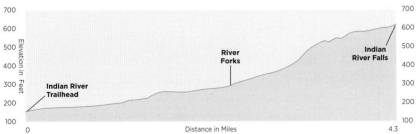

The 4.3-mile trail travels through the forest with a picturesque clearwater stream and waterfall, within walking distance of downtown Sitka.
SARAH STEHN

MILES AND DIRECTIONS

0.0   Begin at the trailhead, past the waterworks building.

0.5   A muskeg opening provides a view of The Sisters.

1.5   Cross the forks of Indian River.

3.0   Cross Billy Creek.

4.3   Arrive at Indian River Falls.

Shorter hikes: Head for the muskeg viewpoint, 0.5 mile one way, or the river forks, 1.5 miles one way.

Fishing: The river is closed to all salmon fishing, but anglers can take a shot at landing Dolly Varden. Dolly fishing is best in early spring and from midsummer through fall.

90. **SITKA NATIONAL HISTORICAL PARK**

WHY GO?

Two walking loops provide an introduction to Southeast forest and water environment, plus local Native culture and history at Alaska's oldest national park.

THE RUNDOWN

Distances: West Loop to Shiskeenue fort site: 1-mile loop. East Loop to Russian Memorial: 0.6-mile loop

Special features: An outdoor museum of Native totem poles, Native and Russian American history, salmon viewing, a visitor center. Day use only and pets on leash only

Location: A mile east of downtown Sitka, adjacent to Sheldon Jackson College

Difficulty: Easy

Trail type: Accessible

Total elevation gain: Insignificant

Best season: Mar through Nov

Fees/permits: Fee for visitor center entry, none for hiking

Maps: USGS Sitka A-4 (SW) (trails not shown); NPS brochure and trail map

Contact: Sitka National Historical Park, 103 Monastery Street, Sitka, AK 99835; (907) 747-0110; www .nps.gov/sitk

---

FINDING THE TRAILHEAD

 From Lake and Lincoln Streets in downtown Sitka, travel east on Lincoln, past the small boat harbor and Sheldon Jackson College, about 0.6 mile to the park visitor center. The trails begin on either side of the visitor center. Most people walk the West Loop counterclockwise, beginning on the west (sea, or right) side of the visitor center; to walk it clockwise, or to cross the Indian River trail bridge for the most direct route to the East Loop, stroll east out of the parking area, to the left of the visitor center. There is also a trailhead for the East Loop on Sawmill Creek Road, about 0.2 mile southeast of the Indian River Bridge.

WHAT TO SEE

Sitka National Historical Park, Alaska's oldest national park, commemorates the 1804 Battle of Sitka, when a force of Russians and Aleuts fought the local Tlingit people and established Sitka as the capital of Russian America. The site of Shiskeenue, the fort the Tlingits defended against the Russian invaders, is on the West Loop.

The West Loop meanders through a "forest" of Southeast Alaska Native totem poles. The carved cedar poles were collected and brought to Sitka in the early 1900s. Many of them are Haida poles from Prince of Wales Island, an island in southern Southeast Alaska. They are no longer in their cultural context but are preserved as in a museum. The booklet Carved History, available in the park bookstore, is a guide to the poles in the park.

The park trails are more of a stroll than a hike. They're a good, undemanding introduction to the look, smell, and feel of Southeast's water-and-forest environment, as well as a showcase of local history and Native culture. The park offers naturalist-led walks in summer.

West Loop: Starting the 1-mile West Loop on the sea side of the visitor center, the trail leads into the forest, through the park's collection of totem poles, and eventually to the fort site. The site of the Tlingit stronghold is a broad opening in the forest on the point of land at the mouth of the Indian River. Past the fort the trail circles back along the Indian River to the visitor center. There are several points along the first half of the loop where you can step out onto the stony beach a few yards off the trail and take in the view of Sitka Sound.

Near the end of the loop, a bridge spans the Indian River, leading to the East Loop. In late summer and fall, the river runs thick with salmon, a traditional Tlingit food source. Now the river is closed to all salmon fishing to protect fish stocks.

East Loop: The 0.6-mile East Loop features the Russian Memorial, a plaque and Russian cross placed in honor of the Russian sailors who died in the Battle of Sitka.

A visit to the park isn't complete without taking a look at the exhibits in the park visitor center. The Southeast Alaska Indian Cultural Center, located inside the visitor center building, offers demonstrations of woodcarving and other local Native arts. The Russian Bishop's House, at 501 Lincoln Street, is also part of the park and worthy of a visit.

The Ten-Cent Treatise on Totems: Totem poles, those tall, elaborately carved cedar poles, comprise one of the most striking art forms imaginable. Crests of human and animal figures, stacked one on top of another, are a window into a different reality—who can look at the figure of a grinning orca, with a tiny human face as the blowhole, without being pulled into the Tlingit and Haida world for just an instant?

These Northwest Coast Native creations are part history, part literature, and part art. It's commonly thought that they developed from family histories carved into the house posts that supported the traditional Northwest Coast communal homes.

The poles generally tell a story—of a family, a legend, or an event—but only the characters of the story are discernible from the pole alone. The Tlingit erected poles as monuments or to mark grave sites, to describe special events or visions, or to ridicule someone for not repaying a debt, sort of an artsy way of turning the person's name over to the collection agency of public opinion. Wealthy Tlingits also commissioned artists to carve poles for special events, such as potlatches, which were public celebrations of feasting and gift giving.

Totem carving has seen a revival in recent years, and the poles are again common in Southeast and in other parts of Alaska. Sitka National Historical Park and Totem Bight State Historical Park north of Ketchikan offer beautiful short hikes to see totem poles in their natural environment.

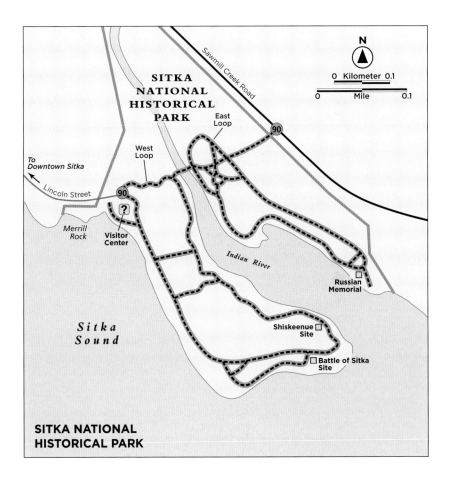

91. HARBOR MOUNTAIN AND GAVAN HILL

WHY GO?

A thru-hike traversing open ridgeline above Sitka Sound, with views of the surrounding wild peaks of Tongass National Forest.

THE RUNDOWN

Distance: 6.3 miles one way

Special features: Subalpine and alpine hiking, views, and a trail shelter on an alpine ridge

Location: Immediately above Sitka

Difficulty: Moderate from Harbor Mountain Trailhead; strenuous from Gavan Hill Trailhead

Trail type: More developed

Total elevation gain: 800 feet from Harbor Mountain; 2,700 feet from Gavan Hill

Best season: Mid-June through Sept

Fees/permits: None

Maps: USGS Sitka A-4 (SW) and A-5 (SE) (trail not shown)

Contact: Tongass National Forest, Sitka Ranger District, 204 Siginaka Way, Sitka, AK 99835; (907) 747-6671; www.fs.usda.gov/tongass/

FINDING THE TRAILHEAD

Harbor Mountain Trailhead: From the intersection of Lake Street and Sawmill Creek Road in Sitka, follow Sawmill Creek and its extension, Halibut Point Road, north about 4 miles and turn right onto Harbor Mountain Road. Follow the winding road a bit over 5 miles to the trailhead in subalpine country at 2,000 feet in elevation. Harbor Mountain Road, a narrow gravel road with pullouts, is not suitable for RVs or trailers.

Gavan Hill Trailhead: From Lake Street and Sawmill Creek Road, travel east 0.2 mile on Sawmill and turn left onto Baranof Street. Follow Baranof 0.2 mile to the end of the street; find the trailhead on the right. The trailhead is an easy walk from downtown Sitka.

Another access to the trail is via the Sitka Cross Trail, a route connecting multiple trails from downtown Sitka.

WHAT TO SEE

The Harbor Mountain–Gavan Hill hike traverses the open ridgeline above Sitka, skirting the watershed of Cascade Creek and leading to great sea, island, and peak views, including a close look at Baranof Island's wild, icy summit range. Other highlights are a side trip to climb the first peak of Harbor Mountain, a fine wildflower slope on the south side of the mountain, and stretches of alpine heather around the head of Cascade Creek. Eagles ride thermals above the heights, and deer wander the high country in summer.

A boardwalk in the dense forest along the 6.3-mile Harbor Mountain and Gavan Hill trail.
SARAH STEHN

A small, enclosed trail shelter (no reservation, no fee) in the saddle connecting the Harbor Mountain and Gavan Hill ridges is the best overnight spot. The shelter has a commanding view, and the knob behind it has an even better view of the dark, rugged peaks that form the backbone of Baranof Island.

Most of the sites suitable for pitching a tent on the ridge are exposed to wind and weather. The weather can change dramatically at this elevation, so be prepared for rain, cold winds, and poor visibility. The trail is well defined, but it could be difficult to follow in places when it's still snow-covered early in summer. Please don't build campfires in the easily damaged subalpine zone. There is no water on the high ridges after the snowpack melts, typically by midsummer.

From the Harbor Mountain Trailhead, 0.2 mile of boardwalk climbs to the ridge west of Harbor Mountain. Subalpine vegetation mixes with montane forest in this northern section of the hike. At 1.5 miles the trail joins the Harbor Mountain summit ridge, where a steep path leads to the first peak; there is no easy route to the true summit beyond.

The trail passes stunted, twisted hemlocks as it curls around the south side of Harbor Mountain into subalpine and alpine terrain. Past the shelter at 2.5 miles, the trail crosses the flat, open summit of Gavan Hill, a fine overlook, and descends on boardwalk and stairsteps into the forest, eventually reaching the Baranof Street trailhead. A mile above the trailhead is a good view of the south side of Sitka.

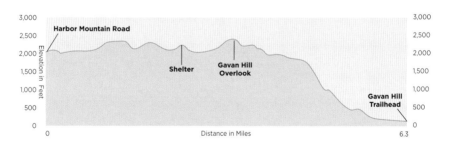

MILES AND DIRECTIONS

Harbor Mountain Trailhead		Gavan Hill Trailhead
0.0	Begin/end at the Harbor Mountain Trailhead.	6.3
1.5	The trail joins the Harbor Mountain ridge.	4.8
2.5	Reach the trail shelter, the best spot for overnighting.	3.8
3.3	Cross the open summit of Gavan Hill.	3.0
5.3	Look south for a good view of Sitka.	1.0
6.3	End/begin at the Gavan Hill Trailhead.	0.0

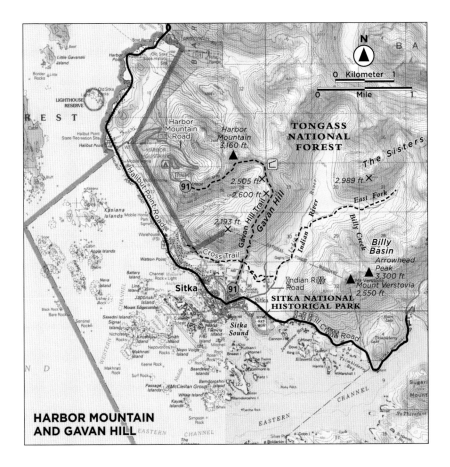

**HARBOR MOUNTAIN
AND GAVAN HILL**

Shorter hikes: On the Gavan Hill side of the trail, try the Mile 1 viewpoint, or if you're feeling energetic, do the steep hike to the Gavan Hill Overlook, 3 miles one way. At Harbor Mountain there are decent views just 0.2 mile up the trail, and the much more difficult jaunt to the south summit of the mountain is about 2 miles one way.

> **TIDBIT**
> Take a look at the elevation profile before deciding which trailhead to begin from.

92. STARRIGAVAN BAY

WHY GO?

Easy interpretive loops winding through forest and coastline in scenic Starrigavan Bay.

THE RUNDOWN

Distances: Estuary Life Trail: 0.4 mile one way. Forest and Muskeg Trail: 0.7 mile one way. Mosquito Cove Trail: a 1.5-mile loop

Special features: Birding, salmon viewing, saltwater meadows, coastal scenery, rain forest, an interpretive brochure, and an adjacent campground

Location: 7.5 miles north of Sitka, at the north end of the Sitka road system

Difficulty: Easy

Trail type: Estuary Life: accessible. Forest and Muskeg: more developed. Mosquito Cove: more

developed with an accessible section

Total elevation gain: Estuary Life: insignificant. Forest and Muskeg: 150 feet. Mosquito Cove: 100 feet

Best season: Mar through Nov

Fees/permits: None

Maps: USGS Sitka A-5 (trails not shown); Forest Service/Alaska State Parks map/brochure *Starrigavan Recreation Are*

Contact: Tongass National Forest, Sitka Ranger District, 204 Siginaka Way, Sitka, AK 99835; (907) 747-6671; www.fs.usda.gov/tongass/

FINDING THE TRAILHEAD

 From downtown Sitka, drive west and north from the corner of Sawmill Creek Road and Lake Street. Sawmill Creek becomes Halibut Point Road; follow it to the Starrigavan Recreation Area, about 7.5 miles from town and just past the state ferry terminal. The Starrigavan Campground and the three trailheads are all within a mile of the terminal.

WHAT TO SEE

These three trails, a cooperative project of Tongass National Forest and Alaska State Parks, are short, easy hikes adjacent to the Starrigavan Campground at the north end of Sitka's road system. The Estuary Life Trail and Forest and Muskeg Trail are interpretive trails. You'll need the area map/brochure, available at the trailheads, to get the most out of these hikes.

The south trailhead for the Forest and Muskeg Trail is across from the Old Sitka boat ramp. There are trailheads for the Estuary Life Trail just south of the T in the road near the campground and in the campground's Estuary Loop. The two trails join Road 7578 (also known as Nelson Logging Road) on opposite sides of the road, at a point about 0.3 mile from its intersection with Halibut Point Road. Park in the parking area on the east side of Road 7578, and you can access either trail from there. The Mosquito Cove Trailhead is in the Bayside Loop of the campground, west of the T in the road.

Connecting the three trails by way of the campground roads, Road 7578, and the pedestrian walkway along Halibut Point Road, you can string together a hike of 3 to 4 miles here. Starrigavan is a good place for travelers without cars; you can walk from the ferry terminal, 0.7 mile, set up camp in the Backpacker Loop in the campground, and entertain yourself on the trails in the recreation area. Don't forget the binoculars.

Estuary Life Trail: The Estuary Life Trail, entirely boardwalk, features a bird-viewing shelter and a river-viewing deck. From the Halibut Point Road trailhead, it's just a few feet to the birding shelter, which overlooks Starrigavan Creek's estuary. Estuaries are biologically rich areas where streams meet the sea, exchanging saltwater and freshwater in rhythm with the tides. Waterfowl like mergansers and great blue herons use the estuary year-round, and many other species of birds can be seen here too.

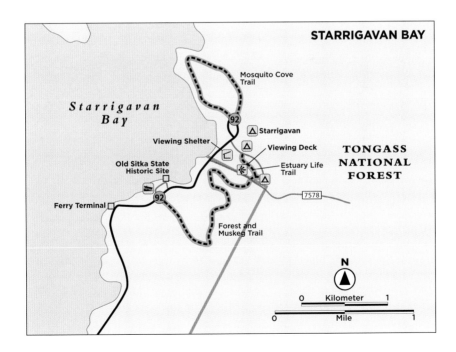

North of the viewing shelter, the trail leads through forest and meadows of tall grasses, passing the connecting path to the Starrigavan Campground's Estuary Loop. The river-viewing deck to the east overlooks the shallow stream. Spawning salmon crowd the creek in late summer and fall (pinks in August and September and silvers in September and October, but the creek is closed to all salmon fishing). Just before reaching Road 7578, the trail crosses the stream on a footbridge.

Forest and Muskeg Trail: The trail leads through forests of hemlock, spruce, and cedar and across muskegs with scattered, stunted shore pine. The interpretive theme here is the biology of northern Southeast Alaska's forests and muskegs. The trail winds along boardwalk and gravel tread, climbing gradually into muskeg openings with views of the mountains at the heart of Baranof Island.

Mosquito Cove Trail: For about half its distance, the hike more or less follows the shorelines of Starrigavan Bay and Mosquito Cove. The trail passes through the usual impressive Baranof Island forest and by a few stout sedimentary rock outcrops. Along the water, look for seabirds and shorebirds.

TIDBIT

Bring your binoculars for this scenic stroll with opportunities to view seabirds and shorebirds.

---

93. BEAVER LAKE AND HERRING COVE TRAIL

WHY GO?

Trails suitable for all hiking abilities, with routes traveling through forests, by muskegs and a lake.

THE RUNDOWN

Distances: Between 1.7 to 6 miles

Special features: Forest, muskegs, marshes, lake, mountain views, picnic tables, and a rowboat

Location: About 5 miles east of Sitka

Difficulty: Easy to moderate

Trail type: More developed

Total elevation gain: 250 feet

Best season: Mar through Nov

Fees/permits: None

Maps: USGS Sitka A-4

Contact: Tongass National Forest, Sitka Ranger District, 204 Siginaka Way, Sitka, AK 99835; (907) 747-6671; www.fs.usda.gov/tongass/

FINDING THE TRAILHEAD

Herring Cove Trailhead: From downtown Sitka, head east for 6 miles on Sawmill Creek Road. Continue past the Sawmill Cove Industrial Park and Blue Lake Road to the gate and trailhead parking area.

Beaver Lake Trailhead: From downtown Sitka, head east for 5 miles on Sawmill Creek Road. At Mile 5.5, across from the pulp mill, turn left onto a gravel road heading uphill. Continue 1.5 miles to Sawmill Creek Campground. The trailhead is across Sawmill Creek Bridge on the south side.

WHAT TO SEE

A favorite among Sitka locals, the Beaver Lake and Herring Cove Trail is a maintained, accessible route traveling through stunted forests, beautiful muskegs, and along marshes with waterfalls and gorgeous views of Bear Mountain. These trails provide a variety of options. An out-and-back from either trailhead, including opportunity to hike around Beaver Lake, or a through-hike option from one trailhead to the other.

For hikers looking for the shortest hike, start at the Sawmill Creek Campground walk around Beaver Lake for a 1.7-mile loop. The first 0.25 mile of the mostly gravel

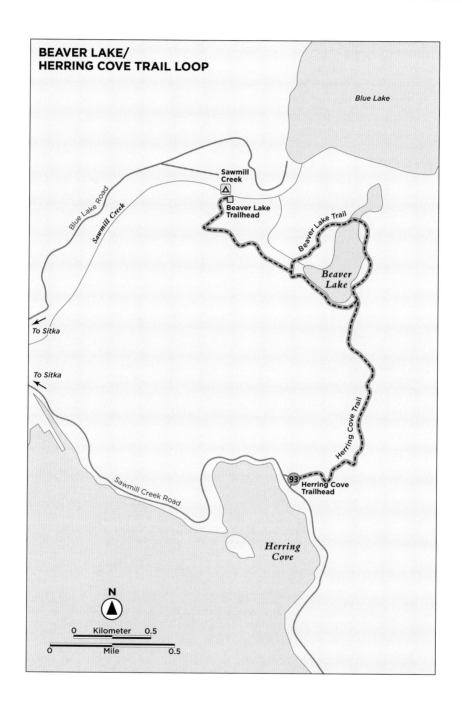

**BEAVER LAKE/
HERRING COVE TRAIL LOOP**

Blue Lake

Blue Lake Road

Sawmill Creek

Sawmill
Creek

Beaver Lake
Trailhead

Beaver Lake Trail

*Beaver
Lake*

To Sitka

To Sitka

Herring Cove Trail

Sawmill Creek Road

93 Herring Cove
Trailhead

*Herring
Cove*

N

0   Kilometer   0.5

0   Mile   0.5

trail climbs about 200 feet in elevation, via switchbacks, through beautiful forest of hemlock, Sitka spruce and yellow cedar, paralleling marshes and the Beaver lake outlet stream. The loop route circles around the lakefront and open forests, and returns to the start at the fishing platforms on the south end of the trail.

The intermediate, 4.6-mile out and back hike starts at the campground, to Herring Cove. The advanced loop is about 6 miles from Herring Cove to Beaver Lake, returning along the Blue Lake Road and Sawmill Creek Road to the Herring Cove Trailhead.

At Beaver Lake, use the public rowboat and picnic tables, for day use in the area.

Longer hikes: For those looking for a bigger adventure, there's a loop route of about 10 miles, starting from Herring Cove to Beaver Lake, connecting with Blue Lake Road to the 1.6-mile Thimbleberry Lake Trail, and returning via Sawmill Creek Road.

One of the top hikes in Sitka, the Beaver Lake and Herring Cove Trail travels through forests, muskegs, and by marshes with waterfalls and gorgeous views of Bear Mountain.
SARAH STEHN

PETERSBURG

PETERSBURG, THE CLOSEST THING in Alaska to a Norwegian village, is all about fish and fishing. The town's economy revolves almost completely around fishing, and most of the nearby trails lead to fishing holes. The Forest Service's Mitkof Island Road Guide map is a big help for finding your way around on the island road system. Petersburg, like most Southeast towns, is accessible from the outside world only by sea or air.

In addition to the two trails described in this section, try the Raven Trail, a 4-mile one-way hike that begins behind the airport and ends at a recreation cabin in high, wet meadows above town. Across Wrangell Narrows (same trailhead as that for Petersburg Lake) is the steep, 4-mile one-way hike to the top of Petersburg Mountain.

For travelers without cars, the most accessible trips are the Raven Trail and the boat-in trips to Petersburg Lake and Petersburg Mountain.

94. THREE LAKES AND IDEAL COVE

WHY GO?

The trails link three lakes, named after sandhill cranes, each equipped with a picnic table, a rowboat, and a trail shelter, which overlooks the Frederick Sound.

THE RUNDOWN

Distance: 0.4 mile one way to a loop of about 7.5 miles

Special features: 3 lakes, each with a picnic table and rowboat; a trail shelter; fishing; coast hiking and camping

Location: 27 miles south of Petersburg

Difficulty: Three Lakes: easy. Three Lakes with a side trip to Ideal Cove: moderate

Trail type: More developed (entirely planked)

Total elevation gain: 50 to 300 feet, depending on the route chosen

Best season: Mid-Apr to mid-Oct

Fees/permits: None

Maps: USGS Petersburg C-3 (NE) and C-2

Contact: Petersburg Visitor Information Center, First and Farm, PO Box 649, Petersburg, AK 99833; (907) 772-4636; www.fs.usda.gov/tongass/

FINDING THE TRAILHEAD

Follow the Mitkof Highway 21 miles south of Petersburg to Three Lakes Loop Road (signed) and turn left (east). The three trailheads are 6.3 miles (Crane Lake), 6.7 miles (Hill Lake), and 7.2 miles (Sand Lake) from the Mitkof Highway. Three Lakes Loop Road is a winding, single-lane gravel road with turnouts; drive with caution.

WHAT TO SEE

The Three Lakes trails connect Sand, Hill, and Crane Lakes and the smaller Shelter Lake via three trailheads and 4.5 miles of boardwalk in a figure-eight loop. The three larger lakes get their names from the sandhill cranes that stop here on their migrations. The Ideal Cove Trail, a Civilian Conservation Corps trail first cleared in the 1930s and have since rebuilt, leading down Hill Creek to the coast of Frederick Sound.

Three Lakes: Sand, Hill, and Crane Lakes are each equipped with a wooden platform, picnic table, and rowboat. There is a refurbished, Civilian Conservation Corps-era three-sided trail shelter at Shelter Lake. All the lakes are at about 150 feet in elevation.

The Three Lakes area is entirely wet forest and meadow, so tenting isn't a good option, except possibly setting up a free-standing tent on one of the platforms at the lakes. Flowers and berries are abundant. The bogs bloom early with shooting stars, marsh marigolds, bog orchids, and other flowers.

For the shortest hike, pick one of the Three Lakes and simply hike straight there, no more than 0.4 mile one way. A two-lake loop is about 2.5 miles round-trip, including a short road walk back to the trailhead where you started. A long loop touching all the lakes is about 2.8 miles plus a 0.9-mile road walk. A bicycle is a reasonable shuttle vehicle if you have one along.

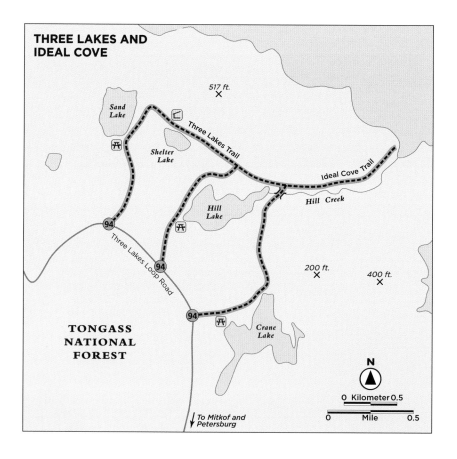

Ideal Cove Trail: Just below Hill Lake, at the bridge over Hill Creek, the Ideal Cove Trail takes off toward the coast. About 1.5 miles one way, the trail served as access to Three Lakes before the Mitkof Highway was built in the early 1970s; the lakes, appropriately, were once known as the Ideal Lakes. After the highway was built, Forest Service and youth crews gradually built the trail system to and around the lakes from the road.

The trail follows Hill Creek and reaches the coast at the mouth of the creek. Ideal Cove, mostly state land with a private cabin, is around the next point to the south, but the ideal campsites are to the north, about 0.5 mile beyond the end of the trail and behind the next point in that direction. Find a campsite in the forest back of the point and a small stream for water just around the point. Plan to hike the coastline no higher than mid tide. Doing this side trip from the Three Lakes loop can yield up to a 7.5-mile round-trip hike, the longest possible hike on this trail system.

Fishing: The Three Lakes offer decent cutthroat trout and Dolly Varden fishing.

> **TIDBIT**
>
> At each lake, you'll find a picnic table, a fire ring, and a rowboat. Plan a hike/rowboat to a picnic adventure, walking between 0.4 mile and about 7.5 miles.

95. PETERSBURG LAKE

WHY GO?

A trail traveling by a creek, wildflower meadows, old-growth forest, and a lake, with one of the few low elevation, longer hiking trails in all of Southeast Alaska.

THE RUNDOWN

Distance: 10.3 miles one way

Special features: Forests, meadows, a large lake, stream and lake fishing, a fee cabin. The trailhead is accessible by boat, a mile across the Wrangell Narrows from Petersburg

Location: On Kupreanof Island, west of Petersburg

Difficulty: Moderate

Trail type: More developed

Total elevation gain: About 500 feet in and 400 feet out

Best season: Mid-Apr to mid-Oct

Fees/permits: Fee for cabin use

Maps: USGS Petersburg D-3 (SW) and D-4 (SE)

Contact: Petersburg Visitor Information Center, First and Farm, PO Box 649, Petersburg, AK 99833; (907) 772-4636; www.fs.usda.gov/tongass/

FINDING THE TRAILHEAD

The hike begins at the Kupreanof state dock, a mile west of the Petersburg waterfront and accessible by powerboat or sea kayak. Contact the Petersburg Visitor Information Center, see "Contact" above, or check www.petersburg.org for information on hiring a ride to the trailhead.

There is also a high-tide trailhead suitable for small boats; it meets the trail 4.4 miles up from the state dock. Skiffs need a tide of at least 14 feet, and kayaks about 12 feet, to make it all the way there. The hike along the lower creek, though, is highly recommended, so don't despair if you can't make it to the high-tide trailhead.

WHAT TO SEE

The Petersburg Lake Trail is one of only a very few longer, low–elevation hikes in Southeast Alaska. The hike's diversity is pretty remarkable, considering that the net elevation gain is only 100 feet. The creek, wildflower meadows, old–growth forests, and mile-long Petersburg Lake make this a premier hike. At the lake, there is a fee cabin and a rowboat for cabin occupants to use (it's available to anyone when the cabin isn't occupied). For cabin reservations, log on to www.reserveusa.com or call (877) 444-6777.

The trip offers good fishing and a chance to see swans and other waterfowl, eagles, black bears, and forest birds. Four species of salmon, spring and fall steelhead, cut-throat trout, and Dolly Varden use the lake and stream. Eagles and bears are especially plentiful when the salmon are thick in late summer and fall.

The creek changes personalities several times on the way to the lake. It's a wide, slow, meandering stream in the estuary, or tidally influenced section; a swift, rocky creek; a dark stream in deep forest with pretty pools and riffles; and a slow, deep, marsh-fringed stream flowing out of the lake. The fork that enters from the south at 9.5 miles is actually a larger stream.

The lower trail jogs out of the forest now and then onto the strip of coastal meadow along the estuary. The meadows are thick with wildflowers in summer. The forest in this reach of the valley is deep and mossy, like something out of J.R. Tolkien. Mini Forests of skunk cabbage line the boardwalk trail (see "Our Friend the Skunk Cabbage" below).

Just before Mile 3 is the only significant climb on the hike, a quick up and down to avoid a piece of private land. At 4.5 miles, the trail enters the Petersburg Creek–Duncan Salt Chuck Wilderness. Between the wilderness boundary and Shaky Frank Creek, about Mile 7, the hike crosses three beaver dams; two are bridged and one is not. The undeveloped crossing is a frequently flooded section of the trail, and the Forest Service trail crew has to reroute it occasionally. Keep your eye out for flagging or other markers that indicate the current route, and be sure you're on it before you stray too far off the beaten path.

Just beyond Shaky Frank Creek is a 0.5-mile-long muskeg bordered by lodgepole pine. Del Monte Peak is visible to the east. Take care on a few high log bridges in this section of the trail.

The developed trail ends at the cabin, in the trees near the lakeshore. The 3,600-foot alpine summits of Portage Mountain make up the view across the lake. The cabin is also accessible by a short floatplane trip from Petersburg, so non hikers use it as well.

The two landslides on the trail, at about Miles 3 and 10, cut loose on the same day in late October 1993. The upper slide partially dammed Petersburg Lake, and although the dam has more or less washed out now, it raised the level of the lake enough after the slide to drown a band of trees around the perimeter of the lake; their skeletons are still visible. The trail does some fancy footwork across fallen logs through this slide.

Much of the Petersburg Creek valley is wet, so tent camping is fairly limited. A few possibilities are the meadows on the lower creek (in dry weather), sandbars on the middle reach at lower water levels, and a few possible sites in the brushy forest by the lake.

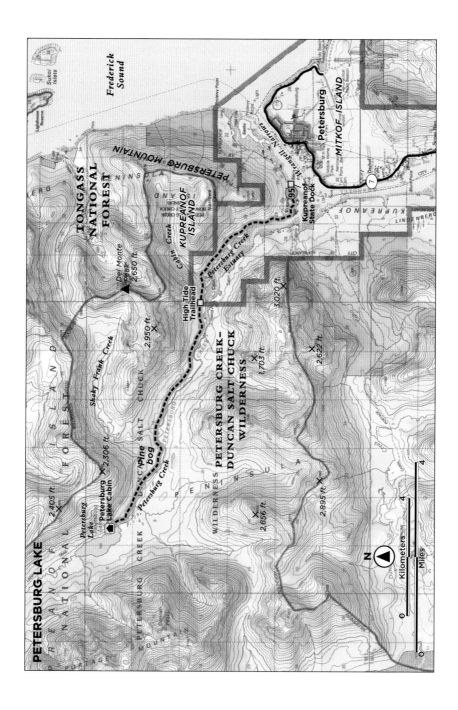

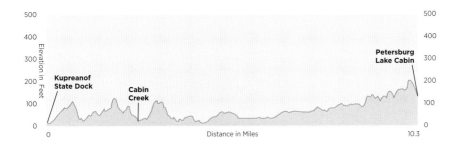

MILES AND DIRECTIONS

0.0 Begin at the Kupreanof state dock.

0.8 Arrive at Petersburg Creek.

3.0 Cross Cabin Creek after a short climb.

4.4 Reach the high-tide trailhead.

4.5 Cross the boundary into the Petersburg Creek–Duncan Salt Chuck Wilderness.

7.0 Cross Shaky Frank Creek.

7.5 Hike through a pine bog.

9.5 Pass the south fork of Petersburg Creek.

10.3 Reach Petersburg Lake Cabin.

Shorter hikes: A day hike on the lower trail, up to 4.5 miles one way, makes a good jaunt for exploring the estuary and coastal meadows.

Fishing: Of the many fishing opportunities, the Department of Fish and Game notes the spring steelhead and fall silver-salmon runs as highlights.

OUR FRIEND THE SKUNK CABBAGE

The skunk cabbage's wet forest habitat may be less than glamorous, but this is a plant with charisma. Its thick, shiny leaves, growing to 4 or 5 feet long, make it impossible to miss on Southeast trails, and its banana-yellow, leaflike "spathes" that pop out of the mud in March are the first sign of the Southeast spring.

The spathe opens to reveal a prominent floral spike, which blossoms with hundreds of tiny flowers. The pollen these flowers shed is responsible for the slightly skunky odor that gives the plant its name and its undeserved reputation.

For humans, skunk cabbage is inedible without careful preparation, but animals love it. Bears, deer, and Canada geese eat the leaves and roots, and Steller's jays munch on the seeds. In traditional times Southeast Alaska's Native people roasted the roots to destroy the irritating chemical, and ground them into flour.

WRANGELL

WRANGELL IS A SMALL, friendly town that is a bit off the beaten path of big industrial, cruise-ship tourism. The portion of the Tongass National Forest south of town has a forest management road system like the Pacific slope forests of Oregon and Washington, making it a good area for a vacation of car camping, fishing, and short hikes. Buy a copy of the Forest Service's Wrangell Island Road Guide if you want to explore the trails and lakes outside Wrangell. The Wrangell area also has several remote Forest Service trails and cabins accessible only by boat or floatplane.

The best trips for travelers without cars are Rainbow Falls and Institute Creek, and the 0.4-mile hike to the top of Mount Dewey, the northernmost green bump behind Wrangell, from the trailhead on Third Street above downtown.

96. **RAINBOW FALLS AND INSTITUTE CREEK**

WHY GO?

A trail with a variety of options, a short hike to waterfalls, or longer overnight adventures into the high country above Wrangell.

THE RUNDOWN

Distances: Rainbow Falls: 0.6 mile one way. Shoemaker Bay Overlook Shelter: 3.3 miles one way. North Wrangell High Country Trail: 6 miles one way

Special features: Rainbow Falls, montane forest and wet meadows, ridgetop views, 3 trail shelters

Location: Just south of Wrangell

Difficulty: Moderate to strenuous

Trail type: More developed, to a route in the alpine

Total elevation gain: Rainbow Falls: 500 feet. Shoemaker

Overlook: 1,600 feet. North Wrangell shelters: 2,600 feet

Best season: Falls: Mar through Oct. Institute Creek and North Wrangell Trails: mid-May through Sept

Fees/permits: None

Maps: USGS Petersburg B-2 (NE), B-1 (NW); Forest Service *Wrangell Island Road Guide*

Contact: Tongass National Forest, Wrangell Ranger District, 525 Bennett Street, PO Box 51, Wrangell, AK 99929; (907) 874-2323; www.fs.usda.gov/tongass/

FINDING THE TRAILHEAD

The trailhead is 4.5 miles south of the state ferry terminal via the Zimovia Highway. Look for the trail on the left (east) side of the highway, across from the Shoemaker Bay Recreation Area (small boat harbor and camp, picnic, and parking areas). Park in the trailhead parking area on the west side of the highway. For travelers without cars, taking a taxi or bike to the trailhead are viable options.

WHAT TO SEE

The Rainbow Falls Trail is a short, steep hike to see Rainbow Creek in freefall in a lush hemlock forest. If you're interested in a longer hike, the trail continues beyond the falls as the Institute Creek Trail, which leads to a trail shelter at an overlook of Shoemaker Bay. A branch of the trail climbs into higher country as the North Wrangell Trail, leading to the High Country and Pond Shelters.

The trails are almost entirely surfaced with stairs, log steps, and "step and run" boardwalk. A masochistic Forest Service employee once counted the stairsteps to Shoemaker Bay Overlook: There are 1,849 of them. If this is your first boardwalk hike, keep in mind that all the stair stepping can be tough on people with knee or hip injuries.

The three trail shelters (no reservation, no fee, first-come, first-served) are open-air, three-sided structures that sleep about four. Each site has a picnic table and outhouse. All the shelters are in wet areas, so there are few if any decent tent sites nearby. You may have to share your shelter with a few pesky mosquitoes, so bring some insect netting along if you plan to sleep in one of them.

Rainbow Falls: Staircases, log steps, and boardwalk steps make up the 500-foot climb to Rainbow Falls. Bring a lunch to eat on one of the two viewing decks, one

The trail is almost entirely surfaced with stairs, log steps, and "step and run" boardwalk. Keep in mind that all the stair stepping can be tough on people with knee or hip injuries. CHARITY HOMMEL

From the Trailhead 0.6 mile in, view the waterfall of Rainbow Creek, in a lush hemlock forest.
CHARITY HOMMEL

below the falls at 0.6 mile and one above at 0.7 mile. The better view of the falls is from the lower deck.

Shoemaker Overlook: The trail beyond Rainbow Falls follows Institute Creek (named for the defunct Wrangell Institute, a former Bureau of Indian Affairs school on the Zimovia Highway), passing a falls-and-cascades section on a set of switchbacks. Above the switchbacks the trail emerges from hemlock/cedar forest into a series of wet meadows fringed with yellow-cedar, spruce, and shore pine. At about 2.2 miles from the trailhead, the North Wrangell Trail forks north.

The Institute trail then crosses Institute Creek and curls around to the south and west, traversing more meadows on the way to the overlook and the shelter, about 3.3 miles from the trailhead. The overlook is a very scenic spot for a long lunch or overnight, but be cautious near the edge as the bluff ends in a vertical drop-off. There is no water at the overlook; besides small trickles and ponds between Institute Creek and the shelter, the best source is Institute Creek, about a mile back on the trail.

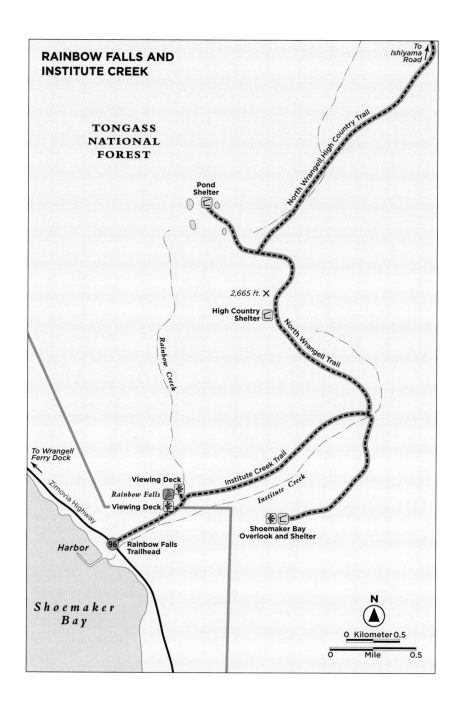

RAINBOW FALLS AND
INSTITUTE CREEK

TONGASS
NATIONAL
FOREST

To
Ishiyama
Road

North Wrangell High Country Trail

Pond
Shelter

2,665 ft. ✕

High Country
Shelter

North Wrangell Trail

Rainbow Creek

To Wrangell
Ferry Dock

Institute Creek Trail

Institute Creek

Viewing Deck

Zimovia Highway

Rainbow Falls

Viewing Deck

Shoemaker Bay
Overlook and Shelter

96

Rainbow Falls
Trailhead

Harbor

Shoemaker
Bay

N

0   Kilometer 0.5

0   Mile   0.5

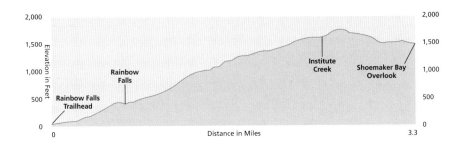

MILES AND DIRECTIONS

0.0   Start from the Rainbow Falls Trailhead.

0.6   View Rainbow Falls from the lower observation deck.

2.2   Pass the North Wrangell Trail junction and cross the bridge over Institute Creek.

3.3   Reach Shoemaker Bay Overlook and Shelter.

North Wrangell High Country Trail: From the trail fork at 2.2 miles on the Rainbow Falls/Institute Creek Trail, the primitive North Wrangell High Country Trail climbs the ridge that rises to the west of the headwaters of Institute Creek. The High Country Shelter is near the top of the ridge, 1.3 miles beyond the trail fork, in open country at about 2,600 feet in elevation, with no nearby water source.

Shortly after the shelter, the trail steeply climbs to an intersection. To the left, a spur trail leads 0.5 mile to the Pond Shelter, set in a high, wet meadow dotted with small ponds. To the right, the main North Wrangell High Country Trail continues to the other end of the trail. The route is an additional 2 miles to Ishiyama Road (formerly North Wrangell Spur Road). This unmarked end of the trailhead is about 4.5 miles from town, so plan transportation accordingly. Check with the Forest Service on the current conditions of the high country trail.

MILES AND DIRECTIONS

0.0   Start from the Rainbow Falls Trailhead.

0.6   View Rainbow Falls from the lower observation deck.

2.2   Turn north on the North Wrangell Trail.

3.5   Climb to the High Country Shelter.

4.0   Trail junction, main North Wrangell Trail to the right, left to Pond Shelter.

6.0   Arrive at unmarked trailhead on Ishiyama Road.

KETCHIKAN

KETCHIKAN, ALASKA, LIES ON the southwest corner of Revillagigedo ("Revilla") Island, where it basks in more than 13 feet of rain a year. The city is so far south, it's closer to Seattle than to Anchorage. Accessible only by air or sea, Ketchikan is the first Alaska state-ferry stop on the trip up from the south.

Besides the trails described here, try the Connell Lake Trail off Revilla Road (2 miles one way), the Dude Mountain Trail at the end of Revilla Road/Brown Mountain Road (1 mile one way, steep), and the short, easy trail at Totem Bight State Historical Park 10 miles north of town on the North Tongass Highway (0.3 mile, an interpretive trail with Tlingit and Haida totem poles and a clan house).

Travelers without cars can walk to the Deer Mountain Trailhead from the dock/downtown area of Ketchikan. Another option is to head for the Ward Lake Recreation Area, about 7 miles north of the ferry terminal, for campground-based hiking or a short backpack (Ward Lake and Ward Creek, and Perseverance Lake and the Connell Lake Trail).

97. DEER MOUNTAIN

WHY GO?

A trail within walking distance of downtown Ketchikan, with mountains, lakes, and a variety of trip options, from day hikes, to overnight treks in picturesque alpine terrain.

THE RUNDOWN

Distance: Deer Mountain: 2.5 miles one way. Blue Lake: 4.5 miles one way. Traverse: 12.5 miles

Special features: Mountain scenery, an alpine traverse, trail shelters below Deer Mountain and at Blue Lake. The trailhead is accessible on foot from downtown Ketchikan

Location: A mile southeast of downtown Ketchikan

Difficulty: Deer Mountain and Blue Lake: strenuous. Traverse: very strenuous

Trail type: Deer Mountain: more-developed trail. Blue Lake and traverse: more-developed trail lower; less-developed trail/route on the alpine ridges

Total elevation gain: Deer Mountain: 2,600 feet. Blue Lake: 2,700 feet. Traverse: 4,700 feet

Best season: Deer Mountain: June through Sept. Blue Lake and traverse: Late June through mid-Sept

Fees/permits: None

Maps: USGS Ketchikan B-5; Forest Service *Ketchikan Area Hiking Guide*

Contact: Tongass National Forest, Ketchikan–Misty Fjords Ranger District, 3031 Tongass Ave., Ketchikan, AK 99901; (907) 225-2148; www.fs.usda.gov/tongass/

FINDING THE TRAILHEAD

Deer Mountain: From the Southeast Alaska Discovery Center (SEADC, at the corner of Main and Mill by the city dock), travel east and south on Mill and Stedman Streets, the main route through town, 0.4 mile to Deermount Street. Turn left (east) and continue 0.4 mile to Ketchikan Lakes Road; turn right and climb steeply 0.4 mile to the top of the hill. Cross Nordstrom Drive and turn right into the trailhead parking area about 100 feet beyond the intersection. A series of hiker signs leads to the trailhead from Stedman Street.

Silvis Lakes: From SEADC, follow Mill and Stedman Streets east and south through Ketchikan. The route becomes the South Tongass Highway; follow it

13 miles to the end of the road at the Beaver Falls Power Plant. Drive down the hill, just beyond the end of road sign, and leave your vehicle in the Silvis Lakes parking area on the right. The trail follows the gated, graveled road that begins 50 feet to the east.

WHAT TO SEE

Popular with both locals and visitors, the Deer Mountain Trail climbs a 3,001-foot peak above Ketchikan with a panoramic view of mountain peaks, forests, islands, and ocean. From there, you can continue to alpine Blue Lake and beyond; the route crosses the island on high ridges to the Silvis Lakes Trailhead on George Inlet. Whatever your destination, this is a good hike for travelers, as the trailhead is a walk of only a mile from downtown Ketchikan.

The traverse across the island is a fine alpine ramble. Experienced backpackers can do it in one extremely long day, but if the weather is decent and you're okay with carrying a full pack on a steep hike, a 2-to-3-day backpack into the Deer Mountain–John Mountain high country is an unforgettable a trip. Even if it's sunny, pack good rain gear and warm layers of clothing; Ketchikan is one of the wettest places in Southeast, and the weather can change quickly.

Deep snow often lingers on the trail until mid-June, and north-facing slopes on the high ridges hold snow well beyond that. Near Deer Mountain a section of trail on a steep sidehill is prone to snow slides early in the season, and slipping off the trail and falling through a wind-formed cornice are also potential hazards. On the traverse the north-facing sections north of Northbird Peak and south of Silvis Saddle are steep enough to be a slip-and-slide hazard if they're still holding hardened snow. Be prepared to turn back if you encounter dangerous snow conditions, and consider carrying an ice ax if you're doing the traverse early in the summer.

Deer Mountain Summit and Blue Lake: The trail climbs steadily up a moderate grade through hemlock and cedar forest. There are some fine rock and log steps on the lower trail, and many switchbacks on the way. There are viewpoints at about 1 and 2 miles, but by far the best is from the peak. Above the second viewpoint the trail traverses an open subalpine slope with good views to the north, across Ketchikan Lake. Take the spur trail to the summit at 2.2 miles; 0.2 mile farther on the main trail is the spur to the shelter, which sits in the saddle northeast of and well below the summit.

Past Deer Mountain, the fancy trail work ends, but the hike continues along a rough alpine footpath marked variously with stakes, rods, rock cairns, and orange diamonds. Take a deep breath, and you may be able to smell both mountain heather and salty sea air at the same time; this is not an everyday experience. The path descends a bit, climbs to a high point at 3,000 feet in elevation, and then drops into a saddle above icy, spectacular Blue Lake. The shelter, a small A-frame with sleeping space for a maximum of four hikers, sits on a promontory on the northwest side of the lake, down the slope from the saddle. There is also fair camping potential on the southwest and west shoreline.

Deer Mountain–Silvis Lakes Traverse: If the weather is at all questionable, Blue Lake is the place to turn around. Beyond Blue Lake the trail is less defined, more of a marked route with intermittent sections of tread, and the markers may not be spaced closely enough to follow if heavy weather or fog moves in. Be prepared for bad weather, and be sure to have a topo map and compass along.

Be prepared for some wild mountain beauty too. The traverse stays high in alpine country for about 7 miles, from Deer Mountain to a point below Mahoney Mountain, climbing peaks and dropping into saddles through a land of snowfields, tarns, and tumbling streams. The steepest descent is the drop into Silvis Saddle from the south; it's so steep that there is a fixed rope in place for assistance.

The best overnight spots are the Deer Mountain Shelter, Blue Lake and the Blue Lake Shelter, the basin between John and Mahoney Mountains, and a few partially protected spots along the ridge. With Blue Lake, snowmelt ponds, and a nice stream running down from Silvis Saddle, water is rarely a problem here. The spur trails to John and Mahoney Mountains make good side trips, but there are plenty of fine, scenic spots on the route if you don't take the extra time to bag the two peaks.

With about 2.5 miles of power project road, two dams, a powerhouse, a pipeline, and fluctuating lake levels, the Silvis Lakes portion of the hike is probably too industrial for some hikers' tastes. Add to that the very long, rough descent from the Mahoney Mountain spur trail to the Upper Silvis Lake Dam, plus the hassle of the shuttle back from the Silvis Lakes Trailhead, and it's tempting to do the trip as an out-and-back from Ketchikan to Mahoney Mountain, about a 15-mile round-trip. It's shorter overall, however, to continue to Silvis Lakes.

If you're looking for a challenging day hike to a summit, try Mahoney Mountain from the Silvis Lakes Trailhead, a strenuous 6 miles one way with 3,300 feet of elevation gain.

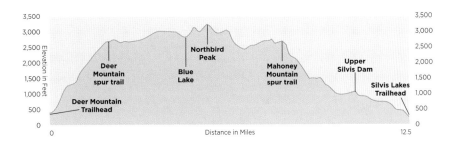

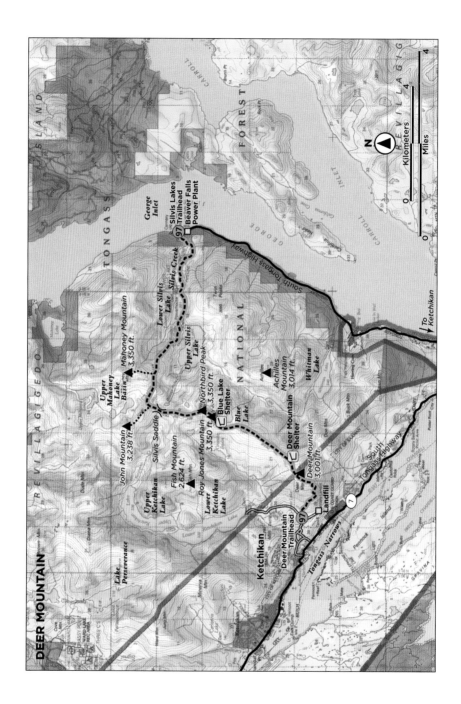

DEER MOUNTAIN

MILES AND DIRECTIONS

Deer Mountain
Summit

0.0	Begin at the trailhead.
1.0	Arrive at the lower viewpoint.
2.0	Reach the second viewpoint.
2.2	Follow the spur trail to the summit of Deer Mountain.
2.5	Take in the view from the Deer Mountain summit.

Deer Mountain–Silvis
Lakes Traverse

2.4	Arrive at the Deer Mountain Shelter.
4.5	Reach the saddle above Blue Lake and the Blue Lake Shelter.
5.5	Summit Northbird Peak.
6.5	Descend to Silvis Saddle.
6.7	Meet the John Mountain spur trail.
7.5	Intersect the Mahoney Mountain spur trail.
9.5	Pass the Upper Silvis Lake Dam.
10.0	Descend to the shoreline of Lower Silvis Lake.
12.5	End the hike at the Silvis Lakes Trailhead.

Shorter hikes: Try the trek to the second, very scenic viewpoint on the Deer Mountain Trail, 2 miles one way.

98. **WARD LAKE AND WARD CREEK**

WHY GO?

These trails are among the most popular in the area and travel by old-growth forest, Ward Creek and Ward Lake.

THE RUNDOWN

Distance: 1.3 to about 6 miles round-trip

Special features: Old-growth forest, wildlife, fishing, viewing decks, an interpretive trail, and a popular recreation area

Location: 8 miles north of downtown Ketchikan

Difficulty: Easy

Trail type: Ward Lake: more developed. Ward Creek: accessible

Total elevation gain: Up to 100 feet

Best season: Mar through Nov

Fees/permits: None

Maps: USGS Ketchikan B-6 (NE); Forest Service *Ketchikan Area Hiking Guide*

Contact: Tongass National Forest, Ketchikan–Misty Fjords Ranger District, 3031 Tongass Ave., Ketchikan, AK 99901; (907) 225-2148; www.fs.usda.gov/tongass/

FINDING THE TRAILHEAD

 Travel 7 miles north on the North Tongass Highway from the dock/downtown area of Ketchikan; turn right onto Revilla Road, the signed intersection just past the highway bridge over Ward Creek. Follow Revilla Road 1.3 miles to Ward Lake Road and turn right. Join the Ward Lake Nature Trail at the Ward Lake Day Use Area (0.5 mile from Revilla Road), the Grassy Point Picnic Area (0.6 mile), or at the back of the left loop of the Signal Creek Campground (about 1 mile). All of these trailheads are on the right (west) side of the road.

Join the Ward Creek Trail at the signed trailhead on the east side of Revilla Road, about 1.9 miles from the North Tongass Highway, or at the Ward Lake Day Use Area on Ward Lake Road. You can also access the trail at the back of the Last Chance Campground, at Mile 2.3 of Revilla Road.

WHAT TO SEE

Although these are Ketchikan's most popular trails, it's still possible to enjoy the quiet of an old-growth forest, relax by a beautiful creek, and hear and glimpse wildlife on these short trails. You can do the Ward Lake Nature Trail, a 1.3-mile loop, the Ward Creek Trail, about 2.5 miles one way, or a combination of the two by circling Ward Lake and backtracking on the Ward Creek Trail, adding up to about 6 miles round-trip.

Ward Lake Nature Trail: The trail skirts the shoreline around Ward Lake, elevation 52 feet. On the east side of the lake, the trail connects picnic areas and campgrounds near the road; the west side is away from the road and is quieter. The bridge over the lake's outlet stream, a short walk from the west side of the Signal Creek Campground, offers a good view of the lake and the rocky stream.

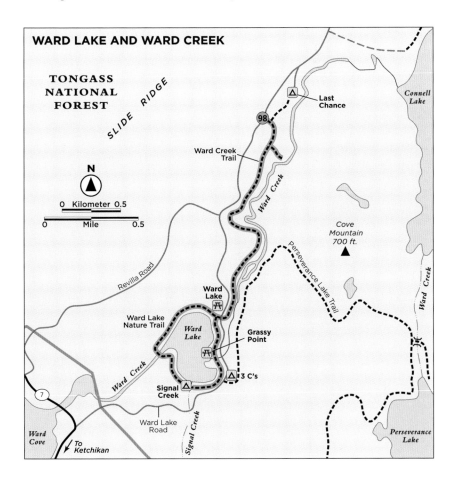

Giant spruces and hemlocks line the trail, many with huge root buttresses. Salmonberry, wood violets, dogwood, huckleberry, mosses, ferns, and other plants thrive in the understory, and forest birds like thrushes, winter wrens, and Steller's jays are common. Salmon spawn in Ward Creek in late summer and fall. Hikers commonly see deer, beavers, and red squirrels. Swans, geese, ducks, and loons all use the lake in spring and early summer.

Interpretive signs along the trail describe the ancient forest. If it's raining, stay dry under one of the covered picnic shelters on the east side of the lake at the Ward Lake and Grassy Point sites.

Ward Creek Trail: The wide, graded and graveled trail more or less parallels Revilla Road to the east, following Ward Creek. The creek is the main event; the trail features several benches and fishing and viewing decks overlooking the cascades and deep, dark pools of the creek, which in most other parts of the world would qualify as a river.

The Ward Creek Trail also connects with other short trails on the west side of Revilla Road; see the Forest Service's area hiking guide for details.

Fishing: Pink, red, and silver salmon, steelhead, Dolly Varden, and cutthroat trout use Ward Creek and Ward Lake at different times of the spring, summer, and fall. Check current regulations before wetting a line.

99. PERSEVERANCE LAKE

WHY GO?

A short trail traveling by forest, streams, and muskeg, ending at a lake.

THE RUNDOWN

Distance: 2.4 miles one way

Special features: Forest and lake scenery, fishing, a connecting trail to high country to the west

Location: 8 miles north of Ketchikan

Difficulty: Moderate

Trail type: More developed

Total elevation gain: 500 feet in, 100 feet out

Best season: Mar through Nov

Fees/permits: None

Maps: USGS Ketchikan B-6 (NE) and B-5 (NW); Forest Service *Ketchikan Area Hiking Guide*

Contact: Tongass National Forest, Ketchikan–Misty Fjords Ranger District, 3031 Tongass Ave., Ketchikan, AK 99901; (907) 225-2148; www.fs.usda.gov/tongass/

FINDING THE TRAILHEAD

Travel 7 miles north on the North Tongass Highway from the dock/downtown area of Ketchikan and turn right onto Revilla Road, the signed intersection just past the highway bridge over Ward Creek. Follow Revilla Road 1.3 miles to Ward Lake Road and turn right toward the Ward Lake Recreation Area (see the Ward Lake and Ward Creek hike). In 0.8 mile park on the right (west) side of the road in a parking area just beyond the Grassy Point Picnic Area. The trail starts approximately 100 feet beyond the entrance to the 3 C's Group Use Campground.

WHAT TO SEE

The 2.4-mile Perseverance Lake Trail is a wide, gravel tread traveling through a landscape of ancient forest, small streams, and muskeg. About 0.2 mile from Perseverance Lake, a bridge takes you across Ward Creek, the lake's outlet stream. Just before the bridge, the Minerva Mountain Trail cuts away to the south and west, eventually climbing to the high alpine ridge to the west of the lake.

At the lake a big logjam by the outlet and several rocks, meadows, and points along the lakeshore make good casting spots for anglers; otherwise the lakeshore is fairly thick with vegetation. It's tough to get very far around the lake without

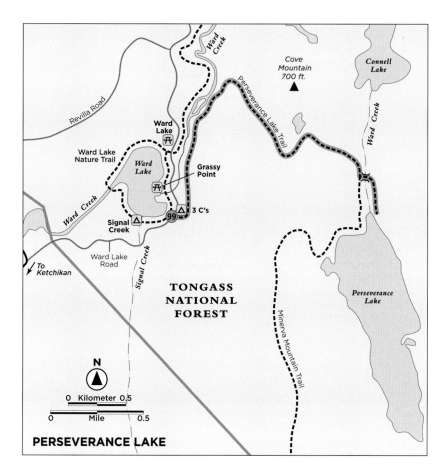

PERSEVERANCE LAKE

Revilla Road

Ward Creek

Cove Mountain 700 ft.

Connell Lake

Perseverance Lake Trail

Ward Creek

Ward Lake Nature Trail

Ward Lake

Ward Lake

Grassy Point

3 C's

99

Signal Creek

Ward Lake Road

Signal Creek

To Ketchikan

N

TONGASS NATIONAL FOREST

Minerva Mountain Trail

Perseverance Lake

0   Kilometer   0.5

0   Mile   0.5

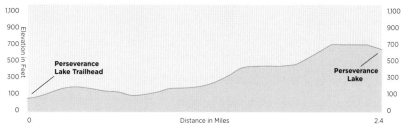

1,100

900

700

500

300

100

0

Elevation in Feet

Perseverance Lake Trailhead

Perseverance Lake

1,100

900

700

500

300

100

0

0

Distance in Miles

2.4

bushwhacking, so most hikers stay close to the end of the trail at the north end of the lake. The Forest Service has put in two tent platforms, one on either side of the outlet stream, for overnighters.

Minerva Mountain Trail: This high-country trail, climbs more than 2,000 feet in about 4 miles to Ward Mountain (2,670 feet), and a clear route continues along the ridge from Ward Mountain to Minerva Mountain and beyond. The first 0.5 mile or so skirts the edge of Perseverance Lake.

Fishing: Fishing in the lake is fair for brook and rainbow trout most of the spring, summer, and fall.

THE MUSKEGS OF SOUTHEAST ALASKA

One of the first things hikers new to Southeast Alaska notice is that rain forest isn't all there is to the plant world here. The forest is nearly everywhere broken up by open, sunny, soggy, boot-sucking muskegs. Muskeg isn't a scientifically approved term, but it's what most people call these landscapes of small ponds with floating lilies, deep blankets of mosses and sedges, a few stunted trees, and lots of low-growing plants with "bog" in their common names, like bog blueberry, bog rosemary, and bog orchid.

One of the few trees that can survive in a muskeg, the shore pine, provides a clue to how muskegs work.

Known by its other common name, lodgepole pine, this tree is a dominant pine in many of the Lower 48's western mountains, where it thrives in dry, rocky country. The common thread: The lodgepole/shore pine does well in marginal situations where other trees just can't make it.

Muskegs are "marginal" because they're sopping wet, acidic, and nutrient-poor. They've built up over thousands of years on top of thick layers of silt left behind when the mantle of ice retreated from Southeast Alaska after the last great glaciation. Southeast's heavy rains leach out the minerals in the soil, and the sphagnum mosses that thrive in the muskegs release acids that retard natural decomposition, starving other plants of nutrients. The ones that survive are mostly tough and tiny.

Muskegs, however, are full of animal life. They're havens for diving beetles, dragonflies, water striders, and yes, mosquitoes, as well as birds like the great blue heron, greater yellowlegs, snipe, kingfisher, and many insect-eating songbirds. To top it off, most of Southeast's richest salmon streams lie in watersheds with extensive muskegs and other wetlands.

100. **NAHA RIVER**

WHY GO?

A remote trail winding by lakes, a river, and a saltwater lagoon, with opportunities for fishing and wildlife viewing, just north of Ketchikan.

THE RUNDOWN

Distance: 5.4 miles one way

Special features: A saltwater lagoon, a beautiful Southeast river, 2 lakes, 2 fee cabins, wildlife, and fishing. Access is by boat from Ketchikan

Location: 25 miles north of Ketchikan and about 8 miles north of the end of the Ketchikan road system

Difficulty: Easy/moderate

Trail type: More developed, much of it planked

Total elevation gain: About 400 feet

Best season: Apr through Oct

Fees/permits: Fee for cabin use

Maps: USGS Ketchikan C-5

Contact: Tongass National Forest, Ketchikan–Misty Fjords Ranger District, 3031 Tongass Ave., Ketchikan, AK 99901; (907) 225-2148; www. fs.usda.gov/tongass/

FINDING THE TRAILHEAD

The trail begins about 8 miles north of the end of the Ketchikan road system, at the dock near the head of Naha Bay. Access is by boat, and the simplest way to get there is to arrange a charter drop-off and pickup at Knudson Cove Marina (407 Knudson Cove Road, Ketchikan, AK 99901; 907-247-8500 or 800-528-2486; www.knudsoncovemarina.com). You can also rent a skiff with an outboard at the marina. Knudson Cove is about 15 miles north of downtown Ketchikan; drive to North Point Higgins Road at Mile 14.2 of the North Tongass Highway and turn left. Then take an immediate right onto Knudson Cove Road and follow it about 0.4 mile to the marina.

It's also possible to kayak to the dock to start the trip, although it's a long out-and-back paddle to combine with a hike unless you plan to spend at least one night out. Experienced kayakers can rent from Southeast Exposure (37 Potter Rd., Ketchikan, AK 99901; 907-225-5829; www.southeastexposure.com), a guiding and kayak-rental business located just past Knudson Cove Road off the North Tongass Highway.

WHAT TO SEE

The Naha River Trail features a saltwater lagoon, a fine river with rapids and wa-terfalls, good fishing, two lakes, and a Forest Service fee cabin with a skiff and oars at each of the lakes. The Jordan Lake and Heckman Lake cabins are the best overnight options (fee and reservation required; go to www.reserveusa.com or call 877-444-6777). As for tenting, the forest is brushy and usually wet, and there are no established campsites, but a determined backpacker can make do. The trail is mostly planked, with only a few ups and downs in this lower, hilly country; Heckman Lake is only 139 feet above sea level.

The river's lake-dominated watershed is one of the richest aquatic environments in Southeast Alaska, providing homes for a terrific variety of fish. Besides the two lakes on the trail, there are five other significant lakes in the watershed, and the river is full of riffles and pools and other habitat. Grayling and trophy-worthy cutthroat trout inhabit the high mountain lakes beyond the trail, while the lower watershed supports Dolly Varden and cutthroat, four species of salmon, and abundant steelhead trout runs. Local anglers and families commonly use the lower river, especially on weekends, so if you want maximum solitude, plan to spend most of your time on the upper part of the trail.

The pools below the rapids at Mile 2.5 and the falls at Mile 5.0 are two of the choice spots along the river; watch especially for black bears in those areas when fish are running. Black bears, deer, beavers, bald eagles, and waterfowl are commonly sighted in the Naha valley, and if you're in the right place at the right time, you might be lucky enough to hear a wolf howling in the distance

From the dock, climb the gangway into the forest to start the hike. Almost im-mediately a side trail splits off toward the water, to the right. It's a 0.2-mile loop that leads to a picnic shelter and the tide race at the mouth of Roosevelt Lagoon. The narrow slot at the end of the lagoon becomes a chute of roaring white water when the tide is changing; try to be there soon after high slack tide to see it at its best.

At the tide race the trail joins a plank tramway, which runs between the sea and the lagoon, bypassing the tide race. When it was better equipped, the tramway provided a route for moving small boats into the lagoon from Naha Bay. Now, many steelhead fishermen leave small boats on the shore of the lagoon, hike in with electric motors, and zip across the lagoon to the river when the fish are running. If you're in a kayak, you could lug your boat over the 100-yard tramway portage, paddle across the lagoon, and join the trail along the northwest shore of the lagoon.

The trail arcs around the north side of Roosevelt Lagoon and emerges on the bank of the river above the head of the lagoon. Shortly after, it passes through the Orton Ranch church camp, complete with lawn and volleyball net, at about 2.4 miles. Stay on the lower edge of the lawn as you hike through this small piece of private property. The camp uses powerboats to transport visitors and supplies, but beyond Orton Ranch the valley is quiet.

Just out of sight of the camp, a short side loop leads to the river rapids and picnic shelter at Mile 2.5. (The 1948 USGS map calls this spot the "Black Bear

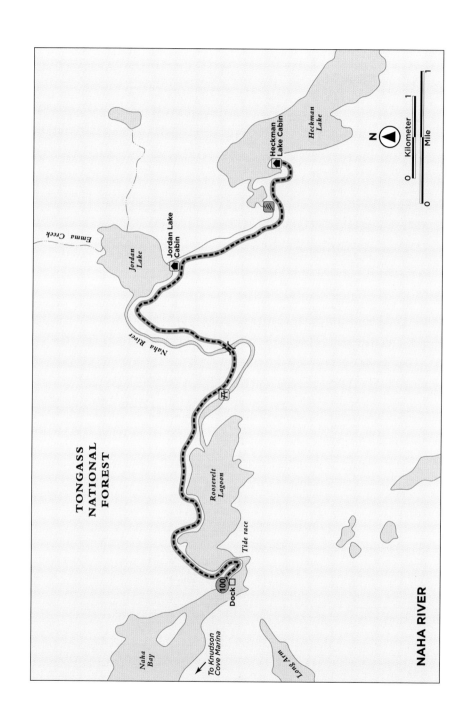

TONGASS
NATIONAL
FOREST

Emma Creek

Jordan
Lake

Jordan Lake
Cabin

Heckman
Lake Cabin

Heckman
Lake

Naha River

Roosevelt
Lagoon

Tide race

100
Dock

Naha
Bay

To Knudson
Cove Marina

Long Arm

N

Kilometer   1

0

Mile

0   1

NAHA RIVER

Observation Post.") Beyond the shelter the country feels much wilder. The bridge over the river at about Mile 3, the two lakes, and the falls at about Mile 5 are the highlights of the upper trail. There are also a few rough anglers' side trails to the river, and all of them are worth the trip.

Heckman Lake is the larger and more scenic of the two lakes, but it's hard to beat the refurbished cabin at Jordan Lake, with its big covered deck overlooking the water. One warning to lake visitors: The rowboats at the cabins are larger and heavier than the ones the Forest Service supplies at many other cabins, and so are significantly more difficult to pull out of the water.

MILES AND DIRECTIONS

0.0 Begin at the Naha Bay Dock.

0.1 A side loop leads to the tide race.

2.0 Arrive at the east end of Roosevelt Lagoon.

2.4 Pass the Orton Ranch.

2.5 A short side loop leads to a picnic shelter and rapids.

4.0 Arrive at Jordan Lake Cabin.

5.0 Hike by the falls, a choice spot along the river.

5.4 Reach the end of the trail at the Heckman Lake Cabin.

Fishing: The premier fishing on the Naha is for spring and fall steelhead, but anglers can fish for Dollies, rainbows, and cutthroat all spring, summer, and fall. From July through September the river hosts runs of silver, pink, red, and chum salmon.

A hiker explores above the Alatna
River in the central Brooks Range
on a late June evening.
NATHANIEL WILDER

OFF THE BEATEN PATH: DISCOVERING WILDERNESS ALASKA

Traveler, there is no path; paths are made by walking.

—Spanish proverb

In the rest of the United States, wilderness exists as islands in a human-dominated landscape, but in Alaska the human landscapes are the islands, floating in a sea of wilderness. That "sea" is so big that a lifetime wouldn't be long enough to explore it all.

Much of the remote wilderness in the state offers good if very tough hiking; this section includes brief entries for a few areas that fit that description. In most of these areas, there are no trails or any facilities of any kind, so your route is up to you. Discovering Alaska this way, on your own initiative and taking complete responsibility for your own trip and your own safety, can be the experience of a lifetime.

You'll need to carefully plan your route from hundreds of possible hikes by studying topographic maps and gathering information from land managers and from air taxi operators who fly into the areas. (The topographic maps listed under each entry are from the U.S. Geological Survey's 1:250,000-scale series; for a few remote areas, that's as detailed as the map coverage gets.) For many, a guided trip may be the best introduction to Alaska's real wilderness. Park and refuge managers have lists of the guiding and air taxi services that operate in their areas.

It's best to be an experienced trail hiker and have at least a few longer, road-accessible alpine ridge hikes under your belt before attempting a remote, fly-in trip. Many people, even experienced Lower 48 backpackers, feel a twinge of wilderness shock as the bush plane pulls away from their drop-off point, leaving them on their own with nothing but a pack full of gear assembled back in the city. Alaska's park managers have become concerned in recent years over the lack of experience of many of the people who are going out into truly wild country, so be sure you're ready before you tackle a trip like this.

There are many possibilities for remote trips, including a two-week march with a pack weighing sixty to eighty pounds, a base camp and day hikes in a choice spot, a combination journey of hiking and river floating, and a shorter backpack trip with lots of side-hike options, limiting the miles you have to cover with a heavy pack. What's right for you depends on how much ground you want to cover and how heavy a pack you're willing to carry.

There are many considerations for trips into remote, trail-free areas. Be sure to read the "Hiking in Alaska" introductory section to this guide. The websites of the parks and refuges listed below are good sources of information as you start to plan your trip.

Stream crossings: Stream courses that don't even show up as perennial streams on USGS maps can become impassable torrents during periods of heavy rain. Leave yourself a way out in case you can't cross a stream on your route, and ask for advice from someone familiar with the area if your route involves crossing a larger stream or river. Don't rely entirely on pilots for this information; they normally see streams only from far above and are not always experienced in river crossings.

Backup plans: In case you don't return on schedule, leave your itinerary and a plan with a responsible person in addition to your air taxi operator. Be sure to discuss alternate pickup points with your pilot in case you can't reach your destination. Consider carrying a small two-way radio for ground-to-air communication in case of unavoidable delays, route changes, or injury.

Planning your route: Cross-country travel is much easier if you can largely avoid the brush and tussocks that can plague an Alaska wilderness hike. ("Tussocks" are wet-tundra cotton grass lumps, and hiking through several miles of them with a full pack is one of the toughest hiking assignments on the planet.) Focus your trip as much as possible on higher alpine areas; elevations above 3,000 feet are generally free of brush and tussocks.

Most Alaska off-trail hiking is rugged and difficult, especially for hikers accustomed to hiking on developed trails. Ridgelines and stream gravel bars are the best hiking routes. For planning purposes and until you know your own pace, count on covering no more than 6 map miles (one township, the survey squares on 1:250,000 topographic maps) per day on a remote trip.

Leaving a margin of safety: Extra food, a good first-aid kit, bear protection, and good clothing and equipment are exponentially more important on a trip into Alaska's true wilderness. The trick is finding the right balance between the gear you may need and the weight of your pack. Be sure to allow more than enough time to reach your pickup point; planning extra time for side trips, rest days, and weather days is a great idea.

GATES OF THE ARCTIC

Description: A national park and preserve in the heart of the Brooks Range, America's northernmost mountains

Location: Arctic northcentral Alaska

Access: Air charter from Bettles or Kotzebue, which are served by scheduled air; scheduled air service to Anaktuvuk Pass; or hiking from the Dalton Highway

Best season: Mid-June to early Sept

USGS maps: Ambler River, Chandalar, Chandler Lake, Hughes, Killik River, Philip Smith Mountains, Survey Pass, Wiseman. National Geographic's Gates of the Arctic National Park and Preserve is a good overview and planning map

Contact: Gates of the Arctic National Park and Preserve, 4175 Geist Rd., Fairbanks, Alaska 99701; (907) 457-5752; www.nps.gov/gaar

Float plane landing on Pingo Lake in Gates of the Arctic National Park, a popular starting point for backpacking and rafting in the Noatak River valley.
HALEY JOHNSTON

THE AREA

The Gates of the Arctic is a remote and undeveloped park of 8.5 million acres, most of which has been designated wilderness. Gates is Bob Marshall country; the early Forest Service wilderness crusader's travels here were the beginnings of the movement to designate a wilderness park in the central Brooks Range. Marshall coined the name for the area, for Frigid Crags and Boreal Mountain, two peaks that form a "gate" of sorts across the North Fork Koyukuk River.

The main ranges in the park are the Endicott Mountains in the eastern part of the park and the Schwatka Mountains in the west. Mount Igikpak in the Schwatka Mountains is the highest point in the park at an elevation of 8,510 feet. The higher parts of the ranges and the north slope are arctic tundra, while the lower valleys on the south side are forested. The park is rugged and mountainous, and millions of grass tussocks make hiking with a heavy pack slow and difficult. There are glaciers only at the highest elevations, so most high passes are glacier-free, and the park's streams run clear except during high water.

The park's many wild valleys and mountains make great hiking. The upper watersheds of the Koyukuk, John, Alatna, and Kobuk south of the range, the Itkillik, Anaktuvuk, Chandler, and Killik north of the range, and the Noatak, which flows west, offer an incredible variety of arctic and alpine tundra rambling. If you have the time and the inclination, bring a collapsible boat with you; do a backpack trip in the mountainous upper reaches of one of the rivers, and then float out to a different pickup point. The typical chartered aircraft drop-off points in the park are lakes and backwater river sloughs.

Park headquarters are in Fairbanks, and the main field operations center is in Bettles. The park recommends that wilderness visitors attend an orientation session in one of the park gateways (Coldfoot, Bettles, Anaktuvuk Pass, or Kotzebue) prior to going out. It's a good idea to call to check on current conditions before you leave home.

ARCTIC NATIONAL WILDLIFE REFUGE

Description: A huge, remote wildlife refuge extending from the south side of the Brooks Range to the Arctic Coast

Location: Arctic northeast Alaska

Access: Air charter to a river gravel bar or tundra landing site from Fort Yukon, Kaktovik, or Deadhorse, all of which are on scheduled air routes from Fairbanks

Best season: Mid-June to early Sept

USGS maps: Arctic, Barter Island, Black River, Chandalar, Christian, Coleen, Demarcation Point, Flaxman Island, Mount Michelson, Philip Smith Mountains, Sagavanirktok, Table Mountain

Contact: Arctic National Wildlife Refuge, 101 12th Ave., PO Box 20, Fairbanks, AK 99701; (907) 456-0250; http://arctic.fws.gov

A rainbow appears to pierce a ridge in the eastern Brooks Range along the Kongakut River in the Arctic National Wildlife Refuge. NATHANIEL WILDER

Hiking in the alpine country of the Upper Kongakut River, south of the confluence with Drain Creek.
HALEY JOHNSTON

THE AREA

The Arctic Refuge, made famous by the debate over oil development on the coastal plain, extends all the way across the Brooks Range from the forested south slope to the Arctic Ocean. It is the only protected area in the United States that spans the whole range of subarctic and arctic ecosystems.

The highest peaks, around 9,000 feet in elevation, and the only significant mountain glaciation in the entire Brooks Range lie in the Romanzof and Franklin Mountains at the heart of the refuge. A smaller but dramatic flanking range, the Sadlerochit Mountains, lies on an east-west axis north of the main ranges. The northwest corner of the refuge includes parts of the Philip Smith Mountains.

Several swift, braided rivers flow north out of the mountains to the ocean through the United States' only protected expanse of arctic tundra plain. The rivers have lyrical names like Ivishak, Okpilak, Aichilik, Kongakut, Jago, and Hulahula, which was named by Hawaiian whalers in the 1890s. The Porcupine caribou herd migrates through the mountains and along the coast on both sides of the international border, calving on the coastal plain from late May to mid-June.

There are only a few lakes in this section of the Brooks Range, so tundra airstrips and gravel-bar landing areas are the typical drop-off points for hikers. As in Gates of the Arctic, ANWR has a number of hike-float possibilities.

WRANGELL–ST. ELIAS

Description: The largest national park in the U.S., encompassing four major mountain ranges

Location: Southcentral Alaska, east of Glennallen

Access: By road via the McCarthy and Nabesna Roads (see Wrangell–St. Elias National Park); or by air charter from McCarthy, Glennallen, Nabesna, Cordova, or Yakutat

Best season: June through Sept, depending on elevation

USGS maps: Bering Glacier, Cordova, Gulkana, Icy Bay, McCarthy, Mount St. Elias, Nabesna, Valdez, Yakutat. National Geographic's Wrangell–St. Elias National Park and Preserve is a good overview and planning map

Contact: Wrangell–St. Elias National Park and Preserve, Mile 106.8 Richardson Highway, PO Box 439, Copper Center, AK 99573; (907) 822-5234; www.nps.gov/wrst

A visitor cooks dinner near a grizzly print close to the Bagley Icefield in Wrangell St. Elias National Park.
NATHANIEL WILDER

THE AREA

Wrangell–St. Elias is a huge, diverse park and preserve with an incredible variety of geology and mountain landscapes, lying at the heart of one of the largest internationally protected areas in the world. The Wrangell and St. Elias Mountains are high, glaciated ranges that form a mountain wall across the center of the park/preserve, broken only by a gap along the Chitina and White Rivers. The Wrangells are volcanoes, while the St. Elias is a coastal range featuring some of the continent's highest peaks, including Mount Logan. Logan, across the border in Canada, is second in height only to Denali in North America. Mount St. Elias, at 18,008 feet, is the highest point in the park.

Rounding out the four major ranges in the park, the Mentasta and Nutzotin Mountains form an eastern extension of the Alaska Range at the northern end of the park/preserve, and the Chugach Mountains rise along the southern coast of the park.

Wrangell–St. Elias is a great place for a fly-in hiking trip. First, the park has a huge number of beautiful hiking routes. Second, there are many aircraft-landing zones on the park's river bars and ridgetops, and there are a number of usable airstrips left from the area's mining days. Third, many good routes are only a short flight from airfields with charter services (in Glennallen, McCarthy, and Nabesna in particular). Fourth, park staff are a very good source of information on specific backcountry routes; the park describes some of them on its website. In addition, there are several public-use cabins in the fly-in backcountry.

One of the air taxi operators, Wrangell Mountain Air of McCarthy, posts an extensive backcountry-trip planning guide on its website (www.wrangellmountainair. com, or call 800-478-1160). Danny Kost, a former ranger, has published a book on hiking in the park, called, no surprise, Hiking in Wrangell–St. Elias National Park.

One trip-planning consideration here is the hunting season for Dall sheep in the preserve, beginning about August 10.

KATMAI

Description: A national park and preserve centered around the Valley of Ten Thousand Smokes, the valley buried in ash by the 1912 Katmai volcanic eruption

Location: Southwest Alaska, east of King Salmon on the Alaska Peninsula

Access: Scheduled air to King Salmon and then scheduled floatplane to Brooks Camp; or air charter from King Salmon or Kodiak to remote locations in the park

Best season: June through mid-Sept

USGS maps: Afognak, Iliamna, Karluk, Mount Katmai, Naknek. National Geographic's Katmai National Park and Preserve is a good overview and planning map

Contact: Katmai National Park and Preserve, #1 King Salmon Mall, PO Box 7, King Salmon, AK 99613; (907) 246-3305; www.nps.gov/katm

The Valley of Ten Thousand Smokes in Katmai National Park, with Mount Griggs and Baked Mountain visible.
HALEY JOHNSTON

THE AREA

Katmai covers four million acres in a swath across the Aleutian Range, from the coast to the lakes region west of the crest of the range. It is a land of steaming volcanoes, big lakes and rivers, a wild Pacific coastline, and a healthy population of brown bears. At least fourteen volcanoes in the park are considered active or potentially active. The spectacular 1912 eruption of Novarupta, a vent on the side of Mount Katmai, buried the Ukak Valley under 700 feet of ash and pumice, creating the Valley of Ten Thousand Smokes.

The valley and its environs—Knife Creek, Windy Creek, the Buttress Range, Novarupta, and Katmai Pass—are the most common backpacking destinations in the park. A concession-operated shuttle bus (fee charged) carries hikers and sightseers over the 23-mile road from Brooks Camp to the Three Forks overlook above the valley. There is a park contact station at the overlook, and visitors can hike down into the valley from there.

Some of the peaks at the head of the valley can be climbed without glacier travel, but others require glacier equipment and experience. High winds and sudden weather changes streaking through Katmai Pass from Shelikof Strait can make backpacking here a challenge.

Facilities at Brooks Camp include a lodge, a campground, a small store, and bear-viewing platforms near the mouth of the Brooks River and a short walk away at Brooks Falls. A trail leads from the campground about 4 miles to Dumpling Mountain, which overlooks the entire Brooks and Naknek Lake area. The lodge and campground are open from June through mid-September. The largest concentrations of salmon and bears in the Brooks Camp area occur in July and September, and those months are also the peak of human visitation.

There are other, more remote hiking destinations, including the Walatka Mountains in the northern part of the park. Backpacking permits are recommended; pick one up at park headquarters in King Salmon or at the visitor centers in the King Salmon airport and at Brooks Camp. Anywhere you travel in Katmai, be prepared for the park's most charismatic inhabitants, its brown bears. The park newspaper, *Novarupta*, is a good overall introduction to the park.

LAKE CLARK

Description: A national park and preserve in the Aleutian and Alaska ranges

Location: Southcentral Alaska, across Cook Inlet from Anchorage and the Kenai Peninsula

Access: Seat-rate fares on flights from Anchorage to Port Alsworth or Iliamna and then air charter into the park; or air charter from Anchorage, Kenai, or Homer

Best season: June through Sept

USGS maps: Lake Clark, Lime Hills, Iliamna, Kenai, Seldovia, Tyonek. National Geographic's Lake Clark National Park and Preserve is a good overview and planning map

Contact: Lake Clark National Park and Preserve, 1 Park Place, Port Alsworth, AK 99653; (907) 781-2117; www.nps.gov/lacl

Aerial view of a stunning turquoise lake in Lake Clark National Park.
SCOTT DICKERSON

THE AREA

The 4-million-acre Lake Clark National Park and Preserve includes Pacific coastline, glacier-covered volcanoes, wild rivers, huge blue-green lakes, precipitous granite peaks, plenty of wilderness hiking country, and some of Alaska's finest mountain scenery. Mount Redoubt and Mount Iliamna, the park's two 10,000-plus-foot volcanoes, are visible from Anchorage. Lake Clark is a 40-mile-long lake west of the mountain chain.

There are many good hiking routes in the park/preserve. Air charters to the string of big lakes in the western foothills, especially Telequana, Turquoise, and Twin Lakes, provide the best hiking access. From the lakes, there are routes into and through the Alaska Range. There are a number of routes that involve glacier travel, which is for experienced and equipped hikers only. The Telequana Trail, a historic route between Lake Clark and Telequana Lake, is not a developed trail. The lakes in the northwest part of the park/preserve are within the preserve and open to hunting during the late summer and fall.

The field headquarters for the park/preserve are at Port Alsworth on Lake Clark. The only developed trail in the park is the 3-mile trail to Tanalian Falls and Kontrashibuna Lake from Port Alsworth.

Lower and Upper Twin Lakes surrounded by peaks of the Neacola mountains, in Lake Clark National Park.
HALEY JOHNSTON

NORTHWEST ALASKA

Description: A few accessible hiking areas in the remote northwest corner of Alaska

Location: Western and Arctic Alaska, in the vicinity of Nome and Kotzebue

Access: Mainly scheduled service from Anchorage or Fairbanks

to Nome or Kotzebue; then air charter into the areas

Best season: Approximately June through Sept

USGS maps: See below

Contact: See below

A hiker explores the undulating terrain of the Great Kobuk Sand Dunes in Kobuk Valley National Park.
HALEY JOHNSTON

THE AREAS

Bering Land Bridge National Preserve near Nome offers remote hiking terrain on ridges near the Continental Divide, among granite pinnacles set in arctic tundra. The preserve is used extensively by local people for subsistence hunting and fishing. Access is by charter flight from Nome; see USGS maps Bendeleben and Kotzebue. Contact: PO Box 220, Nome, AK 99762; (907) 443-2522; www.nps.gov/bela.

Cape Krusenstern National Monument, on the cape just northwest of Kotzebue, records about 9,000 years of human history in a series of 114 beach ridges formed by sea-level changes. A maze of lagoons lie behind the beaches, and behind the lagoons a range of limestone hills rises above the landscape. The best hiking is on the beaches and in the hills. People from Kotzebue and nearby villages own parcels of land on the cape and use the area for subsistence hunting and fishing, so please respect private property and traditional uses. Access is by a short charter flight from Kotzebue; see USGS maps Kotzebue and Noatak. Contact: PO Box 1029, Kotzebue, AK 99572; (907) 442-3760 summer, (907) 442-3890 winter; www.nps.gov/cakr.

Kobuk Valley National Park and Noatak National Preserve, east and northeast of Kotzebue, are best known for their namesake rivers. These NPS areas also include some very remote hiking country in the Baird and De Long Mountains, the westernmost ranges of the Brooks Range, which enclose the Noatak basin. Extensive areas of sand dunes south of the Kobuk River can be explored on foot. Access is mainly by air charter from Kotzebue. See USGS maps Baird Mountains, De Long Mountains, Misheguk Mountain, Ambler River, and Howard Pass. Contact: PO Box 1029, Kotzebue, AK 99572; (907) 442-3760 summer, (907) 442-3890 winter; www. nps.gov/kova and www.nps.gov/noat.

The Kigluaik Mountains, a small, alpine range of sawtooth peaks north of Nome, can be explored from Nome's road system. See USGS maps Nome, Teller, Bendeleben, and Solomon. Contact: Bureau of Land Management, Northern Field Office, 1150 University Ave., Fairbanks, AK 99709; (800) 437-7021.

APPENDIX 1: **INFORMATION SOURCES**

ALASKA PUBLIC LANDS INFORMATION CENTERS

Anchorage
605 West 4th Ave.
Suite 105
Anchorage, AK 99501
(907) 644-3661

Fairbanks
101 Dunkel Street, Suite 110
Fairbanks, AK 99701
(907) 459-3730

Ketchikan (Southeast Alaska
Discovery Center)
50 Main Street
Ketchikan, AK 99901
(907) 228-6220

Tok
Milepost 1314, Alaska Highway
PO Box 359
Tok, AK 99780
(907) 883-5667
APLIC website: www.alaskacenters.gov

Alaska Geographic
241 North C Street
Anchorage, AK 99501
(907) 274-8440
http://akgeo.org/

APPENDIX 2: **CABIN RESERVATIONS**

CHUGACH AND TONGASS NATIONAL FORESTS

For cabin information, contact the Anchorage or Ketchikan branches of the Alaska Public Lands Information Center (see appendix 1) or visit the APLIC website, www.alaskacenters.gov You can also contact the Forest Service office nearest the cabin (listed in the individual hike descriptions), or visit the Chugach and Tongass National Forest websites (www.fs.usda.gov/chugach/ for Southcentral cabins, www.fs.usda.gov/ tongass/ for Southeast cabins).

For cabin reservations, call ReserveUSA or go through the website:

(877) 444-6777 U.S. reservations
(518) 885-3639 international reservations
(888) 448-1474 U.S. customer service
www.reserveusa.com

ALASKA STATE PARKS

For information and reservations for Alaska State Parks cabins, contact the Department of Natural Resources Public Information Center in Anchorage or the nearest state parks office (listed in the individual hike descriptions), or visit the state parks website:

Department of Natural Resources
Public Information Center
550 West 7th Ave.
Suite 1260
Anchorage, AK 99501-3557
(907) 269-8400
http://dnr.alaska.gov/parks/

APPENDIX 3: **FURTHER READING**

BEARS

Alaska Natural History Association. *Bear Facts: The Essentials of Traveling in Bear Country* (brochure).

Herrero, Stephen. *Bear Attacks: Their Causes and Avoidance.* Guilford, CT: Lyons Press, 2002.

Schneider, Bill. *Bear Aware.* Guilford, CT: Globe Pequot, 2012.

Smith, Dave. *Backcountry Bear Basics.* Seattle: The Mountaineers, 1997.

ECOLOGY

O'Clair, Rita M., et al. *The Nature of Southeast Alaska.* Anchorage: Alaska Northwest Books, 2014.

FAMILY HIKING

Ross, Cindy, and Todd Gladfelter. *Kids in the Wild.* Seattle: The Mountaineers, 1995.

FIRST AID AND WILDERNESS MEDICINE

Carline, Jan, et. al. *Mountaineering First Aid.* Seattle: The Mountaineers, 2004.

Schimelpfenig, Tod, and Linda Lindsey. *NOLS Wilderness First Aid.* Mechanicsburg, PA: Stackpole Books, 2000.

FISH AND FISHING

Armstrong, Robert H. *Alaska's Fish: A Guide to Selected Species.* Anchorage: Alaska Northwest Books, 1996.

Swensen, Evan, and Margaret. *Fishing Alaska.* Guilford, CT: Globe Pequot, 1997.

MAP AND COMPASS

Kjellström, Björn. *Be Expert with Map and Compass.* New York: Collier Books, 2010.

MAP ATLAS

DeLorme: Alaska Atlas & Gazetteer. Yarmouth, ME: DeLorme, 2010.

PLANTS

MacKinnon, Andy, et al. *Plants of the Pacific Northwest Coast.* Vancouver, BC, Canada: Lone Pine Publishing, 2016.

Parker, Harriette. *Alaska's Mushrooms.* Anchorage: Alaska Northwest Books, 1994.

Pratt, Verna. *Alaska's Wild Berries and Berry-like Fruit.* Anchorage: Alaskakrafts Publishing, 1995.

Pratt, Verna. *Field Guide to Alaskan Wildflowers.* Anchorage: Alaskakrafts Publishing, 1990.

Schofield, Janice J. *Alaska's Wild Plants.* Anchorage: Alaska Northwest Books, 2003.

Viereck, Leslie, and Elbert Little. *Alaska Trees and Shrubs.* Fairbanks: University of Alaska Press, 2007.

ROAD GUIDES

Molvar, Erik. *Scenic Driving Alaska and the Yukon.* Guilford, CT: Globe Pequot, 2005.

Morris Communications. *The MILEPOST: All-The-North Travel Guide.* Augusta, GA: Morris Communications, updated annually.

WILDERNESS SKILLS

Harmon, Will. *Wild Country Companion.* Guilford, CT: Globe Pequot, 1994.

WILDLIFE

Armstrong, Robert H. *Guide to the Birds of Alaska.* Anchorage: Alaska Northwest Books, 2008.

Sibley, David A. *The Sibley Field Guide to the Birds of Western North America.* New York: Alfred A. Knopf, 2003.

Smith, Dave, and Tom Walker. *Alaska's Mammals: A Guide to Selected Species.* Anchorage: Alaska Northwest Books, 1995.

APPENDIX 4: **SAMPLE BACKPACKING CHECKLIST**

Use this list as a sample equipment checklist for backpacking. Plan the gear you bring based on your needs, the specific hike, a weather forecast, and the remoteness of the area you're visiting.

- ☐ Pack and pack cover
- ☐ Wool or synthetic layered clothing
- ☐ Synthetic hat, gloves, neck gaiter, socks
- ☐ Waterproof rain gear, rain hat, umbrella
- ☐ Hiking boots, camp shoes, neoprene booties for stream crossings
- ☐ Hiking staff
- ☐ Your FalconGuide
- ☐ Tent and ground cloth
- ☐ Tarp and line
- ☐ Sleeping bag and pad
- ☐ Cook stove, fuel, repair kit
- ☐ Cook kit, mugs, bowls, utensils
- ☐ Waterproof matches, lighters, fire starter, candles
- ☐ Pocketknife
- ☐ Lightweight, high-calorie food
- ☐ Extra food in case of delays or inclement weather
- ☐ Water bottles and water bag
- ☐ Filter or other water-treatment method
- ☐ Fanny pack or other small bag for day hikes
- ☐ Fishing gear, license, and regulations
- ☐ Camera, binoculars
- ☐ Personal toiletries
- ☐ Book, journal, pencil
- ☐ Watch
- ☐ Flares, two-way radio
- ☐ First-aid kit
- ☐ Sunglasses, sun hat, sunscreen, lip balm
- ☐ Bug repellent, head net, bug jacket
- ☐ Trowel, toilet paper
- ☐ Stuff sacks, line for hanging food
- ☐ Bear repellent
- ☐ Compass, maps
- ☐ Flashlight and batteries (optional in midsummer)
- ☐ Small repair kit for tent, pack, and clothing, including duct tape and aluminum tent-pole sleeves
- ☐ Plastic or nylon bags for keeping clothing, camera, and other items dry
- ☐ Garbage bags

Amalga Trail, 374
Angel Rocks, 246
Arctic National Wildlife Refuge, 435
Auke Nu Trail, 367

Beaver Lake and Herring Cove Trail, 397
Bird Ridge, 117
Bold Ridge Trail, 174
Bonanza Ridge, 275
Byers Lake, 212
Byron Glacier, 99

Caines Head, 28
Caribou Creek, 278
Chena Dome, 250
Chilkoot Pass, 313
China Poot Lake, 21
Creamer's Field, 238
Crescent and Carter Lakes, 54
Crow Pass, 111

Dan Moller Trail, 350
Deer Mountain, 415
Devil's Creek, 68
Dewey Lakes, 320

Eagle River Valley, 156
East Glacier and Nugget Creek, 354
Exit Glacier, 34

Falls Creek, 121
Flattop Mountain, 134
Fuller Lakes and Skyline Ridge, 73

Gates of the Arctic, 433
Grace Ridge Trail, 11
Granite Tors, 242
Grewingk Valley, 15
Gull Rock, 89

Harbor Mountain and Gavan Hill, 390
Harding Icefield, 38

Herbert Glacier, 371
Hope Point, 93

Independence Mine, 204
Indian River, 383

Johnson Pass, 50

Kachemak Bay Beach, 3
Katmai, 439
Kenai River, 77
Kesugi Ridge, 215

Lake Clark, 441
Laughton Glacier, 311
Lazy Mountain and Matanuska
    Peak, 184
Lost Lake, 42

McHugh and Rabbit Lakes, 124
McKinley Lake, 304
Mint Glacier Valley, 192
Montana Creek and Windfall Lake, 363
Mount Baldy and Blacktail Rocks, 163
Mount Healy Trail, 229
Mount Juneau and Granite Creek, 345
Mount Riley, 332
Mount Ripinsky and 7 Mile Saddle, 327

Naha River, 426
Northwest Alaska, 443

Perseverance Lake, 423
Perseverance Trail, 341
Petersburg Lake, 404
Pinnell Mountain, 255
Pioneer Ridge, 179
Point Bridget, 378
Portage Pass, 102
Power Creek and Crater Lake, 296
Ptarmigan Lake, 47
Ptarmigan Valley and Roundtop, 167

Quartz Lake State Recreation Trails, 266

Rainbow Falls and Institute Creek, 409
Reed Lakes, 197
Resurrection Pass, 63
Root Glacier and Stairway Icefall, 271
Russian Lakes, 58

Saddlebag Glacier, 307
Savage River Valley, 233
Seduction Point, 337
Seven Lakes, 84
Sheridan Mountain Trail, 301
Ship Lake Pass, 138
Sitka National Historical Park, 387
Skilak Lookout, Bear Mountain, and
    Vista Trails, 80
Skookum Volcano, 285
Snowbird Mine and Glacier Pass, 201
South Fork Eagle River, 151
Starrigavan Bay, 394

Sturgill's Landing, 324
Summit Trail, 260

Talkeetna Lakes Park, 208
Three Lakes and Ideal Cove, 401
Tonsina River, 289
Trail and Lost Creeks, 281
Trail of Blue Ice, 95
Triple Lakes Trail, 224
Turnagain Arm Trail, 129
Twin Peaks Trail, 169

Ward Lake and Ward Creek, 420
West Butte, 189
West Glacier, 359
Williwaw Lakes, 142
Winner Creek, 106
Wolverine Peak, 147
Worthington Glacier, 291
Wrangell–St. Elias, 437
Wynn Nature Center, 8